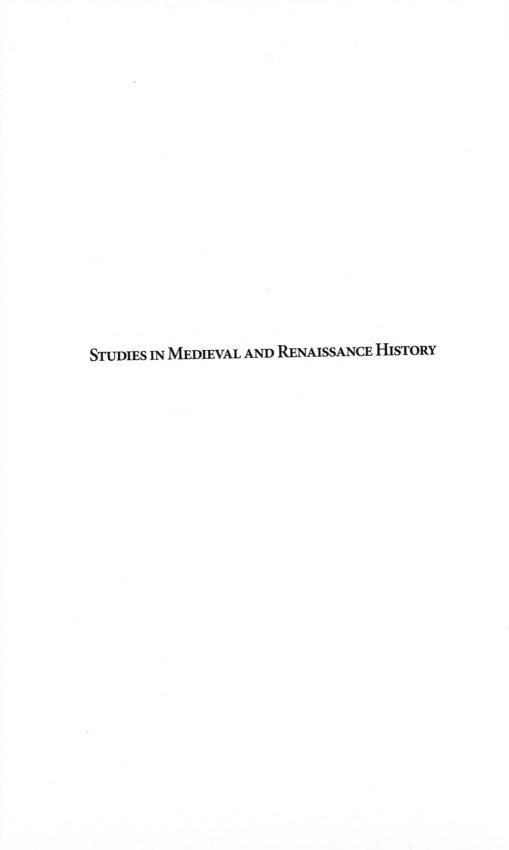

Studies in Medieval and Renaissance History

STUDIES IN MEDIEVAL AND RENAISSANCE HISTORY

Edited by Roger Dahood and Peter E. Medine

THIRD SERIES, VOLUME IV
(Old Series, Volume XXIX; New Series, Volume XIX)

AMS Press, Inc.

New York

Studies in Medieval and Renaissance History
ISSN 0081-8224

Copyright © 2007 by AMS Press, Inc.

Studies in Medieval and Renaissance History is published under the
auspices of the Arizona Center for Medieval and Renaissance Studies.

International Standard Book Numbers

ISBN-13: 978-0-404-64550-2 (Set)
ISBN-10: 0-404-64550-x (Set)

ISBN-13: 978-0-404-64554-0 (Series III.4)
ISBN-10: 0-404-64554-2 (Series III.4)

Library of Congress Catalog Number 63-22098

Manufactured in the United States of America

Roger Dahood and Peter E. Medine, Co-editors

Editorial Board

Table of Contents

Abstracts

A Usable Past: Early Bavarian Hagiography in Context

Jonathan Couser

THIS ARTICLE ANALYZES three saints' lives composed in eighth-century Bavaria before the region was incorporated into the Carolingian Empire. It argues that these hagiographies took shape within the complex, overlapping contexts of Bavaria's political position in Europe, of contact and competition with the cult of St. Boniface centered at Mainz and Fulda, and of the individual backgrounds and concerns of bishops Virgil of Salzburg and Arbeo of Freising, who either wrote the lives or oversaw their writing. Within these contexts, the lives of saints Rupert, Emmeram, and Corbinian asserted the importance of positive relations between Church and duke, promoted a missionary agenda for the Bavarian churches themselves, and constructed a "sacred topography" for the duchy where the holy could be encountered. These conceptions contributed to the development of Bavaria as a "micro-Christendom," possessed of its own resources of sacrality and legitimacy within the larger Christian world.

Knights and Knighthood in Gaelic Scotland, c. 1050–1300

Cynthia J. Neville and R. Andrew McDonald

THE AUTHORS ARGUE that the early reception into Scotland of European ideas about knighthood was more complex and fragmented than scholars have hitherto supposed. Members of the royal family and of the French and European aristocracy newly settled in the kingdom in the

twelfth century eagerly embraced the concept of knighthood and encouraged the spread of Continental ideas about chivalric conduct, but for
some prominent "native" lords—here defined predominantly as Gaelic-
speakers resident in the portions of the kingdom often referred to as the
Scottish *Gàidhealtachd*—European chivalry held, initially at least, more
muted appeal. By c. 1250 European-style knighthood and chivalry had
taken firm root among the secular Gaelic aristocracy but had been adapted to take into account the nature of native society.

The Making of a Myth: Giraldus Cambrensis, *Laudabiliter,* and Henry II's Lordship of Ireland

Anne J. Duggan

FOR THE WHOLE of the Middle Ages and beyond, Adrian IV's bull
Laudabiliter (1155 or 1156) was regarded as the authority behind Henry
II's seizure of Irish territory in 1171–72, an action that had momentous
consequences for the history of England and Ireland over the next eight
hundred years. This article re-examines the text and its context, and it
argues (a) that all known versions derive ultimately from that transmitted by
Gerald de Barri (Giraldus Cambrensis) in his *Expugnatio Hibernica (Conquest
of Ireland)* and other works (supported by the collation: Appendix 1);
(b) that Gerald substantially altered the text by omitting passages that
had been intended to dissuade the English king from any such venture
(supported by a reconstruction of the original: Appendix 2); and (c) that
Gerald falsified the context by making *Laudabiliter* the cornerstone of his
justification for "English" rule over the island of Ireland.

Middle Eastern Apocalyptic Traditions in Dante's *La Divina Commedia* and Mohammed's *Mi^craj* or Night Journey

Brenda Deen Schildgen

THIS ESSAY DISCUSSES the history of critical arguments about the
relationship between Dante's *Commedia* and the *Liber Scale* or *Mi^craj*,
Mohammed's night journey, and the connection between these arguments and more recent criticism of Western Orientalist scholarship. Accepting the likelihood that Dante encountered one of the translations of
the *Mi^craj* circulating in Europe during his lifetime (most likely in Latin,

although there were French and Castilian versions), the essay acknowledges parallels in the system of justice and punishment, the first-person narrator, symbolic reference, and apocalyptic urgency in both works but also highlights the notable differences in their literary repertoires, style, and, most important, their purpose as revealed in the works.

Praying by Numbers
Rachel Fulton

WHY COUNT PRAYERS? For most modern scholars following Huizinga and Weber, late medieval devotional practices such as the numbering of Christ's wounds or the recitation of the 150 Ave Marias of the rosary would seem to have more to do with the commercial development of the European economy and the corollary obsession with calculated exchange than with the spiritual or psychological well-being of their practitioners. Drawing on the history of the rosary, neoplatonic theories of number symbolism, and modern psychological studies of the nature of happiness, this article argues that the late medieval practice of praying by numbers may be seen, on the one hand, as a disciplined effort to participate in God's work of creation and, on the other, as a psychologically astute accommodation of the ideals of prayer to the contingencies of learning a difficult skill.

Agnes Bowker's Cat, the Rabbit Woman of Godalming, and the Shifting Nature of Portents in Early Modern Europe
Philip M. Soergel

DURING THE COURSE of the sixteenth century, most of northern Europe saw the emergence of a vigorous "portent press" that came to comment on nature's wonders and abnormalities for the information they revealed about the future course of events in government, religion, and society. Much of the commentary generated by the purveyors of this information—small and great printers throughout Europe's cities and their natural philosophical and moralist authors—spoke to the contemporary fascination with the imminence of the Apocalypse. At the same time the destabilizing potential inherent in this press meant that its activities were always highly supervised and subject to the censorship of political and religious authorities. This article traces the development of the exploitation of portents and natural wonders in the sixteenth and seventeenth centuries, with particular emphasis on England and Germany, two regions with especially well-developed "portent cultures" at this time. It examines the inchoate nature of these texts' political commentary and in its conclusion explores the reasons for the elimination of portents from the early "public sphere" Jürgen Habermas and others have observed emerging in early eighteenth-century Britain.

The State of the Soul and the Soul of the State: Reconciliation in the Two Parts of Shakespeare's *Henry IV*
Charles R. Forker

A CONCERN WITH reconciliation pervades the tragedies, comedies, and histories of Shakespeare. *1* and *2 Henry IV* focus the theme in the twin scenes in which Prince Hal wins over his disapproving and suspicious father, although the rejection of Falstaff contributes to the theme in a different key. Whereas the comedies and tragedies tend to treat forgiveness with a certain moral, even theological clarity, the chronicle plays often handle the theme in more complicated ways because reconciliation necessarily touches nations as well as individuals, blurring the line between Christian absolutes and political relativism and contingency. The state of the soul becomes entwined with the soul of the state. The tragic strain between a guilty monarch (who has usurped the throne from a legitimate predecessor) and his apparently irresponsible heir makes the moral, political, and emotional issues of the father-son relationship both movingly powerful and disturbingly ambiguous.

A Usable Past: Early Bavarian Hagiography in Context

Jonathan Couser
University of Notre Dame

Introduction

THE OLDEST SURVIVING written literature from east of the Rhine is a cluster of saints' lives composed in Bavaria in the mid-eighth century.[1] At the time, Bavaria was enjoying a period of relative independence under the rule of the Agilulfing Duke Tassilo III. The duchy had only emerged from the shadows of Christendom's fringes to take a place in the mainstream of the Christian world since about 700. As a result, these early hagiographies allow a unique insight into the contours of emergent Christianity

---

[1] Georg Baesecke, "Bischof Arbeo von Freising," in *Beiträge zur Geschichte der deutsche Sprache und Literatur* 68 (1945), 75–134. The following abbreviations will appear in the footnotes: MGH (Monumenta Germaniae Historica); SSRM (Scriptores Rerum Merovingicarum); SSRG (Scriptores Rerum Germanicarum); DD (Diplomata); *ZBLG* (*Zeitschrift für bayerische Landesgeschichte*); *MGSL* (*Mitteilungen der Gesellschaft für Salzburger Landeskunde*); NA (*Notitia Arnonis*); BN (*Breves Notitiae*); *MIÖG* (*Mitteilungen des Instituts für Österreiche Geschichtsforschung*); TF (Theodor Bitterauf, ed., *Die Traditionen des Hochstifts Freising*, 2 vols., Quellen und Erörterungen zur bayerischen und deutschen Geschichte. Neue Folge Band 4. [1905; repr. Munich, 1967]); TP (Max Heuwieser, ed., *Die Traditionen des Hochstifts Passau*, [1930; repr. Aalen, 1988]).

Studies in Medieval and Renaissance History, 3rd Series, Vol. 4 (2007)

on the frontiers of the Frankish world. Soon after their composition, in 788, Bavaria would be absorbed by the Carolingian Empire, and its churches would move in new directions.

Three hagiographies were written in Agilulfing Bavaria: Arbeo of Freising's *Vita sancti Corbiniani* and *Vita vel Passio sancti Haimhrammi*, and a lost *vita* of Rupert of Salzburg, probably composed under Rupert's successor Virgil, which formed the model for the Carolingian *Gesta Hrodberti Episcopi Salisburgensis* and the first chapter of the *Conversio Bagoariorum et Carantanorum* of 870 or 871.[2] Each claims to narrate the career of a churchman who ministered in Bavaria before the formal organization of its four bishoprics by Boniface of Mainz in 739.

The general content of the lost *Vita Hrodberti* can be surmised from the extensive overlap of its derivatives. It describes Rupert as a noble bishop from Worms who came to Bavaria in response to an invitation from Duke Theodo (c. 696–717). Given license to settle anywhere he wished, he made a tour down the Danube to the Pannonian frontier, then turned south to Wallersee, but finally heard of an ideal location at Salzburg. There he restored dilapidated church buildings and organized proper monastic life. He returned to Worms to recruit a group of assistants and a niece of his named Erendruda, who became the first abbess of a convent on the Nonnberg. Foreseeing his death, he returned home, accompanied by visions of angels.

Emmeram's life describes him as a bishop from Poitiers who desired to convert the pagan Avars. When Emmeram reached Bavaria, however, Theodo, who was at war with the Avars, forbade him to continue. He offered Emmeram the opportunity to settle in Bavaria instead and be its pontiff or chief abbot. Emmeram accepted. After three years, however, when the duke's daughter Ota became pregnant by a judge's son,

---

[2] *Arbeonis Episcopi Frisingensis: Vitae Sanctorum Haimhrammi et Corbiniani*, ed. Bruno Krusch, MGH SSRG in Usum Scholarum 13 (Hannover, 1920): *Vita Hrodberti episcopi Salisburgensis*, MGH SSRM VI, ed. Bruno Krusch and Wilhelm Levison (Hannover and Leipzig, 1913), pp. 140–62: Fritz Lošek, ed. and trans., *Die Conversio Bagoariorum et Carantanorum und der Brief des Erzbischofs Theotmar von Salzburg* (Hannover, 1997). A further edition of the *Vita Corbiniani*, with parallel German translation, is available in Hubert Glaser, Franz Brunhölzl, and Sigmund Benker, *Vita Corbiniani: Bischof Arbeo von Freising und die Lebensgeschichte des hl. Korbinian* (Munich and Zurich, 1983), and an edition with German translation of the *Vita Haimhrammi* was published by Bernhard Bischoff, *Leben und Leiden des Hl. Emmeram* (Munich, 1953).

Emmeram took the blame upon himself. He set out for Rome to explain the true situation, but Ota's brother Lantpert caught up with him and executed a grisly vengeance. A series of miracles followed his death, culminating in the translation of Emmeram's relics back to Regensburg.

Corbinian, according to his *Vita*, was a Frankish ascetic who gathered a monastic community around himself near Melun. Two successive pilgrimages to Rome brought recognition of his spiritual gifts, so that the pope gave him an episcopal consecration, a *pallium*, and a commission to preach throughout the world. After the second of these pilgrimages he settled at Freising in Bavaria, where he came into sharp conflict with Duke Grimoald (a son of Theodo, d. 725) and his wife Pilitrud. Corbinian escaped Pilitrud's conspiracies, however, and lived to die of old age under Duke Hucbert (725–35). Initially buried at Mais in the Tyrol, he was later translated to Freising by Arbeo, who believed the saint had saved his life as a young boy.

It is not the purpose of this article to assess the historical reliability of these three narratives.[3] We may say briefly that their trustworthiness varies. In the case of Rupert, the saint's career was known to his successor, Bishop Virgil of Salzburg, through the testimony of Rupert's own disciples and contemporaries.[4] The earliest version of Rupert's *Vita* was probably composed under Virgil, if not by him, and shows a generally restrained character. Thus, the *Vita Hrodberti* can be taken as a sober account of Rupert's career, at least in outline. The *vitae* written by Arbeo of Freising are a different matter. Their accounts are often highly schematic or stereotyped, given to radical hagiographic exaggeration, and show some chronological impossibilities. Still, Arbeo does occasionally indicate sources for individual episodes that might be authentic. Of Emmeram, little can be believed other than that he had been a religious

---

3 This has most recently been done for Emmeram by Carl Hammer, "Arbeo of Freising's 'Life and Passion' of St. Emmeram: The Martyr and His Critics," *Revue d'Histoire Ecclésiastique* 101 (2006), 5–36.

4 See Herwig Wolfram, "Libellus Virgilii. Ein quellenkritisches Problem der ältesten Salburger Güterverzeichnisse," in *Mönchtum, Episkopat und Adel zur Gründungszeit des Klosters Reichenau*, ed. Arno Borst (Sigmaringen, 1974), pp. 177–214; and Heinrich Wanderwitz, "Der Libellus Virgilii und das Verhältnis von Herzog und Bischöfen in Bayern," in *Virgil von Salzburg: Missionar und Gelehrter. Beiträge des internationalen Symposiums vom 21.–24. September 1984 in der Salzburger Residenz*, ed. Heinz Dopsch and Roswitha Juffinger (Salzburg, 1985), pp. 357–61.

figure of some local prominence, perhaps a Frank, who was murdered in the village of Helfendorf (southeast of modern Munich) during Duke Theodo's reign and came to be venerated locally.[5] Corbinian was also probably the leader of some local religious community at Freising in the 720s who forged connections between Bavaria and the Tyrol. He fell afoul of Duke Grimoald but was restored to favor under Hucbert before dying, and came to be venerated almost immediately.[6]

A hagiography, however, is most informative not when sifted for data on the period it purports to describe but when studied as a whole as a document of the era that produced it. Saints represent the ideals of the communities that venerate them. Their hagiographies reveal the values,

---

[5] Gottfried Mayr has attempted to date Emmeram's death to 715 or immediately prior, based on his belief that Ortlaip, the donor in a charter of 772, was a contemporary of the martyrdom. The argument rests on a highly questionable grammatical point—a "temporal *ubi*"—and is interesting, but not compelling. Gottfried Mayr, "Zur Todeszeit des Hl. Emmeram und zur frühen Geschichte des Klosters Herrenchiemsee. Bemerkungen zur Schenkung des Ortlaip in Helfendorf," ZBLG 34 (1971), 358–73, and Gottfried Mayr, "Neuerliche Anmerkungen zur Todeszeit des heiligen Emmeram und zur Kirchenpolitik Herzog Theodos," in *Typen der Ethnogenese unter besonderer Berücksichtigung der Bayern: Teil 1. Berichte des Symposions der Kommission für Frühmittelalterforschung, 27. bis 30. Oktober 1986, Stift Zwettl, Niederösterreich*, ed. Herwig Wolfram und Helmut Pohl (Vienna, 1990), pp. 199–215. See also the criticism of Gertrud Diepolder, "Arbeos Emmeramsleben und die Schenkung Ortlaips aus Helfendorf. Eine Quellenrevision im Lichte archäologischer Befunde," in *Land und Reich, Stamm und Nation: Probleme und Perspektiven bayerischer Geschichte. Festgabe für Max Spindler zum 90. Geburtstag*, ed. Andreas Kraus (Munich, 1984), pp. 269–85.

[6] The value of Arbeo's *vitae* as factual sources has been sharply challenged by Lothar Vogel; in *Vom Werden eines Heiligen: Eine Untersuchung der Vita Corbiniani des Bischofs Arbeo von Freising* (Berlin and New York, 2000), and in "Der Freisinger Bistumspatron Corbinian und seine *Vita*," in *Hagiographica* 11 (2004): 157–222. Vogel's form-critical approach has in turn been challenged in numerous book reviews and by Gertrud Diepolder, "Vom 'historischen Quellenwert' der *Vita* Corbiniani: Zum Umgang Lothar Vogels mit Bischof Arbeo von Freising als Historiograph," ZBLG 64, no. 1 (2001), 3–38, and Stephanie Haarländer, "Von der 'Destruktion' eines Heiligen: Zum Umgang Lothar Vogels mit Hagiographie," ZBLG 64, no. 1 (2001), 39–57. My purpose in this article is not to enter this debate, but it is apparent that the *vitae* are highly literary compositions with only faint traces of historical memory of their subjects. For further discussion of the historical reliability of these texts, see my dissertation, "The Chalice of Christ and the Chalice of Demons: The Making of Christendom in Agilolfing Bavaria, ca. 500–788 AD" (Notre Dame, 2006), cc. 2–3.

assumptions, and aspirations of these communities, as well as their anxieties and the evils they wish to condemn. The life of a church's patron or founder saint creates a "usable past," an account of the community's origins and experience that justifies its existence and practices.[7]

In this article, I will consider each of these saints' lives from Bavaria, asking what light each sheds on the self-image, and self-presentation, of the Bavarian churches. These texts present a variety of models of holiness, but common concerns can be discerned in all. The hagiographers of the Agilulfing era used these texts to tell a story of Bavaria's Christianization, whether this story was based in fact or not. Their narrative of missionaries coming to evangelize Bavaria simultaneously asserted the independence of the Bavarian churches from outside authorities, bound political rulers to the welfare of the church, and constructed a sacred topography for Bavaria itself. They also set a missionary agenda for the Bavarian church to pursue in the 770s. In these ways, the *vitae* created a vision of the duchy as a kind of "micro-Christendom," a zone of autonomous Christian culture with its own traditions, institutions, and sources of sacrality distinct from, but interconnected with, the larger Christian world.[8]

In order to see the significance of these *vitae*, we must situate them in three overlapping contexts: the political context of Bavaria and the Frankish world during the reign of Duke Tassilo III; the biographical

---

[7] Studies on hagiography as a genre and its usefulness for history abound. Useful introductions and relevant recent studies include Hippolyte Delehaye, *The Legends of the Saints: An Introduction to Hagiography,* trans. V. M. Crawford (1907; repr. Notre Dame, IN, 1961); Dieter von der Nahmer, *Die Lateinische Heiligenvita: Eine Einführung in die Lateinische Hagiographie* (Darmstadt, 1994); René Aigrain, *L'hagiographie: Ses sources, ses méthodes, son histoire* (1953; repr. Brussels, 2000); Arnold Angenendt, *Heilige und Reliquien: Die Geschichte ihres Kultes vom frühen Christentum bis zur Gegenwart* (Munich, 1994), pp. 138–48; Ian Wood, "The Use and Abuse of Latin Hagiography in the Early Medieval West," in *East and West: Modes of Communication,* Proceedings of the First Plenary Conference at Merida (Leiden, 1999), pp. 93–110; The expression "usable past" was coined in 1918 by Van Wyck Brooks to advocate a flexible version of American literary history that would inspire rather than discourage new writers: Van Wyck Brooks, "On Creating a Usable Past," *The Dial,* v. 64, no. 764 (April 11, 1918), 337–41. It has since become common coin; I use it broadly here to indicate narratives of the past which, deliberately or not, are framed in such a fashion as to support or justify present agendas.

[8] The concept of a "micro-Christendom" was articulated by Peter Brown, *The Rise of Western Christendom,* 2nd ed. (Malden, Mass., 2003), pp. 13–17 and 355–79.

contexts of Bishops Arbeo of Freising and Virgil of Salzburg, whose personalities shaped the *vitae*; and the hagiographical context of the eighth-century Bavarian churches, particularly in their relationship to saints' cults and church institutions in neighboring areas.

The Three Contexts of the Early Bavarian *Vitae*

The first contextual frame to consider is the political background. These *vitae* were written within a narrow time frame, between 768 and 774.[9] This period represented the high-water mark of Duke Tassilo III's independence and power. Initially under the regency of his mother, Chiltrud, and his uncle, the Frankish palace mayor and (later) King Pippin III, Tassilo came of age around 754 and distanced himself from his royal uncle by 763.[10] Carolingian chronicles claimed that Tassilo deserted the Frankish army that year, an act of treason known as *harisliz*. But although Pippin raised the matter in a Frankish assembly the following year, he took no action, implying that he could not muster a consensus among the Frankish aristocracy that Tassilo's behavior called for punishment.[11]

---

[9] See the individual dating arguments below, pp. 22–23, 30.

[10] The assumption that Tassilo's appearance to swear loyalty to Pippin at Compiègne in 757 represented his coming of age is probably mistaken; Tassilo was already bearing arms in Pippin's service in 755, a mark of adulthood. Most probably he assumed personal rule in 754 upon Chiltrud's death. At fourteen, he would have been legally competent under Bavarian law by this time. See Matthias Becher, *Eid und Herrschaft* (Sigmaringen, 1993), p. 30. Kurt Reindel, "Grundlegung: Das Zeitalter der Agilolfinger (bis 788)," in Max Spindler, ed. *Handbuch der bayerischen Geschichte*, 1. Band: Das Alte Bayern/Das Stammesherzogtum bis zum Ausgang des 12. Jahrhunderts. 2nd edition (Munich, 1981), p. 167. *Annales Mettenses Priores*, MGH SSRG in usum scholarum v. 10, ed. Bernhard von Simson (Hannover, 1905): 748, p. 41; 757, pp. 49–50; and 763, pp. 52–53. *Annales Regni Francorum*, MGH SSRG in usum scholarum v. 6, ed. Friedrich Kurze (Hannover, 1895): 748, pp. 6, 8; 757, pp. 14, 16; and 763, pp. 20–22. On the period of Tassilo's minority, see Jahn, *Ducatus Baiuvariorum: Das bairische Herzogtum der Agilolfinger* (Stuttgart, 1991), pp. 277–334; and Stefan Freund, *Von den Agilulfingern zu den Karolingern: Bayerns Bischöfe zwischen Kirchenorganisation, Reichsintegration und Karolingischer Reform (700–847)* (Munich, 2004), pp. 82–83.

[11] *Annales Regni Francorum* 764, p. 22: *Annales Mettenses Priores* 764, pp. 52–53.

After 763 Tassilo ruled independently and acted as a monarch in all
but title. He married the Lombard princess Liutpirc, forming an alliance
with King Desiderius. As her dowry, she probably brought Tassilo districts of the Tyrol that the Bavarians had lost in 725.[12] Tassilo visited Italy
again in 769, founding the monastery of Innichen on his return. Sometime between 769 and 777 he presided over two Bavarian assemblies on
the Frankish model, which passed reform legislation for both church and
secular law.[13] Both he and Liutpirc made pilgrimages to Rome in 769 and
772. Pope Hadrian baptized their son and heir, a boy named Theodo,
on the second of these visits.[14] In 770 Tassilo met with Bertrada, Pippin III's

---

[12] The year of this wedding is not directly attested and has been set anywhere
from 763 to 769; I have followed Jahn, *Ducatus*, p. 374. See Reindel, "Grundlegung,"
p. 169. That districts in the Tyrol were handed over to Tassilo as Liutpirc's dowry is only
an assumption, but a widely accepted and well grounded one. The relics of Valentinus
were translated from this region in 764; in 767 they were followed by the relics of
Corbinian and in 769 Tassilo was giving land at Innichen to Scharnitz/Schlehdorf
for the founding of a new monastery; Bishop Alim of Saeben/Sabiona appears in
the confraternity of Dingolfing not long thereafter. The date of Valentinus's translation makes an earlier date for the marriage seem more probable than a later one.
Paul the Deacon reports at the very end of his *Historia Langobardorum* that King
Liutprand had captured many fortresses (*castra*) from the Bavarians, so presumably
these were returned by Desiderius. Liutprand may have been operating in alliance
with Charles Martel in one of the campaigns of the 720s. Paul the Deacon, *Historia
Langobardorum*, MGH SSRG in usum scholarum v. 48, ed. Georg Waitz (1878; repr.
Hannover, 1987), 6.58, p. 242.

[13] *Concilium Dingolfingense*, and *Concilium Neuchingense*, ed. Albert Wer-
minghoff, MGH Concilia II (Hannover and Leipzig, 1906), pp. 93–97, 98–105. See
Heinrich Berg, "Zur Organisation der bayerischen Kirche und zu den bayerischen
Synoden des 8. Jahrhunderts," in *Typen der Ethnogenese unter besonderer Berück-
sichtigung der Bayern:* Teil 1, Berichte des Symposions der Kommission für Frühmit-
telalterforschung, 27. bis 30. Oktober 1986, Stift Zwettl, Niederösterreich, ed. Herwig
Wolfram und Helmut Pohl (Vienna, 1990), pp. 181–97; and Wilfried Hartmann und
Heinz Dopsch, "Bistümer, Synoden und Metropolitenverfassung," in *Die Bajuwaren:
Von Severin bis Tassilo 488–788. Gemeinsame Landesausstellung des Freistaates
Bayern und des Landes Salzburg,* ed. Hermann Dannheimer und Heinz Dopsch
Rosenheim/Bayern, Mattsee/Salzburg, 19. Mai bis 6. November 1988, pp. 318–27;
Wilfried Hartmann, *Die Synoden der Karolingerzeit im Frankenreich und Italien,*
Konziliengeschichte, Reihe A: Darstellungen, ed. Walter Brandmüller (Paderborn,
1989), pp. 88–96.

[14] Jahn, *Ducatus*, pp. 390–94. The number of known persons baptized, confirmed, or held as godchildren by early medieval popes is small in any case, compri-
sing King Caedwalla of Wessex and the sons of Pippin III. See Arnold Angenendt,

widow, who constructed a three-way alliance across the Alps with Franks, Lombards, and Bavarians all linked to each other.[15] The balance, however, did not last. In 773 or 774, Charlemagne invaded Italy at Pope Hadrian's request, deposed Desiderius and took the Lombard crown for himself.[16] Tassilo, allied to both sides, stayed out of the conflict.[17] Ultimately, the growth of Charles's power in both Italy and Germany spelled the end of Bavarian independence. Increased Frankish pressure in the 780s ended with Tassilo's deposition in 788, bringing Bavaria under direct Carolingian rule.[18]

Kaiserherrschaft und Königstaufe: Kaiser, Könige und Päpste als geistliche Patrone in der abendländischen Missionsgeschichte (Berlin, 1984), pp. 152–63.

[15] Jahn, *Ducatus*, pp. 394–98. Sturm, the abbot of Fulda, also played a role in this flurry of diplomacy, as his *Vita* credits him with making peace between Charlemagne and Tassilo. *Vita Sturmi*, c. 22.

[16] Noble, *Republic*, pp. 99–132. Janet L. Nelson, "Making a Difference in Eighth-Century Politics: The Daughters of Desiderius," in *After Rome's Fall: Narrators and Sources of Early Medieval History. Essays Presented to Walter Goffart*, ed. Alexander Callander Murray (Toronto, 1998), pp. 171–90, demonstrates that Liutpirc, like at least two of her sisters, exercised political influence long after her father's fall, and thus cannot be seen only as tokens in a game of early medieval marriage politics.

[17] Jahn, *Ducatus*, pp. 465–71.

[18] Jahn, *Ducatus*, pp. 521–50. It is likely that the entire Tassilo affair of 788 caused a crisis of confidence among the Frankish aristocracy that the official chronicles attempted to assuage. In 763 Pippin III was unable to gain enough support to act against Tassilo's supposed desertion (see above, p. 6); a coup was attempted in 792 or 793 under Charlemagne's son Pippin the Hunchback (Einhard, *Vita Caroli Magni*, ed. Georg Waitz, MGH SSRG in usum scholarum v. 25 (1911; repr. Hannover, 1947), c. 20, pp. 25–26), after which Tassilo was brought out of his monastic confinement to renounce all claims to his dukedom, and beg Charles's forgiveness for his offenses, at the Synod of Frankfurt in 794. The *Annales Regni Francorum* and *Annales Mettenses Priores* mention neither the conspiracy nor Tassilo's presence at Frankfurt, but instead give elaborate treatment of Tassilo's debts to the Carolingians, his treasonous conduct, and then treat his deposition of 788 as final. However, at least one document from after 788 (*TF*125) is dated by Tassilo's regnal years, suggesting that the events of 788 were not so final as the chronicles suggest. It is possible that an early redaction of the *Annales Regni Francorum* was composed to prepare for the Frankfurt synod. See Johannes Fried, "Zum Prozess gegen Tassilo," in *794—Karl der Grosse in Frankfurt am Main: Ein König bei der Arbeit*, ed. Johannes Fried (Sigmaringen, 1994), pp. 114–15. The difficulties Tassilo's fall posed for the Carolingians is shown in Stuart Airlie, "Narratives of Triumph and Rituals of Submission: Charlemagne's Mastering of Bavaria," in *Transactions of the Royal Historical Society*, Sixth Series, vol. 9 (1999), pp. 93–119.

Thus, in the late 760s and early 770s, when these *vitae* were being planned and written, Bavaria was ruled by a duke who had established himself as a sovereign in his own right, able to negotiate and form alliances on equal terms with Frankish and Lombard kings and who enjoyed the papal recognition normally reserved for monarchs. Tassilo also worked to develop monasticism in his duchy, founding or consenting to the foundations of numerous houses during the 760s and 770s including Innichen, Schäftlarn, Mattsee, Tegernsee, Kremsmünster, and probably lesser-known houses such as Weltenburg, Metten, and others.[19] The translations of Emmeram, Corbinian, and Rupert into their new shrines probably took place with Tassilo's consent and even with his active participation.[20] His son carried the same name as the duke who would appear as the ideal ruler in the *vitae*. While the texts are not products of the ducal court, they should be seen against this pattern of ducal support for the Bavarian churches.

The hagiographies of the Agilulfing period are also bound to two dominant personalities of the Bavarian churches: the bishops Virgil of Salzburg and Arbeo of Freising. Their careers thus form the second frame within which these texts must be seen.

The main biographic source for Virgil is the *Conversio Bagoariorum et Carantanorum*, composed around 870 but probably based on good documentation from Salzburg. According to its account, Virgil was an Irishman who came to the continent in Pippin's time, probably about 743.[21] At Compiègne he met Pippin III and stayed with him for about two years. Afterwards Pippin sent him to Bavaria. He acted only as abbot of St. Peter's in Salzburg at first, while a companion named Dobdagrecus

---

[19] Prinz, *Frühes Mönchtum*, pp. 317–445, and Ludwig Holzfurtner, *Gründung und Gründungsüberlieferung. Quellenkritische Studien zur Gründungsgeschichte der bayerischen Klöster der Agilolfingerzeit und ihrer hochmittelalterlichen Überlieferung*, Münchner Hist. Studien. Bayer. Gesch. 11 (Kallmünz, 1984).

[20] I have argued that these translations represented an aspect of Tassilo's ecclesiastical policy in my dissertation, "The Chalice of Christ and the Chalice of Demons" (PhD dissertation, Notre Dame, 2006), pp. 309–12.

[21] *Conversio*, c. 2, p. 100. Virgil was in Bavaria by 746, as he complained to the pope of Boniface's actions there. Epp. Bon. 68, pp. 141–42. If the two-year stay with Pippin described in the *Conversio* is accurate, he must have been in Francia no later than 744–46, and perhaps a year or more earlier.

performed episcopal functions, until Virgil was finally consecrated bishop himself in 749.[22]

Although foreign, Virgil adapted to Bavarian conditions. He largely relied on the personnel he found in Salzburg; there are few Irish names among his associates.[23] He challenged criticisms of the Bavarian clergy from the papal legate Boniface of Mainz and gained ducal support. The underlying reason for the conflict between Virgil and Boniface is unclear. The sources do not support an interpretation overdetermined by supposed inherent antagonisms between Celtic and Anglo-Saxon traditions; none of the usual bones of contention (tonsure, calculation of Easter, and so forth) arose between Boniface and Virgil.[24] Possibly they were predisposed to conflict due to simmering rivalry between their Frankish patrons, the brothers Pippin (behind Virgil) and Carloman (behind Boniface). The actual conflict that emerged, however, was based on differing assessments of the Bavarian church itself. Boniface took a strict line, calling for the repetition of incorrectly performed baptisms. Virgil argued that sacraments remained valid if no heresy was intended. Also, Virgil claimed the right

---

[22] The chronology of the sources needs to be disentangled here. The *Conversio* claims that Virgil was consecrated in 767, after three years when Dobdagrecus acted as bishop. *Conversio*, c. 2, p. 100. The date of 767 is probably scribal confusion and may represent when construction began on Virgil's new cathedral in Salzburg, which was completed in 774. The period of Dobdagrecus's "vice-episcopacy" would then be 746–49. See Freund, *Agilolfingern zu den Karolingern*, p. 90 n. 304, and especially Herwig Wolfram, *Salzburg, Bayern, Oesterreich: Die Conversio Bagoariorum et Carantanorum und die Quellen ihrer Zeit* (Vienna, 1995), pp. 258–63.

[23] There is a long-standing tendency to identify Latin and Biblical names from Virgil's Salzburg as concealed Irishmen, like Virgil himself. However, there is no reason to assume that these were Irish rather than Alpine *Romani*. Besides Virgil himself, we know of his companion Dobdagrecus (Dubh-da-Cruich), who had an episcopal consecration but later served as abbot of Chiemsee. Boniface's letters complain of another "Scottus" in Bavaria named Samson. Since Samson was teaching about baptism in terms reminiscent of Pope Zacharias's response to Boniface on the subject, he may have been another member of Virgil's entourage. *S. Bonifatii et Lullii Epistolae*, ed. Michael Tangl, MGH Epp. Selectae vol. 1 (Berlin, 1916), ep. 80, p. 177. Two other members of the community of St. Peter's-Salzburg carry Irish names, monks named Baithanus and Mailprech; these were presumably companions of Virgil's as well. Karl Forstner, "Das Salzburger Scriptorium unter Virgil und das Verbrüderungsburch von St. Peter," in *Virgil von Salzburg*, p. 135.

[24] Cf. Pàdraig P. Ò Néill, "Bonifaz und Virgil—Konflikt zweier Kulturen," in *Virgil von Salzburg*, pp. 76–83.

to succeed to the next available bishopric in Bavaria, whereas Boniface, regarding himself as the region's metropolitan, reserved to himself the right to choose new bishops.[25] Both men were noted educators, but Virgil was more inclined to speculative cosmology while Boniface remained a dogmatic grammarian. Personality conflicts may have exacerbated friction arising from political or ecclesiological grounds.

Virgil founded a scriptorium at Salzburg and was remembered as a teacher and an intellectual.[26] Although he was not, as once thought, the author of the remarkable *Cosmography* of "Aethicus Ister," the work was known and copied in Bavaria during his episcopate, and Virgil probably played a role in its dissemination there.[27] Boniface accused him of teaching the existence of inhabited antipodes; that is, of lands and people on the far side of the world, an idea that Virgil probably learned from late antique pagan sources, such as Martianus Capella, rather than from any Christian writer. The pope summoned Virgil to answer for these views, but whether the Irishman responded is unknown. He succeeded either

---

[25] Epp. Bon. 68 and 80.

[26] Alcuin, *Carmen* CIX, in *Inscriptiones Colonienses et Salisburgenses*, MGH Poetae Latini aevi Carolini, vol. 1., ed. Ernst Dümmler (1881; rep. Munich, 1978), p. 340. On the Salzburg scriptorium under Virgil, see Bernhard Bischoff, *Die südostdeutschen Schreibschulen und Bibliotheken in der Karolingerzeit*, vol. 2 (Wiesbaden, 1960), pp. 54–59.

[27] The identity of the pseudonymous "Aethicus Ister" is unknown. The text is most recently edited and commentated by Otto Prinz, *Die Kosmographie des Aethicus* (Munich, 1993). An older edition is that of Heinrich Wuttke, *Die Kosmographie des Istrier Aithikos im lateinischen Auszüge des Hieronymus* (Leipzig, 1853). The proposal that the text was produced by Virgil as a "literary revenge" on Boniface was offered by Heinz Löwe, "Ein literarischer Widersacher des Bonifatius. Virgil von Salzburg und die Kosmographie des Aethicus Ister," *Abhandlungen der Akademie von Mainz, Geistes- und sozialwissenschaftlichen Klasse* 11 (1951), 903–83. However, the main point of cosmographic contention between Boniface and Virgil, the existence of inhabited Antipodes, is not addressed at all in the Aethicus text. It is now dated to the late seventh or early eighth century. See Kurt Hillkowitz, *Zur Kosmographie des Aethicus* (1934; repr. Cologne, 1973); Heinz Löwe, "Salzburg als Zentrum literarischen Schaffens im 8. Jahrhundert," *MGSL* 115 (1975), 114–43; Michael Herren, "Wozu diente die Fälschung der Kosmographie des Aethicus," in *Lateinische Kultur im 8. Jahrhundert, Traube Gedenkschrift*, ed. A. Lehner and W. Berschin (St. Ottilien, 1989), pp. 145–59; and Marina Smyth, "Das Universum in der Kosmographie des Aethicus Ister," in *Virgil von Salzburg*, pp. 170–82.

in ignoring the summons or in vindicating his beliefs, for he continued unhindered as bishop of Salzburg for another thirty-six years.[28] Virgil was also an active advocate of the rights of his see. He revived the claims of the bishops of Salzburg to the cell of St. Maximilian, a small monastic settlement founded in Rupert's time. It had since come under the control of its secular founders. Despite Virgil's efforts, Salzburg gained control of the cell only after Charlemagne's arrival in Bavaria.[29] In another case, Virgil was invited to consecrate the church for a new aristocratic monastery at Otting. When the founder declined to declare who would have authority over the house, however, Virgil refused to perform the consecration until the right of the bishop of Salzburg to govern its affairs was acknowledged.[30] Together with this activism for property, Virgil also undertook a massive building campaign at Salzburg. Dedicated in 774, the new cathedral he created was, for a time, the largest church in Europe north of the Alps. The sheer scale of the project announced that Bavaria had "arrived" as an entity to be reckoned with in western Christendom.[31]

---

[28] Epp. Bon. 80, pp. 178–79. See John Carey, "Ireland and the Antipodes: The Heterodoxy of Virgil of Salzburg," *Speculum* 64, no. 1 (January 1989), 1–11; Valerie I. J. Flint, "Monsters and the Antipodes in the Early Middle Ages and Enlightenment," *Viator* 15 (1984), 65–80.

[29] The entire affair is related in *Notitia Arnonis* c. 8, pp. 94, 96; and *Breves Notitiae* 3, pp. 8–10. See Fritz Lošek, ed. and trans., *Notitia Arnonis und Breves Notitiae: Die Salzburger Güterverzeichnisse aus der Zeit um 800: Sprachliche-historische Einleitung, Text und Übersetzung* (1990), pp. 104–8 and 112–18. At no point in either text is the conflict over St. Maximilian explicitly said to have been resolved, though they were produced around 790 and 800, respectively; however, *NA* 8.8 states that the *noticiam* (it is unclear if the entirety of the *NA* is meant or only the report on the Maximilian Cell) has been drawn up with Charlemagne's consent in the same year he took control of Bavaria, which presumably means that Charlemagne decided the case in Salzburg's favor in 788 or 789. See Warren Brown, *Unjust Seizure: Conflict, Interest, and Authority in an Early Medieval Society* (Ithaca, NY, 2001), pp. 45–52 and 83–85.

[30] *BN* 13.1–5, p. 120.

[31] The Salzburg Cathedral was excavated in 1956–58 and again in 1966–67. Its axis lay slightly diagonal to the modern structure throughout the Middle Ages, so that the choir stood approximately where the modern north transept is. Interpretation of the earliest layers remains debated, but the excavators believed that Virgil built a three-aisled basilica measuring 33m x 66m between 767 and 774. See Heinz Dopsch, "Der heilige Rupert in Salzburg: Vor 1300 Jahren kam der 'Grunderheilige'

Finally, Virgil took responsibility for Christian missions to the Carantanian Slavs to Salzburg's southeast. After the Bavarians wrested the overlordship of Carantania from the Avars, the Slavic Duke Boruth handed over his son Cacatius and his nephew Cheitmar as hostages, to be raised as Christians.[32] Each succeeded to the ducal office in turn. Cheitmar brought a priest named Maioranus as chaplain. Soon, he asked Virgil to send a bishop for his people; Virgil declined to come himself, but sent a chorepiscopus named Modestus, who ministered there in the years between 752 or 757 and 763, with a team of priests and other clergy.[33] After Modestus's death, however, a series of pagan uprisings disrupted the mission between 763 and their final suppression by Tassilo in 772.[34] Thereafter a regular rotation of clergy went from Salzburg to Carantania. It appears that the Carantanian mission was a prize project of the church at Salzburg, but also one that could be thrown into doubt by political setbacks.

Virgil is a difficult puzzle to solve. He came to the continent as an Irish *peregrinus*, but made his way in continental style without the tensions associated with other *peregrini* like Columbanus.[35] Yet he did not simply

---

aus Worms am Rhein," in *Hl. Rupert von Salzburg: 696–1996. Katalog der Ausstellung im Dommuseum zu Salzburg und in der Erzabtei St. Peter, 16. Mai 1996–27. Oktober 1996*, ed. P. Petrus Eder OSB and Johann Kronbichler (Salzburg, 1996), p. 74; Wolfram, *Geburt*, pp. 136–37; F. Wagner, "Bemerkungen zur Aufrisskonstruktion des ersten Salzburger Dombaus," *MGSL* 120/121 (1980/1981), 289–303; Hermann Vetters, "Die mittelalterlichen Dome Salzburgs," in *Virgil von Salzburg*, pp. 286–316; and Fritz Moosleitner, "Neue Ergebnisse zu den Salzburger Domgrabungen," in *Virgil von Salzburg*, pp. 317–25, who believes the western façade used to define the cathedral's scale actually dates from the episcopate of Arn or possibly Archbishop Hartwik (991–1023), and that Virgil's church was smaller than generally believed.

[32] *Conversio*, c. 4, p. 104. Odilo is not named nor is the date given in the text, but its references to "King" Pippin mean that the events must have occurred after Charles Martel's death at the end of 740. It is unlikely that the subjection of the Carantanians occurred after Odilo's death, during Tassilo's minority from 749–56.

[33] *Conversio*, c. 5, p. 106. The dates for this period must be calculated backward from later references in the text. Modestus was presumably a chorepiscopus, an "auxiliary" or (literally) "field bishop" operating under the local diocesan, Virgil.

[34] *Conversio*, c. 5, p. 108. The timing suggests that this uprising may have been the cause of Tassilo's sudden withdrawal from Pippin's forces in Aquitaine.

[35] Michael J. Enright, "Iromanie-Irophobie Revisited: A Suggested Frame of Reference for Considering Contintental Reactions to Irish *peregrini* in the Seventh and Eighth Centuries," in *Karl Martell in seiner Zeit*, ed. Jörg Jarnut, Ulrich Nonn, and Michael Richter (Sigmaringen, 1994), pp. 367–80.

assimilate, either; when he commissioned a confraternity book to com-
pile those for whom the monks of Salzburg prayed, a list of Irish abbots'
names shows that he remembered his roots.[36] It was Pippin who sent him
to Bavaria, perhaps initially to keep tabs on Odilo and then to supervise
Tassilo's minority; but he won Odilo's favor, and operated under Tassilo
with no discernible friction, even at the height of Tassilo's independence.

Arbeo of Freising came from very different origins, but was a close
associate of Virgil's. His birth must have fallen shortly before 718, as he
was dedicated to clerical life by his family around 727 and was thus still a
child at that time, but had received a priestly ordination by 748.[37] At least
part of his childhood was spent in the Tyrol, but he thought of himself
as a Bavarian.[38] When he was a priest at Freising, he served as a scribe
for charters of land donations. As these charters use formulae similar to
those of Lombard documents, an Italian education has been hypothe-
sized for Arbeo but cannot be proven.[39] He might have learned the forms

---

[36] There are a few symptoms of insular script in early manuscripts from the
St. Peter's scriptorium, although the Salzburg script is not overwhelmingly "insu-
lar." See Karl Forstner, *Die karolingischen Handschriften und Fragmente in den
Salzburger Bibliotheken* (Salzburg, 1962), p. 18. Verses composed by Alcuin for the
Salzburg cathedral emphasize Virgil's impressive Irish education. Alcuin, *Carmen
CIX*, p. 340.

[37] Arbeo was given to the church at Freising a year after the death of St. Corbinian,
so he could not have been over twelve at that time, the age of majority in Bavarian law. As
Corbinian lived into Duke Hucbert's reign, his death can have occurred no earlier
than 725. Since Arbeo was a priest (and therefore thirty years old) by 748, Corbinian
was being venerated as a saint no later than 730. This is reinforced by Arbeo's statement that the spring at Weihenstephan was dry for forty years from Corbinian's
death until his translation back to Freising (*Vita Corbiniani*, c. 28, pp. 219–20). If the
figure is precise, which it need not be, Corbinian died in 727.

[38] He identified the Bavarians as "our people" (*gens nostra*), *Vita Corbiniani* c.
15, p. 203.

[39] On Arbeo's background and education see Heinz Löwe, "Arbeo von Freising:
Eine Studie zu Religiösität und Bildung im 8. Jahrhundert," in Löwe, *Von Cassiodor
zu Dante* (Berlin, 1973), pp. 75–110; Löwe, following Baesecke, argues for an Italian education for Arbeo on pp. 77–84. See also Hubert Glaser, "Bischof Arbeo von
Freising als Gegenstand der neueren Forschung," in *Vita Corbiniani: Bischof Arbeo
von Freising und die Lebensgeschichte des hl. Korbinian,* ed. Hubert Glaser, Franz
Brunhölzl, and Sigmund Benker (Munich and Zurich, 1983), pp. 32–33, which follows the suggestion that Arbeo simply employed forms already in use in Bavaria.
Under Bishop Joseph, a cell was founded at Isen dedicated to St. Zeno (*TF* 4, 6). This

in the Tyrol as part of his elementary education before being given to the church, but Lombard influences in Freising predated Arbeo's activity, so he may have learned these formulae there.[40]

At any rate, Arbeo was certainly in Freising by 748 and a priest there.[41] He became archpriest later and head of a newly founded monastery at Scharnitz (later moved to Schlehdorf) in 764.[42] He described Bishop Ermbert, who died in 748, as his *nutritor*; but most of his career that we can trace occurred under Joseph, Ermbert's successor.[43] Joseph in turn died in 765, so that Arbeo left Schlehdorf and became the new bishop of Freising. He had the relics of St. Corbinian brought to Freising from Mais in 767 and probably wrote the *Life of St. Corbinian* for the saint's feast day soon thereafter.[44]

We hear of fewer conflicts involving Arbeo than Virgil, but the tempestuous nature of Corbinian's *Vita* suggests that the existing charters may conceal more property disputes than they admit. He pursued the

---

dedication reveals a connection to Mais in the Tyrol (St. Corbinian's resting place, where Arbeo spent his boyhood) but possibly also to Verona. It also appears that Spanish canon law collections were making their way to Bavaria through northern Italy in the mid-eighth century; see Peter Landau, "Kanonessammlungen in Bayern in der Zeit Tassilos III. und Karls des Grossen," in *Regensburg, Bayern und Europa: Festschrift für Kurt Reindel zu seinem 70. Geburtstag*, ed. Lothar Kolmer und Peter Segl (Regensburg, 1995), pp. 137–60.

[40] Herwig Wolfram, "Intitulatio I: Lateinische Königs- und Fürstentitel bis zum Ende des 8. Jahrhunderts," *MIÖG* 21 (1967), 156–84.

[41] *TF 2*.

[42] Arbeo appears with the title of "archpriest" in *TF 7* (June 24, 754). He received the leadership of Scharnitz/Schlehdorf in *TF 19* (June 29, 763). The document assigns Arbeo responsibility for the leadership of Schlehdorf but never actually names him abbot. This has raised the question as to Schlehdorf's constitutional status and whether Arbeo ever functioned as abbot there. Atto, however, was clearly abbot of Schlehdorf during Arbeo's episcopate and succeeded Arbeo as bishop of Freising, suggesting that Arbeo set a precedent for a career track from Schlehdorf to Freising.

[43] *Vita Corbiniani*, c. 30, p. 222.

[44] *Vita Corbiniani*, cc. 41–42, pp. 228–31. The first document to witness the presence of Corbinian's relics at Freising is dated to October 1, 767 (*TF 24*). According to the *Vita Corbiniani*, the translation of Corbinian was prompted by the removal of Valentinus's relics from Mais, which occurred in April of 767. Corbinian had asked to be buried in Mais so as to lie near Valentinus; this request was no longer meaningful with Valentinus's departure. So Corbinian's translation must have occurred between April and October of 767. See Jahn, *Ducatus*, pp. 389–90.

welfare of his see aggressively; compared to nineteen charters preserved from his predecessors' reigns, eighty-eight charters from Arbeo's episcopate survive.[45] He died a year before Virgil, in 783.

Scholars have imagined Arbeo in radically different ways. One long-standing view sees him as an anti-Agilulfing activist, agitating on behalf of the Carolingians well before Tassilo's actual fall.[46] This view has been questioned recently, and some more current studies see Arbeo as one of Tassilo's most important supporters, whose death was a blow to the duke's independence in the 780s.[47] The view of him as an anti-Agilulfing propagandist is based on two pieces of evidence; one of these is the portrayal of the Agilulfings in Arbeo's *vitae*, and will be dealt with below.

The other comes from a property dispute of 804, shortly after the Carolingian takeover of Bavaria. One account of the dispute claims that Tassilo and Liutpirc had confiscated certain properties from Freising in Arbeo's time, because Arbeo was less loyal to them than to Charlemagne.[48]

---

[45] *TF* 1–108. This is approximately four charters per year under Arbeo, compared to 0.8 per year under Ermbert and Joseph. Many older charters were probably not preserved; the absence of a foundation document from the bishopric's creation in 739 is curious. Even so, the difference is striking.

[46] Friedrich Prinz saw a pro-Frankish, anti-Agilulfing faction centered on the Huosi kin-group and led by Arbeo in western Bavaria, compared to a pro-Agilulfing party in eastern Bavaria. See Friedrich Prinz, "Herzog und Adel im agilulfingischen Bayern," *ZBLG* 25 (1962), pp. 283–311, repr. in *Zur Geschichte der Bayern*, ed. Karl Bosl (Darmstadt, 1965), pp. 225–63; and Bosl, *Frühes Münchtum*, throughout pp. 317–448 but especially at, e.g., pp. 364–66. The close relationship between Virgil and Arbeo (*Vita Corbiniani*, prologue, pp. 188–89) should already suggest the limitations of such a view (Prinz believed that Virgil was isolated at Salzburg, a judgment which is not borne out by Virgil's very effective career there). Despite criticisms of Prinz's view, the "anti-Agilulfing" Arbeo still appears in scholarship from time to time. See Ian Wood, *The Missionary Life* (Harlow, 2001), pp. 153–54; Kathy Lynn Roper Pearson, *Conflicting Loyalties in Early Medieval Bavaria* (Aldershot, 1999), pp. 75–111. Freund, *Agilulfingern zu den Karolingern*, p. 92, declines to make an argument about Arbeo's loyalties but sees the Bavarian episcopate as a whole supporting the duke. For example, the episcopal successions at Freising and Salzburg in 783 and 784 occurred without strife, and both of the new bishops were native Bavarians who had been groomed for office.

[47] Joachim Jahn has re-imagined Arbeo as a strong ducal supporter. In Jahn's view, the undermining of Tassilo's power was not the result of Arbeo's agitation but a change of course by his successor, Atto. See Jahn, *Ducatus*, pp. 521–27.

[48] *TF* 193b. *TF* 193a presents a version of the *placitum* omitting any mention of Arbeo's loyalties. On the politicization of this dispute, see Brown, *Unjust Seizure*,

This is the only direct statement in any source that Arbeo was hostile to Tassilo. Another account of the same dispute, however, omits any reference to Arbeo's loyalties. The transfer of power may have created a free-for-all "land grab," as Charlemagne explicitly stated that charters and privileges issued by the "wicked men" Odilo and Tassilo would not necessarily be confirmed under the new regime and all property claims would be reconsidered.[49] In this charged environment, it is not hard to suspect Atto, Arbeo's successor at Freising, of embroidering or even concocting a story to explain how baptismal churches in his diocese came to be under the control of a monastery—a story that played along with the current political discourse.

We should not presume a strong anti-Agilulfing agenda in Arbeo's *vitae* on the basis of a single charter produced twenty years after Arbeo's death.[50] At the time of the lives' composition, Tassilo was at the height of his independence, and his Lombard allies had not yet fallen. Indeed, it appeared that an age of transalpine peace had come, with marriages and alliances linking Frankish, Lombard, and Bavarian rulers to each other by 772. Even if Atto told the truth, that Arbeo was penalized for his support of Charlemagne against Tassilo, this does not mean that the bishop of Freising was an inveterate enemy of the duke, for the Carolingians and Agilulfings only came into open conflict in 780, well after the composition date of the Bavarian *vitae*.[51]

Arbeo and Virgil were thus two complex personalities whose backgrounds put them at the crossroads of many different streams of early medieval culture. Virgil was a prestigious outsider, with ties to Celtic traditions and to Carolingian Francia, yet who also could integrate himself into the church of Agilulfing Bavaria without noticeable difficulty. Arbeo, on the other hand, was the product of local culture, but with links to the Tyrolean frontier and perhaps to the Lombard world beyond it. The lives they produced would reflect these various streams of influence.

---

pp. 113–16, and Joachim Jahn, "Virgil, Arbeo und Cozroh. Verfassungsgeschichtliche Beobachtungen an bairischen Quellen des 8. und 9. Jahrhunderts," *MGSL* 130 (1990), 201–92 (here at pp. 231–33).

[49] MGH DD Karolinorum I, ed. Engelbert and Mühlbacher (Hannover, 1906), 162.

[50] Brown, *Unjust Seizure*, p. 115, n. 69.

[51] Jahn, *Ducatus*, pp. 521–50.

A third framework in which to read the lives of Rupert, Emmeram, and Corbinian is their hagiographic context; that is, the background of texts and cults in eighth-century Bavaria that exerted influence on its churches. Most significant of these is the cult of the Anglo-Saxon missionary and papal legate St. Boniface. Boniface had visited Bavaria on four occasions: in 719, the early 730s, 738 or 739, and finally around 746 to 748.[52] In 754 he met his death at the hands of pagan raiders in Frisia and almost instantly became the new martyr-saint of early medieval Europe.[53] His cult, however, was not instantly or universally disseminated. Centers of Boniface-veneration were at Utrecht, the see nearest to his martyrdom and ruled by his disciple Gregory; at Mainz, which had been Boniface's own archiepiscopal see and which was under his disciple Lull; and Fulda, Boniface's favorite monastic foundation where yet another follower, Sturm, was abbot and where his relics finally came to lie.[54] Boniface was also venerated as a martyr in his native England, but his cult would have to wait until Charlemagne's time to come to the Frankish court.[55] Not until the eleventh century would his name start to appear as a patron of churches beyond these early cult centers.[56]

Boniface was not remembered fondly by the leaders of the Bavarian church. His name does not appear in the Salzburg *Confraternity Book*,

---

[52] Willibald, *Vita Bonifatii*, ed. Wilhelm Levison, MGH SSRG in usum scholarum v. 57 (1905; repr. Hannover, 2003), cc. 5 (p. 22), 6 (pp. 35–36), 7 (pp. 37–39). Epp. Bon. 45 (October 29, 739), 68 (July 1, 746), and 80 (May 1, 748). The *Vita* thus attests only three visits, the last in 738 or 739 to 740. However, letter 68 (from Pope Zacharias to Boniface) describes a complaint from Virgil and Sidonius in Bavaria that Boniface has required rebaptism on the basis of a priest's mispronunciation of the formula of the Trinity. Six years seems a very long interval for this complaint to have waited to be brought to Zacharias's attention, but it is hard to imagine how Boniface could have objected to the mispronunciation without being present to hear it. Letter 80 indicates that Boniface continued to press his case on Bavarian affairs over the next two years. I therefore infer a fourth visit of Boniface to Bavaria, at least in 746 and possibly later, from these letters. Boniface's setbacks in this period probably account for the omission of the fourth visit from the *Vita*.

[53] *Vita Bonifatii*, cc. 8–9, pp. 41–57.

[54] Petra Kehl, *Kult und Nachleben des heiligen Bonifatius im Mittelalter (754–1200)* (Fulda, 1993), passim.

[55] Kehl, *Kult und Nachleben*, pp. 77–87.

[56] Hans Ulrich Rudolf, *Apostoli Gentium: Studien zum Apostelepitheton under besonderer Berücksichtigung des Winfried-Bonifatius und seiner Verehrung* (Cöppingen, 1971).

despite his martyrdom and the fact that he had established John as Salzburg's bishop in 739. Bavarian bishops (apart from Willibald of Eichstätt, a special case) did not attend the Anglo-Saxon's reform councils of the 740s.[57] Virgil complained of Boniface's actions to the pope in 746, and Boniface responded by accusing Virgil of heresy and of falsely pretending to have a papal promise of a bishopric in 748. By that time Duke Odilo (Tassilo's father) was already favoring Virgil over Boniface, which the latter attributed to the Irishman's intrigues.[58] Sidonius, Virgil's associate in these disputes, became bishop of Passau in the 750s, suggesting that a partisan role in the conflict did not diminish one's standing among the Bavarian clergy.[59]

Nevertheless, Fulda and the cult of St. Boniface exerted a pull on Bavarians. Fulda's abbot, Sturm, was himself a Bavarian of a very influential family, and an indefatigable promoter of his teacher's cult.[60] Nor was Sturm alone of his countrymen at Fulda. Older attempts to see Fulda as having a "Bavarian stamp," on the evidence of the monks' names, have largely been abandoned, but there were clearly a number of Bavarians among the brothers there; these must have been recruited as oblates from Bavarian families, and probably brought property in Bavaria with them into the cloister's portfolio of landholdings.[61] Fulda held property

---

[57] Episcopal attendance is known for the *Concilium in Austrasia Habitum q.d. Germanicum*, MGH Concilia 2.1, ed. Albert Werminghoff (1906; repr. Hannover, 1979), pp. 1–4: this first of Boniface's reforming councils was attended by bishops from Würzburg, Cologne, Buraburg, Eichstätt, Strasbourg, and either Utrecht or Erfurt. Only Willibald of Eichstätt was linked to Bavaria, but he was one of Boniface's own disciples.

[58] Epp. Bon. 80.

[59] *TP* 5 (August 8, 754), mentions Sidonius's episcopacy at Passau. It is uncertain when he succeeded Vivilo or when he died; he had been succeeded by Wisurih by the time of the synod of Dingolfing, which may have been as early as 769 or 770.

[60] *Vita Sturmi*, MGH SS 2, ed. Georg Heinrich Pertz (1829; repr. Stuttgart, 1976), c. 2, p. 366. On Sturm's Bavarian relations, see Wilhelm Störmer, "Ein Adelsgruppe um die Fuldäer Äbte Sturmi und Eigil und die Holzkirchener Klostergründer Troand. Beobachtungen zum bayerisch-alemannisch-ostfränkischen Adel des 8./9. Jahrhunderts," in *Gesellschaft und Herrschaft, Forschungen zu sozial- und landesgeschichtlichen Problemen vornehmlich in Bayern. Ein Festgabe für Karl Bosl zum 60. Geburtstag* (Munich, 1969), pp. 1–34.

[61] There are very few names in the Fulda memorial rolls that can be identified as specifically Bavarian. However, besides Sturm and his successor, Eigil, several of the early Fulda scribes appear to have come from Bavaria. Both of these early abbots

in Bavaria and Alemannia, although naturally these holdings were not as dense as those in its immediate vicinity around Würzburg.[62] Boniface may have founded Fulda with the deliberate intention of connecting it to Bavaria. He described the monastery as situated in the midst of the four peoples to whom he ministered.[63] Three of the four are certainly the Franks, Thuringians, and Hessians. Which was the fourth remains an open question: as the Frisians are much too far away, Boniface must have meant either the Bavarians or the Saxons. Since he gave it a Bavarian abbot (Sturm) and never actually worked among the Saxons, I surmise that the Bavarians were meant. This suggests that part of Fulda's purpose was the cultivation of Boniface's style of Christian observance among the Bavarians.

There are other indications of the strong pull of Bonifatian connections in Bavaria. The monastery of Benediktbeuern would claim in the eleventh century that it had been founded with Boniface's assistance.[64] Even if untrue, the claim indicates that a sense of Boniface's sanctity

---

were probably relatives of Bishop Baturich of Regensburg. Some practices of the Fulda scriptorium may indicate Bavarian influence, although this is hard to prove amid Fulda's general effort to standardize its spelling. See Dieter Geuenich, *Die Personennamen der Klostergemeinschaft von Fulda im früheren Mittelalter* (Munich, 1976), pp. 247–53. Presumably the monastery's recruitment pattern followed its landholdings, which were most concentrated in the area around Mainz and Worms, up the Main valley to Thuringia; but Bavaria would have been a peripheral zone, along with other regions outside this central area. See also Dieter Geuenich, "Die personelle Entwicklung der Klostergemeinschaft von Fulda bis zum Jahr 1000," in *Kloster Fulda in der Welt der Karolinger und Ottonen*, ed. Gangolf Schrimpf (Frankfurt, 1996), pp. 163–76.

[62] See Werner Rösener, "Die Grundherrschaft des Klosters Fulda in karolingischer und ottonischer Zeit," in *Kloster Fulda in der Welt der Karolinger und Ottonen*, ed. Gangolf Schrimpf (Frankfurt, 1996), pp. 209–24, esp. at pp. 213 and 216. The list of Fulda's older properties compiled by Eberhard in the twelfth century shows eighty-two properties in Bavaria and Alemannia in its fortieth chapter. At least twenty-one of these were Alemannian, while I have only been able to identify seven so far as positively Bavarian, including properties at Freising and Regensburg. To what extent Fulda's Bavarian landholdings dated from the Agilulfing period is difficult to determine. Baturich, Bishop of Regensburg in the early ninth century, enjoyed a close relationship with Fulda (though he probably had not actually been a monk there) and some of the latter's southern holdings probably date from his episcopate. See Freund, *Agilolfingern zu den Karolingern*, pp. 258–67 and 275–99.

[63] Epp. Bon. 86.

[64] See Prinz, *Frühes Mönchtum*, pp. 366–67.

was cultivated there by this time. This veneration would probably have arisen either recently, exported from Fulda during the expansion of Boniface's cult in the eleventh century, or as a tradition going back to the cult's initial growth in the eighth century. The earliest extant manuscript of Willibald's *Vita Bonifatii* comes from the scriptorium at Freising, from the beginning of the ninth century. In the judgment of Wilhelm Levison, who edited the *Vita*, this manuscript was only one generation removed from Willibald's autograph. Boniface's appeal was even stronger at Regensburg. Another early copy of Willibald's *Vita* comes from the St. Emmeram scriptorium in the tenth century, although this is about five generations removed from the autograph. That the *Vita* had been so frequently recopied between the 760s and the tenth century suggests its popularity. However, we do not know whether the intervening generations of manuscripts were copied at Fulda, St. Emmeram, or elsewhere.[65] By the mid-eleventh century, St. Emmeram was a strong center of Boniface's veneration; Otloh of St. Emmeram wrote a new version of the *Vita Bonifatii* here in the 1060s, largely a compilation of passages from Willibald's *Vita*, other minor *vitae* composed in the intervening centuries, and letters from the saint's correspondence.[66] Otloh's work represents a new surge in Fulda's influence, but may also reflect an older interest in Boniface at Regensburg. A letter from the monks of Fulda to Louis the Pious in 817 or 818 names a group of saints who are interceding for the emperor. This list probably reflects the saints venerated at Fulda, and hence the churches that Fulda's monks were connected to. St. Emmeram is on this list.[67]

We need to revise the picture of Boniface's reputation in Bavaria. Virgil and the Bavarian clergy did not simply drive Boniface and his memory from the land. Though the evidence is sparse and sometimes late, it indicates that Fulda and its patron claimed a place in the affections of pious Bavarians. There were sons of Bavarian families at Fulda, and the Anglo-Saxon martyr was known and venerated by at least some Bavarians. The

---

[65] Levison, *Vitae sancti Bonifatii*, pp. xvii–xxvii. The Freising manuscript is Levison's manuscript 1; that from Regensburg is manuscript 4. Both precede the expansion of Boniface's cult in the eleventh century.

[66] Otloh of St. Emmeram, *Vita Bonifatii*, ed. Wilhelm Levison, MGH SSRG in usum scholarum v. 57 (1905; repr. Hannover, 2003), pp. 111–217.

[67] Kehl, *Kult und Nachleben*, pp. 34–35.

Bonifatian cult must be taken into account as a part of the context of Bavarian hagiographic composition in the eighth century. Thus, the *vitae* of ss. Rupert, Emmeram, and Corbinian were written and read within a complex array of contexts. They told of the patron saints of churches whose fortunes were closely tied to a ruling house at the height of its independence and authority, but still linked to Frankish and Lombard authorities. They embodied the aspirations of leaders of religious communities with both monastic and pastoral elements, who were active proponents of the rights of their sees. They also responded to the presence of a new and compelling cult of a recent martyr, who also happened to have been a rival and opponent of one of these shaping personalities.

Models of Sanctity in the Early Bavarian *Vitae*

Salzburg: *The Hagiographic Profile of St. Rupert*

> Synopsis of the *Life of St. Rupert*: Rupert, a bishop of noble descent in Worms, attracts the attention of Duke Theodo of Bavaria through his reputation for sanctity and teaching. Theodo invites the saint to Bavaria, and offers him anyplace he pleases to settle. Rupert travels down the Danube to Lorch, but finding the place unsuitable, proceeds to Salzburg. Theodo gives him all ducal properties within two leagues of the city. There Rupert restores dilapidated Roman buildings and organizes religious life by canonical norms. After some time he returns to Worms to fetch a group of disciples to assist, together with his niece Erendruda, whom he places at the head of a new women's convent on the Nonnberg in Salzburg. Finally, feeling his death drawing near, Rupert returns to Worms, and several chosen disciples experience a vision of angels carrying his soul to heaven.

All the surviving texts that narrate Rupert's career are productions of the Carolingian period.[68] However, at least two texts about Rupert

---

[68] There is a substantial literature on Rupert. See Ignaz Zibermayr, "Die Rupertlegende," *MIÖG* 62 (1954), 67–82; Herwig Wolfram, "Der heilige Rupert und die antikarolingische Adelsopposition," *MIÖG* LXXX (1972), 4–34; Herwig Wolfram, "Vier Fragen zur Geschichte des heiligen Rupert," *Studien und Mitteilungen*

were composed during Tassilo's reign. One was the *Libellus Virgilii*, a report compiled by Virgil of Salzburg on Rupert's work, particularly concerning the background of the cell of St. Maximilian.[69] Parts of it were later incorporated into the *Notitia Arnonis* and *Breves Notitiae*. It was not hagiographic in character and will not enter significantly into our discussion here, although it shows that Virgil had access to more than one eyewitness to Rupert's activity, and it is likely that the two works were meant to complement each other as accounts of the bishopric's early development.[70] The other text was our early *Vita Hrodberti*, the basis of the later *Gesta Hrodberti* and the first chapter of the *Conversio*. This text is not preserved, but a reasonable reconstruction of its contents can be made on the basis of later versions. It is likely that Virgil of Salzburg was involved in the composition of this text, either directly or as a patron. Since the text was revised in the 790s, it is unlikely that the original had only been composed after Virgil's death in 784.[71] We can assume that the original *Vita* of Rupert was composed sometime around 774 (the year of Rupert's translation to Salzburg, which is not mentioned in the *vita*) and reflects Virgil's view of his see's founding saint.

The texts of the *Gesta Hrodberti* and the *Conversio* version of the *Vita* follow each other extremely closely, making it clear that they are

---

des Benediktiner-Ordens und seiner Zweige 93 (1982), 2–25: Heinz Dopsch, "Der heilige Rupert in Salzburg: Vor 1300 Jahren kam der 'Grunderheilige' aus Worms am Rhein," in *Hl. Rupert von Salzburg: 696–1996. Katalog der Austellung im Dommuseum zu Salzburg und in der Erzabtei St. Peter, 16. Mai 1996–27. Oktober 1996*, ed. P. Petrus Eder OSB and Johann Kronbichler (Salzburg, 1996), pp. 66–88; Jahn, *Ducatus*, pp. 48–69.

[69] See Wolfram, "Libellus Virgilii," pp. 177–214, and Wanderwitz, "Der Libellus Virgilii," pp. 357–61.

[70] The founding of the cell of St. Maximilian, which is such a prominent episode of Rupert's career in the *BN* and *NA*, is not narrated in any version of the *Vita*. This absence is best explained if the *Libellus* was composed before the *Vita* and the two were read in conjunction. Arbeo's prologue to the *Vita Haimhrammi* is addressed to Virgil and implies that Virgil himself was a model for Arbeo's writing; if this refers to Virgil's involvement in composing the *Vita Hrodberti*, it would put the text earlier than 772.

[71] A further support for this argument is the complete absence of a translation account from any early version of Rupert's *Vita*. Translations feature heavily in Arbeo's *vitae*, as will be seen below. The absence of a translation from the Rupertine sources could mean that the original *Vita* was composed before 774.

related.[72] Each appears to make its own modifications to an underlying source text.[73] For instance, the *Gesta* adds a vision of angels by Rupert's disciples as his death approaches and adds the Nonnberg to sites where miracles ("beneficia") occurred for the faithful.[74] The *Gesta* identifies Rupert's ancestry as of a "noble and royal line" ("nobili regali progenie"), whereas for the *Conversio* it is simply "royal."[75] The *Gesta* also includes a statement that Rupert bought a property at Piding from Theodo for a princely sum, a transaction not mentioned in the *Conversio*.[76] There are several other such variations that the writer of the *Conversio* would have had no compelling reason to drop but which are explicable if the *Gesta* author elaborated on a prior text in a different way than the *Conversio* author did.

What sort of a profile of St. Rupert emerges if we assume that we can discern an original *Vita* underlying these two texts?[77] How did Virgil, or a writer working under him, portray the founding figure of the see of Salzburg, and hence how did he set an agenda for the bishopric of Salzburg itself?

One striking feature of Rupert's *Vita* is the absence of miracles. Not one specific miracle is attributed to the saint. Both versions of the *Vita* claim that healings occurred at the saint's tomb, but without describing any

---

[72] Lošek's edition of the *Conversio* provides a convenient parallel text of the *Gesta Hrodberti* for the *Conversio's* first chapter. For this discussion I have ignored slight differences of orthography and grammar between the two versions that doubtless reflect an increase of Frankish influence in the Salzburg scriptorium over the course of the ninth century (e.g., the change from the *Gesta's* spelling "Hiltiperhti" to the *Conversio's* "Hildeberti," a classic instance of east vs. west Germanic spelling conventions. On this note, that the more "Bavarian" scribe of the *Gesta* spells his subject's name "Hrodbert" rather than "Hrotperht" is another sign in favor of Rupert's western origins. If he had been a local figure, presumably an eastern form of his name would have been used).

[73] See Helmut Beumann, "Zur Textgeschichte der *Vita* Ruperti," in *Festschrift für Hermann Heimpel zum 70. Geburtstag*, vol. 3, Veröffentlichen des Max-Planck-Instituts für Geschichte 36/III (1972), pp. 166–96.

[74] *Gesta Hrodberti*, c. 10. The vagueness of this reference to tomb miracles may mean that the original *Vita* was written before the translation of 774.

[75] *Gesta Hrodberti*, c. 1; *Conversio*, c. 1, p. 90.

[76] *Gesta Hrodberti*, c. 8. See Wolfram, Herwig Wolfram, "Der heilige Rupert und die antikarolingische Adelsopposition," *MIÖG* 80 (1972), 20ff, on this insertion.

[77] No one has yet published a reconstructed text of the original *Vita* behind the existing versions.

specific instances.[78] Both versions also claim that Rupert performed healings during the Danubian journey that brought him to Lorch, but again no specific cases are recorded.[79] It appears that while the hagiographer had to claim some miraculous power for his subject to assert that he was indeed a saint, miracles were not so significant as to require elaboration. This is a characteristic feature of Carolingian (as opposed to Merovingian) hagiography and reinforces the suggestion above that Virgil's style as a bishop owed much to his connections at the Carolingian court.[80]

One characteristic of the early *Vita*, however, was the importance of nobility as a characteristic of the saint himself and of those among whom he worked. The surviving versions of the *Vita* vary in their emphasis on Rupert's nobility and dealings with nobles; it is possible that the later *Conversio* has toned down the original's emphasis on this theme.[81] That the *Gesta* is closer to the original is suggested by its reference to a "former duke" as compared to a "certain duke" in the *Conversio*.[82] The *Gesta*, for instance, states that Rupert converted many nobles to the true faith and taught them, while the *Conversio* states that Rupert converted both noble

---

[78] *Gesta Hrodberti*, c. 8 ; *Conversio*, c. 1, p. 98.

[79] *Gesta Hrodberti*, c. 5 ; *Conversio*, c. 1, p. 94.

[80] See Ian Wood, *Missionary Life*, pp. 262–64.

[81] Bavarian hagiographies played a key role in defining the concept of the early medieval "noble saint" in modern scholarship. See Karl Bosl, "Der 'Adelsheilige.' Idealtypus und Wirklichkeit, Gesellschaft, und Kultur im merowingerzeitlichen Bayern des 7. und 8. Jahrhunderts. Gesellschaftsgeschichtliche Beiträge zu den Viten der bayerischen Stammesheiligen Emmeram, Rupert, Korbinian," in *Speculum Historiale*, ed. K. Bauer, L. Boehm, and M. Mueller (Freiburg and Munich, 1965), and repr. in Friedrich Prinz, ed., *Mönchtum und Gesellschaft im Frühmittelalter* (Darmstadt, 1976), pp. 354–86. František Graus rejected the concept, arguing that on the one hand, the lives of Bavarian and contemporary Frankish saints did not emphasize the parentage of the saint as highly as Bosl had claimed, and that in any case early medieval society did not yet have a true nobility in the sense of a self-conscious class with hereditary legal privileges. See František Graus, *Volk, Herrscher und Heilige im Reich der Merowinger. Studien zur Hagiographie der Merowingerzeit* (Prague, 1965), pp. 197–210, 363; and Graus, "Sozialgeschichtliche Aspekte der Hagiographie der Merowinger- und Karolingerzeit: Die Viten der Heiligen des südalemannischen Raumes und die sogenannten Adelsheiligen," in *Mönchtum, Episkopat und Adel zur Gründungszeit des Klosters Reichenau*, ed. Arno Borst (Sigmaringen, 1974), pp. 131–76. My intention here is not to revive the "noble saint" model per se, but to point out that the fundamental characteristic of Rupert's sanctity is worldly authority and lordship.

[82] *Gesta Hrodberti*, c. 3 ; *Conversio*, c. 1, p. 90.

and common persons.[83] Beumann thought, plausibly though not prov-
ably, that the simpler phrasing of the *Gesta* is the original, which stresses
Rupert's influence among the powerful of the duchy. The *Conversio*, a
text about mission, emphasized instead the breadth of Rupert's appeal
and influence. There are two occasions where the *Conversio* mentions the
followers of a character simply as "*suis.*" In the *Gesta*, these followers are
specified as "*satellitibus*" (for Theodo) and "*sequacibus*" (for Rupert).[84] If
the terms "satellitibus" and "sequacibus" were part of the original *Vita*,
then it seems to have emphasized the high status of both Rupert and
his host Theodo. Salzburg was a church with a noble founder who had a
noble audience.

While miracles were not important to the image of Rupert as a saint,
preaching was central. In this respect also, the original *Vita* of Rupert
was very Carolingian in character.[85] Both versions of the *Vita* agree in
emphasizing this aspect of Rupert's career. In Worms, Rupert attracted
great crowds of people to hear his preaching and doctrine; it was this that
brought him to Theodo's attention. Rupert, "preacher of the truth," was
compelled by divine love to accept Theodo's invitation, and was received
as the "evangelical doctor." Besides healing, he spent the Danubian journey "preaching the word of the doctrine of life." Thus, a central feature of
Rupert's profile is his eminence as a teacher and preacher.

The *Vita* also insisted that Rupert adhered to canonical order in his
activity. Terms emphasizing proper ecclesiastical order recur frequently
in the description of his restoration of Salzburg. Hence, while restoring
church buildings, Rupert "put into order the ecclesiastical office there, as
appeared right to him."[86] Having rebuilt a church and dedicated it to St.
Peter, Rupert added a cloister to it in accordance with the proper order
for a community of religious. He then ordained priests so that the daily
office would be kept "in the fitting order" (*congruo ordine*).[87] He likewise

---

[83] *Gesta Hrodberti*, c. 4 ; *Conversio*, c. 1, p. 92.

[84] *Gesta Hrodberti*, cc. 4 and 5; *Conversio*, c. 1, p. 92.

[85] Wood, *Missionary Life*, pp. 256–58; Lutz von Padberg, *Mission und Christianisierung: Formen und Folgen bei Angelsachsen und Franken im 7. und 8. Jahrhundert* (Stuttgart, 1995), pp. 125–40. See Arnold Angenendt, *Heilige und Reliquien: Die Geschichte ihres Kultes vom frühen Christentum bis zur Gegenwart* (Munich, 1994), pp. 143–48, on the Carolingian shift from more miraculous to more exemplary saints.

[86] *Gesta Hrodberti*, c. 7 ; *Conversio*, c. 1, p. 94.

[87] Both of these references in *Gesta Hrodberti*, c. 8; *Conversio*, c. 1, p. 96.

arranged the life of the nuns at the Nonnberg "rationally, as the canonical order requires."[88] Thus, canonical order is mentioned four times in the span of about one printed page.

The passages emphasizing order also emphasize Rupert's role as a builder and a restorer of churches. Only one church is explicitly a new foundation of Rupert's, the nunnery on the Nonnberg.[89] The *Vita* text depicts Rupert restoring a dilapidated church building, dedicating it to St. Peter, and adding appropriate auxiliary buildings to it.[90] The implication is that he perhaps reorganized and revitalized an existing religious community rather than created a new foundation from scratch. Even so, the text returns repeatedly to the theme of buildings, and Rupert's renovations and additions to the existing structures. Even as it mentions their declining state, the *Vita*'s language also emphasizes the beauty of the structures involved.[91] Doubtless this description showed respect to the post-Roman inhabitants of Salzburg, who had after all been the ones using these buildings before, while still stressing Rupert's role as a father and benevolent lord to the community there.

Rupert not only rebuilds churches in the *Vita*, but he also is adept at acquiring land. Theodo makes extravagant grants to Rupert in the *Vita*—most dramatically, everything in a two-league (*leuvas*) radius of Salzburg.[92] Prior to this, Theodo is supposed to have given a wide swath of property around the church at Wallersee as well.[93] The *Gesta* adds a report that Theodo sold Rupert property at Piding for a princely sum.[94]

---

[88] *Gesta Hrodberti*, c. 9 ; *Conversio*, c. 1, p. 96.

[89] Ibid.

[90] *Gesta Hrodberti*, c. 8 ; *Conversio*, c. 1, p. 96.

[91] ". . . where many buildings had been marvelously constructed in ancient times, and then had almost collapsed and been overrun by forests." (. . . *ubi antiquis scilicet temporibus multa fuerunt mirabiliter constructa edificia et tunc pene dilapsa silvisque cooperta.*) *Conversio*, c. 1, p. 94; the passage is different in *Gesta Hrodberti*, c. 6. "Then the man of the Lord began to renew those places, building first a beautiful church to God." (*Tunc vir Domini ista cepit renovare loca primo Deo formosam edificans ecclesiam*). *Gesta Hrodberti*, c. 8; *Conversio*, c. 1, p. 96.

[92] *Gesta Hrodberti*, c. 7; *Conversio*, c. 1, pp. 94, 96.

[93] According to the *BN/NA*, it was Theodebert and not Theodo who gave Wallersee to Rupert. The attribution of this grant to Theodo appears in both the Gesta and the *Conversio* and so probably was in the original *Vita* as well. By dropping mention of Theodebert, the *Vita* streamlined the account and strengthened the sense of partnership between the founding duke, Theodo, and the founding saint, Rupert.

[94] *Gesta Hrodberti*, c. 8.

Since this does not appear in the *Conversio*, it is probably a forged property claim that was being made by Salzburg at the time of the *Gesta's* composition, and might be another instance of a "land-grab" mentality that followed Tassilo's fall.[95] Still, the fact that such a forgery was made, combined with Rupert's position at the head of the *Notitia Arnonis* and *Breves Notitiae* as the recipient of numerous ducal grants, indicates that the original *Vita* also saw Rupert as a successful land-baron.

These, then, are the elements that create the profile of Rupert in eighth-century hagiography. Rupert is a "confessor" simply because he is a holy man who was not martyred.[96] His holiness, however, is not mainly evidenced in miracles. Rather, the writer of the original *Vita* presented a man who deserved to be considered a saint because he was a compelling teacher and preacher, a great builder and restorer, a canonically diligent organizer of religious communities, and a skilled land manager.

This profile responds to the contexts of mid-eighth-century Bavaria in several ways. Politically, Rupert's life seems to have stressed cooperation between the Church and the duke, to the point that Rupert seems to deal with Theodo as an equal rather than as his superior. Although Rupert comes from the Frankish kingdom, the *Vita* omits any reference to Frankish rulers; this may recognize the *de facto* independence that Tassilo still enjoyed in the 770s. As an outsider himself, Virgil may have found Rupert to set an important precedent for his own role as head of the Salzburg community. Meanwhile, Rupert's role as a bishop at Salzburg undercut the claims of the Bonifatian tradition that emphasized the Anglo-Saxon's role in creating a canonical episcopal see there; the *Vita* repeatedly stresses that Rupert established everything "in canonical order."

---

[95] On the possibility of a "land-grab" phase after the Carolingian takeover of Bavaria, see Brown, *Unjust Seizure*, pp. 73–102, and p. 21–22 above.

[96] Contra the anti-Carolingian interpretation of Rupert's career, which holds that Rupert was a "confessor" due to his "persecution" by the early Carolingians. Cf. Herwig Wolfram, "Der heilige Rupert und die antikarolingische Adelsopposition," *MIÖG* 80 (1972), 4–34.

Freising: The Profiles of Bishop Arbeo's Saints

Synopsis of the Life or Passion of St. Emmeram: Emmeram, a bishop in Poitiers, hears of the paganism of the Avars and decides to evangelize them. He preaches his way eastward, acquiring a translator named Vitalis along the way. Duke Theodo receives the saint at Regensburg but forbids him to continue on his mission, because the Avars are at war with the Bavarians and have devastated the frontier along the Enns. Instead, he offers Emmeram the position of bishop or abbot of the Bavarian churches, and Emmeram, seeing the richness of the country and the half-Christian state of the people, accepts. After three years, however, he is approached by Theodo's daughter Ota, who has become pregnant by the son of a local judge. Emmeram agrees to help the two by taking the blame for the pregnancy on himself, but sets out for Rome to clear his name before the pope. Theodo's son Lantpert, seeking revenge for his dishonored sister, pursues Emmeram as far as Helfendorf. There Lantpert and his accomplices torture and dismember Emmeram, leaving his still-breathing trunk for dead. Vitalis and his other disciples try to carry him to Ascheim, where there is a church, but he dies at a crossroads en route. Local inhabitants at Helfendorf gather the severed limbs and bury them under a hawthorn tree, but the relics disappear after a visit by two enigmatic horsemen. Meanwhile the site of the death is marked by mild weather until the locals remember the martyr and build a church to him. Much later, when floodwaters threaten the tomb at Ascheim, dreams reveal that Emmeram wishes to be returned to his episcopal city of Regensburg, and his relics are translated there. Various miracles bless the churches dedicated to him.

Synopsis of the Life of St. Corbinian: Corbinian is born to a Frankish couple near Melun. Restoring a church of St. Germanus to enter religious life, he acquires a reputation for sanctity and attracts the attention of many, culminating in the gift of a jeweled robe by the Mayor of the Palace Pippin II. Desiring ascetic withdrawal, Corbinian leaves for Rome, but the pope tells him not to hide his light under a bushel, consecrates him bishop, and sends him home. A second pilgrimage seven years later yields the same result and is marked by several miracles, including the divine punishments of thieves who steal horses from the saint. This time, Corbinian stops in Bavaria on his return journey and attaches himself to the court of Duke Grimoald at Freising. Conflict rises between Corbinian and Grimoald's wife Pilitrud, climaxing with her plotting to have him assassinated when he beats a peasant woman who tried to heal Pilitrud's son by magic. Corbinian escapes the plot and flees to the Tyrol, where Grimoald had helped him found a church at Mais. Grimoald and Pilitrud fall to a coup and Charles Martel's intervention. The new duke, Hucbert, restores Corbinian. When the saint dies a little later, he is buried at Mais near St. Valentinus, until the latter is translated to Passau and Bishop Arbeo of Freising, the author of the *vita*, has Corbinian's relics brought to Freising, where they work various miracles.

Much longer than the *Gesta Hrodberti* or its Virgilian model are the *Vitae* of Ss. Emmeram and Corbinian, written by Arbeo of Freising around 770. The *Vita Corbiniani* was certainly written in conjunction with the translation of that saint's relics to Freising, an event that can be dated to October of 767.[97] Since the *Vita* narrates the translation itself, it must have been composed after this event. Only two chapters describe miracles at the new tomb in Freising.[98] The surviving copy of the older version of this *Life* cuts off in midchapter after these stories, so we do not know whether the original composition carried on much longer; it probably did not. Thus, the composition date was probably not long after 767. The *Vita Haimhrammi* probably followed afterwards, as it is unlikely that Arbeo would have written a *vita* for a saint interred in a neighboring diocese before writing about his own patron. A direct verbal reminiscence of the *Vita Haimhrammi* in a charter of 772, however, suggests that Arbeo had completed this work by then.[99] We can date the *Vita Corbiniani* to roughly 768 or 769, and the *Vita Haimhrammi* to 770 or 772.[100]

Arbeo's *vitae* emphasize that Emmeram and Corbinian are outsiders to Bavaria. Corbinian is a Neustrian Frank, from the area around

---

[97] See n. 44, above.

[98] *Vita Corbiniani*, cc. 45–46, p. 232; the fragmentary c. 47 may also have reported an additional posthumous miracle.

[99] *TF* 50.

[100] See Brown, *Unjust Seizure*, p. 36 n. 10 and p. 56 n. 79; and Vogel, *Werden*, pp. 180–82.

Melun.[101] Emmeram is Aquitainian, supposedly from Poitiers.[102] By emphasizing that they are foreigners, Arbeo creates an image of the saints as *peregrini pro Christo*, abandoning home and family for the sake of Christ. In Emmeram's case, Arbeo even gives the saint an interpreter, Vitalis, to help him communicate after he crosses the Rhine.[103] Corbinian's ascetic career in Francia is described at length, so that the reader is reminded of his outsider status when he comes to Grimoald's court.

Both Emmeram and Corbinian are also of noble background. However, this is not so emphasized as to make them "noble saints" of a distinctive type. In Emmeram's case, the eminence of his birth is introduced only in an off-handed fashion. It is not an aspect of his catalogue of virtues, nor is it brought up when Arbeo describes Emmeram's beginnings in Aquitaine. Rather, Arbeo only mentions his "immense riches" and "crowds of noble relatives" when Emmeram decides to abandon them all in order to preach to the Avars.[104] In other words, in Emmeram's case, nobility is not an aspect of his sanctity, but serves to throw his piety and dedication into relief, as is often the case for *peregrini* or other ascetics. Arbeo never calls Corbinian's parents "noble" at all. However, the saint himself carries an aura of aristocracy with him in his travels. He rides expensive Spanish horses that arouse the envy of noble Lombards, he

---

101 *Vita Corbiniani*, c. 1, pp. 189–90. Again, whether or not the modern critic accepts Arbeo's claim that Corbinian was from a community near Melun, it is significant that Arbeo saw fit to make this claim. As someone who had grown up in the Tyrol himself, it is unlikely that Arbeo was confused by a Tyrolean place name and misidentified it as a Neustrian city, as Vogel argues.

102 *Vita Haimhrammi*, c. 1, p. 27.

103 *Vita Haimhrammi*, c. 3, p. 31. The "historical Emmeram," of course, may have grown up speaking vulgar Latin, or early Romance, despite his Germanic name. The point to be made here is Arbeo's decision to emphasize the linguistic barrier. Early medieval hagiography rarely indicates missionary saints' need for interpreters, either because their linguistic expertise enabled them to communicate independently or because describing language barriers did not serve hagiographic aims. We are sometimes told that missionaries purchased slave boys from peoples they intended to evangelize, but the lives never describe such an unfree translator's activity. Hagiographies of the Carolingian period praised Pirmin and Boniface for their ability to communicate in local vernaculars. *Vita Pirminii*, c. 3, p. 22–23. Liudger, *Vita Gregorii abbatis Traiectensis*, ed. O. Holder-Egger, MGH SS 15.1 (1887; repr. Stuttgart, 1963), pp. 63–79, here at c. 2, p. 68. See von Padberg, *Mission und Christianisierung*, pp. 140–46.

104 *Vita Haimhrammi*, c. 3, pp. 30–31.

dines at court with dukes, beats peasant women for their superstitious ways, and receives rich gifts from Frankish palace mayors.[105] But even though Corbinian still seems to carry these paraphernalia about as he travels, Arbeo insists that renunciation of worldly riches was the saint's true desire. The gift of a jeweled robe from Pippin, in particular, prompts Corbinian to flee Gaul for Rome.

Asceticism is described as an aspect of the saints' Gallic backgrounds but, curiously, seems to be left behind in Gaul. Ascetic rigors play no role in their careers once they come to Bavaria. We are told little of Emmeram's practices, only that he dedicated himself to the study of scripture from a young age and that zealous fasting and prayer were among his virtues.[106] Corbinian was a hermit of sorts before coming to Bavaria, but for him also Arbeo only makes general statements about his piety in prayer and fasting. Even at his "hermitage" at a restored church of St. Germanus, Corbinian's group of disciples included a cellarer, so he does not come across as particularly ascetic.[107] Still, both of Corbinian's visits to Rome are motivated by the desire to live in religious contemplation, evoking a theme of escape from the active world. In this respect, Arbeo's texts vary considerably from contemporary *vitae* from the British isles, where asceticism was still significant, but are compatible with hagiographic writing on the continent.

Arbeo emphasizes that both of his saints are outsiders to Bavaria who grew up in the longer-standing Christian traditions of Frankish Gaul. Both are also noble persons to some degree, although their rank is not specified and the eminence of their families is only mentioned to highlight the piety of the saints who abandon it for Christ. Arbeo also makes a nod to asceticism for each of them, although again his statements are general enough to show that they are not to be venerated as ascetics per se.

More specific than their origins, however, are the dealings that the two saints have with secular rulers. Here Arbeo supplies much more detail. The sainthood of Emmeram and Corbinian is heavily based on their ability to function correctly with holders of political power. Both

---

[105] *Vita Corbiniani*, c. 5, pp. 193–94; c. 8, pp. 196–97; c. 16, pp. 205–6; c. 26, pp. 217–18; c. 29, pp. 221–22. See Bosl, "Adelsheilige," pp. 377–79, and further literature above, n. 6.

[106] *Vita Haimhrammi*, cc. 1–2, pp. 26–30.

[107] *Vita Corbiniani*, cc. 2–4, pp. 190–93.

Lives feature encounters with Agilulfing dukes. Two other sets of rulers, Frankish and Lombard, appear only in the *Vita Corbiniani*.

Emmeram preached his way across Francia and into Alemannia without ever meeting any Frankish rulers.[108] Corbinian's links to Pippin II, however, play a prominent role in his hagiography. His sanctity at "Castrus" attracts the palace mayor's interest and generosity, including the gift of a jeweled robe Pippin had worn at the Marchfield.[109] In Corbinian's career, Pippin's patronage plays a similar role to high birth in Emmeram's; it represents the wealth from which the saint flees. Corbinian decides to undertake his first pilgrimage to Rome in order to escape the cares of wealth and the entanglement with the world that Pippin's favor represents.[110] However, this is not the only role that the ruler plays. After Corbinian's return from Rome, he appeals to Pippin to save the life of the condemned felon Adalbert. By making the sign of the cross on Adalbert's neck, Corbinian saves his life from hanging, for the rope cannot choke him though he is suspended for two days. The palace mayor, for his part, is happy to grant the saint's request and commit the condemned man into his care.[111]

While he stresses Corbinian's ties to Pippin II, we should remember that Arbeo was writing this *Vita* within a year or so of the death of Pippin III, who was the father of the ruling Frankish kings, Charlemagne and Carloman (both still alive at the time of the *Vita*'s composition), and who had been regent for Tassilo III during the duke's minority.[112] We needn't think that Arbeo or his audience would have confused the two Pippins, but names carried ideological implications in the early Middle Ages; for instance, Charles Martel's choice to name his younger son Pippin (III) made a clear claim to the inheritance of Pippin II.[113] That the elder Pippin had favored Corbinian would have carried strong implications in

---

108 *Vita Haimhrammi*, c. 3, pp. 30–31.

109 *Vita Corbiniani*, c. 5, pp. 193–94.

110 *Vita Corbiniani*, c. 6, pp. 194–95.

111 *Vita Corbiniani*, cc. 10–11, pp. 197–99. Friedrich Lotter, "Heiliger und Gehenkter: Zur Todesstrafe in hagiographischen Episodenerzählungen des Mittelalters," in *Ecclesia et Regnum: Beiträge zur Geschichte von Kirche, Recht, und Staat im Mittelalter. Festschrift für Frank-Josef Schmale zu seinem 65. Geburtstag*, ed. Dieter Berg and Hans-Werner Goetz (Karlsruhe, 1989), pp. 1–20.

112 Jahn, *Ducatus*, pp. 283–334.

113 Waltraud Joch, *Legitimität und Integration: Untersuchungen zu den Anfängen Karl Martells* (Husum, 1999), pp. 78–80.

Tassilo's Bavaria. While Tassilo was ruling more or less independently, this was still a time of Franco-Bavarian cooperation, as witnessed in the alliances of 770, and the blessings of an eminent Carolingian were an asset to a Bavarian saint.

As noted above, the relationship of Arbeo's saints to the Agilulfing dukes has been a subject of considerable debate among scholars, as these relationships can be taken to mirror Arbeo's attitude toward the Agilulfing dynasty in general and Tassilo III in particular. One view has held that the Agilulfings appear in a particularly bad light in these *vitae*, and that this representation amounts to a condemnation of the dynasty as a whole and an anti-Agilulfing, pro-Carolingian agenda on the part of Arbeo. This view draws additional support from the Freising dispute charter, mentioned above, which claimed that Tassilo had transferred control of a number of baptismal churches from Freising to Chiemsee because of Arbeo's disloyalty.[114]

As in the case of the Freising dispute account, more recent scholarship has modified or rejected this picture. The Agilulfings are not condemned as a group in Arbeo's *vitae*. In fact, the subjects of censure are almost never ruling dukes. Thus, the villain of the *Vita Haimhrammi* is not Theodo but his son Lantpert, who is punished by the duke for Emmeram's martyrdom by exile and exclusion from the succession.[115] In the *Vita Corbiniani*, Duke Grimoald meets a bad end at the hands of a conspiracy.[116] However, the real villain of the *Vita* is not Grimoald but his wife, Pilitrud; it is she, not her husband, who plots Corbinian's death. Grimoald comes across as a temporizing figure. He promises the saint to put Pilitrud away but then does not follow through, and when Corbinian storms away from the duke's table it is Grimoald who sends gifts to the aggrieved saint until he relents.[117] When Corbinian beats a peasant woman for witchcraft, she flees to Pilitrud, not to Grimoald.[118]

Positive relationships with the Bavarian dukes are far more prominent than hostile ones. Theodo, of course, is the ideal duke; it is he who has the first contact with Emmeram and Corbinian and urges them to stay and strengthen the faith of his people. Theodo gives Emmeram an

---

[114] See above, pp. 21–22.
[115] *Vita Haimhrammi*, c. 28, pp. 67–69.
[116] *Vita Corbiniani*, c. 31, pp. 223–24.
[117] *Vita Corbiniani*, c. 24, pp. 215–16, and c. 26, pp. 217–18.
[118] *Vita Corbiniani*, c. 29, pp. 221–22.

open invitation to become the "pontiff" of the Bavarians or, should he prefer, to be a sort of over-abbot to all the monasteries of the duchy.[119] He banishes Emmeram's persecutor, even though it is his own son. He punishes his daughter Ota as well, whose sexual indiscretion gave rise to the whole situation. Defying Corbinian's wish for poverty and simplicity, Theodo takes a page from Pippin's book and plies the saint with rich gifts.[120] Grimoald would do the same to seek Corbinian's reconciliation, and also assists him to purchase Kuens for himself. Hucbert, on succeeding Grimoald, calls Corbinian back from exile and forges a bond with him through a baptism.

Briefly, then, the interpretation of Arbeo's *vitae* as anti-Agilulfing propaganda can be discarded. The lives of Emmeram and Corbinian do not attempt to undermine the legitimacy of the ruling house of Bavaria, nor to accuse it of incorrigible vice. The villains of both *Lives* are excluded branches of the ruling line, and their exclusion is explicitly the result of their misdeeds toward the saints. Lantpert is exiled, and Pilitrud's son (Grimoald's heir) dies in childhood.[121]

The appearances of the various Agilulfings in Arbeo's *vitae* have the character of a hagiographic "mirror for princes." Various members and associates of the ducal house pass across the stage, representing a spectrum of possible behaviors by those in power. Theodo invites saints to his court, showers them with gifts and privileges and urges them to stay in Bavaria in order to save his people's souls. Ota uses confession to try to hide her own guilt. Lantpert takes the law into his own hands, refuses to listen to God's preacher, and instead persecutes and martyrs him. Pilitrud sees the bishop as a rival to her own power and plots his murder whenever he crosses her. Grimoald equivocates, tries to gain the saint's

---

119 *Vita Haimhrammi*, c. 5, pp. 33–34. We should note in this connection that these lives, in which Duke Theodo is so praised, were written shortly before the baptism of Tassilo's son Theodo at Rome in 772. We do not know the younger Theodo's birth year, so it is hard to tell whether Tassilo's choice of name for his heir may have been influenced by these lives, or if their depiction of the elder Theodo may have been a compliment to the ducal house.

120 *Vita Corbiniani*, c. 15, pp. 202–5.

121 Brown, *Unjust Seizure*, pp. 63–64; Bosl, "Adelsheilige," p. 177; and Glaser, "Arbeo," p. 57. Note, contra the erroneous statement in Wood (*Missionary Life*, p. 153), that Pilitrud was Tassilo III's grandmother, his grandmother was Pilitrud's niece Swanahild. Swanahild herself is not mentioned by Arbeo, even in connection with Pilitrud's departure with Charles Martel.

favor, but fails to follow through on his promises. Hucbert recalls the saint and makes him an ally. Those who befriend the saints are blessed and happy, while those who oppose them bring disaster on their own heads. Arbeo is not subtle about this theme, but makes it explicit in the *Vita Haimhrammi*; "For the wrath of the righteous is to be feared, lest they provoke him who dwells in their bodies (i.e., God) to wrath. The Truth speaks through himself of these matters, 'He who hates you, hates me,' and so forth."[122] The *vitae* are neither pro- nor anti-Agilulfing as such, but teach the common message that good comes to those who honor the church and evil to those who oppose it.[123] It also gives specific examples of ways that a ruler can show his veneration for God and His saints: protection of clergy, support for pastoral ministry, and a liberal flow of gifts to the church are all in order. Unkept promises, disrespect for clergy, seizure of church property, and the cynical use of penance (not to mention outright persecution) are fatal. As for the Carolingians and the Franks, Arbeo does no more and no less than to offer Pippin, the namesake of Tassilo's former regent and father of the present kings, as a further model of correct princely behavior.

The same principle applies to Corbinian's dealings with Lombard authorities. The Lombard king (presumably Liutprand, though he goes unnamed in the *Vita*) receives Corbinian with all due honor and reverence on the southbound leg of his second pilgrimage, and entertains the saint for a week, availing himself of Corbinian's teaching and prayers during this time. The "princeps" of Trent, Husing, however, has such a desire for Corbinian's fine horse that he has it stolen when the pilgrim refuses to sell it.[124] On Corbinian's northward journey, Husing has paid for his crime; the horse's sexual organ is so swollen that the creature is useless for anything. He has to give Corbinian two horses and a sum of gold as

---

[122] "*Cavenda namque est ira iustorum, ne et ipsum ad iracundia provocent, qui inhabitator eorum corporibus existit. De quibus per semet ipsam veritas dicit:* Qui vos odit, me odit *et reliqua.*" *Vita Haimhrammi* 29, p. 69. The biblical allusion is to Luke 10:16, but Arbeo changes "audit" to "odit" to make his point. He continues on this theme at some length thereafter. Note that while the gender of *ipsam* is feminine, I have rendered it masculine in the translation since the "truth" to which Arbeo refers is Christ himself.

[123] Cf. Brown, *Unjust Seizure*, p. 64.

[124] *Vita Corbiniani*, c. 16, pp. 205–6.

composition.[125] The non-noble horse thief from Pavia fares worse, dying the very day he steals Corbinian's second, Spanish horse. In this case the Lombard king himself intervenes to obtain Corbinian's reconciliation, which comes to a return of the stolen horse and 200 *solidi* in cash.[126] The Lombard king's intervention suggests one further aspect of the proper behavior of authorities towards the saint, which is to intervene on behalf of their transgressing subjects to obtain his pardon. Rulers are not only responsible for their own good relations with the saint (and therefore his church), but also for the good relations of their subjects.

Besides political authority figures, Arbeo's *vitae* also connect their protagonists to ecclesiastical authority. Both assert that their subjects went to Rome, or at least tried to, though there is little to give us confidence that they actually did. In neither case are the accounts of these journeys to the eternal city plausible or well-supported. If the *vitae* depict these early Bavarian saints traveling to Rome, it is not because they did so, but because it was important to Arbeo that they should have done so.[127]

While a full doctrine of papal primacy was not yet developed in the eighth century, Rome had long been accepted as the chief of the churches of the west, if not the entire Christian world, and was the touchstone of orthodoxy and correct ecclesiastical order for the Latin churches.[128] Even idiosyncratic Irish churchmen did not deny the claims of Rome, not even when criticizing Roman ecclesiastical practices such as the dating

---

[125] *Vita Corbiniani*, c. 22, pp. 212–14.

[126] *Vita Corbiniani*, c. 21, pp. 211–12. These episodes suggest a pattern of conflict resolution based on submission by the offending party and forgiveness by the aggrieved, which was probably used outside of literary accounts as well. See Warren Brown, *Unjust Seizure* (Ithaca, NY, 2001), pp. 55–64; and Geoffrey Koziol, *Begging Pardon and Favor*, pp. 25–76.

[127] I argue this point in "Virtual Pilgrimage: The Roman Journeys of St. Corbinian of Freising," in *Travel and Movement in Medieval Italy, 500–1500*, ed. Edward Coleman and Bill Day (forthcoming).

[128] For a discussion of the papacy's relationship to the rest of Western Christendom during this period, see Thomas F. X. Noble, "The Papacy in the Eighth and Ninth Centuries," in *The New Cambridge Medieval History*, vol. 2 (c. 700–c. 900), ed. Rosamond McKitterick (Cambridge, 1995), pp. 577–86, with citations there to the extensive literature on this topic, and Arnold Angenendt, "Princeps imperii—Princeps apostolorum: Rom zwischen Universalismus und Gentilismus," in *Roma—Caput und Fons: Zwei Vorträge über das päpstliche Rom zwischen Altertum und Mittelalter*, Gerda Henkel Vorlesung (Opladen, 1989), pp. 7–44.

of Easter or the condemnation of the Three Chapters. Rather, early in the seventh century the Irish monastic founder Columbanus insisted that his people were faithful followers of Peter and Paul (and thus Peter's successor) and that he himself had striven to defend the pope from his detractors.[129]

For the Anglo-Saxon missionaries of Virgil's and Arbeo's time, likewise, Rome had long been the font and measure of the true faith and proper Christian order.[130] The initial missionaries of the Anglo-Saxons had been sent by Pope Gregory the Great. Archbishops of Canterbury had traditionally gone to Rome to obtain the *pallium*, the liturgical cloth that marked their office. Both Willibrord and Boniface had also obtained the *pallium* from the pope, and several of Boniface's disciples had stayed at Rome and at Monte Cassino to learn ideal ecclesiastical and monastic customs.[131] Communion with Rome represented membership in the larger Christian world.

Emmeram's connection with Rome in his *Vita* is only one of intention. When he senses his martyrdom approaching, the saint asks permission to undertake a pilgrimage there.[132] The account is confusing to the reader, because Emmeram knows that he will never reach the tomb of Peter; he has already foreseen his martyrdom. Only after he plans the pilgrimage does Ota bring her difficulty to him, giving Emmeram the motivation to vindicate himself before the pope.[133] Arbeo seems to have introduced the pilgrimage theme partly to transport Emmeram to Helfendorf, but also because a pilgrimage to Rome is part of the saintly profile with which he wishes to endow Emmeram.

---

[129] Columbanus, ep. 5, c. 3, in *Sancti Columbani Opera*, ed. G. S. M. Walker. Scriptores Latini Hiberniae, vol. 2 (Dublin, 1957), pp. 36–57.

[130] Von Padberg, *Mission und Christianisierung*, pp. 69–75. The prestige of Roman authority in spiritual matters could lead, among other things, to a high demand for codices of Roman origin north of the Alps, or even to the creation of fictive Roman provenances for texts to lend them authority; see Rudolf Schieffer, "'Redeamus ad fontem': Rom als Hort authentischer Überlieferung im frühen Mittelalter," in *Roma—Caput und Fons: Zwei Vorträge über das päpstliche Rom zwischen Altertum und Mittelalter,* Gerda Henkel Vorlesung (Opladen, 1989), pp. 45–70.

[131] *Vita Sturmi,* pp. 365–77; *Vita Willibrordi, archiepiscopi Traiectensis,* MGH SSRM 7, ed. Wilhelm Levison (Hannover and Leipzig, 1920), pp. 81–141.

[132] *Vita Haimhrammi,* c. 8, pp. 37–39.

[133] *Vita Haimhrammi,* c. 9, pp. 39–40.

Corbinian makes two pilgrimages to Rome. Structurally, there are important similarities between the two. Both times, Corbinian's intention is to ask the pope for permission to live a contemplative life under papal direction.[134] Both times, his request is refused, lest his light be hidden under a bushel, and he is commissioned to return to the world to preach.[135] The first time, it is the pope himself who gives Corbinian this directive and who invests Corbinian not only with authority to preach but with an episcopal consecration and a *pallium*. The second time, Corbinian's preaching mission is confirmed by an entire Roman synod. However, while the second journey makes no changes in his ecclesiastical status, it differs from the first by providing a narrative framework within which several miracle stories are set. Both of the Lombard horse-theft narratives, with their divine punishments, take place during this second journey. On another occasion, the saint and his companions are fed by a fish delivered by a passing eagle, and yet another time Corbinian's prayers assist his disciple Anseric not only in catching a fish of astonishing size but also in fighting off the local fishermen who try to steal it from him.

The description of Corbinian's reception and commission in Rome is clearly meant as a response to the cult of St. Boniface. Boniface's *Vita* reports three visits to Rome, over the course of which he received ever-increasing ecclesiastical authority. At the first, in 718, he received a preaching commission; he was consecrated bishop in 722; and he made a third visit in 738, having in the meantime received the archepiscopal *pallium* in 732 by messenger.[136] Corbinian's journeys, then, make him the equal of Boniface in authority and legitimacy.[137]

There is another possible hagiographic source for Corbinian's visit to Rome. Arbeo was aware not only of the monastic community at Fulda to his north. He was also in contact with the monastery of St. Amand

---

[134] *Vita Corbiniani*, c. 6, pp. 194–95; c. 14, pp. 201–2.

[135] *Vita Corbiniani*, cc. 8–9, pp. 196–97; c. 20, pp. 210–11.

[136] *Vita Bonifatii*, c. 5, pp. 21–22; c. 6, pp. 28–30 and 34–35.

[137] Boniface also received his letters of recommendation from the pope in 718 in a "pallium"; *Vita Bonifatii*, c. 5, p. 21. Balthasar Arnold, "Zur Vita Corbiniani," in *Wissenschaftliche Festgabe zum zwölfhundertjährigen Jubiläum des heiligen Korbinian*, ed. Joseph Schlecht (Munich, 1924), p. 67, suggests this more ordinary cloth as a parallel for the claim of the *Vita Corbiniani* that its protagonist received a "pallium." However, while Arbeo's account never claims that Corbinian was made an archbishop, it does seem that the reference to his *pallium* was meant as a claim of authority equal to Boniface's.

in Francia, formerly known as Elnone. One of his most promising cler-
ics, Arn, who served as deacon, priest, and archpriest at Freising, went to
St. Amand around 778–79 and became its abbot in 782.[138] This must have
involved a prior relationship between Freising and St. Amand, as Bavaria
was now at the height of its independence under Tassilo and Arn's transfer
is unlikely to have been engineered by Carolingian authorities.[139] Amandus,
the namesake and founder of St. Amand, must have passed through Bavaria
in the mid-seventh century when he attempted a Slavic mission; possibly
some institutional links remained between Bavarian religious communities
and Amand's northern houses from this time.[140]

   There are no direct verbal parallels between the *Vita Corbiniani* and
the earliest version of the *Vita Sancti Amandi*. However, the structural and
thematic parallels are striking.[141] While Arbeo did not copy episodes word-

---

[138] Jahn, *Ducatus*, p. 527. Arn's last appearance at Freising was in June of 778
(*TF* 89), so he must have gone to St. Amand sometime between then and 782. On
Arn's early career, see Wilhelm Störmer, "Der junge Arn in Freising. Familienkreis
und Weggenossen aus dem Freisinger Domstift," in *Erzbischof Arn von Salzburg*, ed.
Meta Niederkorn-Bruck and Anton Scharer (Vienna, 2004), pp. 9–26; and Herwig
Wolfram, "Arn von Salzburg und Karl der Grosse," in *1200 Jahre Erzbistum Salz-
burg: die älteste Metropole im deutschen Sprachraum. Beiträge des Internationalen
Kongresses in Salzburg vom 11. bis 13. Juni 1998, Mitteilungen der Gesellschaft für
Salzburger Landeskunde*, Ergänzungsband 18 (Salzburg, 1998), pp. 21–32.

[139] The absence of charter sources for St. Amand in this period unfortunately
prevents us from tracing the prosopographical connections that presumably played
a role in this relationship.

[140] *Vita Amandi I*, ed. Bruno Krusch, in MGH SSRM 5, ed. Bruno Krusch and
Wilhelm Levison (Hannover, 1910), pp. 428–49: here at c. 16, pp. 439–40: it is possible that Amandus was remembered in Salzburg. The Salzburg *Liber Confraternitatis*
mentions two monks, one of them a priest, named "Amandinus," who had died
before 784. A living priest Amandinus was among Arn's witnesses to the property
holdings of Salzburg around 790 (*NA* 8.8) and a priest Amandus was among those
who had heard the Maximilian-Cell story from his elders in Virgil's time (*BN* 8.14,
p. 114). The name seems to have been peculiar to the Salzburg *Romani*; no variant
of "Amandus" is found in the charter collections for Freising, Regensburg, Passau,
Mondsee, or Schätlarn. This name was clearly popular prior to Arn's arrival from St.
Amand. That its use represents veneration of Amandus at Salzburg is thus possible,
but cannot be proven.

[141] The possibility of a relationship between the *Vita Amandi* and the *Vita Corbiniani* is raised by Theodor Klüppel, "Die Germania (750–950)," in *Hagiographies*,
vol. 2, ed. Guy Philippart, Corpus Christianorum (Turnhout, 1996), p. 175, and by
Wood, *Missionary Life*, p. 42. Wood points out some of the parallels I have mentioned

for-word from the *Vita Amandi*, he may have known it and been influenced by the model of sanctity Amandus represented. Amandus lived as an ascetic at Bourges for fifteen years, a period similar to Corbinian's fourteen years as an ascetic at Chatres.[142] Like Corbinian, Amandus also made two pilgrimages to Rome. In his first pilgrimage, rather than meeting the pope, he had a vision of St. Peter while sleeping on the steps of St. Peter's, who commissioned him to preach the gospel in Gaul.[143] This commission to evangelize became the driving theme in Amandus's career. Amandus left Rome with relics, which suggests that he did have contact with ecclesiastical authorities there. He later received episcopal consecration unwillingly, at the insistence of King Chlothar II.[144] Amandus made a second journey to Rome, although all that the *Vita* tells about it is a set of miracles; a boy who fell overboard was rescued, a massive fish was caught, and St. Peter himself appeared to calm a storm.[145] Thus, as in Corbinian's case, the device of a second journey is used as a framework for miracle accounts.

Like Corbinian, Amandus rescued a convict whom a Frankish count had executed.[146] Amandus also rebuked King Dagobert over his sexual misconduct, but was eventually reconciled and baptized the king's sons, a pattern reminiscent of Corbinian's criticism of Grimoald's marriage and his later restoration under Hucbert.[147] On several occasions, those who mocked Amandus's preaching suffered divine wrath. One woman was struck blind for worshiping a tree, but healed when she cut it down.[148] Like Corbinian,

---

in his discussion of the *Vita Amandi* but does not bring these observations to bear on his interpretation of Arbeo's hagiographic writing.

[142] *Vita Amandi*, cc. 5–6, pp. 433–34. Chatres is generally identified with either modern Arpajon or Chatrettes.

[143] *Vita Amandi*, c. 7, p. 434.

[144] *Vita Amandi*, c. 8, pp. 434–35.

[145] *Vita Amandi*, cc. 10–12, pp. 435–36.

[146] *Vita Amandi*, c. 14, pp. 438–39. See Friedrich Lotter, "Heiliger und Gehenkter: Zur Todesstrafe in hagiographischen Episodenerzählungen des Mittelalters," in *Ecclesia et Regnum: Beiträge zur Geschichte von Kirche, Recht, und Staat im Mittelalter. Festschrift für Frank-Josef Schmale zu seinem 65. Geburtstag*, ed. Dieter Berg and Hans-Werner Goetz (Karlsruhe, 1989), pp. 1–20, who argues that as far as the gallows-miracle is concerned, the *Vita Amandi* and *Vita Corbiniani*, together with the *Vita Fidoli*, form a family structurally distinct from analogous episodes in Gregory of Tours's works and those of later post-Carolingian hagiographies.

[147] *Vita Amandi*, c. 17, pp. 440–42.

[148] *Vita Amandi*, cc. 19, 20, 24, pp. 443–44, 447.

Amandus survived a conspiracy to murder him, hatched by the bishop of Uzés.[149] Even the similarity of names between Amandus and his mother Amantia are reminiscent of Corbinianus and his mother Corbiniana.[150]

Are the parallels between the *Vita Amandi* and the *Vita Corbiniani* simply due to the common fund of hagiographic cliché? Some similarities doubtless could be. There is nothing unusual about divine wrath visiting the persecutors of a saint, for instance, or of reluctant bishops being recruited from the ranks of ascetics. Columbanus had also stirred up trouble over rulers' marital lives. But other parallels are not mere common coin of hagiography, even if they are not strictly unique to these two *Lives*. There are few other saints who make two journeys to Rome, and fewer for whom the first serves to initiate mission work while the second provides a framework for miracle stories. Both confront old peasant witches, rescue victims of capital punishment, and save young boys who have fallen at the risk of their lives (Corbinian, posthumously, the boy who falls off a cliff; Amandus a boy who falls from a ship into the sea). Individually, any one of these similarities could be coincidental or only reflect common models; in combination, together with the known institutional contact between Freising and Elnone represented by Arn, they present a strong case for a relationship between the two texts.

Based on these parallels, it is likely that Arbeo has modeled his portrait of Corbinian on that of Amandus, and this is part of the model for the two Roman pilgrimage narratives. This means that he has not only attempted to respond to the *Life of Boniface*, which Fulda propagated, but that he did so by appealing to an older hagiographic tradition that may have had deeper roots in Bavaria than the Boniface tradition had. By creating a saint for Bavaria on the model of Amandus, Arbeo created a strong rival figure to oppose the Anglo-Saxon martyr.

The strong missionary theme of the *Vita Amandi* also finds resonances in Arbeo's *vitae*. In fact, Arbeo went out of his way to portray his saints as missionaries in ways that were not rooted in whatever local traditions about them he may have had.

The introduction to the *Life of St. Emmeram* shows that Arbeo was conscious of the broad sweep of Christianization of his era. It tells how "the fame of Christ has spread through the world, so that not a small

---

[149] *Vita Amandi*, c. 23, pp. 445–46.
[150] *Vita Amandi*, c. 1, pp. 431–32.

part of Europe is perceived to flourish remarkably with the discovery of holy Christianity, so that so many westerners of the English, of Britain, of Ireland, Gaul, Alemannia, part of Germany, little by little have come to shine constantly with the praise of God in marvelous fashion. Among these provinces Gothia, Septimania, Spain, [and] Aquitaine with their inhabitants, throwing off idolatry, have begun to worship the son of God together. In the region of Poitou of the aforesaid Aquitaine an ancient city is known to be situated, where the boy named Emmeram had his birth."[151] The mention of the English, Irish, and Alemanni here shows that Arbeo was conscious of the missionary work a century past in the British Isles and on the continent, possibly including the traditions of Columbanus, Gall, and perhaps Pirmin, who worked among the Alemanni. The reference to "part of Germany" could be both an acknowledgment of and a swipe at Boniface, who never succeeded in evangelizing the Saxons. In any case, this rapid overview of European Christendom shows that Arbeo wants the story of Emmeram's martyrdom to be read in the context of a larger story, the Christianization of Europe.

The brief report that Arbeo makes in his first seven chapters on Emmeram's life clearly shows that he wants Emmeram to be seen as a participant in that story of Christianization. Spontaneously, beginning around Poitiers, Emmeram sets out to preach through the countryside to all social classes, and great crowds gather to hear him.[152] The references to both high and low-status audience members are based on the *Dialogues* of Gregory the Great.[153] When Emmeram hears that the Avars are pagans,

---

[151] *Vita Haimhrammi*, c. 1, pp. 26–27. "*[Christi] in partibus mundi fama percreverat, ita ut Europae non modica pars insegniter sacris christianitatis indagine florere dinosceretur, ita ut occidentales tot angulorum, Brittaniae, Hiberniae, Galliae, Alamanniae, Germaniae pars, paulatim mirifico modo in Dei laude constanter fulsissent. Inter quas provintias Gotia, Septemania, Spania, Aquitania cum habitatoribus suis deponentes idolatria unicum Dei filium colere coeperunt. In cuius Aquitaniae praedictae partibus Pictavis urbs antiqua sita dinoscitur, ex qua ortus est puer vocabulo Haimhrammus.*" My translation follows two emendations that appear in some manuscripts, reading "insigniter" for "insegniter" and "sacrae" for "sacris."

[152] *Vita Haimhrammi*, c. 2, pp. 28–30.

[153] See above, pp. 33–34. The *Vita's* editor, Bruno Krusch, noticed Arbeo's proclivity to describe Emmeram's preaching in language drawn from Gregory I's *Dialogues*. *Vita Haimhrammi*, at p. 29 n. 1, p. 37 n. 1, p. 38 n. 2, pp. 42–43, 58, 62 marginal notes, p. 69 n. 1, p. 70 n. 3, p. 73 marginal note, p. 86 marginal note, p. 95 marginal note, p. 99 n. 2.

he resolves to go and preach to them, and makes his way across Gaul and Alemannia until he comes to Bavaria.[154] There Theodo forbids him to continue on account of his own recent wars with the Avars that have devastated the borderlands around the Enns, but he invites Emmeram to stay in Bavaria as pontiff or chief abbot of the land.[155] Emmeram is then cast as a missionary to Bavaria as well. "But its inhabitants, neophytes at that time, had not torn idolatry up by the root, since they, like their fathers, collectively and with their offspring drank the chalice of Christ and [that] of demons."[156] Emmeram spends three years correcting this situation, preaching boldly to the proud and humbly to the lowly, as he travels through the cities, towns, and villages of the land (using the same quotation from Gregory the Great that had described Emmeram's activity at Poitiers). It is at this point that the narrative proceeds to the martyrdom account.

In the *Life of Emmeram*, then, Arbeo creates a portrait of a Bavaria in Theodo's generation where Christianity is known, but highly flawed; paganism ("idolatry") persists. Emmeram's story takes place in the context of a master narrative of missionary history, and Emmeram himself becomes a participant in that story. Bavaria in Theodo's time was not "already essentially Christianized," at least not to Arbeo's standards.[157] It was still, at that time, a valid mission field.

Arbeo draws a similar portrait in the *Life of Corbinian*. There, when Corbinian passes through Bavaria on his second journey to Rome, he also preaches the "seed of divine words," because "our folk was only halfway into the Christian religion, as it were still unformed, [still] in the novitiate of its conversion."[158] The expression matches the image Arbeo painted of Theodo's era in the *Vita Haimhrammi*. He does not, however, identify any prior missionary figures who would have initiated Bavaria's conversion prior to Emmeram's or Corbinian's arrival. A half-Christian state is simply a given for Theodo's reign.

---

[154] *Vita Haimhrammi*, c. 3, pp. 30–31.

[155] *Vita Haimhrammi*, cc. 4–5, pp. 32–34.

[156] *Vita Haimhrammi*, c. 7, pp. 36–37. "*Sed habitatores eius neofitti eo namque in tempore idolatriam radicitus ex se non extirpaverunt, quia ut patres calicem Christi commune et demoniorum suisque prolibus propinaverunt.*"

[157] Cf. Wood, *Missionary Life*, pp. 10–11.

[158] *Vita Corbiniani* 15, p. 203: "*. . . quia paene in Christianitatis religione gens nostra, ut ruda adhuc fuerat, novicitate conversionis erat.*"

The actual activity Arbeo reports for Corbinian hardly makes him out as an active missionary. Unlike Emmeram, he does not aspire to find any genuine pagans to preach to. This only makes it the more striking, then, that Corbinian's preaching commission from the pope during his first pilgrimage is an unmistakable missionary mandate: "He was enabled to exercise the office of preaching everywhere throughout the entire world."[159] This may be compared with the commission given to Boniface. The Anglo-Saxon was initially given authorization to preach universally, but his episcopal consecration narrowed his mission field to Germany; only later was this extended to Gaul.[160] Initially Corbinian performed this office in Gaul, but afterwards he did so in Bavaria. This may be another echo of the *Vita Amandi*, for St. Peter had given Amandus a commission in his vision to preach in Gaul (though he was not yet a bishop); Amandus's will and the events of the *Vita* indicate that he thought of his calling as a mission to the entire world.[161] Thereafter, the life ceases to treat Corbinian in terms that evoke a sense of mission to full or semipagans. The episode of the peasant witch, however, echoes the story of the old woman in the *Vita Amandi* who worshiped a tree and may be a reminder of the Christianizing theme of the *Vita Corbiniani*'s earlier sections.

In any saint's life, death is as important to the sanctity of the protagonist as life. The earliest texts of the hagiographic genre were martyrdom accounts from the early church, in which a faithful confrontation with death proved the salvation of the victim. Eventually confessors, who had kept the faith but survived, joined the ranks of the saints, and this category gradually expanded as eminent Christians were felt to have "confessed" even without being persecuted. Nevertheless, a hagiography

---

159 *"Ubique praedicationis officium exercere per universum orbem potuisset."* *Vita Corbiniani* c. 9, p. 197.

160 Boniface's initial preaching commission from Pope Gregory II in 719 was open-ended and authorized him to preach to any peoples imprisoned by the error of disbelief (*"ad gentes quascumque infidelitatis errore detentas"*). Epp. Bon. 12, pp. 17–18. His episcopal commission of 722, however, made him a bishop for peoples east of the Rhine only. Epp. Bon. 17, pp. 29–33. After the tumultuous events of the early 740s (including the Frankish capture and rejection of a papal legate to Bavaria in 743), Boniface's authority was expanded again to include Gaul in 744. Epp. Bon. 58, p. 108.

161 *Vita Amandi*, c. 7, p. 434. *Testamentum Amandi Episcopi*, MGH SSRM 5, ed. Bruno Krusch (Hannover, 1910), pp. 483–85.

could not be written for a living holy man. The way the saint faced death was the final confirmation of his sanctity.[162]

Rupert's *Vita*, as we have mentioned, makes only the slightest reference to his death. Nevertheless, it is not silent on the subject; Rupert foresees the end coming and goes to his rest in peace. According to the version in the *Gesta*, a select few were privileged to see angels welcoming his soul into heaven.[163]

The *Life of Corbinian* is not much more elaborate in its account of the hero's death. Again, it is important that the saint foresees his end coming. He makes arrangements for his burial at the side of St. Valentinus in Mais, drinks a little wine, celebrates a final mass, and passes peacefully.[164] The peacefulness of Corbinian's death is a stark contrast to that of Grimoald, who is murdered by a conspiracy, or Pilitrud, who dies penniless and exiled, or her henchman Ninus, who dies like Arius in the latrine.[165] Pilitrud and Ninus had conspired to murder Corbinian, but he escaped this fate; Arbeo directly contrasts the violent and unhappy deaths of the wicked with the peaceful death of the righteous.

Emmeram, of course, dies a death par excellence, a gruesome martyrdom at the hands of a maddened persecutor in classical fashion. That his persecutor is no pagan does little to weaken this impression. The complex story of his death, with severed limbs buried separately while Emmeram's trunk survives a journey of some miles, creates a multiplication of holy sites, as will be discussed below. Emmeram faces his death with peace and joy, despite the violence, again a characteristic of a true Christian martyr.[166] His followers flee while Emmeram remains to die, so that he dies, in a sense, in their place.[167] He also lives long enough to give final dying admonitions to his disciples, a last reminder of his power as a preacher.[168]

Bearing our hagiographic context in mind, the martyrdom of Emmeram must be compared with that of Boniface. The *Vita Haimhrammi*, in a sense, creates a Bavarian martyr to compete with the new

---

[162] Peter Brown, *The Cult of the Saints* (Chicago, 1981), pp. 69–85. František Graus, *Volk, Herrscher, Heilige*, pp. 91–102.

[163] See above, pp. 29.

[164] *Vita Corbiniani*, cc. 33–34, pp. 224–25.

[165] *Vita Corbiniani*, cc. 30–31, pp. 222–24.

[166] *Vita Haimhrammi*, c. 18, p. 53.

[167] *Vita Haimhrammi*, c. 16, p. 49.

[168] *Vita Haimhrammi*, cc. 19–20, pp. 53–56.

martyr-saint of Fulda. Boniface died in the mission field, killed by pagans while preparing to confirm new converts. He forbade his followers to fight, and many were killed with him.[169] Emmeram does not die while evangelizing, but he does die on pilgrimage, creating a similar aura of sanctity for his activity and a sense of outrage at his killers' action. He also does not defend himself against Lantpert's attack, although his followers flee and so are saved from being killed themselves. The death of Emmeram himself, however, is narrated with much greater and gorier detail than Boniface's.[170] As a result, it evokes a larger martyrdom literature as well as seeking to evoke greater sympathy for its subject. Thus, Arbeo's martyrdom account supplies a literary quality that Willibald's lacks; a vivid, compelling narrative of the actual suffering and death of the martyr.

Events after the deaths of the saints are also important. The Emmeram account seems confused, because of the several locations associated with his martyrdom. He is interred at Ascheim, but the site of the death itself is long forgotten until unusual weather (its remaining warm and sunny even in winter) brings his death there to memory.[171] The saint's severed limbs are at first preserved and venerated by the locals, but when two mysterious horsemen visit, both horsemen and relics disappear without a trace.[172] Arbeo gives the impression that a cult was slow to form around Emmeram, in spite of his dramatic martyrdom. Nevertheless, his anecdotes depict a growing accumulation of miracles that culminate in dreams that Emmeram wishes to be returned to Regensburg, and his subsequent translation.[173]

Corbinian's cult, by contrast, developed in a less dramatic but more direct fashion; soon after his death, his disciples moved his body from Freising to Mais, in keeping with his wishes. At first, Lombard border guards barred them from coming to Mais (an indication that the Tyrol had come under Lombard control in the interim, a development of Liutprand's reign), until a message from the king gave permission for the interment.[174] Signs

---

[169] *Vita Bonifatii*, c. 8, pp. 49–50.

[170] The vivid image of the Anglo-Saxon holding a gospel-book over his head to ward off a sword blow comes from a later *vita*, although it may be based on a genuine memory. *Vita Altera Bonifatii*, c. 16, p. 73; see Wood, *Missionary Life*, pp. 102–7.

[171] *Vita Haimhrammi*, cc. 24–25, pp. 60–64.

[172] *Vita Haimhrammi*, cc. 22–23, pp. 57–59.

[173] *Vita Haimhrammi*, c. 31, pp. 72–74.

[174] *Vita Corbiniani*, c. 37, pp. 226–27.

of sanctity were already present during this first translation, just a month after Corbinian's death; warm blood seemed to flow from the corpse's nose, and three days after he was entombed a display of lights appeared in the church, outshining the candles there.[175] From there Arbeo tells the story of how a young boy (himself) fell from the cliff by the church on the eve of Corbinian's solemnities, which must have happened only a short time after the interment.[176]

The translations of the saints to Regensburg and Freising are important aspects of their posthumous careers. In each case, the translation is occasioned by visions and dreams, in which it is revealed the saint wishes to be moved. Emmeram's body is moved by river, apparently down the Isar and then up the Danube; despite a dramatic thunderstorm, his intercession miraculously enables the boat to move upriver against the wind and prevents the lights from being extinguished.[177] In Corbinian's case, a manifestation of mist and noise terrifies those around the church.[178] When the translation has been accomplished, the saint's hand appears unwithered and raised in blessing.[179]

The posthumous miracles of both saints largely follow rather than precede the translations. In Emmeram's case, miracles that occur before his translation are associated with the sites of the martyrdom and not with the relics at Ascheim. Only after his translation to Regensburg does the body itself become miraculous. In this way, the miracles not only confirm the sanctity of Emmeram and Corbinian, but also the legitimacy of the new tombs to which they have been translated—that is, the episcopal seats of Regensburg and Freising, respectively. Emmeram preserves a captured pilgrim until he attains his freedom, strikes sinners into repentance, and drives a spirit out of a girl that had made her unable to eat.[180] Corbinian's *Life*, in the earlier version, is missing its final chapters, so we

---

[175] *Vita Corbiniani*, cc. 38–39, p. 227.

[176] *Vita Corbiniani*, c. 40, pp. 227–28. On the date of Corbinian's death and the beginning of his veneration, see n. 37, above.

[177] *Vita Haimhrammi*, c. 32, pp. 74–75.

[178] *Vita Corbiniani*, c. 43, p. 231.

[179] *Vita Corbiniani*, c. 44. p. 231–32.

[180] *Vita Haimhrammi*, cc. 36–45, pp. 80–98.

cannot be sure how extensive the posthumous miracle collection was, but it included at least one exorcism.[181]

On the whole, the posthumous accounts of Emmeram and Corbinian are standard hagiographic fare. Emmeram's "afterlife" is notable for the lack of early cult and the way in which the earliest signs of his sanctity attached to local sites: Helfendorf, where the attack took place, the crossroads where he died, and the hawthorn tree where his limbs were initially buried. This may be a case where a Christian bishop is employing a saint's cult to appropriate local "superstitious" fertility practices. Corbinian's cult, on the other hand, developed in an immediate, if rather modest, fashion. In each case, however, it is a liturgical moment—a dramatic translation rite—that causes the cult to take form. These developments also led to the creation of holy sites in the geography of the duchy.

It has long been known that the spread of the cult of saints created a "spiritual topography" in the Roman and then the European worlds.[182] The dissemination of cults and the situation of shrines in particular locations created a geography of the sacred, a sense of space, distance, and location where the powers of the holy could be found and appealed to. Such a sacred topography gradually replaced that of the pagan world that preceded Christianity, with its sacred temples, groves, springs, and grottoes. In some cases, the new cult sites might directly build on the old ones, as when Christian churches were built next to sacred springs or from the wood of felled holy trees. In other cases, the new Christian centers might be entirely new and shift the flow of devotees away from traditional locations.[183]

The lives of Emmeram and Corbinian depict the production of a Christian topography for Bavaria through the activity of the saints, including their posthumous activity. In spite of Arbeo's claim in both

---

[181] *Vita Corbiniani*, c. 46, p. 232.

[182] See Brown, *Rise of Western Christendom*, pp. 145–65, for a discussion of such a process in late antique Gaul. See also the essays in *Topographies of Power in the Early Middle Ages*, ed. Mayke de Jong and Frans Theuws (Leiden, 2001).

[183] See František Graus, *Volk, Herrscher, Heilige*, pp. 171–96. John M. Howe, "The Conversion of the Physical World," in *Varieties of Religious Conversion in the Middle Ages*, ed. James Muldoon (Gainesville, FL, 1997), pp. 63–78, argued for extensive continuity between pagan and Christian sacral landscapes, as opposed to Robert Markus, *The End of Ancient Christianity* (New York, 1990), pp. 139–55, who saw the process as less direct and immediate. As we shall see, the Bavarian sources do not directly identify any of the area's sacred spaces as prior pagan sites.

of the lives that the Bavarians had not become fully Christianized in the time of Emmeram and Corbinian, he does not make any effort to claim that this new topography competed with an older or pagan sense of sacred space.

The city of Regensburg takes on a particular significance at the time of Emmeram's arrival in Bavaria. Arbeo pauses here, as he does for few other locations, to describe the ducal city: "When he had followed the course of this river (the Danube), he arrived at the city of Regensburg, constructed of cut stones, which had grown into the metropolis of this people in its fortress."[184] In fact, he describes Regensburg at three separate points during the *Vita*. The first description occurs on Emmeram's arrival, where Regensburg's urban character and impressive Roman walls are emphasized. In the second, after Theodo has invited Emmeram to stay in Bavaria, the saint is in part persuaded by the great beauty and fertility of the country around the city, which make it a pleasant residence. The third time, the escaped slave's first sight of the city walls and their towers across the Danube brings a climax of relief and joy to the story.[185] Arbeo also mentions that Vitalis, Emmeram's interpreter, returned to Regensburg to live as an ascetic there. By this point in the *Vita* he refers to Regensburg simply as "the city," implying that the reader will understand its metropolitan character.[186] What is noteworthy about the description of Regensburg is that it is the residence of the dukes that

---

[184] "*Cuius dum sequeret fluentis, ad Radasponam pervenit urbem, qui ex sectis lapidibus constructa, in metropolim huius gentis in arce decreverat.*" *Vita Haimhrammi*, c. 4, p. 32. Arbeo's Latin is, as often, irregular here, and reading "decreverat" to mean that the city "had declined" does not make much sense in the context. Several manuscripts and the B version of the *Vita* give "creverat" or "excreverat" here, which I assume reflects Arbeo's intended meaning, and have followed in the translation. The "arce" probably refers to an inner compound, presumably a ducal complex on the northeast or eastern side of the old Roman *castrum*. See Peter Schmid, "Ratispona metropolis Baioariae: Die bayerischen Herzöge und Regensburg," in *Geschichte der Stadt Regensburg*: Band 1, ed. Peter Schmid (Regensburg, 2000), pp. 51–101.

[185] *Vita Haimhrammi*, c. 6, pp. 34–36; c. 43, pp. 92–93. The topos of the fertile setting of the saint's chosen residence runs through much late antique and Merovingian hagiography. See Julia M. H. Smith, "*Aedificatio sancti loci*: The Making of a Ninth-Century Holy Place," in *Topographies of Power in the Early Middle Ages*, ed. Mayke de Jong and Frans Theuws (Leiden, 2001), pp. 361–96, here at 382–83.

[186] *Vita Haimhrammi*, c. 20, pp. 55–56.

receives this panegyrical treatment. Regensburg itself thus takes on an aura of holiness; it is a city for a saint.

In the *Vita Corbiniani*, Freising stands in the place of Regensburg, a site where secular authority overlaps with the supernatural power derived from the saint's presence. It appears to be Duke Grimoald's principal residence, much as Regensburg was Theodo's, and the course of the narrative in the Bavarian section of the *Vita* is driven by the saint's comings and goings from the ducal palace there. Thus, the beginning of Corbinian's conflict with Pilitrud is indicated by his initial refusal to come into Freising itself.[187] The later heightening of this struggle is marked by Corbinian's attempt to storm out of the palace there, which Grimoald prevents by ordering his subordinates to bar the doors until he has mollified the saint.[188] When Pilitrud attempts to have Corbinian murdered, he leaves Freising altogether for his monastic cell at Mais, to return only after Grimoald's death and Pilitrud's exile.[189] Thus, the physical presence or absence of the saint forms a running commentary on the spiritual status of the duchy's rulers.

Freising, of course, was Arbeo's own episcopal see, and his desire to draw attention to Corbinian's activity there can only have served to enhance the reputation of his own office. The few miracles Corbinian worked in Bavaria (rather than in Francia or Italy) took place either at Freising itself or in neighboring Weihenstefan.[190] Arbeo's insistence on the importance of the saint's presence at the ducal palace was relevant to his own time as well as to his image of Corbinian's period, for Freising continued to serve as a ducal center and residence. Tassilo was present at the see on at least two documented occasions during Arbeo's episcopacy, once on September 26, 770, and again on September 8, 772.[191] Two other ducal visits may be attested by older charters, one that may put a teenaged Tassilo at Freising in 757 and another a little later, in 759.[192] By asserting the significance of the saint's favor to ducal fortunes, Arbeo would have asserted his own significance for Tassilo's itinerant court.

---

[187] *Vita Corbiniani*, c. 24, pp. 215–16.
[188] *Vita Corbiniani*, c. 26, pp. 217–18.
[189] *Vita Corbiniani*, cc. 29–32, pp. 221–24.
[190] *Vita Corbiniani*, cc. 27–28, pp. 219–20.
[191] *TF* 39 (September 26, 770) and 48 (September 8, 772).
[192] *TF* 10 (757) and 15 (759, per Jahn, *Ducatus*, pp. 352–56).

The *Vita Haimhrammi* identifies Ascheim as the place of the martyr's initial burial. It may be significant that Ascheim was also a major ducal center—a *locus publicus*—and hosted the first known Bavarian church synod around 754 or 756.[193] It is unclear if Emmeram's relics were still here at the time of the synod or had already been removed to Regensburg. One suspects that they were present, or even that the synod was the occasion for their translation. It would appear, then, that Arbeo's *vitae* draw attention to sites of veneration of his saints—particularly Emmeram— which are also centers of ducal authority, Regensburg and Ascheim. This makes the idea of an anti-Agilulfing Arbeo even more dubious. Rather, it would appear that Arbeo envisions a saint's cult that supports and is supported by the duke.

Corbinian for his part finds Freising delightful, and Kuens, near Mais, where he creates a foundation of his own.[194] The praises of these places are not sounded repeatedly as was the case for Regensburg, but the theme is similar. Arbeo also tells a story that would create a particular holy spot within Freising, rather than the aura that attached to Regensburg as a whole. On one occasion Corbinian struck the ground on the hillside near Weihenstephan, causing a spring to gush forth. This spring dried up the day Corbinian died, only to well up again when the saint was translated back to Freising.[195] Holy wells and springs were typical centers of late Roman paganism, and the attachment of Corbinian's name to this one could represent an effort by Arbeo to Christianize such a cult site. The question must remain open. At any rate, the text of the *Vita* serves to confirm and legitimate the veneration of this spring.

As we have seen, there are several places that the *Vita Haimhrammi* identifies as places where veneration is appropriate. Helfendorf, where Emmeram was attacked and where his limbs were buried under a haw- thorn tree, is one.[196] The crossroads where he finally died is another, man- ifesting remarkable fertility and immunity to bad weather. This became the site of a church.[197] Given the late antique tendency to worship sacred

---

[193] MGH Concilia 2.1, ed. Albert E. Werminghoff (Hannover and Leipzig, 1906), pp. 56–58. The synod is undated but appears to have taken place shortly before Tassilo III came of age, perhaps as early as 754. See n. 10, above.

[194] *Vita Corbiniani*, c. 23, pp. 214–15.

[195] *Vita Corbiniani*, c. 28, pp. 219–20.

[196] *Vita Haimhrammi*, cc. 22–23, pp. 57–59.

[197] *Vita Haimhrammi*, c. 25, 30, pp. 62–64, 70–72.

trees and springs, one may suspect that Arbeo is Christianizing older pagan sites; even if not, it is clear that his *vitae* create a topography for the diocese associated with healing and fertility, under the auspices of the saints.

Thus, the lives create a strong connection between the sanctity of their subjects and local geography. They do not attempt to create a totalistic sacrality ranging across all of the duchy; rather, each is concerned with a particular set of local sites where the divine manifests itself. In the *Life of St. Rupert*, part of the association of the saint with physical place, as we saw, had to do with his role in reconstructing church buildings in Salzburg itself. Another aspect, seen at the Maximilian cell, however, was the direct manifestation of supernatural power. This aspect of divine manifestations associated with a location is a dominant theme in the Emmeram's life, particularly at the hawthorn tree and the crossroads of his death, in Corbinian's life with the marvelous spring at Weihenstefan, and in both lives with Emmeram's and Corbinian's miracle-working tombs. A third aspect to sacrality, besides the architectural or the locus of manifestation, is the indication in all three lives of rich and aesthetically pleasing places attracting the favor of the saints: Salzburg for Rupert, Regensburg for Emmeram, and Freising for Corbinian.

Conclusion: The *Typus* of Bavaria's Eighth-Century Saints

The *vitae* of Bavarian saints written in the eighth century represent a complex array of concerns and themes. In all likelihood, the *Lives* of Rupert, Emmeram, and Corbinian were written within a short span of time, between the translations of Corbinian in 767 and Rupert in 774. This was a period when Bavaria enjoyed a new height of independence from Frankish domination, and the autonomy of the Bavarian church followed suit. The saints' Lives discussed in this essay provided a variety of models of holiness which articulated an ideology of a Christian society. They thus provided the conceptual basis upon which a Bavarian "micro-Christendom" could be constructed.

The "typus," or literary and ideological model, of St. Rupert is the simplest of the three. Rupert appears in his *Vita* as a prince of the church. Miracles are only vaguely alluded to in his *Vita*, and asceticism not at all. Rupert deals on an equal footing with the duke, who must negotiate for the saint's favor. He founds institutions, restores dilapidated buildings, and gathers disciples. Above all, he obtains gifts of property for his churches. Rupert is a bishop's saint, a model for the businesslike church leader, exuding wealth, learning, and authority. His career gives the church at Salzburg a stamp of legitimacy and order that, in the context of the mid-eighth century and Virgil's career, can be seen as a counterpoint to Boniface's accusations of heresy and claims to have founded these institutions reflected in the traditions maintained at Fulda and Mainz.

St. Emmeram's image has some similarities to Rupert's; he also negotiates with dukes and is noted for his learning and doctrine. However, the overwhelming emphasis of his life—or passion—is on his martyrdom. Emmeram's living career is of minor importance compared to his death; in it, he becomes a sacrificial victim, and the drawn-out tale of his murder scatters blood across the Bavarian landscape, sanctifying several locations by its touch: Helfendorf, Ascheim, and the crossroads of his death, which might be Feldkirchen. Associations of healing and fertility spring up at these locations, suggesting that unlike Rupert, who was a saint for bishops and lords, Emmeram may be a saint for more humble people, at least within Arbeo's own diocese. In fact, the attachment of his martyrdom story to these various locations may reveal an effort to Christianize a lingering pagan topography of the region south of Freising. In opening Emmeram's *Vita*, Arbeo clearly has Christianization in mind; he sets the *Vita* in the context of a grand narrative of the conversion of western Europe. Emmeram himself, in the brief portrait we have of his living activity, appears as a missionary, rooting out lingering paganism from the Bavarian people. Nevertheless, Emmeram's story also stands out as a cautionary tale to secular authorities, contrasting the favorable treatment the saint receives from Theodo with the hostility of Theodo's son, and stressing the bad end of the latter and his henchmen.

Most complex of the three figures is Corbinian. The *Life of Corbinian* combines many of the concerns we have seen in the other two Lives. Corbinian is an authoritative bishop and learned teacher, who rebukes dukes, gains amnesty for convicts, and receives rich gifts. He is also a missionary, induced to stay in Bavaria by its half-finished Christianization and driven to wrath by the persistence of superstitious practices there. He escapes martyrdom at the hands of his enemies, but leaves his mark on the landscape in the form of a holy spring at Freising and a tomb at Mais. But Corbinian's life also incorporates themes that had not been as prominent in the other *Lives*. He is the only saint with an ascetic background. He is also the only one to be linked to Rome by not one, but two pilgrimages. These Roman connections are invoked in his *vita* to claim an authority for him that closely matches that wielded by Boniface, with his legatine commission and *pallium*. Corbinian is also, while still living, the most distinguished miracle worker; divine wrath strikes those who oppose or steal from him, and he summons springs out of the ground and causes food to be delivered to his followers. Corbinian is also a churchman who must constantly deal with conflict, particularly from factions within the ducal household. His unyielding posture and the evil ends to which his foes come drives home the message that secular authority must cooperate with the church or face the unpleasant consequences.

By laying out a model of cooperation between ducal and ecclesiastical authority, by linking the patrons of the Bavarian churches with the touchstone of Roman legitimacy and orthodoxy, and by using the narrative of saints' lives to generate a Christian sacred topography for Bavaria, where the power of God had manifested and where miracles occur, Arbeo and his anonymous contemporary created a vision of Bavaria as a fully-fledged "micro-Christendom." Such a Christendom had its own resources of sacrality, and was thus able to assert its independence from rival Christendoms such as the one embodied by the powerful cult of St. Boniface at Fulda. At the same time, it could boast of its own connectivity to Christendom at large, not only to Rome but also to the Frankish and Lombard kingdoms. The saints of Bavaria were the interlocutors of Frankish and Italian rulers as well as Bavarian dukes.

This transition to a Bavarian Christendom also meant that the eighth-century hagiographers rewrote the story of Bavaria's own Christianity. The writers held back from asserting that Rupert, Emmeram, and Corbinian had actually founded the churches over which they presided. But the promotion of these three saints' cults meant that any past Christian identity, whether a survival of Roman times or imported from Francia, Italy, or elsewhere, was devalued. The people to whom Emmeram and Corbinian came were still in the "novitiate" of their Christianity; they had not yet rooted out idolatry, but mixed the cup of Christ with that of the demons. The beautiful churches of Roman times that Rupert found at Salzburg lay in ruins and derelict until he restored them.

In the process of recasting Bavaria's own history in this manner, the hagiographers also recast their saints as missionaries. The lives give little evidence that the saints in question really did act as missionaries, in any sense of the word. But they show that by the 760s, the idea of the missionary had become important to the Bavarian church. We should remember that Bavarian missionaries had faced pagan uprisings from the Carantanian Slavs since 763. Suppressed twice, a renewed outbreak of anti-Christian violence in 769 may have cast the entire mission project into doubt, precisely at the time Arbeo was writing his hagiographies.[198] Duke Tassilo's final defeat of the rebellious Slavs only occurred after the composition of Arbeo's lives, in 772. But rather than giving up the mission, the hagiographers, and Arbeo in particular, responded by making missionary prerogatives (Emmeram's desire to evangelize the Avars, Corbinian's commission to universal preaching) a central feature of his saints' holiness, and thus asserted mission as a central value for the communities that venerated these saints. In a sense, the periphery shaped the center; the greater challenge posed by the mission field prompted the promotion of mission itself as a defining feature of the central Bavarian churches' identity. This newly formulated missionary identity for the Bavarian church would continue to shape the direction of its efforts for the remainder of the Agilulfing era and to set the agenda for these churches through the transition to Carolingian rule and into the ninth century.

---

[198] See above, pp. 16–17.

Knights and Knighthood in Gaelic Scotland, c. 1050–1300

Cynthia J. Neville
Dalhousie University

R. Andrew McDonald
Brock University

Introduction

In the summer of 1215, a dramatic episode occurred in the far north of Scotland, when a local warrior named Ferchar Maccintsacairt smashed a dangerous and well-supported rebellion against the boy king, Alexander II. According to the near-contemporary *Chronicle of Melrose*, Ferchar "mightily overthrew these enemies of the king; he cut off their heads, and presented them as an offering to the new king. . . . And because of this, the lord king made him a new knight."[1] The event is noteworthy for many reasons, not least because it attests the loyalty to the Scottish crown of a

The authors would like to acknowledge with thanks the financial support of the Social Sciences and Humanities Research Council of Canada in the research undertaken for this article.

[1] *The Chronicle of Melrose from the Cottonian Manuscript, Faustina B. IX in the British Museum: A Complete and Full-sized Facsimile in Collotype*, ed. Alan Orr Anderson and Marjorie Ogilvie Anderson (London, 1936), pp. 59–60.

Gaelic magnate in a period when the ruling dynasty could by no means take for granted the allegiance of the native elite of the northern reaches of the realm.[2] As William Croft Dickinson observed some years ago, it is also of interest since, as a consequence of his support, this same Maccint-sacairt apparently won the honorable status of a knight.[3] Moreover, by 1230 he had achieved the dignity of an earldom and with it a prominent role in royal efforts to control the north.[4]

The figure of the knight and the various social, political, and cultural practices associated with it originated in the old Carolingian heartland of Europe. Knighthood, then, was a characteristically Frankish concept that was carried to other parts of Europe through the processes of conquest, colonization, and assimilation that Robert Bartlett has so comprehensively explored.[5] Although the particulars of Bartlett's arguments remain the subject of some debate, scholars in general agree that the idea of the knight as both a mounted warrior and a member of an exclusive social order gained currency in the British Isles soon after the Norman Conquest of England in 1066.[6] A new "roving" aristocracy,[7] French-speaking and endowed with sometimes extensive gifts of land and privilege, quickly extended its influence over the Conqueror's new kingdom and, in

---

[2] See here R. Andrew McDonald, *Outlaws of Medieval Scotland: Challenges to the Canmore Kings, 1058–1266* (East Linton, 2003), pp. 43–44.

[3] William Croft Dickinson, *Scotland from the Earliest Times to 1603*, 3rd ed. (Oxford, 1977), p. 4.

[4] R. Andrew McDonald, "Old and New in the Far North: Ferchar Maccintsacairt and the Early Earls of Ross, c. 1200–74," in *The Exercise of Power in Medieval Scotland c. 1200–1500*, ed. Steve Boardman and Alasdair Ross (Dublin, 2003), pp. 23–45; Alexander Grant, "The Province of Ross and the Kingdom of Alba," in *Alba: Celtic Scotland in the Medieval Era*, ed. Edward J. Cowan and R. Andrew McDonald (East Linton, 2000), pp. 117–26.

[5] Maurice Keen, *Chivalry* (New Haven, 1984), esp. pp. 18–82; Robert Bartlett, *The Making of Europe: Conquest, Colonization and Cultural Change 950–1350* (Princeton, 1993).

[6] Keen, *Chivalry*, pp. 27–28; D. Crouch, *The Image of Aristocracy in Britain 1000–1300* (London, 1992), pp. 20–63; D. Crouch, *The Birth of Nobility: Constructing Aristocracy in England and France 900–1300* (Harlow, 2005). For an interesting view of the changes effected to noble society in England following the Conquest, see John Gillingham, "1066 and the Introduction of Chivalry into England," in *Law and Government in Medieval England and Normandy: Essays in Honour of Sir James Holt*, ed. George Garnett and John Hudson (Cambridge, 1994), pp. 31–55.

[7] Bartlett, *Making of Europe*, p. 51.

the generations thereafter, penetrated the neighboring regions of Wales, Scotland, and Ireland. "Such was the supremacy of this 'French' culture," one historian has opined, "that even the outlying parts of the British Isles were sucked into its vortex."[8]

Widespread though the idea of the knight and its attendant ethos may have been, it is nevertheless the case that Gaelic magnates who were also knights do not feature prominently in the chronicles of the medieval British Isles. Early twelfth-century observers of the Celtic peoples of Wales, Scotland, and Ireland, most of them writing from England, or at least from an English perspective, occasionally remarked (with surprise and no little curiosity) that native lords were capable of exhibiting genteel behavior. Walter Map, for example, grudgingly allowed that the highland Scots had a notion (albeit odd) of knightly conduct,[9] and Orderic Vitalis expressed some admiration for King Malcolm III's understanding of a promise honorably made.[10] By the middle years of that same century, however, curiosity had begun to harden into hostility. William of Newburgh commented acidly that King David I (1124–53) was a "civilized king of an uncivilized people."[11] Within a generation, the writings of chroniclers as diverse as John of Worcester, Henry of Huntingdon, John of Hexham, and even Aelred of Rievaulx, a friend and admirer of David, signaled a linguistic turn that marked the emergence of a "great socio-cultural divide" between the "civilized" English and the "barbarous" Celts that was to characterize relations between the peoples for centuries to come.[12] The portrayal of the Gaelic populations as political, cultural, and linguistic Others has been the subject of close and fascinating study during the last two decades, and the findings of scholars such as Rees Davies, Robert Bartlett, and John Gillingham have done much to shed valuable light on the relations between England and its neighbors in the context of the

---

8 R. R. Davies, *Domination and Conquest: The Experience of Ireland, Scotland and Wales 1100–1300* (Cambridge, 1990), p. 18.

9 Walter Map, *De nugis curialium*, ed. Montague Rhodes James (Oxford, 1914), p. 88.

10 *The Ecclesiastical History of Orderic Vitalis*, ed. Marjorie Chibnall, 6 vols. (Oxford, 1969–80), 2:218.

11 William of Newburgh, *Historia rerum Anglicarum*, in *Chronicles of the Reigns of Stephen, Henry II and Richard I*, ed. Richard Howlett, 4 vols., Rolls Series, 82 (London, 1884–89), 1:72.

12 R. R. Davies, *The First English Empire: Power and Identities in the British Isles 1093–1343* (Oxford, 2000), p. 115.

medieval British polity.[13] Yet work remains to be done on the ways in which the Celtic populations of the British Isles received and internalized these new ideas. Too often, historians have emphasized the "willing and, indeed, optimistic surrender" of native mores to the "exhilarating international world of aristocratic fellowship" that the knightly culture of Europe represented.[14] Welsh, Scottish, and Irish historians themselves, for the most part, have treated the reception of knighthood and its customs and practices in their respective realms as the consequence of an inevitable process of "Europeanization" or "modernization" of the Celtic peoples. As early as the mid-twelfth century, it has been observed, the Gaelic aristocracy of Wales "was being drawn into the orbit of Anglo-

---

[13] The literature here is now very considerable, but is dominated by the works of Bartlett, Davies, and Gillingham: Robert Bartlett, *Gerald of Wales 1146–1223* (Oxford, 1982), pp. 158–77; Bartlett, *Making of Europe*; Davies, *Domination and Conquest*; Davies, *First English Empire*; R. R. Davies, "Law and National Identity in Thirteenth-Century Wales," in *Welsh Society and Nationhood: Historical Essays Presented to Glanmor Williams*, ed. R. R. Davies, R. A. Griffiths, I. G. Jones, and K. O. Morgan (Cardiff, 1984), pp. 51–69; John Gillingham, "1066 and the Introduction of Chivalry"; John Gillingham, "The Beginnings of English Imperialism," *Journal of Historical Sociology* 5 (1992), 342–409; John Gillingham, "Conquering the Barbarians: War and Chivalry in Twelfth-Century Britain," *Haskins Society Journal* 4 (1993 for 1992), 67–84; John Gillingham, "The Context and Purposes of Geoffrey of Monmouth's *The History of the Kings of Britain*," in *Anglo-Norman Studies 13: Proceedings of the Battle Conference 1990*, ed. Marjorie Chibnall (Woodbridge, 1990), pp. 99–118; John Gillingham, "Foundations of a Disunited Kingdom," in *Uniting the Kingdom? The Making of British History*, ed. Alexander Grant and K. J. Stringer (New York, 1996), pp. 48–64; John Gillingham, "Killing and Mutilating Political Enemies in the British Isles from the Late Twelfth to the Early Fourteenth Century: A Comparative Study," in *Britain and Ireland 900–1300: Insular Responses to Medieval European Change*, ed. Brendan Smith (Cambridge, 1999), pp. 114–34; John Gillingham, "The Travels of Roger of Howden and His Views of the Irish, Scots and Welsh," in *Anglo-Norman Studies 20: Proceedings of the Battle Conference in Dublin, 1997*, ed. Christopher Harper-Bill (Woodbridge, 1997), pp. 151–69. See also W. R. Jones, "England Against the Celtic Fringe: A Study in Cultural Stereotypes," *Cahiers d'histoire mondiale* 13 (1971), 95–111; W. R. Jones, "The Image of the Barbarian in Medieval Europe," *Comparative Studies in Society and History* 13 (1971), 376–407; and Matthew Strickland, "Securing the North: Invasion and the Strategy of Defence in Twelfth-Century Anglo-Scottish Warfare," in *Anglo-Norman Studies 12: Proceedings of the Battle Conference 1989*, ed. Marjorie Chibnall (Woodbrdge, 1989), pp. 177–98.

[14] Davies, *Domination and Conquest*, pp. 47, 51.

French cultural life";[15] by the closing decades of that same century, Robin Frame has argued, the influence of "Anglo-Norman military and economic entrepreneurs" in Ireland had begun to spread from Leinster into Munster, Ulster, and Connaught.[16]

R. L. Graeme Ritchie's seminal work on the "Normanization" of Scotland, published in 1954, set the tone for a new generation of historians whose influence continues to shape interpretations of the impact of European culture on the northern kingdom. The scholarship of Archibald Duncan, Keith Stringer, and, above all, Geoffrey Barrow has much clarified the political, military, and legal status of the knight in Scotland.[17] This work, however, has been concerned primarily with analyzing the spread of tenure by knight's feu rather than with exploring the status, manners, and social significance of knighthood within the kingdom, or with answering questions about the degree to which the native aristocracy in particular accepted European notions about knightly conduct and behavior. Some twenty-five years ago, Barrow's contention that a "cut-and-dried, ready-to-wear feudalism" came to Scotland in the wake

---

15 R. R. Davies, *The Age of Conquest: Wales 1063–1415* (Oxford, 2000), p. 105; R. R. Davies, "Henry I and Wales," in *Studies in Medieval History presented to R. H. C. Davis*, ed. Henry Mayr-Harting and R. I. Moore (London, 1985), pp. 133–47; A. D. Carr, *Medieval Wales* (London, 1995), pp. 46–49.

16 Robin Frame, *The Political Development of the British Isles 1100–1400* (Oxford, 1990), p. 35. For a survey of the process of colonization in a specific region of Ireland, see Brendan Smith, *Colonisation and Conquest in Medieval Ireland: The English in Louth, 1170–1330* (Cambridge, 1999).

17 Robert Lindsay Graeme Ritchie, *The Normans in Scotland* (Edinburgh, 1954). Barrow's works on this subject are extensive, but see especially "The Beginnings of Feudalism in Scotland," *Bulletin of the Institute of Historical Research* 29 (1956), 1–28, revised and reprinted as "The Beginnings of Military Feudalism," in G. W. S. Barrow, *The Kingdom of the Scots: Government, Church and Society from the Eleventh to the Thirteenth Century*, 2nd ed. (Edinburgh, 2003), pp. 250–78; G. W. S. Barrow, *The Anglo-Norman Era in Scottish History* (Oxford, 1980); and his masterful Introductions to *Regesta Regum Scottorum, 1: The Acts of Malcolm IV King of Scots 1153–1165* (Edinburgh, 1960), and *Regesta Regum Scottorum 2: The Acts of William I King of Scots, 1165–1214* (Edinburgh, 1971). Hereafter cited as *RRS* I and *RRS* 2, respectively. See also A. A. M. Duncan, *Scotland: The Making of the Kingdom* (Edinburgh, 1975); Keith J. Stringer, *Earl David of Huntingdon, 1152–1219: A Study in Anglo-Scottish History* (Edinburgh, 1985); Keith J. Stringer, "Scottish Foundations: Thirteenth-Century Perspectives," in *Uniting the Kingdom?*, ed. Grant and Stringer, pp. 85–96; Bruce Webster, *Medieval Scotland: The Making of an Identity* (Basingstoke, 1997), pp. 21–49; A. D. M. Barrell, *Medieval Scotland* (Cambridge, 2000), pp. 16–19.

of English and Continental aristocratic settlers initiated a debate that has kept scholarly discussion closely focused on the political, economic, and tenurial significance of knighthood and the extent to which Scotland was or was not "feudalized."[18] So little has been written on the subject of knighthood among the native elite, in fact, that recent surveys of the Middle Ages in Britain, although scrupulously informed about myriad aspects of the social and cultural experiences of the aristocracy, still have remarkably little to offer on concepts of knightly rank and status among the Gaelic magnates. Many of these works imply a more seamless absorption by native landholders of the trappings of European-style knighthood than the extant evidence would suggest.[19]

Only in recent years have a few scholars turned their attention to the political and social environments of the great native lordships situated in the "land of earls" north of Forth that played such a prominent role in the making of the medieval Scottish polity.[20] These studies reveal that the Gaelic magnates' attitudes toward European ideas of knighthood were at once more complex and multifaceted than some analyses have indicated. Simply put, acceptance of Continental notions about the knight and his place in society required that native lords consider in novel ways not merely fundamental practices such as warfare, military obligation, and land ownership, but also that they reinterpret deeply ingrained notions of social status, manhood, and self-identity. This article explores the subject of knights, knighthood, and the ethos of European knighthood in twelfth- and thirteenth-century Scotland. It begins by examining the evidence for knighthood among the Scottish royal kindred and reviews briefly recent findings about the spread of the institutions widely associated with the figure of the knight into portions of the kingdom in the wake of the settlers whom Ritchie identified generally (if erroneously) as

---

[18] Barrow, *Anglo-Norman Era*, p. 139. As recently as 2003, the annual meeting of the Scottish Medievalists was devoted to the theme of "Fiefs and Vassals: Scottish Feudalism Reappraised." See Susan Reynolds, "Fiefs and Vassals in Scotland: A View from Outside," *Scottish Historical Review* 82 (2003), 176–93.

[19] See, for example, Crouch, *Image of Aristocracy*, pp. 54–55; and David Carpenter, *The Struggle for Mastery: Britain 1066–1284* (London, 2003), pp. 423–24.

[20] Duncan, *Making of the Kingdom*, p. 164. See here Cynthia J. Neville, *Native Lordship in Medieval Scotland: The Earldoms of Strathearn and Lennox, c. 1140–1365* (Dublin, 2005); the essays collected in *Exercise of Power*, ed. Boardman and Ross and R. Andrew McDonald, *The Kingdom of the Isles: Scotland's Western Seaboard, c. 1100–c. 1336* (East Linton, 1997).

"Scotland's Norman aristocracy." The emphasis of this study, however, lies in an examination of the extent to which members of the kingdom's Gàidhealtachd absorbed, internalized, and in turn gave expression to the manners, customs, and values of European-style knighthood.

This study draws heavily on written sources such as chronicles and especially charter texts, as well as on the courtly literature of the years between the mid-twelfth and the late thirteenth centuries. Just as valuable as evidentiary materials are the waxen seals that, from the 1150s, medieval Scottish noblemen began to adopt. Although these survive in relatively small numbers, the symbols with which they were impressed reveal in telling fashion the ways in which English and European images of the knight interacted with native systems of belief. Collectively, these sources reveal that the Gaelic aristocracy of Scotland understood clearly the significance that European culture attached to the figure of the mounted fighting man. Yet they indicate also that native lords mediated the foreign culture of Europe through the filter of their own mores. More intriguingly, they suggest that knightly status was not, to all members alike of the aristocracy in Scotland, an unrivalled exemplar.[21] Until the mid-thirteenth century at least, the men of the Scottish royal family saw in knighthood an important mark of their membership of an international elite, and they enthusiastically encouraged their followers, native and newcomer, to adopt its trappings. Yet, it is apparent that many of the native lords who were among their most powerful subjects were not prepared to discard native traditions and customs wholesale in favor of European practices and ideas. Extant evidence reveals that there was much in the material culture of the chivalric ethos of Europe that they found attractive and inviting, but it is equally clear that Gaelic ideas about status, honor, and manly conduct endured alongside the European

---

21 This was very much the case in the medieval lordship of the Isles, where, as John Bannerman has shown, knighthood as a social marker touched Gaelic society only lightly. Rank and status were measured, instead, according to distinctly different criteria. See here "The Scots Language and the Kin-based Society," in *Gaelic and Scots in Harmony: Proceedings of the Second International Conference on the Languages of Scotland*, ed. Derick S. Thomson (Glasgow, 1988), pp. 1–19; and "The Lordship of the Isles," in *Scottish Society in the Fifteenth Century*, ed. Jennifer M. Brown (London, 1977), pp. 209–40. See also the tentative conclusions of Dauvit Broun concerning the accommodation between Gaels and Europeans in lowland Scotland, in "Anglo-French Acculturation and the Irish Element in Scottish Identity," in *Britain and Ireland 900–1300*, ed. Smith, esp. pp. 137–43.

well into the thirteenth century. The final section of the article seeks to explain why this was so and why it is not entirely appropriate to describe the native aristocracy of Scotland in the period between 1150 and 1300 as thoroughly "Europeanized" in its outlook and practices.

The Political Background

Scotland in the twelfth century was a kingdom in a state of profound political, social, economic, and ecclesiastical change during which, scholars agree, it moved decisively into a new era as a self-conscious western European state. From 1097 until 1286 it was ruled by the descendants in the direct male line of King Malcolm III (1058–93) and his second wife, Margaret, a period sometimes referred to as that of the MacMalcolm dynasty. After a brief civil war following the deaths of Malcolm and Margaret in 1093, their son Edgar gained the kingship in 1097; he was followed in turn by his brothers Alexander I (1107–24) and David I (1124–53). David's grandsons, first Malcolm IV (1153–65) and then William I (1165–1214), consolidated the hold of the MacMalcolms on the throne; thereafter, the royal line descended directly in the male line to Alexander II (1214–49) and Alexander III (1249–86). The early MacMalcolm kings, in particular David I, initiated a thoroughgoing transformation of Scottish society, a process that their successors continued and that is often described in terms of the Europeanization of the kingdom.[22] As a consequence of these changes, Scotland joined a confraternity of the more or less culturally homogeneous kingdoms of medieval Europe, theoretically at least united under the spiritual leadership of the papacy as well as under the political leadership of powerful secular rulers.

In Scotland, as elsewhere, the process had several defining characteristics. The division of the kingdom into clearly defined units of diocesan and parish administration, together with the foundation of a host of monasteries for the reformed religious orders, wrought momentous change in the

---

[22] See, for example, Bartlett, *Making of Europe*, pp. 53–54, 104–5; Barrell, *Medieval Scotland*, pp. 15–16; Thomas Owen Clancy and Barbara E. Crawford, "The Formation of the Scottish Kingdom," and David Ditchburn and Alistair J. Macdonald, "Medieval Scotland, 1100–1550," both in *The New Penguin History of Scotland from the Earliest Times to the Present Day*, ed. R. A. Houston and W. W. J. Knox (London, 2001), pp. 88, 140; McDonald, *Outlaws of Medieval Scotland*, p. 153.

ecclesiastical sphere. The erection of a series of impressive border abbeys consciously modeled on architectural styles then current in England and the Continent gave visual expression to the "new vigour" with which the royal family welcomed spiritual reform.[23] In the economic realm, the rapid growth of towns (many of royal foundation) and the introduction of a standardized coinage bore witness to an equally profound series of transformations.[24] In political and secular matters, the most significant feature of the Europeanization of Scotland was the settlement, throughout the region south of the Forth as well as in distant Moray, of adventurers from England and the Continent. King David I, reared at the English court, granted estates of varying size to many of the newcomers, ranging from the vast lordship of Annandale that became the foundation of the Bruce family's fortunes to the more modest lands in East Lothian with which he endowed another follower, Alexander de St. Martin.[25] From most of these tenants David and his successors on the Scottish throne demanded military service, and it was concurrent with the settlement of such foreigners largely south of the River Forth that the knight's feu, succinctly described as "a notional valuation of the land needed to support a knight in the king's service," first gained currency in Scotland.[26] From the time of Malcolm IV onward, other terms and concepts associated throughout Europe with the figure of the knight begin to appear regularly in records written in, and relating to, Scotland south of Forth, from castles to plate armor, and armorial bearings to tournaments.

Scottish Kings and Knighthood to 1286

In 1087 Duncan, the eldest son of Malcolm III and his first wife, was released from captivity, having been held hostage by William the Conqueror since 1072. Robert Curthose, acting on behalf of his brother, King

---

[23] Richard Fawcett, "The Architectural Context of the Border Abbey Churches in the Twelfth and Thirteenth Centuries," in *Anglo Norman Studies 25: Proceedings of the Battle Conference 2002*, ed. John Gillingham (Woodbridge, 2003), pp. 85–106.

[24] Elizabeth Gemmill and Nicholas Mayhew, *Changing Values in Medieval Scotland: A Study of Prices, Money, and Weights and Measures* (Cambridge, 1995).

[25] *The Charters of David I: The Written Acts of David I King of Scots, 1124–53, and of His Son Henry Earl of Northumberland, 1139–52*, ed. G. W. S. Barrow (Woodbridge, 1999), nos. 16, 194.

[26] Barrow, *Kingdom of the Scots*, p. 262.

William II, considered the occasion sufficiently noteworthy to "honor" the former prisoner "with military arms."[27] The chronicler John of Worcester's brief mention of the events of 1087 is the first instance on record of a native Scot receiving knighthood, and the earliest written association of the royal kindred with the title.[28] Thereafter, there is increasing evidence that members of the Scottish royal family actively pursued the honor of knighthood, and that they regarded it as a mark of distinction entirely appropriate to their identification with the ruling houses of Europe.

Duncan's half brother, Alexander I, never received arms in a formal ceremony such as that of 1087. Nor is there any indication that, despite his reliance on the support of the English king for his tenure of the throne, he encouraged the introduction into his kingdom of any of the French influences that he encountered at the court of his father-in-law, Henry I.[29] Yet, looking back from the perspective of the later Middle Ages, Scottish chroniclers had no doubt about the knightly qualities of the children of Malcolm III and his saintly second wife, Margaret. The fifteenth-century cleric Andrew of Wyntoun saw in Alexander I a knight in all but name, commanding a force of cavalry at Invergowrie against a fierce contingent of highlanders, riding to war against the Welsh and offering as gifts to the priory of St. Andrews the visible symbols of his rank: "his cumly steide of Araby," together with a fine suit of armor, his shield and his spear.[30] In a flight of literary fancy Wyntoun's contemporary, Walter Bower, portrayed all three sons as "noble knights," all gleaming in armor.[31] Yet there is nothing to suggest that either Alexander or his predecessor, Edgar, was a member of the knightly order. Much less doubt surrounds the status of

---

[27] *Florentii Wigornensis monachi Chronicon ex chronicis*, ed. Benjamin Thorpe, 2 vols. (London, 1848–49), 2:21.

[28] Macbeth is said to have received a band of Norman knights ejected from the Welsh marches in 1052, but the king himself has never been identified as a knight. G. W. S. Barrow, "Macbeth and Other Mormaers of Moray," in *The Hub of the Highlands: The Book of Inverness and District* (Inverness, 1975), p. 117.

[29] Duncan, *Making of the Kingdom*, p. 128. Ritchie's claim that Alexander was a "typical early twelfth-century Norman knight" is not supported by extant evidence. R. L. G. Ritchie, *Chrétien de Troyes and Scotland* (Oxford, 1952), pp. 4–5.

[30] *The Original Chronicle of Andrew of Wyntoun*, ed. F. J. Amours, 6 vols., Scottish Text Society, 50, 53–54, 56–57, 63 (Edinburgh, 1903–14), 4:371, 373, 375, 377; Duncan, *Making of the Kingdom*, p. 128.

[31] *Scotichronicon, vol. 5: Books IX and X, by Walter Bower*, ed. Simon Taylor and D. E. R. Watt, with Brian Scott (Aberdeen, 1990), p. 337.

Alexander's successor, David I. The youngest son of Malcolm and Margaret spent his early years at the court of Henry I. Here, according to William of Malmesbury, "he rubbed off all tarnish of Scottish barbarity" and learned to emulate the ways of a baron in the European style. Here, too, wrote his admirer, Aelred of Rievaulx, he developed the refinement in dress, manners, and moral character that were to prove so influential later in his life.[32] For Graeme Ritchie, moreover, David was a paragon of European knighthood, "more Norman than the Normans."[33] The prince acquired his polish as the recipient of much royal favor, including appointment as a justice, a generous grant of land in Normandy, a wife in the person of Maud, daughter of Waltheof of Northumbria and grand-niece of William the Conqueror (together with the earldom with which her father had been associated), and, as a mark of his newly exalted status, the arms of a knight.[34] Henry I's munificence was by no means benign, and David himself developed a shrewd appreciation of his own value as both potential ally and enemy in the context of English diplomacy.[35] The game of international politics, however, was open only to men of recognized status, and the order of knighthood endowed the Scottish prince with the *gravitas* that he needed to play a role in this cosmopolitan world. Twenty-five years after he had left the English court, David had secured a sterling reputation as a respected and successful ruler. During the troubled period of the civil wars of Stephen's reign, the supporters of Empress Maud and her son, Henry of Anjou, regarded him as something

---

[32] *Willelmi Malmesbiriensis monachi De gestis regum Anglorum*, ed. William Stubbs, 2 vols., Rolls Series, 90 (London, 1887–89), 2:477; *Eulogium Davidis Regis Scotorum ex Allredi Revalensis Genealogia regum Anglorum*, in John Pinkerton, *Vitae antiquae sanctorum qui habitaverunt in ea parte Brittaniae nunc vocata Scotia* (London, 1789), p. 450.

[33] Ritchie, *Chrétien de Troyes*, p. 4.

[34] Aelred of Rievaulx, *Relatio de Standardo*, in *Chronicles of the Reigns of Stephen, Henry II, and Richard I*, ed. Richard Howlett, 4 vols., Rolls Series, 82 (London, 1886), 3:193; *Ecclesiastical History of Orderic Vitalis*, ed. Chibnall., 4:274; *Early Sources of Scottish History A.D. 500 to 1286*, ed. Alan Orr Anderson, 2 vols. (Edinburgh, 1922), 2:147–48; Duncan, *Making of the Kingdom*, p. 134.

[35] See Keith J. Stringer, "State-Building in Twelfth-Century Britain: David I, King of Scotland, and Northern England," in *Government, Religion and Society in Northern England 1000–1700*, ed. John C. Appleby and Paul Dalton (Stroud, 1997), pp. 40–62; Judith Green, "David I and Henry I," *Scottish Historical Review* 75 (1996), 1–19; Stringer, *Earl David*, p. 2; Davies, *Domination and Conquest*, pp. 50–51.

of an elder statesman and a special friend, and in 1149 they urged the fifteen-year-old Henry to leave the relative security of Normandy for the Scottish court at Carlisle.[36] There, David welcomed him with much fanfare and ceremony, and there he bestowed on Henry the arms and the insignia of knighthood.[37]

David I's openness to the chivalric culture of his day was an important legacy to his successors. Malcolm IV and William I in turn demonstrated genuine enthusiasm in achieving the honor. David ensured that his son, Henry earl of Northumberland, should be exposed to chivalric culture from a very early age. He arranged for his elevation to knighthood as a young man, and both Aelred of Rievaulx and William of Newburgh later wrote with unabashed praise of Henry's exploits.[38] More ardent still in his admiration of the brotherhood of arms was the young king Malcolm IV, who succeeded to the throne in 1153 at about the age of twelve. Scholars have frequently commented on the "burning ambition" and the "indecent anxiety" that Malcolm demonstrated for securing the status of a knight, as indeed did his contemporaries.[39] There seems little doubt, moreover, that King Henry II ruthlessly exploited Malcolm's aspirations to wrest from him a series of territorial gains and political promises.[40] On at least one, and probably two, occasions, Henry dangled before the young king the prospect of a grant of arms. So manifest was Malcolm's disappointment at his failure to achieve his ambitions that one chronicler was moved to comment that at Christmas time in 1157, he departed Carlisle "not well reconciled" with Henry, and "not yet . . . a knight."[41]

---

[36] *Gesta Stephani*, ed. K. R. Potter (Oxford, 1976), pp. 214, 215; G. W. S. Barrow, *Kingship and Unity: Scotland 1000–1306*, 2nd ed. (Edinburgh, 2003), p. 46.

[37] *Chron. Melrose*, ed. Anderson and Anderson, p. 35; *Chronica magistri Rogeri de Houedene*, ed. William Stubbs, 4 vols., Rolls Series, 51 (London, 1868–71), 1:211; *The Chronicle of Richard Prior of Hexham (A.D. 1135 to A.D. 1139)*, in *Symeonis monachi opera omnia*, ed. Thomas Arnold, 2 vols., Rolls Series, 75 (London, 1882–85), 2:322–23; William of Newburgh, *Historia rerum Anglicarum*, in *Chron. Stephen*, ed. Howlett, 1:105.

[38] Aelred of Rievaulx, *Relatio de Standardo*, ed. Howlett, 3:196–97; William of Newburgh, *Historia regum Anglorum*, ed. Howlett, 1:71. See also the comments of St. Bernard of Clairvaux, in *Early Sources*, ed. Anderson, 2:185.

[39] Davies, *Domination and Conquest*, p. 51; Ritchie, *Normans in Scotland*, p. 349; *RRS 1*, ed. Barrow, pp. 10–12; Duncan, *Kingship of the Scots*, p. 72.

[40] Duncan, *Making of the Kingdom*, pp. 224–26; Barrow, *Kingdom of the Scots*, pp. 119, 147; Barrow, *Kingship and Unity*, p. 47.

[41] *Chron. Melrose*, ed. Anderson and Anderson, p. 35.

Malcolm's wish was finally fulfilled when he followed Henry on an expedition to France in 1159. At Périgueux, one chronicler noted, "Henry girded the king of Scots with the belt of knighthood . . . [and] the new knight in turn conferred knighthood on the sons of thirty noblemen."[42] It is entirely likely that among the youths honored that day was Malcolm's brother and eventual successor, William, whose admission to the ranks of knighthood is not specifically recorded in any chronicle sources but who in 1159 would certainly have been old enough to accept the honor.[43] Thereafter, William made a name for himself within and beyond Scotland as an ardent devotee of knighthood and chivalry. He traveled to France again in 1166 and returned home after winning renown in a series of tournaments.[44] Jordan Fantosme's account of the rebellion of the Young King and the war with the Scots in 1173–74, although not overtly sympathetic to William's actions, never fails to depict the Scottish king in anything but the most chivalrous of terms. Thus, in 1173, although compelled to retire before a superior force led by Richard de Lucy, William nonetheless proved himself "a good knight of surpassing valour"; at Alnwick, the following year, he was "a valiant knight and prodigiously bold."[45] Anxious, moreover, to see that his younger brother, David, should not suffer the humiliation that Malcolm IV had known, William took advantage of a brief period of cordial relations with Henry II in 1170 to secure David's elevation to the ranks of knighthood.[46] In Jordan Fantosme's estimation, David earl of Huntingdon became "the noblest of warriors."[47] A generation after the ceremony that honored Henry of Anjou, King John was responsible for bestowing the insignia of knighthood on William's thirteen-year-old son, Alexander, at Windsor, during the Christmas celebrations of 1212.[48] This time,

---

[42] *Annals of the Reigns of Malcolm and William Kings of Scotland A.D. 1153–1214*, ed. A. C. Lawrie. (Glasgow, 1910), pp. 43–44.

[43] Jordan Fantosme implies that William accompanied his brother on campaign to Toulouse. See *Jordan Fantosme's Chronicle*, ed. R. C. Johnston (Oxford, 1981), p. 94, 95; *RRS 2*, ed. Barrow, p. 4; Ritchie, *Normans in Scotland*, p. 350.

[44] *Chron. Melrose*, ed. Anderson and Anderson, p. 37.

[45] *Jordan Fantosme's Chronicle*, ed. Johnston, pp. 54, 55, 132, 133.

[46] *Chron. Melrose*, ed. Anderson and Anderson, p. 37; *Chron. Hoveden*, ed. Stubbs, 2:4.

[47] *Jordan Fantosme's Chronicle*, ed. Johnston, pp. 82, 83.

[48] *Rogeri de Wendover liber qui dicitur Flores historiarium*, ed. Henry G. Hewlett, 3 vols., Rolls Series, 84 (London, 1869–89), 2:60; *Chron. Melrose*, ed. Anderson and Anderson, p. 57.

the ceremony celebrated the strength of the political alliance that the two rulers had forged, and the prince returned to Scotland with a band of well-equipped warriors in his following.[49] His son, Alexander, similarly received the arms of knighthood from the king of England in person, at York on the day before his marriage to Henry III's daughter.[50] The chronicler Matthew Paris added an interesting anecdote to his account of the dubbing ceremony, claiming that the English earl marshal, Sir Roger Bigod, demanded of the new knight his palfrey and saddle, "not for a price or for greed, but for the ancient custom in similar cases, lest it should be lost in time through his remissness." Although still a boy, Alexander was shrewd enough to see in the request a challenge to his authority as the ruler of an independent Scotland, and stated unequivocally that his knighting at Henry's hands was a matter of choice, rather than necessity or compulsion.[51]

The keen interest of the MacMalcolm kings of Scotland in the status of knighthood reflected perhaps more than anything a sound appreciation of contemporary politics, and all must have been uncomfortably aware that accepting the symbols of knighthood from the hands of their most powerful rival signaled a measure of deference that was potentially damaging to their pretensions to sovereign status. Yet each in turn was prepared to submit, if only ceremoniously, to the English king. The social and political allure of knighthood and the advantages that would accrue to a knighted king of Scots evidently outweighed all other considerations. As Maurice Keen and others have so convincingly shown, by the twelfth century the idea of an international brotherhood of knights, separated by rank, status, and accomplishments from lesser men, had become deeply embedded among the rulers of western Europe, an idea powerful enough to efface, in some contexts, even "the palpable difference of rank between a king and a knight."[52] David I, in particular, seems to have been inspired by such a sentiment and despite his knighting by Henry I proved remarkably successful in preserving the independence of Scotland against the territorial

---

[49] Duncan, *Making of the Kingdom*, p. 251; Duncan, *Kingship of the Scots*, pp. 111–12.

[50] *Chron. Melrose*, ed. Anderson and Anderson, p. 109; *Johannis de Fordun, Chronica gentis Scotorum*, ed. William F. Skene, 2 vols., The Historians of Scotland, 1 (Edinburgh, 1871–72), 1:293.

[51] *Matthei Pariensis, monachi S. Albani, Chornica majora*, ed. Henry Richard Luard, 7 vols., Rolls Series, 57 (London, 1872–83), 5:269.

[52] Keen, *Chivalry*, p. 73; Crouch, *Image of Aristocracy*, pp. 132–40.

ambitions of Henry I and Stephen. His grandsons faced a more dangerous threat to the integrity of their kingdom in Henry II, yet each was also
prepared to accept knighthood from the ruler of England. In the political
world of the twelfth century, all knew that status as a knight and thus
social equality with the rulers of other European states was a minimum
requirement for recognition of their own position as sovereign.

The chivalric ethos of the day was also in and of itself powerfully
attractive. Malcolm IV was so proud of his exalted new social position
that he referred to it specifically in the notification clauses of a handful
of charters dated just after his knighting in France, and neither he nor
his brother could conceive of any figure more worthy to bestow knighthood upon them than the king of England.[53] William I was even more
captivated by the customs, conventions, and practices associated with the
figure of the knight and deeply concerned with shaping his reputation as
the most renowned warrior of his day. The feats of arms that took him to
France in 1166 provided him with the opportunity to lay the basis for his
fame as a tourneyer. Less than a decade later, he was back on the tournament circuit on the Continent in the company of such illustrious fight-
ers as William Marshal.[54] Participation in these competitions, in fact,
was an especially important means of restoring William's reputation as
a knight following his humiliating capture at Alnwick in 1174, when he
had been presented to Henry II with his feet ignominiously tied under his
horse's belly.[55] Jordan Fantosme, who was well informed about the events
of 1173–74, leaves no doubt that throughout his life William was scrupu-
lous in his observance of knightly conduct. On one occasion he offered
to prove his title to the lands of Northumberland by the sword of a single knight in battle. He issued a formal summons to the keeper of Wark
castle, then gave him a period of respite before launching an assault; he
avoided any situation that might give the appearance of cowardice. On

---

[53] *RRS 1*, ed. Barrow, p. 76, and nos. 183, 184, 195, 198; Barrow, *Kingdom of the
Scots*, p. 255.

[54] *L'histoire de Guillaume le Maréchal*, ed. Paul Meyer, 3 vols. (Paris, 1899–
1901), 1:48–49; *Chron. Wyntoun*, ed. Amours, 5:3.

[55] Carol Edington, "The Tournament in Medieval Scotland," in *Armies, Chivalry and Warfare in Medieval Britain and France: Proceedings of the 1995 Harlaxton
Symposium*, ed. Matthew Strickland (Stamford, 1998), p. 47; Matthew Strickland,
*War and Chivalry: The Conduct and Perception of War in England and Normandy,
1066–1217* (Cambridge, 1996), p. 150; Duncan, *Making of the Kingdom*, p. 230.

several occasions he granted clemency to his enemies when he might more wisely have taken advantage of their weakness.[56] Throughout his account Fantosme is careful to contrast the conduct of men he identifies as William's knights, for whom the king had nothing but love and admiration, with the behavior of the Gallovidians and "the Scots who dwell north of Forth," on whom the king depended out of necessity alone. Toward the end of the reign, an English chronicler could remark in specific reference to William that "the more recent kings of Scots profess themselves to be rather Frenchmen, both in race and in manners, language and culture."[57] Fantosme, however, identified similar sentiments more than a generation earlier, when he wrote of King William that "[h]e cherished, loved, and held dear people from abroad. He never had much love for those of his own country."[58] Extant records from the reign of William I suggest that the king showed genuine interest in the customs and practices of his Gaelic predecessors; his enthronement, for example, is believed to have combined the drama of traditional Gaelic and more recent European ceremonies.[59] There can be little doubt, though, that by 1214 the king of Scotland and many of those whom he counted his intimates had thoroughly embraced the knightly culture of Europe and were actively encouraging its dissemination throughout the realm.

William's reign saw the Scottish monarchy establish a firm claim to be the peer of its European counterparts in its chivalric accomplishments. His thirteenth-century successors, Alexander II and Alexander III, further refined the image of warrior kings. Success in campaigns against their enemies, in this period Scottish rebels in the north, as well as threats of invasion from Norway in the west, undoubtedly contributed to their strong reputation, but each was conscious also of modeling his own conduct, as well as that of his court, on the most recent norms dictated by European knightly culture. Alexander II deliberately cultivated the public spectacle as an appropriate stage for the display of munificence. In a lavish feast held on Whitsunday 1219 in Roxburgh, he

---

[56] *Jordan Fantosme's Chronicle*, ed. Johnston, pp. 26, 27, 36–41, 52, 53, 122, 123; Strickland, *War and Chivalry*, p. 220.

[57] *Memorialie fratris Walteri de Coventria*, ed. W. Stubbs, 2 vols., Rolls Series, 58 (London, 1872–73), 2:206.

[58] *Jordan Fantosme's Chronicle*, ed. Johnston, pp. 48, 49.

[59] Duncan, *Kingship of the Scots*, p. 98.

celebrated the accession of John of Huntingdon to his father's estates by investing a group of noble youths with the honor of knighthood.[60] In a similarly magnanimous gesture (one that had clear political resonance), he exercised the privilege that permitted one knight to make another by ennobling a relative of the papal legate, Ottobuono, when he bestowed on him the belt of knighthood and a gift of land.[61] Like his father, Alexander III grasped fully the political currency that he might accrue in making new knights. In a series of ceremonies, he bestowed the honor on Colban earl of Fife and David of Strathbogie earl of Atholl at Christmas 1264; Donald, son and heir of William earl of Mar, at Michaelmas 1270; and William, son and heir of Nicholas de Soules, at Michaelmas 1271.[62] It was perhaps he, moreover, who in 1273 gave arms to Malcolm II earl of Lennox.[63] From the very beginning of their respective reigns, Alexander II and Alexander III journeyed to England, to the court of their neighbor and rival, King Henry III, only in the company of "a great bevy of knights,"[64] acutely aware of the need to support their claims to sovereign authority with the visual evidence of their royal and knightly rank.

The Alexandrian period, however, also witnessed an important shift in the identification of kingship with knighthood. While the twelfth-century rulers of Scotland had believed that the title of *miles* befitted their status as kings and had eagerly pursued it, Alexander III was of a different mind. The chronicler Walter Bower described in detail the events that attended the young king's enthronement in the summer of 1249, dwelling in particular on the dissent that erupted among the assembled nobles when one group wished to bestow the honor of knighthood on him before his inauguration. Further enmity was avoided when Walter Comyn earl of Menteith, "a man far-seeing in his counsel and steadfast in spirit," offered the argument that a king was by right of his office a knight, inasmuch as the insignia of the crown and scepter that he wore symbolized his knightly dignity. The earl's opinion won the day, and Bishop Bernham of St. Andrews duly invested Alexander with those symbols

---

[60] *Chron. Fordun*, ed. Skene, 1:282.

[61] Matthew Paris, *Chron. majora*, ed. Luard, 3:414.

[62] *Scotichronicon, vol. 5*, ed. Taylor and Watt, pp. 348–49, 366–67, 380–81, 382–83.

[63] *Cartularium comitatus de Levenax*, ed. James Dennistoun, Maitland Club, 24 (Edinburgh, 1833), pp. 14–15.

[64] *Chron. Fordun*, ed. Skene, 2:284.

of the royal office.[65] Alexander seems to have taken to heart Comyn's views on the nature of knighthood and in doing so gave expression to a new awareness on the part of the Scots of the unique figure of the king, who, in so many respects, stood above all men. Thus, while the young Alexander agreed to become a knight, he also made manifest his intention to celebrate more openly his Gaelic antecedents. The enthronement ceremony of 1249 resembled in many respects the coronations of other thirteenth-century European kings, with the royal candidate attired in "silk cloths embroidered in gold" as well as a robe of purple, and bishops and high ranking magnates allotted prominent roles in the rituals that transformed the young Alexander into a full-fledged king. Yet at the inauguration feast the new monarch also made a powerful appeal to his Gaelic past, in the persons of the inaugural nobles, Malcolm of Fife and Malise of Strathearn, a "venerable, grey-haired" master poet who recited the royal pedigree, and a harpist who accompanied him.[66]

The enthronement of Alexander III did not signal a diminution in the luster accorded to knighthood among the Scottish aristocracy, and the honorific titles *dominus* and *miles* continued to inspire ambitious young men for centuries to come. After 1249, however, and more apparently still after the struggle for sovereignty in the wars of independence, Walter Comyn's wise words concerning the dignity inherent in kingship became part and parcel of the concept of monarchy, and knighthood no longer a prerequisite for the royal office.

Knighthood and the European Newcomers to Scotland, 1093–1214

The close political and social affiliations of the Scottish royal family with its English counterpart made well nigh inevitable the dissemination of ideas about knights, knighthood, and chivalric culture from the larger realm to the smaller. It is no surprise that many of the Anglo-Norman and Continental magnates who settled in Scotland between the mid-twelfth and

---

[65] *Scotichronicon*, vol. 5, ed. Taylor and Watt, pp. 290–93. The incident is discussed in Duncan, *Kingship of the Scots*, pp. 131–33; and A. Young, *Robert the Bruce's Rivals: The Comyns, 1212–1314* (East Linton, 1997), pp. 47–49.

[66] John Bannerman, "The King's Poet and the Inauguration of Alexander III," *Scottish Historical Review* 68 (1989), 120–49.

the early thirteenth centuries should themselves have been knights. Professor Barrow's research has treated in exhaustive detail the evidence relating to the European colonists who contributed so much to the shaping of the "Anglo-Norman era" of Scottish history and more particularly to the entrenchment in the southern reaches of the kingdom of knight service, the knight's feu, and the feudal host.[67] There is no need to repeat his findings here; a few strategic examples will suffice to demonstrate that knighthood was well known in the twelfth century among the incoming elite.

The author of the chronicle known as the *Gesta Annalia* mentioned knights in the entourage of King Malcolm III, but in some of these passages he listed these together with "thanes," "chiefs," and "magnates," clearly intending a generic use of the terms in such contexts.[68] In his account of the treachery of an unnamed Scottish nobleman, the chronicler was a little clearer in arguing that the concept of proper knightly behavior was a feature of Malcolm III's rule.[69] Later still, Walter Bower also conceived of a knight-like Malcolm III, resplendent in armor, in his account of a vision that inspired Sir John Wemyss in 1263.[70] A different, and much earlier, reference dates from the reign of David I, when in 1127 the Céli Dé brethren of Loch Leven found themselves engaged in dispute with their neighbor, the newcomer Robert of Burgundy. Of especial interest here is the fact that Robert was styled *miles* in the charter that recorded the case. The scribe's choice of the honorary title was clearly intended to emphasize Robert's high rank. On this occasion, knightly status concealed a wicked heart, and Robert's title did not protect him from the condemnation of the holy men, who described him as "the furnace and burning fire of all iniquity."[71] Later in the twelfth century Jordan Fantosme wrote at length of the knightly contingent that accompanied William I on the campaigns of 1173–74. In describing the embassy that the king sent to Henry II in

---

67 Barrow, *Anglo-Norman Era*; Barrow, *Kingdom of the Scots*, pp. 250–95.

68 *Chron. Fordun*, ed. Skene, 1:186, 206. On the authorship of the *Gesta*, see now Dauvit Broun, "A New Look at *Gesta Annalia* Attributed to John of Fordun," in *Church, Chronicle and Learning in Medieval and Early Renaissance Scotland: Essays Presented to Donald Watt on the Occasion of the Completion of the Publication of Bower's Scotichronicon*, ed. Barbara E. Crawford (Edinburgh, 1999), pp. 9–30.

69 *Chron. Fordun*, ed. Skene, 1:207–8.

70 *Scotichronicon*, vol. 5, ed. Taylor and Watt, p. 337.

71 *Early Scottish Charters prior to A.D. 1153*, ed. Archibald C. Lawrie (Glasgow, 1905), no. 80.

Normandy, he noted that the Scottish monarch promised to deliver "a thousand armed knights"; similarly, Fantosme wrote that the Scottish assault on Carlisle witnessed the fall of "many blood-stained knights" and the loss of their shields, hauberks, and helmets.[72] The chronicler's thoughtful critique of the role of good fortune and moral character in the bitter conflicts of the mid–1170s enabled him to devote a great deal of attention to such qualities as honor, courage, and martial skill, and led him to identify by name knights from Scotland (and England) who distinguished themselves by virtue of their conduct.[73] Such, for example, were Richard de Melville, William de Mortimer, Ralph Rufus, and Alan de Lascelles, the last, although "very old" in 1174, "a most excellent knight."[74]

The numerous charters of enfeftment that survive from the reigns of Malcolm IV and William I attest not merely the settlement of men of knightly rank in new estates, but the raising by royal (and eventually aristocratic) fiat of lesser men to new, honorable status.[75] The rapid standardization of holding clauses such as "[to be held] as freely as the king's other knights hold their feus in the kingdom," or " . . . as the king's other knights hold their feus of the king," or ". . . as any knights hold their lands of the king in the realm of Scotland" bears witness not merely to the proliferation of new forms of tenure but also to a new awareness of the exalted rank of the men who were so privileged.[76] There was no doubt whatsoever in the minds of some contemporary observers that knightly conduct was a moral standard to which all genuinely Christian fighting men should aspire. Jordan Fantosme, for example, was unequivocal in his opinion of the native contingents that made up significant portions of the armies of William I and his son, David earl of Huntingdon. He consistently excoriated the men of "that wicked race" and sharply con-

---

[72] *Jordan Fantosme's Chronicle*, ed. Johnston, pp. 24–25, 48–51.

[73] Two different but equally compelling assessments of Jordan Fantosme's unique chronicle are offered in Antonia Gransden, *Historical Writing in England c.550 to c.1307* (Ithaca, 1974), pp. 237–38, and Matthew Strickland, "Arms and the Men: War, Loyalty and Lordship in Jordan Fantosme's Chronicle," in *Medieval Knighthood IV: Papers from the Fifth Strawberry Hill Conference, 1990*, ed. Christopher Harper-Bill and Ruth Harvey (Woodbridge, 1992), pp. 187–220.

[74] *Jordan Fantosme's Chronicle*, ed. Johnston, pp. 136–39.

[75] Barrow, *Kingdom of the Scots*, pp. 254–60.

[76] See, for example, *RRS 2*, ed. Barrow, nos. 42, 43, 125, 137, 140.

trasted the acts of sacrilege, savagery, and cruelty of "the Gallovidians and the Scots who dwell north of the Forth" with the gallant, honorable, and courteous behavior of their knights, barons, and "finest warriors."[77] Aelred of Rievaulx, Richard of Hexham, and others likewise devoted considerable space in their accounts of the battle of the Standard (1138) to juxtaposing the barbarities committed by David's native soldiery with the more temperate acts of his knights, emphasizing time and again the disregard of the "naked" Gaels for the conventions that governed warfare in their day.[78] Nearly identical accounts of atrocities again preoccupied English chroniclers who wrote of the reign of William I.[79] Thus had knightly status come, by the late twelfth century, to acquire not merely social but more generally racial, linguistic, and national dimensions.

Other features associated throughout Europe with knightly practices emerged in the parts of Scotland settled by newcomers in this period. King William's offer to settle his claim to Northumbria by recourse to single combat has already been noted.[80] As early as the reign of Alexander I, the monks of Scone had secured the privilege of overseeing judicial ordeals and had apparently set aside an islet on the River Tay on which to conduct them, but there is no evidence that duels were held here.[81] Before the turn of the twelfth century, trial by combat as a method of dispute settlement among honorable men as well as in the context of the ordeal appears to have become widespread in parts of Scotland. At least one of the handful of men who challenged the MacMalcolm title to the kingship perished in single combat in 1154.[82] In 1242, the Scottish nobleman Walter Bisset insisted on defending himself against the charge of murdering

---

[77] *Jordan Fantosme's Chronicle*, ed. Johnston, pp. 52–53, 84–85, 138–41. For a discussion of this topic, see Strickland, *War and Chivalry*, pp. 291–340.

[78] *Scottish Annals from English Chroniclers A.D. 500 to 1286*, ed. Alan Orr Anderson (Stamford, 1991), pp. 179–213.

[79] See, for example, *Radulfi de Diceto decani Lundoniensis opera historica*, ed. William Stubbs, 2 vols., Rolls Series, 68 (London, 1876), 1:376.

[80] *Jordan Fantosme's Chronicle*, ed. Johnston, pp. 26–27.

[81] *Early Scottish Charters*, ed. Lawrie, no. 49; *Liber ecclesie de Scon*, ed. Cosmo Innes, Maitland Club, 62 (Edinburgh, 1843), no. 36. In any case, it would have been highly unusual for monks to be directly involved in armed encounters between knights. For a review of the use of the trial by combat in lowland Scotland, see George Neilson, *Trial by Combat* (New York, 1981), pp. 76–86.

[82] *A Scottish Chronicle known as the Chronicle of Holyrood*, ed. Marjorie Orr Anderson, Scottish History Society, 3rd. ser., 30 (Edinburgh, 1938), p. 37.

a political opponent in a judicial duel.[83] In the early thirteenth century, moreover, the practice of defending claims by recourse to arms became an important feature of the nascent laws of the Anglo-Scottish borderlands. Here, the custom endured well into the medieval period despite royal (and papal) censure, because it was regarded as a particularly appropriate way for noble litigants from two distinct allegiances to resolve disputes.[84] Yet the use of knightly champions in the judicial context was not a custom indigenous to Scotland,[85] and the native nobility, whose responsibilities as heads of extensive kinship networks included the dispensation of justice, did not favor it. To have done so would have threatened the crucial role they played within a legal system that required great lords to act above all as arbitrators between disputing tenants rather than as judges and executioners.

The growth in popularity of jousting in the thirteenth century among some segments of the Scottish nobility further attests the spread of European practices within the realm. Indeed, one scholar has aptly noted that the public spectacle of the tournament reveals "a changed attitude to fighting; formerly there had been knights, now there was knighthood."[86] King William was an enthusiast of the joust, seeking opponents in lists as distant as France, perhaps because he could not find men to match his skills at home. By the time of his son's reign, tournaments were being hosted in Scotland. Matthew Paris, who was unusually well informed about such matters, notes that the by mid-twelfth century in what he identified as the northern parts of Scotland (perhaps Moray, or perhaps more generally the region north of Forth), hastiludes were infamous for their "calamitous" nature.[87] Paris, and later Bower, recounted with dismay the feud that erupted between two important families after Thomas of Galloway unhorsed Walter Bisset at the tournament of 1242.[88] The scale of military activity on which Alexander III embarked in his efforts to wrest control of the western parts of his kingdom from the rulers of Norway suggests

---

[83] *Scotichronicon, vol. 5,* ed. Taylor and Watt, pp. 132–33; Matthew Paris, *Chron. majora,* ed. Luard, 4:200–202.

[84] Cynthia. J. Neville, *Violence, Custom and Law: The Anglo-Scottish Border Lands in the Later Middle Ages* (Edinburgh, 1998), pp. 4, 6, 8, 40, 76–77.

[85] Neilson, *Trial by Combat,* p. 75.

[86] Duncan, *Making of the Kingdom,* p. 445.

[87] Matthew Paris, *Chron. majora,* ed. Luard, 4:200.

[88] Ibid., 4:200–202; *Scotichronicon, vol 5,* ed. Taylor and Watt, pp. 178–83.

that tourneys remained popular well into the century. Such events would have offered valuable training to the king's mounted forces, and informal battles in the lists may have kept Alexander's knights entertained on the campaigns that he led into England in 1264 and against Norwegian invaders in 1263 and 1264.[89] On the latter occasion, Alexander Comyn earl of Buchan, William Comyn earl of Mar, and Alan Durward all joined the royal army with "no mean band of knights."[90] The wars of independence offered a host of new opportunities for Scottish knights to test their skills in the lists against English opponents, and from the early years of the fourteenth century onward, the border region became part of a lively tournament circuit in Britain and western Europe.[91] Yet, Thomas of Galloway apart, the evidence for participation in jousts and tourneys on the part of Gaelic magnates and their followings is slender. Such foreign games, introduced into Scotland by Anglo-Norman and Continental newcomers, obviously had little appeal among their native fellows.

In thirteenth-century Europe, the honorable status of knighthood was strongly associated with the Christian duty to embark on crusade. St. Bernard, it has been aptly noted, first articulated the idea that the soldier of Christ embodied the highest and most exclusive ideals of the true knight; thereafter, all across western Europe crusading propaganda "gave Jerusalem and the defence of the Holy Places a unique position of significance in the mental world of knighthood."[92] Scottish response to the major crusades of the period 1095–1292 was muted, though by no means negligible. Aristocrats such as Robert de Quincy, his son Saher, David de Strathbogie earl of Atholl, Adam de Kilconquhar earl of Carrick, Patrick II earl of Dunbar, and possibly Alan son of Walter the Steward all took the cross at various times between the First and the Eighth Crusades, some perishing of disease or in battle before they could return to their homes.[93] They were joined on occasion by their countrymen. Lagmann king of Man and the Western Isles died on the first expedition to Jerusalem, and Ranald son of Somerled of Argyll is said to have received a cross

---

[89] Matthew Paris, *Chron. majora*, ed. Luard, 4:379–80; *Early Sources*, ed. Anderson, 2:630.

[90] *Chron. Fordun*, ed. Skene, 1:301.

[91] Edington, "The Tournament in Medieval Scotland," pp. 49–62; Neville, *Violence, Custom and Law*, pp. 77, 103.

[92] Keen, *Chivalry*, pp. 5, 50.

[93] Alan Macquarrie, *Scotland and the Crusades* (Edinburgh, 1985).

from the Holy City before he died around 1207.[94] Guibert of Nogent and an unnamed Premonstratensian canon wrote famously of the "ferocious" and "ridiculous" appearance of the common Gaels who passed through their lands on their way to fight God's enemies.[95] To their numbers should be added the poet Muireadhach Albanach Ó Dáiligh, who departed his Lennox home soon after the death around 1217 of his patron,[96] Earl Maldoven, and possibly Earl Malise II of Strathearn, who was in the French port city of Cahors in 1259. Although clearly not part of the expedition that Louis IX of France launched in 1244, Malise's undertaking to pay 100s "in subsidy to the Holy Land" should he default on a loan he had transacted there points at least to an awareness of the Christian act of pilgrimage.[97] Yet Alan Macquarrie, who has studied the participation of the Scots in the crusading movement, has shown that, by and large, native Scots were slow to take up the call of the Holy Land, and that evidence of enthusiasm for the crusade in Scotland has a distinctly "Anglo-Norman appearance."[98]

Knights and Knighthood among the Native Elite—The Documentary Evidence

Collectively, the records relating to the appeal of knightly status and knightly involvement in judicial duels, tournaments, and the Crusades strongly suggest that, as historians have now long held, the period between roughly 1124 and 1250 saw the smooth integration of Scotland into the

---

[94] Ibid., pp. 11, 124; McDonald, *Kingdom of the Isles*, pp. 78–79.

[95] Alan Macquarrie, "The Crusades and the Scottish *Gaidhealtachd* in Fact and Legend," in *The Middle Ages in the Highlands*, ed. Loraine Maclean (Inverness, 1981), pp. 133–35; A. A. M. Duncan, "The Dress of the Scots," *Scottish Historical Review* 29 (1950), 210–12.

[96] Derick S. Thomson, "The MacMhuirich Bardic Family," *Transactions of the Gaelic Society of Inverness* 43 (1966), 279–80; and G. Murphy, "Two Irish Poems Written from the Mediterranean in the Thirteenth Century," *Éigse* 7 (1953), 73–79. A more recent translation of some of these poems is found in *The Triumph Tree: Scotland's Earliest Poetry AD 550 to 1350*, ed. Thomas Owen Clancy (Edinburgh, 1998), pp. 247–54.

[97] The National Archives, London, E 368/34, m. 29.

[98] Macquarrie, *Scotland and the Crusades*, pp. 123–26; R. A. McDonald. "'Far is Rome from Lochlong': Gaels and Scandinavians on Pilgrimage and Crusade," *Scripta Mediterranea* 18 (1997), 3–34.

European cultural world. Nevertheless, there is good reason to scrutinize extant source materials closely and to ask if these do indeed reflect as seamless a process as might first appear. The Scotland of David I, Malcolm IV, and William I was by no means a homogeneous land; it was still a realm in which people of varied ethnic and linguistic backgrounds lived side by side. At no level was the multicultural nature of Scottish society more apparent than among its highest ranks, which included Gaels, Britons, Norsemen, Anglians, and, most recently, Anglo-Norman and French magnates. As a potent reminder of the racial admixture of their subjects, until well into William's reign Scottish kings routinely addressed their charters and brieves to all their good men, "French and English and Scots," sometimes also adding the Gallovidians to the pertinent clause.[99]

The highest-ranking members of the Scottish aristocracy were the earls, of whom there were some eight in the middle of the twelfth century, increasing to thirteen in 1286. Between them, these descendants of the great mormaers of the past governed a vast portion of the kingdom north of Forth. Most of their lands consisted of territorially compact lordships of a kind virtually unknown south of the border. Unlike the conquest of England in 1066, which witnessed the near total displacement of the Anglo-Saxon nobility, the arrival of newcomers to Scotland did not signal the end of the dominance of the native elite. The research of a handful of scholars in recent years has done much to illuminate the ways in which dignitaries interacted with, influenced, and in turn were influenced by the political and cultural changes that swept through the kingdom in the two centuries after 1124. Their conclusions are varied, but all generally agree that the introduction of a foreign element into the upper ranks of Scottish society generated complex and, in many cases, highly localized responses on the part of native landholders. Some, like the earls of Fife, took advantage of their close kinship with the Scottish royal family to adopt new ways. Descended from the line of Maelcoluim I and Cinaed III, in return for recognition of their special status the earls of Fife became the most "feudalized" of the Gaelic lords at the royal court.[100] At the other

---

[99] See, for example, *Charters of David I*, ed. Barrow, nos. 41, 44, 53, 57, 66, 70; *RRS 1*, ed. Barrow, nos. 131, 154, *RRS, 2*, ed. Barrow, nos. 27, 39, 46, 48, 61, 74, 75, 78, 80, 81–83, 96, 106, 116, 140, 144, 179, 218, 507.

[100] G. W. S. Barrow, "The Earls of Fife in the 12th Century," *Proceedings of the Society of Antiquaries of Scotland* 86 (1952), 51–62.

end of the political spectrum, the rulers of Galloway maintained a fierce resistance to royal interference well into the thirteenth century, yet their most prominent members did not believe that accepting the honorific title associated with knighthood was incompatible with their standing as independent native princes. In between these extremes of accommodation with the new political and cultural landscapes of twelfth- and thirteenth-century Scotland lay the vast majority of Gaelic magnates and lordlings.

The extent to which the Gaelic elite accepted European ideas about the knight and the ideals of European chivalry is no easy matter to assess, for surviving evidence is exiguous, at once suggestive of, and contradictory to, the notion that new social and cultural norms and customs were diffused outward from the royal court. Some Gaelic lords, for example, willingly settled new men within their territories, but in doing so they adopted strategies designed to isolate strangers from their native tenant neighbors. Sigillographic evidence and other kinds of written sources, likewise, offer strong indications that Gaelic magnates readily assumed some of the trappings of European-style knighthood, yet here, too, closer examination of source materials reveals that the spread of new ideas was a nuanced process in which native custom gave way only slowly and only partly to innovation.

Proximity to the royal family by blood and to the king's court by political affiliation was an important factor in the transmission of European ideas and practices, and some magnates saw clear personal advantage in emulating the crown's policy of enfefting new families within their lands or in accepting a formal vassalic relationship with the king, or both. The early earls of Fife, who moved easily among the Anglo-Norman and Continental newcomers at court, were quick to appreciate the interest that David I demonstrated in establishing in Scotland a knightly order modeled on the one he had known in England. As early as 1136, Earl Duncan I agreed to accept title to the earldom of Fife itself from the king in the shape of a royal charter, granted in return for military service.[101] Duncan's "submission" was a shrewdly calculated move. There followed a series of other gifts of land and privilege that secured for the earl and his successors an impressive lordship spread over Fife, East and West

---

[101] *Facsimiles of the National Manuscripts of Scotland*, ed. Cosmo Innes, 3 vols. (London, 1867–72), 1: plate 50; Barrow, *Kingdom of the Scots*, p. 253.

Lothian, and Moray and, far more important within the strongly kin-based society of twelfth-century Fife, formal recognition of the family's special blood relationship with the MacMalcolm dynasty.[102] Duncan I and his immediate descendants in turn created knights' feus for incoming settlers, among them William de Holderness, Miles de Raiville, and William de Wyville,[103] just as the king's new magnates were doing elsewhere south of Forth.

Another prominent (though in this case Northumbrian) noble family was that of the earls of Lothian, later Dunbar. Like the Fifes, its members claimed a blood relation to the royal house and were also prominent at court. Like the earls of Fife, moreover, the earls of Dunbar owed their wealth and prestige to the MacMalcolms and had good reason to portray themselves as firm supporters of the crown and its policies. Of Anglo-Saxon origin, the first earl had been Cospatrick of Northumbria, who fled England about 1069 and around 1072 was granted extensive lands in Lothian by Malcolm III.[104] Later members of the family accumulated vast estates in England and Scotland and played prominent roles as cross-border landholders. The connections that they cultivated in Northumberland and southern Scotland kept them in close touch with cultural developments that were drawing the frontier region into the orbit of European influence. Patrick II embarked on crusade in 1248 and perished at Marseille,[105] and in Lothian, French and English knights rubbed shoulders with native lords on estates that combined the generic Middle English term *tun* with the personal names of the newcomers, such as Philpington (West Lothian), Clermiston (Midlothian) and Penston (East Lothian).[106]

Across the Forth, the story was more complex. In the early twelfth century the native earls of Strathearn already laid claim to a long, distinguished, and impeccably Gaelic history. Descendants of mormaers of the ancient kingdom of Fortriu, they played a leading role in the formal enthronement of the kings of Scotland and preserved within their

---

102 Barrow, *Anglo-Norman Era*, pp. 84–86; John Bannerman, "MacDuff of Fife," in *Medieval Scotland: Crown, Lordship and Community*, ed. Alexander Grant and Keith. J. Stringer (Edinburgh, 1993), pp. 24–38.

103 Barrow, *Anglo-Norman Era*, p. 87.

104 *Chron. Howden*, ed. Stubbs, 1:59.

105 Macquarrie, *Scotland and the Crusades*, p. 48.

106 Barrow, *Anglo-Norman Era*, pp. 36, 38.

lordship a social and political structure that complemented their leadership of an extensive network of kinsmen and clients. In fact, the first earl on record, Malise I, was overtly hostile to the adoption of foreign manners and customs. In 1138 he joined David I's campaign into northern England at the head of a force of men mustered not according to any "feudal" obligation but performing, rather, the traditional duty to serve in the common army of the king.[107] Aelred of Rievaulx's detailed account of the battle of the Standard made much of the dissension that erupted within the ranks of the assembled Scottish army. According to the chronicler, the king wished to give his "knights" (that is, his heavily armed mounted warriors) pride of place in the encounter, only to be derided by the men of Galloway, who claimed the ancient privilege of occupying the front line, and mocked by the earl of Strathearn, who stated in no uncertain terms that he was of like mind.[108] David's decision to acquiesce in the face of his Gaelic warriors' protest, Aelred concluded sententiously, doomed the Scottish effort that day.[109]

This manifestation of Strathearn conservatism was not unique. A generation after 1138 Earl Ferteth led a more dangerous rising of Gaelic magnates against the Scottish crown in 1160, after Malcolm IV, eager to secure the knighthood that continued to elude him, joined the English king, Henry II, on a campaign to Toulouse. The Melrose chronicler, writing a century and a half after the event, considered the rebellion distasteful and best forgotten. The Holyrood chronicler did not mention it at all.[110] But the author of the *Gesta Annalia* was more perceptive. He noted that the earls' disquiet sprang from "their king's too great intimacy and friendship with Henry, king of England," and the fear that "this intimacy would bring them shame and disgrace."[111] In some contrast to its dealings with the family of Fife in the twelfth and thirteenth centuries, the Scottish crown never succeeded in establishing a formal vassalic relationship with the native earls of Strathearn in respect of the lands that comprised their lordship, nor did it consider it wise to press the matter.[112] Earl Gilbert acquired

---

[107] The common army is discussed in Duncan, *Making of the Kingdom*, pp. 110–11; and G. W. S. Barrow, "The Army of Alexander III's Scotland," in *Scotland in the Reign of Alexander III*, ed. Norman H. Reid (Edinburgh, 1990), pp. 132–47.

[108] Aelred of Rievaulx, *Relatio de Standardo*, ed. Howlett, 3:189–90.

[109] Ibid., 3:198–99.

[110] *Chron. Melrose*, ed. Anderson and Anderson, p. 36.

[111] *Chron. Fordun*, ed. Skene, 1:256.

[112] Neville, *Native Lordship*, p. 22.

some estates by royal grant in return for military service,[113] and, following his marriage to the daughter of a prominent Anglo-Norman lord, Sir William D'Aubigny, he invited into his territories a handful of English and Continental newcomers.[114] Yet two observations may be made in respect of the spread of tenure by knight's feu in Strathearn down to the middle years of the thirteenth century. One is that the earls carefully controlled the number of landholders of non-native origin in their midst, the other that they deliberately settled newcomers in the peripheries of their territories, frequently on estates that they had added to patrimonial lands by gift, grant, or good fortune.[115] In short, in Strathearn there was no expropriation of the sitting tenantry and no sudden influx of new ideas, customs, or practices into the heartlands of the lordship. It was not, in fact, until the time of Earl Malise II (d. 1271) that noblemen who could claim descent from Anglo-Norman and European ancestors gained a strong foothold across the full extent of the earls' territories.

More intriguing still is the measured pace with which the honorific titles associated with knighthood, *dominus* and *miles*, gained currency among the upper ranks of the nobility of Strathearn. Malise son of Ferteth (d. before 1214) became a tenant of King William I and of his own father-in-law, David earl of Huntingdon, in a series of holdings located in Strathtay and Strathmore, as well as of his brother, Earl Gilbert, in estates within Strathearn proper.[116] He held those lands in return for performing knight service, yet he never styled himself *miles*, preferring throughout his life to identify himself specifically with his kindred and his ancestral lands, either as "Malise son of Earl Ferteth" or "Malise brother of Earl Gilbert."[117] It was not until well into the thirteenth century and

[113] *RRS 2*, ed. Barrow, nos. 206, 258; Cynthia J. Neville, "A Celtic Enclave in Norman Scotland: Earl Gilbert and the Earldom of Strathearn, 1171–1223," in *Freedom and Authority: Scotland c.1050–c.1650*, ed. Terry Brotherstone and David Ditchburn (East Linton, 2000), pp. 76–78.

[114] Neville, *Native Lordship*, pp. 44–45, 75–78.

[115] Ibid., p. 53.

[116] *RRS 2*, ed. Barrow, nos. 136, 524; Neville, "A Celtic Enclave," p. 78; Stringer, *Earl David*, p. 82.

[117] See, for example, *RRS, 2*, ed. Barrow, nos. 147, 149, 153, 273, 335, 338, 348, 373, 393, 403, 432, 464; *Charters, Bulls and Other Documents relating to the Abbey of Inchaffray*, ed. William Alexander Lindsay, John Dowden, and John Maitland Thomson, Scottish History Society, 56 (Edinburgh, 1908), nos. 3, 9, 11, 12, 25; Robert Sibbald, *The History, Ancient and Modern, of the Sheriffdoms of Fife and Kinross*, new ed. (Edinburgh, 1803), p. 229.

a generation after the time of Gilbert and Malise sons of Ferteth that charter evidence reveals a change of practice among the earls' immediate kindred in respect of the use of the honorific title of *miles*. Fergus and Malise, the sons of Gilbert, became successive tenants of the earl in the lands that had belonged to their uncle, Malise,[118] and each in turn assumed, as adults, the honor of knighthood. For the youngest of his sons, his namesake Gilbert, the earl had created a generous feu consisting of lands in Inverness-shire that he had acquired (or perhaps over which he had regained control) by royal grant.[119] By 1250 the lord of Glencarnie had become Sir Gilbert of Glencarnie, after securing title to further lands in the region from the bishop of Moray and Alan Durward.[120] The establishment of Earl Gilbert's sons as wealthy lords in their own right had the twin consequences of thrusting them into the cosmopolitan milieu of a royal court thoroughly imbued in European ideas about knighthood and of making them attractive prospects as patrons in the endless stream of lesser men scrabbling for a foothold on the tenurial ladder that defined the landholding elite of their day. Gilbert's sons certainly did not shed their Gaelic identities altogether in the mid-thirteenth century, but a hundred years and more after their predecessor, Malise I, had voiced open opposition to the influence of foreigners within the kingdom, they had begun to embrace the cultural norms of European society. Moreover, in seeking to achieve knighthood, they initiated a process of integrating traditional Gaelic custom and new European ideas that was to transform the upper echelons of the Scots nobility as a whole.

The penetration of European ideas into the nearby Gaelic lordship of Lennox followed a pattern strikingly similar to that of Strathearn, though resistance to change here endured even longer. After a period of minority, during which the earldom fell under direct royal control, Earl Ailin II regained the title in the 1190s.[121] If William I expected him to imitate the

---

[118] Neville, *Native Lordship*, p. 47.

[119] *RRS 2*, ed. Barrow, no. 206; Neville, *Native Lordship*, pp. 46–47. Alasdair Ross has suggested that Kinveachy and Glencarnie had been in the possession of one of Earl Gilbert's predecessors, acquired perhaps by marriage. The argument is interesting but must rest on conjecture. Alasdair Ross, "The Lords and Lordship of Glencarnie," in *Exercise of Power*, ed. Boardman and Ross, pp. 161–66.

[120] *Registrum episcopatus Moraviensis*, ed. Cosmo Innes, Bannatyne Club, 58 (Edinburgh, 1837), no. 80; William Fraser, *The Chiefs of Grant*, 3 vols. (Edinburgh, 1883), 3:nos. 6, 11.

[121] Neville, *Native Lordship*, p. 25; Stringer, *Earl David*, pp. 16–17.

royal policy of enfeffing foreigners within his territories, he must have been disappointed, for Ailin (d. c. 1217) and his successor, Maldoven (d. c. 1250), introduced new tenants only cautiously in the course of the later twelfth and the early thirteenth centuries. Like the earls of Strathearn, moreover, they were careful to create estates for the newcomers only in the peripheral regions of their lordship: in the borderlands of the neighboring Stewart holdings in Strathgryfe, on the Rosneath peninsula in Loch Long and, in the east, in Stathblane. The new tenants were also settled hard by lands belonging to members of the earls' kindred, so that even in the distant reaches of Lennox foreigners had to share local prominence with native worthies who had close ties to the earl.[122]

There is no clear evidence that either Ailin II or Maldoven held the earldom of Lennox by royal charter in return for specified military service. In 1238 Alexander III took advantage of his decision to exert direct royal control over the fortress of Dumbarton to define in writing the terms by which Maldoven held his remaining lands. Yet the royal charter in which he did so demanded merely that he perform the forensic service that all Gaelic magnates traditionally owed the king's common army.[123] Indeed, neither Maldoven nor any of his direct descendants held his lands for mounted military service and, as in Strathearn, for the remainder of the thirteenth century knight service was never more than a notional concept within the lordship of Lennox.[124] Knighthood, moreover, held only limited attraction for the kinsmen of the earls or their tenants, at least until the latter part of that same century. Maldoven's brother, Amelec, appears with the title *dominus* in witness lists of 1238 and 1240 x 1249,[125] but it was not until the next generation that native dignitaries began in significant numbers actively to pursue the rank of knight. Maldoven's son, Malcolm, appears as *miles* in a charter dating from just before his death in 1248,[126] but the important tenant families of Luss and Beg and the progenitors of the later medieval families of Colquhoun and Galbraith made no effort to pursue the honor until the closing decades of the thirteenth century.[127] Clearly,

---

122 Neville, *Native Lordship*, pp. 54–58.
123 *Lennox Cart.*, ed. Dennistoun, pp. 1–2.
124 Neville, *Native Lordship*, p. 57.
125 *Lennox Cart.*, ed. Dennistoun, pp. 26–27, 30–31.
126 William Fraser, *The Lennox*, 2 vols. (Edinburgh, 1874), 2:11–12.
127 Neville, *Native Lordship*, pp. 58–59. John de Luss first appears as *miles* in a charter of the 1290s, Robert Colquhoun in the 1280s (*Native Lordship*, pp. 39–40),

the Gaelic elite of Strathearn and Lennox measured status, position, and authority according to markedly different standards than did the Anglo-Norman and Continental noblemen of their day. Yet the second half of the thirteenth century was certainly a period of transition in Scotland, as it was elsewhere in Europe. As notions of rank and status themselves became more sharply focused, the exclusivity associated with knighthood gained currency among the sons of men who had once considered it superfluous or irrelevant.

So far, this discussion has been restricted primarily to eastern and central Scotland where, in the years 1124 to 1250, the processes and institutions of Europeanization were felt most strongly. Shifting the focus toward the west and north of the kingdom into Galloway, Argyll and the Isles, and Ross reveals a land of continuing contrasts. These were rugged and sparsely populated regions, the outer or "Atlantic" zone of the realm, further removed still than Strathearn and Lennox from the centers of power established by the MacMalcolm kings and, at the end of the twelfth century, only lightly touched by foreign influences and military innovations. Knighthood here was not unknown, but it is apparent that its evolution was deeply influenced by native customs and mores.

From the middle years of the twelfth century the Hebrides, the islands lying off Scotland's west coast, were home to a powerful dynasty of Gaelic-Norse rulers who claimed descent from the mighty Somerled of Argyll. Somerled perished in 1164 in an invasion of the Scottish mainland. Much like the rebellion of 1160 led by Ferteth of Strathearn, the invasion quite possibly represented a reaction against "the dynamic forces of Europeanisation that were sweeping the Scottish kingdom."[128] If this was the case, then there is evidence that several generations after 1164 the descendants of Somerled (commonly known as the MacSorleys) had finally begun to come to terms with the social, political, and cultural changes that were

---

and William Galbraith in 1278 (*Lennox Cart.*, ed. Dennistoun, pp. 39–40, 46–47; William Fraser, *The Stirlings of Keir, and Their Family Papers* [Edinburgh, 1858], pp. 404–5). Malcolm Beg and his sons never witnessed grants as *milites* or *domini*.

[128] McDonald, *Outlaws of Medieval Scotland*, p. 97; R. Andrew McDonald, "The Death and Burial of Somerled of Argyll," *West Highland Notes and Queries*, 2nd ser., 8 (1991), 6–10; *Carmen de morte Sumerledi*, in *Symeonis monachi opera omnia*, ed. Arnold, 2:386–88; *Highland Papers*, ed. J. R. N. MacPhail, 4 vols., Scottish History Society, 2nd ser., 5, 12, 20, 3rd ser., 22 (Edinburgh, 1914–34), 1:9–10.

then spreading into other traditionally conservative areas of the realm. Chronicle and charter sources of the mid-thirteenth century leave little doubt that Ewen of Argyll, a great-grandson of Somerled, was a member of the knightly order. Describing Ewen's dealings with King Alexander II in 1249, Matthew Paris called him a "vigorous and very handsome knight."[129] The chronicler may have been practicing literary license rather than representing reality, but there are good reasons for arguing that this was not the case. Matthew and Ewen were both in Norway in 1248 and may have made each other's acquaintance. Matthew, then, may have been writing about Ewen from personal experience.[130] Charter evidence, moreover, corroborates that of the chronicle. A deed of 1240 describes Ewen as *miles*; another, dated 1255, styles him *dominus*,[131] a title that, by this time, is usually (if not inevitably) taken as an indication that its bearer had been knighted. Altogether, then, the evidence for Ewen having been formally knighted is very strong. Like some of his young contemporaries in Fife, Strathearn, Lennox, and elsewhere, he appears as a man of two worlds, in this instance a Hebridean sea king who was nonetheless in tune with European cultural trends. Later MacSorleys emulated him in this respect. Ewen's son, Alexander, and his grandson, John, feature prominently in documents originating both in western Scotland and the royal chancery, where they are identified as knights.[132] English Exchequer accounts indicate payments to "Sir John of Argyll, knight."[133] In the late thirteenth century, moreover, neither tenure by knight service nor the rank of knight was quite as exotic in this part of the realm as it had once been. Angus Mór, a great-grandson of Somerled, had accepted the

---

[129] Matthew Paris, *Chon. majora*, ed. Luard, 5:88–89.

[130] McDonald, *Kingdom of the Isles*, pp. 146–47.

[131] A. A. M. Duncan and A. L. Brown, "Argyll and the Isles in the Earlier Middle Ages," *Proceedings of the Society of Antiquaries of Scotland* 90 (1956–57), 219; *Acts of the Parliaments of Scotland*, ed. Thomas Thomson and Cosmo Innes, 11 vols. (Edinburgh, 1814–44), 1:115.

[132] Ewan swore fealty to Edward I in 1296 as a knight. *Calendar of Documents Relating to Scotland Preserved in Her Majesty's Public Record Office*, ed. Joseph Bain, 4 vols. (Edinburgh, 1881–88), 2:no. 791 and no. 823, p. 195.

[133] Ibid., 3: nos. 303, 355; See also *Edward I and the Throne of Scotland 1290–1296*, ed. E. L. G. Stones and Grant G. Simpson, 2 vols. (Oxford, 1978), 2:368, which indicates that John had not yet been knighted in 1291.

honorific title by 1293, and the Ragman Rolls of 1296 include the names of at least one West Highland lord identified as knight.[134]

The reigns of Alexander II and Alexander III saw the enfeftment in lands around Loch Awe and Loch Fyne of Gillascop MacGilchrist in return for the service of a full knight, and some twenty years later Dugald Mac-Sween granted estates within his own lands in Knapdale, Cowal, and Kintyre to Walter Stewart earl of Mar for the service of "two-thirds of a knight in the king's army."[135] References to the "barons of Argyll," moreover, begin to appear regularly in extant record materials from the region in the last quarter of the thirteenth century,[136] an indication not merely of a sense of cohesion among the magnates of the region, but of an understanding of the political and judicial authority inherent in the term "baron." By the year 1300, then, the ideas, practices, and values associated with European-style knighthood had begun to merge smoothly with native Gaelic concepts of lordship and power to create a uniquely hybrid Scottish aristocracy in the western reaches of the realm. Yet the chronology of these developments remains a point of interest. Knights and knighthood became known in the Highlands and Hebridean Islands, but only several generations after they had taken firm root in the regions of the kingdom south of Forth.

Another powerful and semiautonomous native dynasty was that of the lords of Galloway, in southwestern Scotland. This family represents still another model in the context of Gaelic-European integration, accommodation, and acculturation. Descended from Fergus, the first known lord and a contemporary (and a relation through marriage) of Somerled of Argyll, the Galloway dynasty ruled a "kingdom within a kingdom" until the death of Alan in 1234.[137] Recent historiography has

---

[134] *Instrumenta publica sive processus super fidelitatibus et homagiis Scotorum,* ed. Thomas Thomson, Bannatyne Club, 47 (Edinburgh, 1834), p. 162. Many of the seals appended to the homage rolls include armorial bearings, suggesting, perhaps, that some Highland subscribers were also knights. See Bruce A. McAndrew, "The Sigillography of the Ragman Roll," *Proceedings of the Society of Antiquaries of Scotland* 129 (1999): 663–72.

[135] *Highland Papers,* ed. MacPhail, 2:121–24; Barrow, *Anglo-Norman Era,* p. 138.

[136] *CDS,* 2, ed. Bain, no. 55; 3:no. 80; *Rotuli Scotiae in turri Londoniensi et in domo capitulari Westmonasteriensi asservati,* ed. David MacPherson, John Caley, and William Illingworth, 2 vols. (London, 1814–19), 1:32; *Documents Illustrative of the History of Scotland 1286–1306,* ed. Joseph Stevenson, 2 vols. (Edinburgh, 1870), 2:nos. 445, 610; *Inchaffray Charters,* ed. Lindsay, Dowden, and Thomson, no. 73.

[137] Duncan, *Making of the Kingdom,* p. 187.

emphasized the role of the lords of Galloway as "modernizers," and has made much of their willingness to adopt the new manners and modes of Scottish courtly society. The period of Alan of Galloway in particular has been portrayed as witnessing the "acceleration of the process by which the Scottish crown sought to integrate the lordship of Galloway into the kingdom," an alignment of interests that had already begun under Fergus.[138] Yet an assessment of the family of Galloway from a perspective that focuses specifically on the penetration and spread of European ideas about knighthood reveals a considerably more complex interaction between these Gaelic rulers and Anglo-Norman and Continental newcomers than historians have to date acknowledged.

There is no clear evidence to suggest that Fergus was receptive to the conventions of knighthood. He is nowhere styled *miles*, and indeed, within the territories west of the River Urr that constituted his patrimonial lands, he openly resisted the introduction of tenure by knight service and the military and political obligations consequent on it.[139] Despite his military support of David I in 1138,[140] Fergus's later record of rebellion against the crown has been interpreted as an active campaign to prevent foreign ideas and practices from intruding into his lordship.[141] Contemporary English chroniclers singled out for the severest censure the savageness and barbarity of the soldiers whom he led to the battle of the Standard in 1138. Their comments leave little doubt that they considered the fighting style of the Gallovidian, their dress, their language, in essence their very Gaelicness, the antitheses of acceptable knightly conduct.[142]

---

[138] Richard D. Oram, *The Lordship of Galloway* (Edinburgh, 2000), p. 135; Keith J. Stringer, "Periphery and Core in Thirteenth-Century Scotland: Alan, Son of Roland, Lord of Galloway and Constable of Scotland," in *Medieval Scotland*, ed. Grant and Stringer, pp. 98–101; Keith J. Stringer, "Acts of Lordship: The Records of the Lords of Galloway to 1234," in *Freedom and Authority*, ed. Brotherstone and Ditchburn, pp. 211–12.

[139] Oram, *Lordship of Galloway*, pp. 193–94, 211.

[140] See here Richard Oram's arguments about the nature of the Gallovidian army at the battle of the Standard, in "Fergus, Galloway and the Scots," in *Galloway: Land and Lordship*, ed. Richard D. Oram and Geoffrey P. Stell (Edinburgh, 1991), pp. 123–27.

[141] R. Andrew McDonald, "Rebels Without a Cause? The Relations of Fergus of Galloway and Somerled of Argyll with the Scottish Kings, 1153–1164," in *Alba*, ed. Cowan and McDonald, pp. 166–86. See also the balanced discussion of Fergus's later years in Oram, *Lordship of Galloway*, pp. 74–82.

[142] Strickland, *War and Chivalry*, pp. 291–340. See also the text at note 13 above.

The tenure of land by knight service did not make a definitive appearance in Galloway until after the death of Fergus in 1161, and then in rare and unusual circumstances.[143] His son Uhtred's acquisition of the lands of Desnes Ioan by royal grant brought with it the responsibility to render mounted military service. This obligation in turn required that Uhtred settle new colonists in this portion of his territories,[144] and a grant of land in Kirkudbrightshire dated 1166 × 1172 to Richard fitz Troite marked an early effort to put this policy into effect.[145] Yet, knight service remained an anomaly in the traditional heartlands of Galloway west of the Urr, not merely in Uhtred's time but until well into the thirteenth century,[146] and it was not until the last years of that same century that native noblemen beyond the kindred of Fergus of Galloway began to aspire to the rank of knight in considerable numbers.[147]

As in other regions of Gaelic Scotland, then, foreign ideas penetrated into Galloway only gradually, if not against the overt resistance of the ruling family, then more generally under their careful control and direction. When such ideas did begin to gain currency, moreover, they did not displace preexisting concepts about lordship, authority, and power. Indeed, in many parts of the Gàidhealtachd an association between headship of a kindred and the honorific title of knight was slow to develop. Alan of Galloway took pride in the office of constable, which he inherited through his de Morville mother,[148] and his close links with the crowns of both England and Scotland bear witness to a magnate able to move with confidence (and much royal trust) in the rarefied circles of the two courts. As was the case in late twelfth- and thirteenth-century Strathearn and Lennox, the title *miles*, considered throughout the Europeanized parts of Britain a prize well worth pursuing, held limited allure for the native rulers of Galloway. By 1300, the presence in the entourages of all these magnates of men who boasted this distinguished status bears eloquent testimony to the absorption of foreign social customs among the elite of the kingdom of

---

[143] Oram, *Lordship of Galloway*, pp. 200–203.

[144] Ibid., p. 196.

[145] Stringer, "Acts of Lordship," p. 215.

[146] Ibid., pp. 205–6; Stringer, "Periphery and Core," pp. 82–84.

[147] Oram, *Lordship of Galloway*, pp. 203, 207–8.

[148] *Scotichronicon, vol. 4: Books VII and VIII, by Walter Bower*, ed. David J. Corner, A. B. Scott, William W. Scott and D. E. R. Watt (Aberdeen, 1994), pp. 412–13; Stringer, "Periphery and Core," p. 101.

Scotland. Yet neither Fergus of Galloway nor his increasingly cosmopolitan descendants believed that the dignity would add much luster to their already exalted positions. Neither did the earls of Strathearn, nor the earls of Lennox until 1273. Malcolm I earl of Lennox, who succeeded his grandfather Maldoven around 1250, was the first among the thirteenth-century rulers of either lordship to hold the title of knight.[149] The reasons for this were many and varied. These magnates may all have rejected the honor merely because it was so profoundly foreign and so obviously linked to values, beliefs, and customs that competed with indigenous notions of lordship, kinship, and power. They may simply have considered the title of *miles* beneath them in their roles as mormaers in the Gaelic tradition; alternatively, like Alexander III, they may have believed that the dignity of earl already incorporated the qualities, the nobility, and the personal honor associated with the title. For others, perhaps like Ferchar Maccintsacairt, who seems to have lacked the pedigree and inherited status of the Galloways, Strathearns, and Lennoxes, the perquisites of European-style knighthood and service to the crown that was integral to them offered new opportunities for advancement by bestowing on them the noble status that their contemporaries elsewhere in the British Isles associated with the rank of knight. This may explain the enthusiasm with which Ferchar embraced the title that the king granted him, then sought to use it as a basis for further political gain.[150]

Mistrust of the military obligations that contemporary practice imposed on the holders of knight's feus must also have been a potent force. Glimpses of this sense of wariness are visible occasionally in the earls' own written deeds, as well as in the terminology of the few charters of infeftment that the native magnates received by royal grant. Almost inevitably, the documents included clear statements in their holding clauses to the effect that the new feus were to be possessed "as free and quit" as these Gaelic lords held their earldom lands.[151] In their own charters to native tenants, the earls sometimes equated themselves with the greatest of the king's incoming magnates, specifying that estates were to be held "as freely as any land is held of any baron in the kingdom of

---

149 *Lennox Cart.*, ed. Dennistoun, pp. 14–15.
150 Grant, "Province of Ross," pp. 106–9.
151 See, for example, *RRS 2*, ed. Barrow, no. 206; *Lennox Cart.*, ed. Dennistoun, pp. 1–2.

Scotland."[152] The choice of such words was not arbitrary; it spoke, rather, to a thoughtful and well-conceived strategy on the part of the native magnates to secure recognition of their unique status in a cultural world that they found changeable and potentially threatening. Paradoxically, however, these same written acts also reveal that military service counted for little in the Gaelic magnates' conception of lordship and authority. Scholars have long remarked on the tendency of Scottish grantors to make gifts of land either in blench ferm or in return for suit of court alone, that is, free of the obligation to perform military service other than that required of all free men in the kingdom.[153] North of the Forth, the size of a man's following mattered, just as it did elsewhere in the British Isles, but the status of the men who made up the retinue was measured according to different criteria.[154]

Sigillographic and Literary Evidence

The argument that the Gaelic nobility of twelfth- and thirteenth-century Scotland absorbed European ideas about knighthood only cautiously is at first glance negated by sigillographic evidence, which is at once plentiful but challenging. Waxen seals appear as early as the mid-twelfth century, more or less contemporaneously with the diffusion of such devices across England and the Continent more generally. Symbols of royal, then lordly, authority, with the spread of the practice of charter writing, they also became signs of specific identity and of authentication.[155] From the outset, the mounted warrior was the image of choice for seals, symbolizing the role of the king and the nobleman as a leader in war, but also his membership in an exclusive social order. Early Scottish seals closely

---

[152] *Lennox Cart.*, ed. Dennistoun, pp. 68–69.

[153] See, for example, Duncan, *Making of the Kingdom*, pp. 391–409; Alexander Grant, "Service and Tenure in Late Medieval Scotland, 1314–1475," in *Concepts and Patterns of Service in the Later Middle Ages*, ed. Anne Curry and Elizabeth Matthew (Woodbridge, 2000), pp. 145–79.

[154] Neville, *Native Lordship*, pp. 109–11.

[155] John Horne Stevenson, *Heraldry in Scotland*, 2 vols. (Glasgow, 1914), 1:17; Michael Clanchy, *From Memory to Written Record: England 1066–1307*, 2nd ed. (Oxford, 1993), p. 315; Brigitte Bedos Rezak, "Medieval Seals and the Structure of Chivalric Society," in *The Study of Chivalry: Resources and Approaches*, ed. Howell Chickering and Thomas H. Seiler (Kalamazoo, 1988), pp. 317–18.

resembled their counterparts elsewhere in western Europe at this time, and the reverse of the royal seals of Duncan II (d. 1094) and Alexander I (d. 1124) include depictions of these kings in what was fast becoming "typical" fashion, as equestrian figures bearing chain mail, helmet, shield, and lance. David I and his twelfth- and thirteenth-century successors likewise portrayed themselves on their seals as mounted warriors, though the lance had given way to a sword by William's time.[156]

The practice of authenticating written acts by appending seals to parchment was current (if not yet common) among the ranks of the English nobility by the year 1100, and the proliferation of noble seals in Scotland under King David I owed much to the influence of men of Anglo-Norman and Continental origin accustomed to using these devices. [157] The oldest surviving examples of equestrian seals include those of Walter the Steward (attached to a document of c. 1170), his son, Alan (also c. 1170), and Eustace de Balliol (c. 1190).[158] Among the native aristocracy, equestrian seals also begin to appear in the twelfth century. Cospatric II of Dunbar (d. 1138), his son, Cospatrick III (d. 1166), and his grandson, Waldeve (d. 1182) all used such symbols, though it is worth noting here that the documents their seals authenticated were all issued in favor of the church of Durham,[159] where the practice of charter writing was already well established in the late twelfth century. Firm evidence that Scottish magnates were familiar with the equestrian seal and its iconographic associations dates only from the very last years of the twelfth century, some two or three generations after the settlement in Scotland of a new aristocracy. Moreover, only in the early thirteenth century did the use of the seals and armorial bearings more generally begin to spread among the ranks of the native elite.

In the year 1200, Gilbert of Strathearn and Duncan II of Fife alone are known to have possessed equestrian seals.[160] More intriguing still is

---

[156] John Horne Stevenson and Marguerite Wood, *Scottish Heraldic Seals*, 3 vols. (Glasgow, 1940), 1:1–3.

[157] P. D. A. Harvey and Andrew McGuiness, *A Guide to British Medieval Seals* (Toronto, 1996), p. 43; Crouch, *Image of Aristocracy*, pp. 154, 242–43.

[158] Stevenson and Wood, *Scottish Heraldic Seals*, 2:238; 3:600.

[159] Ibid., 2:333–34.

[160] Often cited is the seal of Alan of Galloway (d. 1234), but see also the seals of Malcolm earl of Fife (d. 1228), Angus Mór of Argyll (d. c. 1292), Donald earl of Mar (d. c. 1297) and Malcolm II earl of Lennox (d. c. 1303). Crouch, *Image of Aristocracy*, pp. 240–41; Stevenson and Wood, *Scottish Heraldic Seals*, 2:354; 3:454, 483, 491.

the simplicity of heraldic detail characteristic of each of these artifacts. The obverse of Gilbert's seal shows a figure in chain mail with a shield marked with a plain cross. It is blank on the reverse, although the practice of impressing both sides of a seal was by then becoming common. Soon after the year 1200, Gilbert abandoned his first seal in favor of a new design. The obverse of this one was simpler still, with the shield now portrayed devoid of any marking.[161] The earls of Strathearn did not adopt the armorial bearings of two chevronells that became the family's device until after 1250; before that time, the iconography of their seals varies considerably.[162] The earls of Fife likewise used simple devices on their seals, not adopting decisively the lion rampant that so eloquently linked them to the Scottish royal house until the period of Earl Duncan IV (d. 1353).[163]

The equestrian seal, then, was something of a late influence on Gaelic Scotland and probably not widely used until the second half of the thirteenth century. One is left to wonder, nonetheless, why the native elite did eventually come to conform to European practice in adopting the seal and its attendant heraldic devices as visual representations of their place in Scottish society, especially in view of the fact that they regarded the use of the honorific title of *miles* beneath their rank. Part of the answer lies, surely, in the increasing use of written documents within the kingdom in this period (a phenomenon explored at length by Geoffrey Barrow) and, concomitantly, greater reliance on the waxen seal as proof that the granter of a written deed was "legally committing himself" to its contents.[164] The practice of writing within the secular ranks of the Scottish Gàidhealtachd was a novelty, and it is perhaps small wonder, therefore, that the trappings of this new technology—the Latin language of the written instrument, the charter and brieve styles, and the authenticating seal—should have filtered into the Gaelic lordships only gradually.[165]

---

[161] Stevenson and Wood, *Scottish Heraldic Seals*, 3:625.

[162] Ibid., 3:625–26; *Inchaffray Charters*, ed. Lindsay, Dowden and Thomson, no. 87.

[163] Stevenson and Wood, *Scottish Heraldic Seals*, 2:354.

[164] Rezak, "Medieval Seals," p. 317. For Barrow's discussion of the spread of written documents, see especially *RRS* 1, pp. 57–59, *RRS* 2, pp. 57–59, and "The Pattern of Non-Literary Manuscript Production and Survival in Scotland, 1200–1330," in *Pragmatic Literacy, East and West 1200–1330*, ed. Richard Britnell (Woodbridge, 1997), pp. 131–45.

[165] On this subject generally, see Dauvit Broun, *The Charters of Gaelic Scotland and Ireland in the Early and Central Middle Ages*, Quiggan Pamphlets on the Sources

Admittedly an inexact science, the study of heraldic signs and symbols offers tantalizing glimpses of this process of infiltration at work. Like many Anglo-Norman and European magnates, the earls of Dunbar, Fife, and Strathearn experimented widely with the devices that they impressed on their seals. Patrick II of Dunbar (d. 1272) eventually settled on a lion rampant for the shield on the obverse of his seal over the undecorated shield that his two predecessors had used. Like the earls of Fife, who would also use the lion rampant (if not until the later thirteenth century), the Dunbars claimed descent from the Scottish royal family, and the lion symbol portrayed that affinity in striking fashion.[166] Gilbert of Strathearn's adoption of chevronells, however, suggests that the indigenous Gaelic culture in which he was steeped offered few reference points when it came to fashioning a device that would represent unambiguously his family's lineage. The chevronells were borrowed wholesale from the family of his first wife, Maud D'Aubigny.[167] The later thirteenth-century lords of Galloway, likewise, borrowed the lion rampant, not from the royal house but from the Anglo-Norman family of de Morville, of whom one was the mother of Alan son of Roland.[168] Malcolm I earl of Lennox chose the saltire, perhaps out of admiration for St. Andrew, but perhaps also as a mark of respect for the Bruce family, whose patriotic claim to the Scottish throne he supported unwaveringly throughout the years of the Great Cause and beyond.[169] Ranald MacSorley and other descendants

---

of Medieval Gaelic History (Cambridge, 1995); Cynthia J. Neville, "Charter Writing and the Exercise of Lordship in Thirteenth-Century Celtic Scotland," in *Expectations of the Law in the Middle Ages*, ed. Anthony Musson (Woodbridge, 2001), pp. 67–89; and several of the essays collected in *Literacy in Medieval Celtic Societies*, ed. Huw Pryce (Cambridge, 1998).

[166] Stevenson and Wood, *Scottish Heraldic Seals*, 2:334, 354. The lion rampant was first adopted by King William I.

[167] See the depiction of several thirteenth-century shields from Matthew Paris's *Chronica majora*, British Library MS Cotton Nero Di, fol. 171, in Keen, *Chivalry*, plate 32. The D'Aubigny family in turn was probably indebted for its arms to a link through marriage with the Clares. See John Horace Round, *Feudal England: Historical Studies in the XIth and XIIth Centuries* (London, 1895), pp. 473–76, 575.

[168] Stevenson, *Heraldry in Scotland*, 1:18.

[169] Stevenson and Wood, *Scottish Heraldic Seals*, 2:262; Neville, *Native Lordship*, p. 32. Of the identity of Malcolm's wife, Marjorie, nothing beyond her given name is known, but the name was also popular with the Bruces, and the saltire may represent a marital association with the family.

of Somerled of Argyll, as well as Ragnvald king of Man (d. 1229), found a unique accommodation between Gaelic and European custom and imagery on their seals, which they marked on the obverse with an equestrian figure and on the reverse with a depiction of that "indispensable tool" of the sea-based rulers of the west, the galley.[170] Indeed, Ragnvald of Man serves as a potent reminder of the extent to which the outlying parts of the British Isles participated in contemporary cultural trends. Ragnvald had considerable dealings with the English kings, John and Henry III, and held lands in Ulster for the service of one knight. There is no evidence that he was knighted, but several of his successors as kings of Man and the Isles are said to have enjoyed the privilege. Thus, the thirteenth-century *Cronica Regum Mannie et Insularum* claims that Olaf Godresson (d. 1237), Harald Olafsson (d. 1248), and Magnus Olafsson (d. 1265) all received knighthood from the English king.[171]

The earldom of Carrick, which did not achieve formal identity as a distinct political unit until at least 1200, offers a unique opportunity to examine the changing semiotics of early thirteenth-century armorial bearings. The first earl, Duncan son of Gilbert son of Fergus of Galloway (d. 1250), was a nobleman who moved easily between the Gaelic and European worlds of his day. He called himself Duncan fitz Gilbert, consciously choosing the French style then current at the English court, where he spent several years as a hostage.[172] Like other English magnates he adopted the waxen seal as a tangible symbol of his high status, yet despite his investiture with the arms of knighthood he chose not to use on his seal either the image of the mounted warrior with which he would have

---

[170] McDonald, *Kingdom of the Isles*, pp. 75–76; R. Andrew McDonald, "Images of Hebridean Lordship in the Twelfth and Thirteenth Centuries: The Seal of Raonall Mac Sorley," *Scottish Historical Review* 74 (1995), 120–43. For Ragnvald, see "Opinion of Clarenceux King of Arms, On the Arms of the Isle of Man, on the Accession of James, Duke of Atholl, to the Government thereof, 1st Feb 1735," in *Monumenta de Insula Manniae or A Collection of National Documents Relating to the Isle of Man*, ed. John Robert Oliver, 3 vols., Manx Society, 4, 7, 9 (Douglas, 1860–62), 2:118–19. See also Denis Rixson, *The West Highland Galley* (Edinburgh, 1998), esp. ch. 9, on seals, heraldic devices, and illuminations.

[171] *Cronica Regum Mannie et Insularum, Chronicles of the Kings of Man and the Isles BL Cotton Julius Avii*, ed. George Broderick, 2nd ed. (Douglas, 1996), fols. 46r–49r; Andrew McDonald, *Manx Kingship in its Irish Sea Setting, 1187–1229: King Rognvaldr and the Crovan Dynasty* (forthcoming).

[172] Oram, *Lordship of Galloway*, pp. 100–104.

been well acquainted from his years at the Angevin court or the device of a shield of arms. Instead, he preferred the symbol of a griffin,[173] a creature of mixed breeding. The choice was perhaps significant: unfamiliar with the European custom of employing visual symbols to represent the family, Duncan may have adopted the griffin both because it was already a widely used heraldic device and so easily recognizable,[174] and because it bore eloquent testimony to his own hybrid upbringing.

Although more extensive work is needed, this brief review suggests that the sigillographic evidence so far points in the same direction as other kinds of evidence considered in this essay.[175] At the very least, the artifacts examined above reveal that resistance to sudden change among the Gaelic nobility may be found even in small pieces of wax. They also suggest that a study of the minutiae of writing technology may yet yield valuable information about the ways in which Gaelic lords absorbed and internalized the cultural changes that they encountered in the wake of the migration of foreigners to Scotland in the century and more after 1124. Incoming noblemen did not, apparently, transplant to Scotland, *mutates mutandis*, the sealing practices with which they were familiar in England. Future studies should make it possible to understand more clearly whether the waxen seal acquired unique social and cultural significance when it traveled north from England.

More than a quarter of a century ago, Archibald Duncan opined that the literary styles associated with the chivalric culture of twelfth- and thirteenth-century France and England probably never had much influence in Scotland.[176] Much of this argument depended on Duncan's assessment of the reception within the kingdom of the genre known as romance, for which the evidence is slender at best. The only French language work of this type that may have had its origins in Scotland is the poem called the *Roman de Fergus*, though scholarly opinion is deeply divided on the nature and purpose of this work. Composed in the early years of the thirteenth century, perhaps on the occasion of Alan of Galloway's second marriage in 1209 to Margaret, daughter of

---

[173] Stevenson and Wood, *Scottish Heraldic Seals*, 2:278.

[174] George Henderson, "Romance and Politics on Some Medieval English Seals," *Art History* 1 (1978), 29.

[175] Cynthia Neville is currently at work on such a study.

[176] Duncan, *Making of the Kingdom*, pp. 447–49.

Earl David of Huntingdon,[177] *Fergus* recounts the adventures of a poor lad who, in typical quest fashion, achieves fame and wealth (and gets the girl) after a series of trials and tribulations. Whether it was written in Scotland or merely set there, the poem was not well known in courtly circles in the thirteenth century. More tellingly, neither were French language works of romance generally. Historians are accustomed to lamenting the lack of charter and chronicle materials that survive from the medieval period in Scotland, but they seldom seem aware that the literary remains of the so-called "Anglo-Norman era" are even scarcer.[178] The nobles and knights who settled in parts of Scotland in the century and a half after 1124 may have begun to abandon the French language soon after 1200, and so have doomed the *Roman de Fergus* to an audience no longer able to understand and enjoy it.[179] But even if this was the case—and dating the demise of spoken French is another historical matter fraught with difficulty—it does not explain why *Fergus* and the many other romances that either were set in Scotland or that wove Scottish figures into their plots never found fertile soil in the northern kingdom.[180]

---

[177] Mary Dominica Legge, *Anglo-Norman Literature and Its Background* (Oxford, 1963), pp. 161–62; and M. Dominica Legge, "Sur la genèse du *Roman de Fergus*," in *Mélanges de linguistique romane et de philologie médiévale offerts à M. Maurice Delbouille*, ed. Jean Renson and Madeleine Tyssens, 2 vols. (Gembloux, 1964), 2:399; but see Joan Greenberg, "Guillaume le Clerc and Alan of Galloway," *Proceedings of the Modern Language Association* 66 (1951), 524, 526; Neil Thomas, "The Old French *Roman de Fergus*: Scottish *Mis-en-scène* and Political Implications," *Parergon*, new ser., 11, no. 1 (1993), 100; Oram, *Lordship of Galloway*, pp. 53–54; and Tony Hunt, "The *Roman de Fergus*: Parody or Pastiche?" in *The Scots and Medieval Arthurian Legend*, ed. Rhiannon Purdie and Nicola Royan (Woodbridge, 2005), pp. 55–56.

[178] On the restricted use of the French language in high medieval Scotland, see Duncan, *Making of the Kingdom*, pp. 447–51, and G. W. S. Barrow, "French after the Style of Petithachengon," in *Church, Chronicle and Learning*, ed. Crawford, pp. 187–93.

[179] D. D. R. Owen, *William the Lion, 1143–1214: Kingship and Culture* (East Linton, 1997), pp. 116, 152.

[180] The setting of Scotland as a background for romance stories and the appearance in them of Scottish persons are discussed in Guillaume le Clerc, *Fergus of Galloway: Knight of King Arthur*, ed. D. D. R. Owen (London, 1991), p. xiii; Legge, "Sur la genèse du *Roman de Fergus*," p. 405; and Ritchie, *Chrétien de Troyes*, pp. 5–24.

Nor does it explain why other genres of literature that were popular in both England and France never found a home in "Anglo-Norman" Scotland. The history of the genre that eventually became known as the *roman lignagère* was already old when William of Normandy conquered England. The establishment there of a new ruling order quickly generated considerable demand for ancestral romance and produced such well-known works as *Guillaume d'Angleterre* (c. 1170), the *Estoire de Waldef* (probably the 1190s), *Boeve de Haumtone* (late twelfth century), and *Guy de Warewic* (1232 × 1242).[181] Such stories provided rulers lacking close ties to their newly conquered land with a legitimacy and sense of historicity that reflected and responded to their social aspirations, and simultaneously obscured the status of *parvenus* of many of the newcomers.[182] Like the romance style generally, however, *romans lignagères* were never popular in Scotland.

It is difficult to credit Duncan's suggestion that thirteenth-century Scots were quite simply "out of things" and "rustics," unable to absorb the sophisticated literate culture of England and Europe.[183] His assessment flies in the face of other evidence, military, tenurial, and sigillographic. Some features of European-style knighthood found a ready reception among the newly arrived magnates and eventually also among members of the Gaelic elite. Recent archaeological work, for example, reveals that the story of Tristram and Isolde—and probably other figures of literary romance—had at least some appeal among urban dwellers,[184] and the appearance of personal names associated with the romance literature of Europe in places such as Strathearn and Lennox speaks to the popularity of these stories in regions dominated by native landholders.[185] A more

---

[181] Legge, *Anglo-Norman Literature*, pp. 138, 141–62; and R. S. Loomis, "Scotland and the Arthurian Legend," *Proceedings of the Society of Antiquaries of Scotland* 89 (1955–56), 1–21.

[182] Legge, *Anglo-Norman Literature*, pp. 174–75.

[183] Duncan, *Making of the Kingdom*, p. 447.

[184] Mark A. Hall and D. D. R. Owen, "A Tristram and Iseult Mirror Case from Perth: Reflections on the Production and Consumption of Romance Culture," *Tayside and Fife Archaeological Journal* 4 (1998), 150–65.

[185] One of the early thirteenth-century tenants of the earls of Strathearn, for example, bore the name Tristram; he probably settled as the follower of Earl Gilbert's wife, Maud D'Aubigny. In nearby Lennox, the name Arthur was already well established as a Galbraith family name in the early years of that century, a reflection, in part, of the widespread dissemination across western Europe of Romance

satisfactory explanation for the failure of the romance to secure a place in Scotland lies in an acknowledgment of the strength of the Gaelic literary tradition there, one that confronted and survived challenges presented to it by the influx of foreigners. In the twelfth century the Gaels laid claim to a venerable tradition of prose and poetry, some of it closely resembling the *romans lignagères* in its purpose of celebrating royal, family, and tribal genealogies. The custodians of this literary heritage, moreover, members of the *oes dána*, still exerted a powerful influence within the Gàidhealtachd, in offices such as those of the *maer*, the *breitheamh*, the *archipoeta*, the hereditary medicine man, the *senchaidh*, the *ollamh ríg Alban,* and the *filidh*.[186] As occurred in Ireland and Wales, ecclesiastical reforms and foreign influence together precipitated the transition from purely oral practices to a written Latin language tradition in Scotland,[187] but the strength of native poetic and historical expression remained remarkably vibrant throughout and beyond the period of Anglo-Norman and Continental settlement.[188] The resilience of the Gaelic learned orders, then, must be understood as an important factor in shaping the

---

names. Neville, *Native Lordship,* p. 44; W. D. H. Sellar, "The Earliest Campbells— Norman, Briton or Gael?" *Scottish Studies* 17 (1973), 109–25; R. S. Loomis, "Scotland and the Arthurian Legend," *Proceedings of the Society of Antiquaries of Scotland* 89 (1955–56), 1–21.

[186] D. S. Thomson, "Gaelic Learned Orders and Literati," *Scottish Studies* 12 (1968), 57–78; Bannerman, "The Scots Language and the Kin-based Society," pp. 1–19.

[187] David E. Thornton, "Orality, Literacy and Genealogy in Medieval Ireland and Wales," in *Literacy in Medieval Celtic Societies,* ed. Pryce, pp. 83–98. The transition in all three realms had particularly important implications for native genealogists. See here Donnchadh Ó Corrain, "Celtic Narrative Tradition: Historical Need and Literary Narrative," in *Proceedings of the 7th International Congress of Celtic Studies held at Oxford, from 10th to 15th July, 1983,* ed. D. Ellis Evans, John G. Griffiths, and E. M. Jope (Oxford, 1986), pp. 141–58; Edward J. Cowan, "The Scottish Chronicle in the Poppleton Manuscript," *Innes Review* 32 (1981), 3–21; Dauvit Broun, "Gaelic Literacy in Eastern Scotland between 1124 and 1249," in *Literacy in Medieval Celtic Societies,* ed. Pryce, pp. 188–201; John Ellis Caerwyn Williams, "Gildas, Maelgwyn and the Bard," in *Welsh Society and Nationhood,* ed. Davies, Griffiths, Jones, and Morgan, pp. 30–32; John MacInnes, "Gaelic Poetry and Historical Tradition," in *The Middle Ages in the Highlands,* ed. Maclean, pp. 142–48.

[188] Studies of the making of Campbell family history in the Middle Ages have been particularly rich. See MacInnes, "Gaelic Poetry," pp. 148–61; William Gillies, "Some Aspects of Campbell History," *Transactions of the Gaelic Society of Inverness* 50 (1976–78), 256–95 and, most recently, Steve Boardman, *The Campbells 1250–1513* (Edinburgh, 2006).

aristocratic culture of twelfth- and thirteenth-century Scotland and in limiting the degree to which foreign ideas about chivalry infiltrated the literary culture of the region north of Forth.

Conclusions

When, in 1296, Edward I set about securing the loyalty of the Scots nobility he claimed to have conquered, he accepted as visible (and legally binding) evidence of submission the seals of more than 1,500 individual attestors, each bearing distinctive symbols that identified its bearer. By then, the use of waxen seals had become so commonplace in Scotland that even men (and women) of relatively modest means possessed them.[189] By 1296, moreover, the heraldic conventions that governed the decoration of these objects in Scotland closely followed those of England, and noblemen from across the kingdom now regularly identified their familial and tenurial connections on them.

A century earlier, however, the relationship between the Gaelic elite and the Anglo-French newcomers was still in its initial stages of development. A sudden and wholesale adoption of the many trappings of European-style knighthood entailed a shift of mentality that the Gaelic earls were not prepared to make. Moreover, the settlement of foreigners within Scotland was a process that was accomplished for the most part peacefully, which meant that the indigenous nobility was not required to embrace change either suddenly or forcefully. In Scotland, then, the reception of novel ideas about knighthood proceeded only piecemeal. It is also clear that new concepts were absorbed most quickly and comprehensively when these did not threaten the existing social order. A new emphasis on writing on the part of later twelfth-century kings, for example, gradually filtered downward into the landholding ranks, and for several generations coexisted alongside an older, oral tradition in conservative regions such as Strathearn, Lennox, Argyll, and Galloway. Adaptation to the culture of the written word and its association with the conveyance of land wrought profound changes in all these areas, but

---

[189] See, for example, Stevenson and Wood, *Scottish Heraldic Seals*, 2:242, 350; 3:570 (Geoffrey Baxter, Alexander de Estreville, and William Rutherford parson of the church of Lillisleaf, Roxburghshire). The seals are examined closely in McAndrew, "Sigillography of the Ragman Roll," pp. 663–752.

its consequences did not have a dislocating effect on native notions of lordship, power, and authority. Indeed, it may well have done much to enhance all three.[190] Similarly, the increasing use of seals as a means of authenticating written instruments and the concomitant acceptance of European conventions that linked imagery and symbolism with family and other allegiances may have been new and strange in the late twelfth century, but both might be fairly easily grafted onto Gaelic notions of identity without danger of diminishing native concepts of the great lord.

In other respects, however, the stakes were higher, and acceptance of the ideas and customs associated with knighthood represented a much more significant challenge to fundamental notions of Gaelic status and identity. Chief among these was the privilege that contemporary European society accorded to the mounted warrior in battle. Preoccupied as they were with describing in lurid detail the savagery and uncouthness of the Gallovidians and the wild Scots who accompanied King David I to England in 1138, then William I in 1173–74, English chroniclers never sought to ponder the implications of what they saw as Scottish intransigence in the face of European "civilization." Most notably, they failed to appreciate that the organization of the common army of Scotland and the strategies that its leaders employed were already old, well tried, and well tested in 1138. Gaelic warfare had always accorded a primary role to lightly protected infantrymen carrying only shields, spears, and short broad-edged swords, rather than to a heavily armored, slower cavalry force of the type familiar to the Anglo-Norman and Continental newcomers.[191] The preponderance of foot soldiers gave the Scottish army mobility and speed and made it possible for warriors to turn to good advantage the mountainous terrain that covered much of the kingdom. Of specific importance to the mormaers was the position of privilege that traditional warfare accorded them in the vanguard. Mounted and elaborately attired, their horses set them apart visually from their fighting men and reinforced their exclusivity in native society. Among the Gaels, then, warfare presented a singular opportunity for men of magnate rank to display their unique martial skills and their exalted social status. So, too, of course, did

---

[190] Neville, "Charter Writing," pp. 67–89.

[191] Neil Aitchison, *The Picts and the Scots at War* (Stroud, 2003), pp. 47–61, 67–69; J. M. Hill, "The Distinctiveness of Gaelic Warfare, 1400–1750," *European Studies Quarterly* 22 (1992), 325–28.

it perform such a function among the incoming Europeans, and the new figure of the mounted warrior must have represented a powerful challenge to the native lords' sense of exclusivity, lordship, and rank. Likewise, the European-style knight threatened other, even more fundamental, concepts of Gaelic self-identity. Henry of Huntingdon recounted the ceremony in which King David I raised his grandnephew, Henry of Anjou, into the ranks of knighthood. David, the chronicler noted, "gave the arms of manhood" to young Henry.[192] Orderic Vitalis used similar language in describing the Conqueror's investiture of his son.[193] The juxtaposition of concepts of manhood, knighthood, and mounted military service, part and parcel of the cultural baggage that the MacMalcolms' favored foreigners brought with them to Scotland, presented the indigenous Gaelic nobility of the realm with an alternative model of identity that some may have considered threatening and that many found little reason to welcome openly. It is perhaps from this perspective that the bitter squabbling that erupted in the ranks of David I's army in 1138 is best understood. Aelred of Rievaulx, it has been noted, related at some length the Gallovidians' resistance to the king's plan to make up for his army's inferior numbers by placing his knights in the front line of the opening attack against the English and their bitter objection to David's refusal to accord them this time honored prerogative. Mistrust and animosity were manifest also in a mutiny of the Gallovidian infantrymen at Durham and in a heated exchange between Sir Alan de Percy and Earl Malise I of Strathearn.[194] For the same reasons that Gaelic magnates interpreted recourse to knightly champions and the use of trial by combat as encroachments on some of their most cherished prerogatives as heads of kindred, they saw in the knight's military role still another threat to their identity as great lords. It is small wonder that, despite the myriad attractions of the knightly ethos of Europe, so few of the native leaders from the region north of Forth should have sought to throw themselves willy-nilly into the "vortex" to which Rees Davies has referred.[195]

---

[192] *Henrici archidiaconi Huntendunensis Historia Anglorum*, ed. Thomas Arnold, Rolls Series, 74 (London, 1879), p. 282.

[193] *Ecclesiastical History of Orderic Vitalis*, ed. Chibnall, 4:121.

[194] *Historia Ricardi prioris ecclesie Haugustaldensis de gestis Regis Stephani*, in *Chron. Stephen*, ed. Howlett, 3:155–56; Aelred of Rievaulx, *Relatio de Standardo*, ed. Howlett, 3:190.

[195] See note 8 above.

The dislocating experience of the wars of independence, it has often been noted, saw the Scots forge new concepts of sovereignty and nationhood. It also saw them embark on the urgent task of refining existing traditions about their origins to fashion a distinct identity,[196] a process that in turn had long-lasting effects on deeply rooted notions about lordly authority and power. In the two centuries before 1296, however, there was plenty of room in the Scotland of the MacMalcolms for cultural diversity. The establishment of a *modus vivendi* between Gaelic and European made it possible for members of the native elite to borrow from the cultural practices of the Anglo-French without having to abandon altogether deeply ingrained beliefs and customs drawn from their Gaelic antecedents.[197] The cult of knighthood was at once threatening and alluring to the native magnates who first came into contact with it in the twelfth century. By the end of the thirteenth, many of these dignitaries had found a way to incorporate at least some of its features into the native culture of the realm. That the process of accommodation and acculturation was uneven and at times piecemeal reveals just how powerful was the hold of the Gaelic past when confronted with the dynamism of contemporary European culture.

---

[196] See here the important work of Dauvit Broun, most cogently presented in *The Irish Identity of the Kingdom of the Scots in the Twelfth and Thirteenth Centuries* (Woodbridge, 1999).

[197] Dauvit Broun, "Anglo-French Acculturation," pp. 152–53; Neville, *Native Lordship*, esp. pp. 222–26. On the need to portray the encounter between Gaels and Europeans as a more integrative process, see, most recently, Matthew Hammond, "Ethnicity and the Writing of Medieval Scottish History," *Scottish Historical Review* 85 (2006), 1–27.

The Making of a Myth:
Giraldus Cambrensis, *Laudabiliter*, and Henry II's Lordship of Ireland

Anne J. Duggan
King's College London

FOR MORE THAN a century, scholars have wrestled with the problem of disentangling fact from fiction in Gerald de Barri's account of Henry II's acquisition of the lordship of Ireland in 1171–13, as different parts of his story have been challenged in different ways by different people— rather as a wrongly assembled jigsaw puzzle is broken up and rearranged. The difficulty with this jigsaw, however, is that two crucial pieces (Adrian IV's letter *Laudabiliter*, which allegedly granted Ireland to King Henry in the first place, in late 1155 or early 1156; and *Quoniam ea*, its alleged confirmation by Pope Alexander III in 1172) sit rather awkwardly in the frame created for them by Gerald,[1] thereby distorting the whole historical

---

[1] For *Laudabiliter*, see the critical edition (based on eight manuscript copies of Giraldus Cambrensis, *Expugnatio Hibernica* and three manuscripts of Ralph de Diceto's *Ymagines historiarum*) in *Pontificia Hibernica (i), Medieval Papal Chancery Documents concerning Ireland, 640–1261*, ed. Maurice P. Sheehy (Dublin, 1962), pp. 15–16 no. 4. For both texts, as presented by Giraldus, see *Expugnatio Hibernica; The Conquest of Ireland by Giraldus Cambrensis*, ed. and trans. A. B. Scott and F. X. Martin, Irish Medieval Texts, 1 (Dublin, 1978), pp. 144–47. For a text based on MSS P and R (below, at nn. 143 and 144), see Michael Haren, "*Laudabiliter*: Text and Context," in *Charters and Charter Scholarship in Britain and Ireland*, ed. M. T. Flanagan and J. A. Green (Basingstoke, 2005), pp. 140–63, at 160–63.

picture. What follows is an attempt to sort out the puzzle by reexamining the evidence of the primary sources, the genesis of Henry II's Irish project, and the authenticity of *Laudabiliter* and *Quoniam ea*. It will be argued not only that *Laudabiliter* has been forced into the wrong part of the puzzle but that it was reshaped to fit the picture that Gerald was delineating in his *Expugnatio Hibernica*, and that *Quoniam ea* was confected to make the fitting more exact. And it is further argued that the version of *Laudabiliter* used in Hiberno-English controversies from the mid- to late thirteenth century onwards was ultimately derived not from an official source but from Gerald himself.

The Sources

John of Salisbury

The starting point for any consideration of Adrian IV's grant is John of Salisbury's unambiguous assertion, made in the last chapter of his *Metalogicon*,[2] that it was at his request *(ad preces meas)* that Pope Adrian IV had "granted and given Ireland to the illustrious Henry II king of the English to be held by hereditary right, as his letters testify to this day," since "All islands are said to belong to the Roman Church by ancient right from the donation of Constantine, who established and endowed it"; and also that it was by John's agency that Adrian had sent a "golden ring set with a fine emerald by which investiture of the right to rule in Ireland should be made; and this ring was ordered to be kept in the public treasury until now."[3] Since John was writing

---

[2] *Ioannis Saresberiensis. Metalogicon*, iv. 42, ed. J. B. Hall and K. S. B. Keats-Rohan, *CCCM* 98 (1991), p. 183; cf. the translation (from the earlier edition by Webb) by Daniel D. McGarry, *The Metalogicon of John of Salisbury: A Twelfth-Century Defense of the Verbal and Logical Arts of the Trivium* (Berkeley, 1955; repr. 1962), pp. 274–75. The earliest surviving MS is London, BL Royal MS 13 D. iv (cf. fol. 161), which was copied for Abbot Simon of St. Albans between 1167 and 1183 (cf. fol. iir).

[3] *Metalogicon*, iv. 42 (ed. Hall and Keats-Rohan, p. 183), "Ad preces meas illustri regi Anglorum, Henrico secundo, concessit et dedit Hiberniam iure hereditario possidendam, sicut litterae ipsius testantur in hodiernam diem. Nam omnes insulae de iure antiquo ex donatione Constantini, qui eam fundauit et dotauit, dicuntur ad Romanam Ecclesiam pertinere. Anulum quoque per me transmisit aureum, smaragdo optimo decoratum, quo fieret inuestitura iuris in regenda Hibernia, idemque adhuc anulus in cimiliarchio publico iussus est custodiri."

(in late 1159) within four years of the event and spoke as participant and eyewitness, his evidence must be seriously weighed. The problem is that this description does not square with the text of *Laudabiliter*, which Gerald presents as the *privilegium* obtained by John. For the latter does not "give" or "grant" anything, and there is no mention either of "hereditary right" or of a ring, emerald or otherwise. If John were thinking of *Laudabiliter*, how could he, a highly educated clerk who drafted Archbishop Theobald's legal letters, have transmitted a summary so misleading? Either there was another (lost) letter that corresponded with his description, which Maurice Sheehy argued,[4] or, as I believe, John was guilty of considerable verbal economy, which both amplified the nature of the "concession" and suppressed the conditions attached to it. John's statement cannot be set aside; but it should be interpreted in the context of his own motives in recording the event, as well as in the light of the reconstruction of *Laudabiliter* suggested below. John's purpose in referring to the matter of Ireland was to proclaim the extent of his own influence with the recently deceased Pope Adrian, not to provide a legally accurate summary of the document. He was at pains to point out that it was he who obtained the *litterae*, implying that he was successful where others (members of the mission led by the abbot of St. Albans) were not, and that it was to him that the pope entrusted the emerald ring with which an investiture could be made.

Gerald de Barri (Giraldus Cambrensis)

The second witness to Adrian's grant, Gerald de Barri, provides a very much fuller account of Henry's Irish venture, for he devoted a whole treatise to the Irish conquest. His *Expugnatio Hibernica* was written in the last year of Henry II's life (1188–89) and dedicated to Richard I after July 6, 1189,[5] seventeen to twenty years after the events of 1169–72 and more than thirty years after the events of 1155–56. Gerald could not have been more than nine or ten years old when *Laudabiliter* was supposedly issued. For the story of the conquest itself, however, he relied on information provided by the successful conquerors, especially members of his own family, the Geraldines, who played so distinguished a part in the

---

    [4] Below, at n. 111.
    [5] *Expugnatio* (ed. Scott and Martin), p. 285 n. 2; Michael Richter, *Giraldus Cambrensis* (Aberystwyth, 1976), p. 7.

enterprise. He had first gone to Ireland in 1183, in the company of his brother Philip, to visit his transplanted relatives.[6] He was offered, and rejected, the bishopric of Ferns, but his Irish experience as well as his excellent education and good connections made him an obvious choice to accompany the young Prince John on his ill-omened visit to assume the Lordship of Ireland in 1185. Gerald did not return to England with the prince's entourage; instead he remained on the island for about a year, gathering the material that enabled him to write the *Topographia Hibernica*, which he dedicated to Henry II in *c*. 1186.[7] This was followed not long afterwards by the *Expugnatio Hibernica*, in which he first unveiled *Laudabiliter*, supported by a second papal letter *(Quoniam ea)*, attributed to Alexander III.

Having set out the whole story of the Norman invasions and the king's interventions, Gerald recounts how, following the Council of Cashel (in early 1172),[8] the king sent messengers to the Curia with letters from the archbishops and bishops of Ireland and "sought from Pope Alexander III a privilege [*Quoniam ea*] empowering him, with the pope's full authority and consent, to rule over the Irish people and, as it was very ignorant of the rudiments of the faith, to instruct it in the laws and disciplines of the church according to the usage of the church in England *(iuxta Anglicane ecclesie mores)*."[9] This privilege was then conveyed to Ireland by William FitzAldelin (the king's deputy in Ireland from mid-1173) and Master Nicholas, then prior of the St. Albans dependency of Wallingford, and published at an episcopal council convened for the purpose at Waterford.[10] Read out at the same time was "the other privilege . . . which the king had formerly procured from Alexander's predecessor Adrian through the offices of John of Salisbury, afterwards bishop of Chartres,

---

    [6] Through his mother Angharad (who had married his father, William de Barri), he was a grandson of Gerald of Windsor and Nest, daughter of Rhys ap Tewdwr, the ancestors of the Geraldines: Richter, *Giraldus Cambrensis*, pp. 4, 6–7.

    [7] Ibid., pp. 6–7.

    [8] For which see J. A. Watt, *The Church and the Two Nations in Medieval Ireland* (Cambridge, 1970), pp. 38–39 n. 2 (b); M. T. Flanagan, "Henry II, the Council of Cashel and the Irish Bishops," *Peritia: Journal of the Medieval Academy of Ireland* 10 (1996), 184–211.

    [9] *Expugnatio* (ed. Scott and Martin), pp. 142–43. No such phrase occurs in either *Laudabiliter* or *Quoniam ea*.

    [10] *Expugnatio* (ed. Scott and Martin), pp. 142–43. For FitzAldelin, see *Expugnatio*, p. 317 n. 189, pp. 330–31 n. 294.

who had been sent to Rome for this purpose. By John's hand the aforesaid Pope Adrian also sent the king of England the present of a gold ring as a sign of his investiture, and this had been immediately deposited with the privilege in the archives at Winchester."[11] In this awkward way the chronicler introduced both the "privilegium Adriani pape" (*Laudabiliter*) and the "privilegium Alexandri Terch" (*Quoniam ea*).[12] Both documents were, therefore, as Gerald tells it, derived from the royal government, published together in Ireland by royal agents on royal authority, and thus integral to the legitimization of Henry's rule in the island.

Thus did Gerald put considerable flesh on the bare bones of John of Salisbury's brief note. Not only did he provide a good purpose for the king's intervention in Ireland, he supplied what he claimed was the text of the original papal "grant," together with a confirmatory bull of Alexander III. The difficulties with this plausible account are that neither letter is dated, that *Laudabiliter* does not match John's description of the bull he says he obtained and, even more seriously, that the Alexandrine letter is a complete fabrication. Not only does it break one of the fundamental rules of papal diplomatic by addressing the king in the second-person plural (instead of the singular), its form and content are contradicted by not one but three genuine letters from Alexander III. These "September letters" were issued together at Tusculum (Frascati) on September 20, 1172, brought back from the papal Curia by the royal clerk, Archdeacon Ralph of Llandaff,[13] transmitted to Ireland, and published at Waterford. As at least one scholar has remarked, the demonstrable falsity of *Quoniam ea*

---

[11] Ibid., pp. 144–45. The dependence of this account on John's is self-evident, although John does not say where the letter (as distinct from the ring) was lodged, and he did not identify Winchester.

[12] *Expugnatio* (ed. Scott and Martin), pp. 143–47.

[13] *Pontificia Hibernica (i)*, pp. 19–23 nos. 5–7; see below, at nn. 189–91. W. L. Warren (*Henry II* [London, 1973], p. 198) implies some diplomatic dexterity on the part of Alexander III in the light of the recent murder of Thomas Becket (December 29, 1170), but the "September letters" were issued fully four months after Henry II's formal reconciliation at Avranches on May 21, 1172, and almost three weeks after Alexander II's acknowledgement of the king's submission, issued on September 2, 1172: Anne J. Duggan, "*Ne in dubium*: The official Record of Henry II's Reconciliation at Avranches (May 21, 1172)," *EHR* 115 (2000), 643–58. Henry was therefore in good standing with the Church when Ralph of Llandaff arrived at the Curia with the evidence of Henry's lawful acquisition of Ireland and his patronage of reform.

throws the question of *Laudabiliter*'s own authenticity into sharp focus;[14] but it also raises the more fundamental question of Gerald's reliability.

In his masterly assessment of Giraldus Cambrensis as historian, F. X. Martin discussed the authenticity of the eight texts that are presented verbatim in the *Expugnatio*. There are four "official" documents (*Laudabiliter*; *Quoniam ea*; Henry II's letter encouraging support for Diarmait Mac Murchada's attempt to win back the kingdom of Leinster;[15] the decrees of the second council of Cashel, 1172[16]) and four "private" letters (Diarmait Mac Murchada to Richard FitzGilbert de Clare [= Strongbow], Earl of Strigoil; Ruaidr' Ua Conchobair to Diarmait Mac Murchada; Strongbow to Henry II; Basilia, wife of Raymond le Gros to her husband). Not one of the eight survives Professor Martin's scrutiny unscathed. Not one of them is thought to be an accurate text, and six at least are

---

[14] Watt, *Church and Two Nations*, pp. 36–38 n. 3. This general consensus has been challenged by Walter Ullmann ("Alexander III and the Conquest of Ireland: A Note on the Background," in *Rolando Bandinelli Papa Alessandro III*, ed. F. Liotta [Siena, 1986], pp. 369–87, at 372); and Haren, "*Laudabiliter*: Text and Context," pp. 153–54. Dr. Haren recognizes the formal falsity of *Quoniam ea*, but he argues that it was "a drafted confirmation that it was intended to impetrate" from Alexander III (although it never was). But why should the king have considered seeking confirmation of *Laudabiliter* in 1173, when he had obtained three genuine papal letters in September 1172 on the basis of the written acknowledgement of his lordship that his envoys had secured from the Irish bishops at Cashel in 1172? And why, having obtained the genuine letters, would he have caused a version of *Laudabiliter* and the "draft" *Quoniam ea* to be read out at Waterford in 1173?

[15] Martin's criticisms (*Expugnatio*, ed. Scott and Martin, p. 280) are wholly convincing, but Warren (*Henry II*, pp. 198–99), writing before the new edition of the *Expugnatio* was published, did not question its authenticity, and quoted it in full. Its unusual diplomatic features (use of the second person plural and "bizarre" address "uniuersis fidelibus suis Anglis, Normannis, Gualensibus et Scottis cunctisque nationibus sue ditioni subditis"), among other peculiar features, have led Professor Vincent to doubt its authenticity.

[16] From the transmission of seven of the clauses in the thirteenth-century *Annals of St. Mary's Abbey* in Dublin (*Chartularies of St. Mary's Abbey, Dublin: With the Register of Its House at Dunbrody, and Annals of Ireland*, ed. John T. Gilbert, 2 vols., RS 80 [London, 1884], 2:263–64), Aubrey Gwynn (*The Irish Church in the 11th and 12th Centuries*, ed. Gerard O'Brien [Blackrock, 1992], pp. 306–8) argued for the authenticity of Giraldus's text in *Expugnatio*, i. 35 (ed. Scott and Martin, pp. 98–102), but, with some omissions, the version in the *Annals*, and much else besides, was derived from Gerald. Gwynn rejected the final sentence of the *Expugnatio* text ("Dignum etenim et iustissimum est . . . abiere"), however, as "pure Giraldus."

deemed to be out-and-out concoctions.[17] Nevertheless, having been convinced by the skillful arguments advanced long ago by Kate Norgate and J. F. O'Doherty,[18] Martin held back from applying the full logic of his conclusions to *Laudabiliter*, contenting himself with the statement, "I doubt if Giraldus's version is fully accurate. I suggest no more than a doubt,"[19] and, in the light of the arguments presented by Michael Richter in 1979, he withdrew further in his splendid chapter on Diarmait Mac Murchada in the *New History of Ireland* (1987).[20] Richter's arguments are not watertight, however.[21] Meanwhile, Martin's earlier conclusions on the unreliability of most if not all of Gerald's *Expugnatio* documents retain their serious implications for the reliability of his text of *Laudabiliter*. Its authority is fatally flawed if it, like the other letters and documents transmitted by him, is no more than an inventive chronicler's construct, akin to the dramatic speeches put into the mouths of the leading players in the conquest of Ireland,[22] or if the text has been falsified in some way. Unlike his contemporaries, Roger of Howden and Ralph de Diceto, he was not an assiduous seeker after official or epistolary records. His sources were oral and literary; and he was much influenced by the "prophecies of Merlin," that is Merlin Ambrosius, which he had garnered from their propagator Geoffrey of Monmouth, and also by the Welsh vernacular version of another Merlin, Celidonius or Silvestris, which he claimed to have translated and which was to furnish the never completed third book of the *Expugnatio*.[23] Gerald's aim was not to deceive, but to give verisimilitude

---

17 *Expugnatio* (ed. Scott and Martin), pp. 278–82. The "rejected" are: *Quoniam ea*, Henry's letter allowing Mac Murchada to recruit, and the four "private" letters; questionable accuracy: *Laudabiliter* and the Cashel decrees. See also, *Expugnatio*, p. 322 n. 231, 232.

18 Kate Norgate, "The Bull *Laudabiliter*," *EHR* 8 (1893), 18–52; J. F. O'Doherty, "Rome and the Anglo-Norman Invasion of Ireland," *Irish Ecclesiastical Record* 42 (1933), 131–45.

19 *Expugnatio* (ed. Scott and Martin), p. 279; cf. *Expugnatio*, p. 323 n. 233.

20 M. Richter, "Giraldiana," *Irish Historical Studies* 21 (1979), 422–37, at 430–31; F. X. Martin, "Diarmait Mac Murchada and the Coming of the Anglo-Normans," in *A New History of Ireland*, vol. 2, *Medieval Ireland 1169–1534*, ed. Art Cosgrove (Oxford, 1987), pp. 43–66, esp. 57–58.

21 See below, at n. 195.

22 "They are not to be taken seriously" (*Expugnatio*, ed. Scott and Martin, p. 278).

23 *Expugnatio* (ed. Scott and Martin), pp. lxiv–lxviii.

and immediacy to his narrative: the documents, letters, and speeches are part of that dramatic storytelling.[24]

It would be easy, in the light of this evidence, to dismiss *Laudabiliter* out of hand, were it not for the fact that Gerald clung to it until his death. He reproduced *Laudabiliter* in two later works (*De instructione principum* and *De rebus a se gestis*),[25] even though he was persuaded by critics to suppress the pseudo-Alexandrine *Quoniam ea,* which was duly omitted from the revised version of the *Expugnatio* and also from *De rebus a se gestis.*[26] More than that, in his second preface to the *Expugnatio,* addressed to King John in 1209–10, Gerald spoke of the *Privilegium* and *licentia,* still to be found in the royal archives at Winchester, whose terms he urged the king to fulfil out of piety for his father.[27] If *Laudabiliter* were a complete forgery, would Gerald have appealed to it in an address to Henry's son? Two answers may be proposed: either that *Laudabiliter* was indeed a fake, constructed, perhaps, as a stylistic exercise by some unknown student of papal *dictamen,* which Gerald believed to be the privilege described by John of Salisbury;[28] or, that *Laudabiliter* is not *falsa* but *ficta*—not fake but falsified. Either conclusion would go far towards explaining both the unsatisfactory nature of the text and Gerald's loyalty to it, but the balance of the evidence tends towards the latter rather than the former.[29]

---

[24] Lynn H. Nelson (*The Normans in South Wales, 1090–1191* [Austin and London, 1966], p. 145) called Giraldus "a masterful romanticist."

[25] *De principis instructione,* ii. 19 (*Giraldi Cambrensis Opera,* vols. 1–4, ed. J. S. Brewer; vols. 5–7, ed. James F. Dimock; vol. 8, ed. George F. Warner, RS 21 [London, 1861–91], 8:196–97); *De rebus a se gestis,* xi (*Opera,* 1 [1861], pp. 62–63).

[26] In *De principis instructione,* ii. 19 (*Opera,* 8:197), composed *c.* 1215–16, Giraldus wrote revealingly that "others denied that it [*Quoniam ea*] had ever been obtained (*ab aliis autem unquam impetratum fuisse negatur*)"; cf. *Expugnatio,* ed. Scott and Martin, pp. lix–lxi; *De rebus a se gestis,* ii. 11 (*Opera* 1: 62–63).

[27] *Expugnatio* (ed. Scott and Martin), pp. 263, 323 n. 233. Gerald had some access to royal documents. He inserted a copy of Henry II's Waltham will into his *De principis instructione* (ii. 17: *Opera* 8:191–93). Drawn up in triplicate in early 1182, one copy was, like *Laudabiliter,* kept at Winchester. I am grateful to Professor Nicholas Vincent for this information, and for communicating his opinion that Giraldus had access to "official" sources.

[28] As proposed long ago by P. Scheffer-Boichorst, "Hat Papst Hadrian IV. zu Gunsten des englischen Königs über Irland verfügt?" in *Gesammelte Schriften von Paul Scheffer-Boichorst,* i, [Eberings] Historische Studien, 32 (Berlin, 1903), pp. 132–57, esp. 154, 157.

[29] Below, after n. 133. For the distinction between *ficta* and *falsa,* see *Original*

Ralph de Diceto

A second twelfth-century chronicler transmitted the text of *Laudabiliter.* Ralph de Diceto, the dean of St. Paul's (London) and author of one of the best chronicles of the age, put a copy of *Laudabiliter* in his *Ymagines historiarum.* But it appears there entirely without context. Diceto inserts it, without a single word of explanation or comment, as the very last item in "1154," immediately after a brief record, taken from Robert of Torigny, of Louis VII's pilgrimage to Santiago de Compostela, although the *capitula* that precede the work transmit the comment, "Adrianus papa litteras novo regi direxit (Pope Adrian sent letters to the new king)."[30] The entire record for 1154 comprises seven events, of which only three short notices seem original to Diceto, the remainder being compiled from Robert of Torigny's *Chronica,* Ivo of Chartres' *Panormia,* Ailred of Rievaulx's *De genealogia regum Anglorum,* and *Laudabiliter* itself.[31] Indeed, Pope Adrian's letter constitutes almost one third of the entry for the year. Diceto's learned editor, Bishop Stubbs, thought it quite likely that Diceto derived his text independently of Gerald,[32] although he allowed the possibility that the opposite was the case.[33] That possibility is in fact a strong probability. As we have seen, Gerald wrote his *Expugnatio* in 1188–89. Diceto did not begin his historical work until some time in the 1180s; the *Abbreviationes chronicorum,* which preface the *Ymagines historiarum,* were completed after 1193, for the list of archbishops of Canterbury ends with Hubert Walter, who did not attain that rank until May 30, 1193;[34] and the two earliest surviving manuscripts end in January 1198 and May 1199, respectively.[35]

Papal Documents in England and Wales from the Accession of Pope Innocent III to the Death of Pope Benedict XI (1198–1304), ed. J. E. Sayers (Oxford, 1999), p. lxxiv.

[30] *Radulfi de Diceto decani Lundoniensis opera historica* [= Diceto], ed. W. Stubbs, 2 vols., RS 68/i–ii (London, 1876), 1:268; cf. London, BL, Royal MS 13 E. vi (fol. 55rb–va), written for St. Albans, *c.* 1200, before Diceto's death. Copied from London, Lambeth Palace, MS 8, Royal 13 E. vi was used successively by Roger of Wendover and Matthew Paris.

[31] Diceto, 1:297–301.

[32] This view is also held by Watt, *Church and Two Nations,* p. 36 n. 3.

[33] Diceto, 1:300 n. 1.

[34] Diceto, 1:17. Hubert died in 1205.

[35] London, BL, MS Cotton Claudius E. iii (MS B in the Stubbs edn); London, Lambeth Palace, MS 8 (MS A in the Stubbs edition). Both were products of the St. Paul's scriptorium: cf. Diceto, 2:159, 166.

It is perfectly possible that Diceto had seen Gerald's *Expugnatio* before the *Ymagines* were completed. His own account of Henry's Irish visit combines Gerald's emphasis on the introduction of English ecclesiastical customs to Ireland[36] with additional details from Roger of Howden's *Gesta*.[37] But he did not link the Irish invasion with *Laudabiliter*. Instead, the letter was used, without comment, to expand the rather thin record of the first year of the king's reign; and it was not associated with any particular action or consequence.

Peter of Blois

Further evidence of knowledge of the bull in the twelfth century was presented by the late Walter Ullmann, who drew attention to its presence among the letters of Master Peter of Blois (d. 1211), who served three successive archbishops of Canterbury from *c.* 1175 to 1205.[38] More important, though, he was, one might say, loosely attached to the royal court during the same period and had also served as secretary to Archbishop Rotrou of Rouen *c.* 1172–*c.* 1175.[39] More than Giraldus Cambrensis, therefore, he had access to archiepiscopal and royal archives, and the presence of *Laudabiliter* among his letters could be evidence of early circulation outside the narrative sources. The letter does indeed occur in the vulgate edition of Peter's letters reprinted by Migne in *Patrologia Latina*, but it was unknown to early copyists, and occurs only in Cambridge, Trinity College, MS B. I. 18, fols. 59vb–60ra, no. 97, which transmits a truncated text.[40] Its unique occurrence there, in only one, very late

---

[36] Diceto, 1:350–51; cf. *Expugnatio* (ed. Scott and Martin), p. 100, lines 47–48.

[37] Compare Diceto, 1:348 and 350–51 with *Gesta regis Henrici secundi Benedicti abbatis*, ed. W. Stubbs, 2 vols., RS, 49/i–ii (London, 1867), 1:24–30.

[38] Ullmann, "Alexander III and the Conquest of Ireland," 376 n. 19.

[39] Lena Wahlgren, *The Letter Collections of Peter of Blois*, Studia Graeca et Latina Gothoburgensia, 58 (Göteburg, 1993), p. 11. For the adjustment to the generally received date of 1212 for Peter's death, see *The Later Letters of Peter of Blois*, ed. Elizabeth Revell, Auctores Britannici Medii Aevi, 13 (Oxford, 1993), p. xxix: 30 Nov. 1211.

[40] The Trinity College MS lacks one clause *per homoioleuton* (Christus illuxit ... ad ius) and suspends the transcription at "ecclesie Romane," omitting "de singulis domibus ... in seculis obtinere." These details are obscured by *PL* 207, no. 226, which refers the reader to Adrian's letters in *PL* 188. For its place in Peter's letter collections, see E. S. Cohn, "The Manuscript Evidence for the Letters of Peter of Blois," *EHR* 41 (1926), 43–60, at 50, 55; Wahlgren, *Letter Collections of Peter of Blois*, pp. 27, 197 no. 51.

(fifteenth-century) transcription, among more than two hundred manuscripts of Peter's letters, suggests later interpolation; but even if it had appeared in the early manuscripts, Peter's known propensity for literary invention would have rendered it suspect. The latest scholar to wrestle with the complexities of the Blois letters has described Peter's collections as "a mixture of the genuine and the literary";[41] and the composition of a pseudo-bull would have been well within the capacities of a man with Peter's literary skills. Moreover, his service of Archbishop Rotrou had brought him into close contact with the man who, as bishop of Évreux, had obtained *Satis laudabiliter*, the rescript that could have formed the basis for the construction of a fake.[42] Peter could certainly have concocted such a letter, but there is no evidence that he did.

The St. Albans Tradition

In the thirteenth century, *Laudabiliter* re-emerged in the St. Albans historical tradition in Roger of Wendover's *Flores historiarum*,[43] from which it passed to Matthew Paris, who placed it *sub anno* 1155 in his *Chronica majora*[44] and its abbreviation, the *Historia Anglorum*.[45] The textual connection between these works is easily established, since all three transpose the sentence "Sane omnes insule . . . non est dubium pertinere" to before the final clause, "Si ergo quod . . . obtinere" and omit "Unde . . . exigendum." In all three, moreover, the letter is set in the context of Henry II's plans for the reform of the barbarous Irish, although Matthew accentuated that aspect by inserting even stronger terms into his adaptation of Wendover's contextual narrative.[46] Whether this St. Albans segment

---

41 Wahlgren, *Letter Collections of Peter of Blois*, p. 16.

42 Below, n. 112.

43 Roger of Wendover, *Flores historiarum*, ed. Henry G. Hewlett, 3 vols., RS 84 (London, 1886–89), 1 (1886), pp. 11–13.

44 Matthew Paris, *Chronica majora*, ed. Henry R. Luard, 7 vols., RS 57 (London, 1872–83), 2 (1874), pp. 210–11.

45 Matthew Paris, *Historia Anglorum*, ed. F. Madden, 3 vols., RS 44 (London, 1866–69), 1 (1866), pp. 304–5.

46 Where Wendover had written "Hiberniam insulam hostiliter intrare et terram subjugare (to enter the island of Ireland in hostile fashion and conquer the land)," Matthew wrote "Hiberniam insulam intrare, et terram illam, locum videlicet horroris et vastae solitudinis, utpote limbum mundi, sibi et Dei cultui subjugare

of the *Laudabiliter* story is independent of the Cambrensis–Diceto tradition discussed above is not easy to determine. The rearrangement of the text in the former might be an argument in favor of independence, but thirteenth-century compilers were not immune from the tendency to improve their sources, and the repositioning of the "Sane omnes insule" clause certainly improves the structure of the text. Derivation from Diceto is a strong probability, since St. Albans had a copy of Diceto,[47] and Wendover based much of the early part of his *Flores* on Ralph's *Ymagines*. The little contextual commentary, however, seems to be his own; but it adds nothing that could not be derived from the letter itself.

Yet what one may call "pure" St. Albans tradition adds an illuminating twist to the story. The *Gesta abbatum Sancti Albani*, compiled by Matthew Paris, but exploiting the work of Adam the Cellarer (*c.* 1140–67 x 76), and appended among the *Additamenta* to his *Chronica Majora* in one manuscript, describes the triumphant visit of Abbot Robert of St. Albans to Pope Adrian at Benevento in 1155–56.[48] The principal achievement of the mission, from the point of view of St. Albans, was the abbot's acquisition of at least thirteen privileges and letters of commendation, which proclaimed the abbey's primacy among English Benedictine houses, reinforced its independence from all episcopal authority (except the pope's), and confirmed to the abbot the right to wear pontifical insignia.[49] But Robert had travelled to the papal Curia not only on his own account. As the *Gesta* tell it, Robert was the head of the royal embassy that had been sent to the Curia in October 1155 "to promote certain difficult royal matters *(quaedam ardua negotia regalia . . . expedirent)*."[50] Although the business is not specified, it is probable that, as the Wendover-Paris introduction to *Laudabiliter* states, the acquisition of papal authority for an

---

(to enter the island of Ireland and subject that land—manifestly a dreadful place of desolate wilderness, since it was the edge of the world—to himself and the worship of God)." Such additions were characteristic of what Richard Vaughan *(Matthew Paris* [Cambridge, 1958; repr. 1979], p. 32) called Matthew's "usually colourful and tendentious" "improvement" of his source.

[47] One of the best witnesses to Diceto's works, London, Brit. Libr., MS Royal 13 E. vi (*c.* 1200), was written for St. Albans, and it contains marginal notes in a hand attributed to Matthew Paris.

[48] For discussion of Paris's use of the "ancient roll," see Vaughan, *Matthew Paris,* pp. 182–85, esp. 183.

[49] *PUE,* iii, 234–54 nos. 100–110, 112–13.

[50] *Gesta abbatum S. Albani,* 1:126.

Irish venture was one of its objectives;[51] but whereas the abbot obtained a whole dossier of privileges for himself and his abbey, he was, if John of Salisbury's statement is true, less successful on the king's behalf in respect of Ireland, for John attributed the impetration of the *litterae* to his own *preces*. But what would have led the recently crowned English king to consider such a venture?

The Genesis of Henry II's Intervention in Ireland

The particular circumstances of Henry II's approach to Adrian IV have generated considerable controversy, since some[52] of the leading experts on Anglo-Irish affairs have concluded that Henry had no particular interest in Ireland in 1155–56—and indeed, that the need to establish his authority forcefully throughout his diverse lordships, both in England and across the "Angevin empire," would have been a considerable disincentive. John of Salisbury's proud but enigmatic boast that he had obtained the papal "grant" of Ireland has caused some scholars so to concentrate on his possible motivation that they have transferred the initiative from Henry to Archbishop Theobald of Canterbury and transformed the venture from a secular plan for conquest into a clerical scheme to establish (or re-establish) Canterbury's primacy over the Irish Church. This line of argument has allowed the creation of a Canterbury hypothesis, in which the idea for an Irish domination was traced to Archbishop Theobald, anxious, it is said, to recover Canterbury's jurisdiction over the *ecclesia Hibernica,* recently destroyed by the legislation of the legatine council held at Kells-Mellifont in 1152, which had laid down the structure of an independent Irish Church.[53] John of Salisbury was the agent (if not the Machiavellian originator) of the plan;[54] *Laudabiliter* was the "privilege"

---

51 The other was dispensation from the oath he had taken in the presence of his father's dead body to grant Anjou to his younger brother, Geoffrey: John Gillingham, *The Angevin Empire* (London, 1984), 25.

52 Though not all: see Graeme J. White, *Restoration and Reform 1153–1165: Recovery from Civil War in England* (Cambridge, 2000), pp. 4, 5.

53 Watt, *Church and Two Nations,* p. 28 and n. 3.

54 O'Doherty, "Rome and the Anglo-Norman Invasion," p. 140; O'Doherty, "St. Laurence O'Toole and the Anglo-Norman Invasion," *Irish Ecclesiastical Record* 50 (1937), 449–77, 600–25 at 459, 601; Warren, *Henry II,* pp. 195–96; Michael Richter, "The First Century of Anglo-Irish Relations," *History* 59 (1974), 195–210, esp. 200,

that he obtained; his subsequent disgrace in mid-1156[55] was the direct consequence of the king's displeasure at the tenor of that letter;[56] and it was that letter, allegedly lodged in the royal treasury in Winchester, that Gerald inserted into three of his historical works at the end of the century.[57] Skillfully marshaled by experts, the story is plausible enough; but its neat linking of events and texts is full of holes.

Despite its constant and confident reiteration by distinguished historians, there is no evidence to show that Theobald of Canterbury was particularly concerned to establish primacy over the Irish Church. Canterbury's principal aims, from the days of Lanfranc, had been to define its supremacy, first over York, and then over the Church in Wales. The title (used in six professions of the period) of *Britanniarum primas* (primate of the British isles)[58] could perhaps be interpreted to include Ireland,[59] but it had last been used in 1108, and it was generally replaced, from Anselm's pontificate onwards, with the more restricted *totius Britannie*

206–8; Richter, "Giraldiana," pp. 430–31; Martin, "Diarmait Mac Murchada and the Coming of the Anglo-Normans," pp. 56–57; Marie Therese Flanagan, *Irish Society, Anglo-Norman Settlers, Angevin Kingship: Interactions in Ireland in the Late Twelfth Century* (Oxford, 1989), pp. 7–55, esp. 51–55; R. R. Davies, *Dominion and Conquest* (Oxford, 1990), p. 67. Warren's embrace of the clerical plot theory was part of his strategy to exonerate Henry "from the charge of acquisitive ambition" in respect of Ireland (*Henry II*, p. 206).

[55] *The Letters of John of Salisbury*, volume 1, *The Early Letters (= JohnS)*, ed. and trans. W. J. Millor and H. E. Butler, Nelsons Medieval Texts (London, 1955; repr., Oxford, 1986), nos. 18–21, 27–28, 30–31; cf. 257–58.

[56] This link is specifically made by Millor and Brooke, *JohnS*, 1:257–58: "John may have owed his disgrace to the readiness with which he fell in with the Pope's arrangements" (p. 257), following Giles Constable, "The Alleged Disgrace of John of Salisbury in 1159," *EHR* 69 (1954), 67–76; cf. Klaus Guth, *Johannes von Salisbury (1115/20–1180). Studien zur Kirchen-, Kultur- und Sozialgeschichte Westeuropas im 12. Jahrhundert* (St. Ottilien, 1978), pp. 132–35.

[57] *Expugnatio* (ed. Scott and Martin), pp. 144–46; *De principis instructione*, ii. 19 (*Opera*, 8:96–7); *De rebus a se gestis*, xi (*Opera*, 1:62–63).

[58] *Canterbury Professions*, ed. M. Richter, Canterbury and York Society, 67 (Torquay, 1973), pp. 29–31, 33 nos. 36, 38, 40, 41, 47 (to Lanfranc); p. 35 no. 55 (to Anselm). For alternative primatial formulae under Lanfranc, see *totius Brittannice regionis primas* (pp. 28–29 no. 35); *primas totius Britannice insule* (pp. 32 no. 44); and *Brittaniarum primas* (p. 33 no. 47). Donatus did not use the phrase in 1085 (p. 31 no. 42). Cf. pp. xciii–xcvi.

[59] Flanagan, *Irish Society*, pp. 41–42. Cf. Gwynn, *The Irish Church*, pp. 68–83, "Lanfranc and the Irish Church."

primas (primate of all Britain).[60] Moreover, the evidence for active pursuit of primacy over the whole "British Isles" is somewhat slight. It is true that whenever an Irish bishop sought consecration at the hands of an archbishop of Canterbury, he was obliged to make a profession of obedience; but such approaches were few in number, geographically isolated, and discontinuous. There were, in fact, only six consecrations of Irish bishops at Canterbury in the whole period 1074–1140 (four for Dublin, one each for Waterford and Limerick), and they were all at the request of Irish petitioners, and explained not by Canterbury's claims to primacy over the Irish Church, but by special circumstances within the island.[61] If Ireland had fallen into Canterbury's lap, there would no doubt have been rejoicing among the monks at Christ Church, but it is difficult to see that any archbishop of Canterbury, after Lanfranc, made much effort in that direction, despite Eadmer's conviction that Canterbury was "mother of the whole of England, Scotland, and Ireland, and also of the adjacent islands" and his ascription to Anselm of the claim that the archbishop of Canterbury was "primas . . . totius Angliae, Scottiae, Hiberniae, et adjacentium insularum."[62]

Marie Therese Flanagan's splendid study on the relations among Irish society, Anglo-Norman settlers, and Angevin kingship provides evidence more for the political connections between southern Ireland (especially the Hiberno-Norse) and the Anglo/Cambro-Normans than for Canterbury's claims; and her extensive investigation of "Canterbury and the Irish Church" establishes no more than an intermittent interest on the part of Canterbury's archbishops in the twelfth century. Significantly, the impetus for the consecration of Irish bishops in England came not from Canterbury, but from secular and/or separatist elements in that region, including the Ua Briain kings[63] and the Hiberno-Norse city of Dublin.[64] She assumes

---

[60] *Canterbury Professions*, pp. 34–37, nos. 50a, 50b, 51, 52, 53, 54 (Waterford), 56, 57, 58, 59, 60, 61. There is only one example of *Britanniarum primas* in an Anselmian profession: see p. 35 no. 55 (1107).

[61] *Canterbury Professions*, pp. xciii–xcvi, 29, 31, 34–35, 39 nos. 36, 42, 51, 54, 69, 81; Flanagan, *Irish Society*, pp. 18–22, 30–33; Flanagan, "Henry II," pp. 196–97. For the wider context of the diversity of Irish contact with England and the Continent, see Martin, "Diarmait Mac Murchada and the Coming of the Anglo-Normans."

[62] Eadmer, *Historia Novorum in Anglia*, ed. Martin Rule, RS 81 (London, 1884), pp. 26, 189; cf. Watt, *Church and Two Nations*, pp. 217–25.

[63] Flanagan, "Henry II," pp. 196–97.

[64] Flanagan, *Irish Society*, pp. 18–22, 29–33.

that it was Canterbury interests that prevented the conferment of *pallia* on Armagh and Cashel in 1140; but a far stronger case could be made for the opposition of Diarmait Mac Murchada and the Dubliners, since the proposed metropolitan structure implied the suppression of the (Hiberno-Norse) bishopric of Dublin and its amalgamation with Glendalough, and there was considerable disaffection between Dublin and Armagh.[65] Indeed, as her account of the matter demonstrates, it was precisely such opposition that had impelled Bishop-elect Gréne to seek consecration in Canterbury in 1121 (with the consequence that the archbishop of Armagh administered the see for a number of years); and the next (and last) Irish candidate for consecration, Patricius of Limerick (1140), was the product of a disputed election, and he seems to have remained in England.[66] Some time in the following nine years, however, agreement was reached within the Irish Church, and in 1151 four *pallia* were requested (for Armagh, Cashel, Tuam, and, importantly, Dublin, which thereby began its progressive supercession of Glendalough), and delivered by Cardinal John Paparo in 1152.[67] Although Dr. Flanagan implies that there was opposition to the Irish segment of his legation, the evidence is of the thinnest.[68] The only chronicler to consider the creation of the four Irish metropolitans detrimental to Canterbury's ancient rights was Robert of Torigny,[69] but he made no connection between the Paparo legation and Henry's invasion plans. Motivation for the venture was placed in an entirely secular context: the proposal was Henry's and the opposition the Empress Matilda's. Ralph of Diceto, the constitutionally minded dean of St. Paul's, merely recorded the results of the mission to Ireland in a wholly neutral manner, with no reference to Canterbury's claims.[70]

---

[65] This followed from the decisions of the Council of Rath Breasail (1111): Watt, *Church and Two Nations*, pp. 15–19 and map 1. There were to be two metropolitans, Armagh, as primate, and Cashel.

[66] Flanagan, *Irish Society*, pp. 29–32.

[67] Watt, *Church and Two Nations*, pp. 28–31 and map 2.

[68] Flanagan, *Irish Society*, pp. 36–38.

[69] Cf. below, n. 97.

[70] Diceto, 1:295: "Johannes Papiro cardinalis, legatione fungens in Hyberniam, quatuor ibi constituit archiepiscopos, qui dum transitum habuisset per Angliam fidelitatem juravit regi Stephano (Cardinal John Paparo, discharging a legation in Ireland, established four archbishops there; as he passed through England, he swore fealty to King Stephen)." According to John of Hexham's continuation of Symeon of Durham, *Historia regum* (ed. Thomas Arnold, 2 vols., RS 75 [London, 1882–85],

More significant still, John of Salisbury—who had been a frequent visitor to the papal court between 1150 and 1153,[71] who had met and did not trust John Paparo, and who had seen the copy of the decrees of the council of Kells-Mellifont, which the legate had brought back with him and deposited in the papal archives (then in S. Giovanni in Laterano)[72]— made no adverse comment at all on the Irish mission, either in his letters, or anywhere else in his voluminous writings between 1153 and 1159, or in his *Historia Pontificalis*, which may have been completed as late as 1167,[73] although he did record the cardinal's support for the elevation of St. Andrews in Scotland.[74] Given that John was Archbishop Theobald's principal secretary and legal adviser, and in close touch both with what was happening at the papal court and with the thinking at Canterbury, such silence implies indifference on Canterbury's part to the formal organization of the Irish Church. The same silence extends to Archbishop Theobald himself, who raised no recorded objection to the Kells-Mellifont settlement.[75] Dr. Flanagan's conclusion, that "If it was Canterbury that had proposed a conquest of Ireland in order to associate the king of England with its attempts to re-establish its links with the Irish Church, which had been terminated by the synod of Kells, then the plan had backfired,"[76] indicates her own hesitation on the question.

2:326, 227), Paparo refused to take any oath and went by ship from Flanders to Tynmouth and thence to the court of King David of Scotland, who gave him safe passage to Ireland; cf. John of Salisbury, *Historia Pontificalis*, ed. and trans. Marjorie Chibnall (London, 1956; revised repr. Oxford, 1986), 71–72.

[71] *JohnS*, 1:253–55.

[72] *Historia Pontificalis*, pp. 6, 12, 71–72.

[73] Cf. Marjorie Chibnall's foreword to the 1986 edition.

[74] *Historia Pontificalis*, p. 72, "... he ... promised that he would persuade the lord pope to grant the pallium to the bishop of St. Andrews, so that his see might become the metropolitan of Scotland, Orkney and the adjacent islands. For, although from the time of Pope Calixtus, the archbishop of York should, according to his privileges, have presided over them, the Scots refused to obey him."

[75] Although he had ample opportunity. John of Salisbury was at the Curia at least three times during the critical period 1150–53: between Nov. 1150 and summer 1151 (at Ferentino); in spring 1152 (at Segni); and, during Anastasius IV's brief papacy, in Dec. 1153, at Rome: *JohnS*, 1:255.

[76] Flanagan, *Irish Society*, pp. 53–54.

If the "Canterbury hypothesis"[77] is a weak link in the chain of cause and consequence, the attempt to link John of Salisbury's disfavor with the grant secured from Pope Adrian is even weaker. John's statement in the *Metalogicon* has the character of self-congratulation, inserted to demonstrate his influence with the pope whose early death had deprived him of great expectations.[78] The implication is that *his* prayers (*preces meas*) had been successful where others (Henry II's embassy) had failed, and that *he* had brought back the emerald ring, which was deposited in the treasury. Had that letter led to his disgrace in 1156, one might have expected less self-congratulation. In fact, there is no evidence to link the one to the other. Indeed, in his various letters complaining at the time about his disgrace to Pope Adrian, Peter of Celle, Master Ernulf (keeper of the royal seal), and the king's chancellor, Thomas Becket, he made not the slightest allusion to the Irish affair. The most explicit reference to the cause of the king's displeasure is in *Occasionem scribendi*, written confidentially to his closest friend, Peter, abbot of the Benedictine house of Montier-la-Celle near Troyes. "If you ask the reason," he wrote, "perhaps I have favoured him more than was just, and worked for his advancement with greater vigour than I should; for I sighed for this with all my heart's longing, namely that I might behold him whom I deemed to be kept in exile by the malice of Fortune, reigning by God's mercy on the throne of his fathers, and giving laws to peoples and nations."[79] This could be read as an allusion to working for the Irish grant, as Constable thought,[80] but it is much more likely to refer to John's earlier support, with Archbishop Theobald, for the Angevin succession to King Stephen.

The passage in any case is an ironic thrust against the devious Arnulf, bishop of Lisieux, named in a slightly later letter to Pope Adrian as the man who had incited the king against him: "He has heaped up the king's indignation against my poor self to such an extent that the king himself has denounced me both to the archbishop of Canterbury and to his

---

[77] Haren, "*Laudabiliter*: Text and Context," p. 152: "The 'Canterbury hypothesis' has always had the instability of an inverted pyramid."

[78] That John was hopeful of some preferment is suggested by his reminding the pope "for I continually recall with joy and exultation the words which proceeded from your lips, when at Ferentino [probably winter 1150–51] you gave me your own ring and belt as a pledge of things to come" (*JohnS*, 1:90 and n. 1).

[79] *JohnS*, 1:31.

[80] Constable, "Alleged Disgrace," p. 75.

chancellor[81] for abasing the royal dignity."[82] Such an accusation was rich, coming from a man who had opposed the Angevins, even to the extent of challenging the legitimacy of Matilda's marriage to Geoffrey of Anjou at the Second Lateran Council in 1139.[83] Whichever "work" John had in mind, however, he categorically rejected it as the cause of his disgrace a couple of sentences later:

> This is not the fault of which I am accused, but, innocent as I am, I am charged with a crime far beyond my power to commit and one which might excuse one so insignificant as myself by its very magnitude. I alone in all the realm am accused of diminishing the royal dignity. When they define the act of offence more carefully, these are the charges that they hurl at my head. If any among us invokes the name of Rome, they say it is my doing. If the English Church ventures to claim even the shadow of liberty in making elections or in the trial of ecclesiastical causes, it is imputed to me, as if I were the only person to instruct the lord of Canterbury and the other bishops what they ought to do.[84]

Or, as he later wrote to the same Peter when the storm had abated, "If you ask the cause, my crimes are, that I profess freedom and defend the truth . . . I am conscious of no other fault as far as the king is concerned . . . [it is God's] Church, for whose sake I suffer."[85] These are the most explicit statements that John made about the causes of the king's displeasure—and he was writing confidentially to friends at the very time that he was experiencing the chill wind of royal disfavor. They refer to John's involvement in general ecclesiastical policy—indeed to the tensions between royal and ecclesiastical rights and jurisdiction that would erupt into the

---

[81] Thomas Becket.

[82] *JohnS*, 1:48.

[83] *The Correspondence of Thomas Becket, Archbishop of Canterbury 1162–1170*, ed. and trans. A. J. Duggan, 2 vols., Oxford Medieval Texts (Oxford, 2000), 2:1364–65.

[84] *JohnS*, 1:31–32. The key Latin reads, "Huius tamen culpae non arguor. . . . Solus in regno regiam dicor minuere maiestatem. . . . Quod quis nomen Romanum apud nos inuocat, michi inponunt. Quod in electionibus celebrandis, in causis ecclesiasticis examinandis uel umbram libertatis audet sibi Anglorum ecclesia uendicare, michi inputetur. . . ."

[85] *JohnS*, 1:50–51.

Becket controversy a few years later in 1163–64 (and in which John was one of the first to suffer). Whatever written document was brought back to England, neither it nor the emerald-set ring was the cause of Henry II's anger. The *agent provocateur* was a member of the impressive embassy that Henry sent to discuss "difficult royal matters" with the new Pope Adrian in 1155,[86] perhaps jealous of the evident familiarity between a mere archiepiscopal secretary and the pope. One can imagine the three Norman bishops, all from the nobility, feeling aggrieved that John was chosen to eat at Adrian's table.[87] Whether or not he was a member of their mission, and in the absence of firm evidence one way or the other, I incline to the view that he was at the Curia on his own and perhaps also Theobald's account, not the king's,[88] and the royal envoys, and especially the watchful Arnulf, may well have been disturbed at the influence that John was seen to exercise over the new pope, especially since it was not impossible that John might be brought into the Sacred College.[89] They would almost certainly have known about the rebuke that Adrian inserted, probably on John's instigation, into the mandate about the blessing of the abbot of St. Augustine's issued to Archbishop Theobald in January 1156, since it was established practice for such documents to be issued *in publica audientia*,[90] and the king's emissaries would have been interested in the contents of papal mandates addressed to England. The most offensive

---

[86] Consisting of three Norman bishops (Rotrou of Évreux, Guillaume de Passavant of Le Mans, Arnulf of Lisieux) and Abbot Robert of St. Albans, the mission set out on 9 Oct. 1155. Robert remained at Benevento after the bishops departed, and did not return to St. Albans until the octave of the Ascension (May 31, 1156): *Gesta abbatum*, 1:125–29. See also at nn. 48–50.

[87] *Metalogicon*, iv. 42 (ed. Hall and Keats-Rohan, p. 183); McGarry, trans., *The Metalogicon of John of Salisbury*, p. 274.

[88] The reason for John's presence at the papal court is obscure. His own record, written in 1156–59 (*Policraticus sive de nugis curialium*, vi. 24 (ed. Clement C. J. Webb, 2 vols. [Oxford, 1909], 2:67), speaks somewhat vaguely of his "journey to Apulia to visit the lord Pope Adrian IV (*causa visitandi dominum Adrianum pontificem quartum profectum in Apuliam*)." Had he been a member of the royal embassy, one would expect him to have said so.

[89] See John's own hopeful words to Adrian (*JohnS*, 1:90 and n. 1): "I continually recall with joy and exultation the words which proceeded from your lips, when at Ferentino [probably winter 1150–51] you gave me your own ring and belt as a pledge of things to come."

[90] Cf. John of Salisbury, *Historia Pontificalis*, p. 45, for cases being discussed "in consistorio."

sentence from the king's point of view declared, "the right of appeal is so smothered by you and the king of England that no-one dares to appeal to the apostolic see in your presence or his."[91] Here, I think, we should find the cause of John's great disgrace, not in the ambiguous favor obtained from Adrian IV.[92]

The late Professor Warren was convinced that Canterbury interests lay behind the impetration of the letter, which, he wrote, reads like an "attempt to encourage a hesitant king."[93] The text, however, asserts that the pope was granting a petition made by the king. Its central clause reads: "granting our generous assent to your petition (*petitioni tue benignum impendentes assensum)*"; and that tone is continued throughout the text:

> Your magnificence is thinking about . . . you propose . . . you seek the counsel and favour of the Apostolic see . . . you have indicated . . . that you wish to enter the island of Ireland, to make that people obedient to the laws . . . *you are willing to pay St. Peter an annual tax of one penny from every household, and to preserve the rights of the churches of that land intact and unimpaired* . . . as we support your pious and praiseworthy intention . . . what you have conceived in your mind. . . .[94]

It was only by ignoring the responsorial character of the letter, which ties it to requests made by the king, and omitting from his quotation the

---

91 *Historia monasterii S. Augustini Cantuariensis by Thomas of Elmham*, ed. C. Hardwick, RS 8 (London, 1858), pp. 411–12 no. 42, at 412, ". . . ita apud te et apud regem Angliae appellatio sit sepulta, quod aliquis non est, qui in tua vel in illius praesentia ad sedem apostolicam audeat appellare."

92 In fact, John's own statement *(JohnS,* 1:50) that only through the mediation of Archbishop Theobald could he hope to be restored to favor seems to rule out the "Canterbury hypothesis."

93 *Henry II*, pp. 195–96; cf. Ullmann (who agrees with Warren), "Alexander III and the Conquest of Ireland," 385 n. 59.

94 *Expugnatio* (ed. Scott and Martin), pp. 144–47. The key Latin phrases are: "tua magnificentia cogitat . . . intendis . . . consilium apostolice sedis exigis et favorem . . . significasti . . . te Hibernie insulam ad subdendum illum populum legibus . . . velle intrare, et de singulis domibus annuam unius denarii beato Petro uelle soluere pensionem, et iura ecclesiarum illius terre illibata et integra conseruare . . . pium et laudabile desiderium tuum cum fauore congruo prosequentes . . . peticioni tue . . . ingrediaris . . . exequaris . . . quod concepisti animo. . . ."

key clauses that refer to the rights of the local churches and the payment of Peter's Pence to Rome (which are italicized above) that Warren could turn *Laudabiliter* into the product of a Canterbury-inspired plot.

The concept of the "Canterbury plot" was predicated not only on the belief that Archbishop Theobald lay behind the obtaining of *Laudabiliter,* but on the assumption that Henry II had no Irish ambitions before the late 1160s. Central to this argument is dismissal of Robert of Torigny's record that at a council at Winchester around Michaelmas 1155, Henry had discussed with his nobles *(cum optimatibus suis)* a conquest of Ireland, to confer on his youngest brother William, and that he had abandoned the idea because of his mother's opposition.[95] Professor Warren dismissed Robert's account on five grounds: that no English chronicler records it; that Robert was ill-informed about English affairs; that it would have been very unlikely for Henry to have contemplated so great a promotion for his youngest brother when he had just deprived his middle brother (Geoffrey) of his hoped-for inheritance in Anjou; that Henry had no particular interest in Ireland; and, more important, that the idea of an Irish conquest came not from the king but from the church of Canterbury, intent on establishing its primacy over the whole of Britain. But the case is not so watertight as it appears.

The silence of English chroniclers proves nothing, since they have little to say about the early years of Henry's reign, and, in fact, independent evidence that an Irish venture was discussed at Winchester has been presented by Dr. Flanagan.[96] Nor was Robert of Torigny so out of touch with cross-channel affairs as Warren implies. He recorded Cardinal John

---

[95] *The Chronicle of Robert of Torigni*, ed. R. Howlett, *Chronicles of the Reigns of Stephen, Henry II and Richard I*, RS 82/iv (London, 1889), p. 186. The Winchester council was an important assembly of great lay and ecclesiastical magnates, which included the two archbishops (of Canterbury and York) and at least three bishops, as well as six earls: R. W. Eyton, *Court, Household, and Itinerary of King Henry II* (London, 1878), pp. 12–13.

[96] Flanagan, *Irish Society*, p. 40, citing a charter of Count John of Eu (London, BL, Harley Charter 83 C. 25), which recorded a grant made "apud Wintoniam eo anno quo verbum factum est de Hibernia conquirenda (at Winchester in the same year in which there was discussion about the conquest of Ireland)." For the full text, see *Irish Society*, pp. 305–7. Evidence that William was with his brother Henry is provided in the witness lists of two charters listed by Eyton, *Itinerary*, pp. 12–13 nos. 1 and 5. The Empress is mentioned in the text of no. 5.

Paparo's legation to Ireland in 1152,[97] for example, and his *Chronicle* was quarried extensively in the late 1180s by Ralph de Diceto, dean of St. Paul's, for his own *Ymagines historiarum*.[98] What Geoffrey was deprived of in 1155–56 was his claim to Anjou, Maine, and Touraine, the very core of the Angevins's ancestral lands, which Henry, as the eldest son, wanted to keep for himself. Far from discouraging his brother's ambitions, however, Henry promoted his candidacy for the county of Nantes in 1156, since that would have advanced his own strategy for domination of the duchy of Brittany.[99] Similarly, an Irish appanage under his own lordship for the still younger William would not have been contrary to his interests. In the light both of the Nantes promotion of Geoffrey and of his later proposal to marry William to the widowed Countess Isabella de Warenne, Warren's assertion that Henry "never did much for his brothers" requires reassessment.[100]

Equally, the suggestion that Henry had no interests in Ireland before the late 1160s ignores what has been called his "Irish Sea diplomacy." It is true that he was drawn into the Irish problem by Diarmait Mac Murchada's struggle with Tiernan O'Rourke, prince of Breifne (Meath). Seeking outside support for his cause, Diarmait approached Henry II in 1166–67 and was allowed to seek recruits among the king's *fideles*.[101] His recruitment drive secured three stalwart leaders—Richard FitzGilbert de Clare, Earl of Strigoil (Strongbow), and the half-brothers Robert FitzStephen and Maurice FitzGerald[102]—for all of whom Ireland offered great opportunity. The possibility that Strongbow might become an independent and dangerous ruler in Leinster, following his marriage to Diarmait Mac Murchada's daughter and defeat of the high-king, Ruaidr' Ua Conchobair, outside Dublin in spring 1171, drew King Henry into Irish affairs,

---

[97] *Robert of Torigny*, p. 166.

[98] See above, at n. 31.

[99] Warren, *Henry II*, p. 76.

[100] The marriage was forbidden on canonical grounds by the new archbishop, Thomas Becket, and William died, it was said, of a broken heart in 1164; Isabella and what Warren called "the vast honor of Warenne" were given to the king's remaining (illegitimate half-) brother, Hamelin: Warren, *Henry II*, pp. 66, 195.

[101] Warren, *Henry II*, pp. 192–93. The authenticity of Henry's writ, quoted by Warren (pp. 198–99) from Giraldus, has been seriously, if not fatally, challenged by F. X. Martin: see above, at n. 15.

[102] Sons of the Welsh princess Nesta by different fathers: see the genealogical tables "The Children of Nesta," in *Expugnatio* (ed. Scott and Martin), p. 266.

to assert his overlordship of his vassals and their conquests.[103] Indeed, in an important addition to his source (Roger of Howden's *Gesta*), Gervase of Canterbury said that Henry in 1171 was responding to an appeal from Irish kings who were themselves fearful of Strongbow's unrestrained ambitions.[104] But it was also the continuance of an Irish association that had already served the Angevins well. Henry's links with Diarmait Mac Murchada, king of Leinster, explained by the commercial links between Dublin and Bristol, reached back to the mid-1140s and Diarmait's support for the Angevins.[105] One might add, *pace* Warren, that it was also politically advantageous for Henry to be outside his own realms in the immediate aftermath of Becket's murder, as Gervase of Canterbury said,[106] and to portray himself as the bringer of peace and order to a troubled land.

The only "evidence" for clerical involvement in the venture in 1155 comes from an anonymous Flemish continuator of the *Chronicon* of Sigebert of Gembloux, who was writing at the monastery of Afflighem before 1189. The relevant entry reads, *sub anno* 1156, "Henry the younger, king of England, turned against the French king the large and well-equipped army that he had prepared to lead into Ireland in order to subjugate it to his lordship and, with the advice of bishops and men of religion, to establish his brother as king for that island."[107] Contrary to some recent

---

[103] For the prelude to Henry II's intervention in October 1171, see Lynn H. Nelson, *The Normans in South Wales, 1090–1191* (Austin/London, 1966), pp. 131–50; Watt, *Church and Two Nations*, p. 36, "there is no evidence to warrant any linking of the Invasion with any plot to resurrect the primacy of Canterbury in Ireland"; Flanagan, *Irish Society*, p. 76.

[104] *The Historical Works of Gervase of Canterbury*, ed. W. Stubbs, 2 vols., RS 73 (London, 1879–80), 1:234. For the suggested collaboration of Bishop Christian of Lismore, see below, at n. 138.

[105] Flanagan, *Irish Society*, pp. 69–76; L. Hays and E. D. Jones, "Policy on the Run: Henry II and Irish Sea Diplomacy," *Journal of British Studies* 29 (1990), 293–316, esp. 294–99.

[106] Gervase of Canterbury, 1:235, "Tertia vero, summa, ut aestimo, erat et praecipua, videlict ut sententiam interdicti, si forte daretur, facilius declinaret vel occultius observaret."

[107] *MGH SS*, 6 (Hannover, 1844), p. 403: "Heinricus iunior rex Anglorum, exercitum copiosum et magnum belli apparatum, quem proposuerat ducere in Hiberniam, ut eam suo dominio subiugaret, fratremque suum consilio episcoporum et religiosorum virorum illi insule regem constitueret, convertit contra regem Francorum."

interpretations,[108] this passage supports the argument for secular rather than clerical motivation,[109] both for the proposal and for its abandonment. The "advice of bishops and men of religion" was to be used after the conquest, in the establishment of his (unnamed) brother's kingdom; and there is, of course, not a whiff of Canterbury involvement. There is thus no evidence to support the argument that the initiative for an Irish conquest came from the clergy, or from Canterbury. The concept of a "British Isles" united under the lordship of the English king was certainly current,[110] but its focus was political, not ecclesiastical.

Laudabiliter

Although Gerald identified *Laudabiliter* as the "privilege" obtained by John of Salisbury, its text does not match John's description. It does not "grant" or "give" Ireland to King Henry, nor does it contain the key phrase *iure hereditario possidendam*; and it was only by omitting that phrase from the passage, which he borrowed more or less verbatim from

---

108 Denis Bethell, "English Monks and Irish Reform in the Eleventh and Twelfth Centuries," *Historical Studies* 8 (1971), 111–35, at 135; Martin, "Diarmait Mac Murchada and the Coming of the Anglo-Normans," p. 56; Flanagan, *Irish Society*, p. 40 (which omits the references to the raising of an army and its diversion to France). The anonymous writer may in any case have been confused: Henry did not muster troops against Louis VII until 1161; but he did campaign in Anjou in mid-1156, putting down his brother Geoffrey's rebellion.

109 As O'Doherty recognized; see "Rome and the Anglo-Norman Invasion," p. 140; see now Haren, "*Laudabiliter*: Text and Context," pp. 150–52.

110 R. R. Davies, *The First British Empire: Power and Identities in the British Isles 1093–1343* (Oxford, 2000; repr. 2002), "Island Mythologies," pp. 31–53; cf. Walter Ullmann, "On the Influence of Geoffrey of Monmouth in English History," in *Speculum historiale: Geschichte im Spiegel von geschichtsschreibung und Geschichtsdeutung*, ed. C. Bauer, L. Boehm, and M. Müller (Freiburg, 1965), pp. 257–76; Ullmann, "Alexander III and the Conquest of Ireland," pp. 382–84 (suggesting that Geoffrey of Monmouth's description of King Arthur's British kingdom could have provided grounds for the idea of Henry's "hereditary right" over Ireland: see below, at n. 193); R. William Leckie, *The Passage of Dominion: Geoffrey of Monmouth and the Periodization of Insular History in the Twelfth Century* (Toronto/Buffalo, 1981). For Anglo-Saxon "imperialism," see H. R. Loyn, "The Imperial Style of the Tenth-Century Anglo-Saxon Kings," *History* 40 (1955), 111–15; Janet L. Nelson, "Inauguration Rituals," in *Early Medieval Kingship*, ed. P. H. Sawyer and I. N. Wood (Leeds, 1977), pp. 50–71.

the *Metalogicon*, that Gerald could make the text conform—at least on a quick reading—with John's account. Even if one were to accept Maurice Sheehy's suggestion that *Laudabiliter* was not the formal grant to which John referred but an accompanying letter of exhortation,[111] the text still raises difficulties. Nowhere is it dated, and nowhere does it appear in official communications before the mid- to late thirteenth century. Nevertheless, it is hard to condemn it on purely diplomatic grounds, especially since its earliest transmission is through narrative sources, whose textual accuracy may be doubted.

J. F. O'Doherty demonstrated not only its broad conformity with prevailing papal style, but its employment of part of an *arenga* that occurs, otherwise uniquely, in another of Adrian's letters, *Satis laudabiliter*, issued from the Lateran on February 18, 1159, and addressed to Louis VII of France.[112] The similarities between the prologues of the two letters led O'Doherty to argue that the existence of *Satis laudabiliter* tended to

---

[111] M. P. Sheehy, "The Bull *Laudabiliter*: A Problem in Medieval Diplomatic and History," *Galway Archaeological and Historical Society Journal* 29 (1961), 45–70, esp. 63. Dr Sheehy argued that *Laudabiliter* functioned in the same way as Innocent III's letter to King John (*Selected Letters of Pope Innocent III Concerning England*, ed. and trans. C. R. Cheney and W. H. Semple, NMT [London, 1953], pp. 168–70 no. 63, *Sicut ab Archa*, 4 Nov. 1213) that accompanied the privilege of the same date (*Rex regum*: *PL*, cccvi, 923–24, Reg. xvi, 131), a thesis carefully re-evaluated, and rejected; Haren, "*Laudabiliter*: Text and Context," pp. 145–47.

[112] *PL*, clxxxviii, 1615–17 no. 241 (1158); cf. JL 10546, *sub anno* 1159. JL's ascription of the letter to 1159 is the more likely, since it follows the (temporary) establishment of good relations between the two kings in 1158: Warren, *Henry II*, p. 77. Its *arenga* reads (medieval spellings restored), "Satis laudabiliter et fructuose de Christiano nomine propagando in terris et eterne beatitudinis premio tibi cumulando in celis, tua magnificencia cogitare, dum ad dilatandos terminos populi Christiani, ad paganorum barbariem debellandum, et ad gentes apostatices, et que catholice fidei refugiunt veritatem, Christianorum jugo et ditioni subdendos, simul cum charissimo filio nostro Henrico illustri Anglorum rege, in Hispaniam properare disponis. . . . Atque ad id conuenientius exequendum, matris tue sacrosancte Romane ecclesie consilium exigis et fauorem (Laudably enough and profitably does your magnificence contemplate extending the glorious name of Christ on earth and laying up a reward of eternal bliss in heaven, as you propose, together with our dearest son Henry, illustrious king of the English, to hasten to Spain, to enlarge the boundaries of the Christian people, to make war on the barbarity of the pagans, and to subject the apostate nations and those who flee from the truth of the Catholic faith to the yoke and sway of Christians. . . . And the more expeditiously to achieve this end, you seek the counsel and favour of your mother, the holy Roman Church)."

support the authenticity of the Irish bull, which was issued some years earlier (late 1155 or early 1156).[113] That argument is persuasive, but not conclusive, since it could be argued that *Satis laudabiliter* could itself have formed the basis for the confection of an Irish fake. *Satis laudabiliter* responded to Louis VII's proposal to lead a crusade, jointly with Henry II, against the Muslims in Spain, and a fully dated copy was kept by Louis's chancellor, Hugh of Champfleury, in the collection of royal correspondence that he transmitted for copying to the abbey of Saint-Victor in Paris in 1170–71; and there it remained, being incorporated into the abbey's "Collection F" in the late 1170s.[114] Adrian's letter to Louis VII had thus passed from the security of the royal household to the almost public archive of one of the leading schools of Paris, in which city, incidentally, the young Gerald was a student in 1177–79,[115] when "Collection F" was taking shape. An appropriately adjusted version of the letter would have been addressed to Henry II himself, although it has left no traces in English sources.

Equally, *Satis laudabiliter* could have come to the knowledge of Peter of Blois, who had served as secretary to the very Rotrou, then bishop of Évreux, who was named in the pope's letter. Dependence on *Satis laudabiliter* would explain the curiously mixed language of *Laudabiliter,* which oscillates between crusading rhetoric in its *arenga* and reforming terminology in the body of the letter. As for the other details in *Laudabiliter*— the papal claims to special powers in respect of islands, the payment of Peter's Pence, and the reform of Irish morals—this was hardly secret lore. John of Salisbury's brief account named the Donation of Constantine as the source of papal rights over islands; England and Scandinavia paid Peter's Pence; and Gerald had firsthand knowledge of conditions in Ireland.[116] On the other hand, the very crudity of *Quoniam ea,* constructed by Gerald to support *Laudabiliter,* might, paradoxically, be an argument

---

[113] O'Doherty, "Rome and the Anglo-Norman Invasion," pp. 137–38.

[114] Now Città del Vaticano, Biblioteca Apostolica Vaticana, MS Reg. lat. 179: see Gunnar Teske, *Die Briefsammlungen des 12. Jahrhunderts in St. Viktor/Paris. Entstehung, Überlieferung und Bedeutung für die Geschichte der Abtei,* Studien und Dokumente Zur Gallia Pontificia, 2 (Bonn, 1996), pp. 158, 358 no. 100.

[115] Giraldus Cambrensis, *De rebus a se gestis,* ii. 2 *(Opera,* 1 (1861), pp. 45–47); cf. Richter, *Giraldus Cambrensis,* p. 4.

[116] Which he described at length in *Topographia Hibernica,* iii. 19–20, 26–28 *(Opera,* 5 [1867], pp. 164–65, 170–75).

in its favor. A forger who could make such a mess of one papal letter was unlikely to have made a better hand at another—unless, of course, he had a good model with which to work.

Despite O'Doherty's conviction, questions about the bull's authenticity continue to be raised by diplomatic and textual scholars. Jack Watt expressed some hesitations in 1957 and again in 1970,[117] as did Aubrey Gwynn c. 1983[118] and Ian Robinson in 1990;[119] and, as we have seen, F. X. Martin was doubtful about all eight texts in the *Expugnatio*. Such doubts are magnified by the almost total silence of other contemporaries about Adrian's letter. Normally, the argument *ex silencio* is considered the weakest of all; but there are not one but five silences where one would expect to find some kind of reference. The first silence is on the part of Henry II himself. Nowhere is there any hint of anterior papal permission for his invasion of Ireland in 1171, although Henry was keen to secure papal approbation after the event in 1172, and later still, when he petitioned for a crown for his son John.[120] Whatever papal approval had been brought back from Benevento in 1156, Henry did not use it or refer to it in his embassy to Alexander III in 1172, or later. The second silence is in the other chroniclers. No writer before Gerald mentions *Laudabiliter*.[121] Particularly significant in this context is the silence of Roger of Howden, the royal clerk and later chronicler. He accompanied Henry II to Ireland in 1171-72[122] and wrote a detailed account of the king's doings in the island, first in his *Gesta regis Henrici secundi,* then in his

---

[117] J. A. Watt, "*Laudabiliter* in Medieval Diplomacy and Propaganda," *Irish Ecclesiastical Record* 87 (1957), 420–32 at 420: "Whether or not the letter itself was genuine, it is certain that later medieval generations thought it was; at least to the extent to which different parties put it to different uses in support of their causes"; see p. 432: "a final doubt about the authenticity of *Laudabiliter*." Cf. Watt, *Church and Two Nations*, p. 36: "If the celebrated *Laudabiliter* be in fact Adrian IV's"; see p. 40: "if *Laudabiliter* be accepted as his."

[118] Gwynn, *The Irish Church*, p. 293: "the so-called bull."

[119] *The Papacy 1073-1198* (Cambridge, 1990), pp. 311–12.

[120] Cf. Watt, *Church and Two Nations*, pp. 38, 42.

[121] Though Sheehy allows the possibility that Diceto may have got it independently: *Pontificia Hibernica (i)*, 15 n.

[122] John Gillingham, "The Travels of Roger of Howden and His Views of the Irish, Scots and Welsh," *Anglo-Norman Studies* 20 (1997–98), 151–69, esp. 163–65, 167–68.

Chronica.[123] Although put into final form only in the early 1190s, David Corner has argued that the *Gesta* were compiled "almost contemporaneously" between 1169 and 1192, with the possibility of an early "edition" in 1177.[124] Roger was thus closest of all the chroniclers to the court of Henry II at the time of the Irish adventure—and, indeed, an eyewitness of many of the events he describes. Moreover, both in the *Gesta* and in its later derivative, the *Chronica*, Roger displayed an administrator's interest in texts and documents. From him alone we have the texts of Henry II's legal Assizes, for example, the best text of the so-called compromise of Avranches of 1172,[125] and also the "Treaty" of Windsor (1175) between Henry II and Ruaidrí (Roderick), king of Connacht.[126] He was in a much better position than the younger Gerald to know what had transpired in 1171–72, and one would have expected him to have cited the king's papal warrant, if one had been exploited. Even more than his contemporary Ralph de Diceto, the dean of St. Paul's, he preferred to transmit the full texts of letters and decrees without abridgement; and during the crucial years 1171–76 he had access directly, on his own account, and indirectly through colleagues in the royal household, to the archival core of the royal administration.[127] But although he records Alexander III's confirmation of the king's lordship in Ireland (i.e., the "September letters") following receipt of letters from the archbishops and bishops of Ireland, there is no mention of Adrian's grant.[128]

---

[123] *Gesta regis Henrici secundi*, 1:25–30; *Chronica magistri Rogeri de Houedene*, ed. W. Stubbs, 4 vols., RS 51 (London, 1868–71), 2:29–32, 33–34.

[124] David Corner, "The *Gesta Regis Henrici Secundi* and *Chronica* of Roger, Parson of Howden," *BIHR* 56 (1983), 126–44, esp. 126. The 1177 "edition" is represented by London, BL, MS Cotton Julius A. xi, which was copied for Abbot Benedict of Peterborough and covers the period from Christmas 1169 (which Howden dates 1170) to 1177.

[125] Duggan, "*Ne in dubium*" (above, n. 13).

[126] Howden, *Gesta regis Henrici II*, 1:102–3; *Chronica*, 2:84–85: cf. Flanagan, *Irish Society*, pp. 229–72, 312–13.

[127] Duggan, "*Ne in dubium*," n. 50.

[128] Although misplaced *sub anno* 1171: Howden, *Gesta regis Henrici II*, 1:28; *Chronica*, 2:31–32, "Rex vero Angliae misit transcriptum cartarum universorum archiepicoporum Hyberniae ad Alexandrum papam, et ipse auctoritate apostolica confirmavit illi et haeredibus suis regnum Hyberniae, secundum formam cartarum archiepiscoporum et episcoporum Hyberniae (Indeed the king of England sent the written "charters" of all the archbishops of Ireland to Pope Alexander, and he confirmed the kingdom of Ireland to him and his heirs by apostolic authority, according

The third silence is in the three authentic papal letters issued by Alexander III on September 20, 1172. There is no explicit reference in any of them to Alexander's predecessor nor to any previous papal authorization or grant or to the question of Peter's Pence, the subject of two clauses in *Laudabiliter*; but it is possible to see verbal echoes of Adrian's bull (e.g., *ad tue sempiterne glorie . . . quod laudabiliter incepisti . . . coronam merearis suscipere sempiternam . . . iura beati Petri*) in the letter addressed to Henry himself.[129] These "*Laudabiliter* ghosts" suggest that Pope Alexander knew of the letter—that would not be surprising, since he was papal chancellor when it was issued, and there is likely to have been a copy in Adrian's Registers,[130] but they do not imply that either he or King Henry regarded the letter as a precedent or a warrant. The fourth silence is perhaps the most telling of all. Although the three "September letters" of Alexander III were copied, with their proper inscriptions and dates, into the *Black Book of the Exchequer*, which was compiled early in John's reign,[131] there is no mention of *Laudabiliter* in this authoritative book of royal rights and precedents. Of course, it can be objected that Henry II had disliked the terms of *Laudabiliter*, with its reference to papal authority over islands, and that he had therefore disgraced John of Salisbury and set it aside;[132] but John's disgrace was for something else

---

to the form of the "charters" of the archbishops and bishops of Ireland)." Howden's reference to Henry's heirs is an unwarranted gloss. Ullmann's argument ("Alexander III and the Conquest of Ireland," p. 375) that these letters presuppose Adrian's grant has little to commend it, since in all three letters Alexander stated explicitly that he was responding to a *fait accompli* that had been formally notified to him by the interested parties: see below, at nn. 189–91.

[129] *Quantis vitiorum*, to the papal legate, Bishop Christian of Lismore, and the archbishops and suffragans of Armagh, Cashel, Dublin, and Tuam; *Celebri fama*, to Henry II; *Ubi communi*, to the kings and princes of Ireland: see *Pontificia Hibernica [i]*, 19–23 nos. 5–7. For translations of these letters, see *Irish Historical Documents 1172-1922*, ed. Edmund Curtis and R. B. McDowell (New York, 1943; repr. London, 1968), pp. 19–22 nos. 1–3.

[130] That is, if it was considered important enough for registration. C. R. Cheney estimated that only about 10% of the letters issued from the chancery were registered in the thirteenth century: "The Study of the Papal Chancery," Second Edwards Lecture, University of Glasgow (Glasgow, 1966), p. 15.

[131] London, Public Record Office, E. 164/12, fols. 8v–9v; cf. *Liber Niger Scaccarii*, ed. Thomas Hearne, 2 vols. (Oxford 1771–74), 1 (1774), pp. 42–48; *The Red Book of the Exchequer*, ed. Hubert Hall, 2 vols., RS 99 (London, 1896), pp. lvi–lvii.

[132] Constable, "Alleged Disgrace," p. 75; cf. Gwynn, *The Irish Church*, p. 300.

and Alexander's own letter, which Henry had promulgated and officially recorded, spoke of the "special right" that the Roman Church enjoyed in an island, as distinct from a large land mass (*Romana ecclesia aliud ius habet in insula quam in terra magna et continua*).[133] The fifth silence is the hundred-year-long absence of *Laudabiliter* from official debate.

These "silences" are not enough to prove that *Laudabiliter* is a fake; but they suggest that Adrian's letter was shelved, together with the project for which it had been secured. Neither the entry of Cambro-Norman adventurers in the late 1160s nor Henry II's acquisition of lordship in 1171–72 had been motivated by the desire to execute Adrian's bull. If it had not been for Gerald's desire to turn invasion and conquest into something that it was not, nothing more would have been heard of *Laudabiliter* in the context of Henry's Irish conquest.

Non falsa sed ficta: The Geraldine Text of *Laudabiliter*

For the reason stated above, I am disinclined to see *Laudabiliter* as wholly concocted. On the contrary, piecing together the various pieces of contemporary evidence, one can argue that the document from which it was derived was obtained in late 1155 or early 1156, probably by John of Salisbury, who added his own *preces* to those of the royal embassy led by Abbot Robert of St. Albans. What was presented to the pope was a carefully constructed petition that highlighted the ecclesiastical and moral benefits that would follow King Henry's entry into Ireland, supported by the promise of the payment of Peter's Pence. This latter would have been particularly attractive to Pope Adrian who had himself, as papal legate, introduced the custom into the Norwegian Church in 1153.[134] This much is echoed in Gerald's text; but the resulting papal letter, I suggest, contained much else besides.

Here, comparison with *Satis laudabiliter,* cited above, is highly instructive. That letter, issued in 1159, three years later than *Laudabiliter* itself, contained an extremely diplomatic refusal of papal support for the joint Franco-Angevin crusade in Spain proposed by Louis VII

---

[133] *Pontificia Hibernica*, p. 22.

[134] A. Bergquist, "The Papal Legate: Nicholas Breakspear's Scandinavian Mission," in *Adrian IV: The English Pope (1154–1159); Studies and Texts*, ed. B. Bolton and A. J. Duggan (Aldershot, 2003), pp. 41–48, at 42, 45, 46.

and Henry II. With considerable finesse, Adrian contrived both to praise the proposal and strongly advise against its implementation, unless the kings' intervention was requested in advance by the Church, princes, and people of the area. As Adrian said in the version addressed to King Louis (medieval spellings restored):[135]

> (a) Verum cum excellentia tua et consilii maturitate sit prouida, et luce sapientie illustrata, in ordine ipsius facti uidetur plurimum esse festinata. . . .

> (But yet, although your excellency may be both circumspect with an abundance of prudence and illumined with the light of wisdom, you seem to be very hasty in the arrangement of this particular exploit. . . .)

> (b) Accedit ad hoc quod alienam terram intrare nec prouidum uidetur esse nec tutum, nisi a principibus et a populo terre prius consilium requiratur. Tu uero, sicut accepimus, inconsulta ecclesia et principibus terre illius accedere illuc et festinare disponis, cum hoc deberes nulla ratione tentare, nisi cognita per principes terre necessitate et ab eis prius esses exinde requisitus. Unde quia nos honorem et incrementum tuum tota mentis intentione diligimus, et nihil tale a te aggredi, nisi rationabili causa exigente, uellemus, sublimitati tue presentibus litteris suademus ut prius necessitatem terre per principes illius regni inspicias et consideres, et tam illius ecclesie quam principum et populi uoluntatem diligenter inquiras, et ante eis consilium, sicut decet, accipias. Quo facto, si et neces- sitatem terre uideris imminere, et ecclesie consilium fuerit, ipsi etiam terre principes tue sublimitatis auxilium postulauerint, et consilium dederint, iuxta postulationem et consultum eorum pot- eris postea in facto ipso procedere, et laudabile uotum tuum, diuino comitante presidio, adimplere. . . .

> (Add to this, that it would seem to be neither wise nor safe to enter a foreign land without first seeking the advice of the princes and people of the area. But, as we understand it, you are proposing to

---

[135]   *PL*, clxxxviii, 1615–17 no. 241, at 1616–17.

go there in haste, without consulting the Church and the princes of that land, although you should on no account attempt it, unless, having learned the need from the princes of the region, you are then asked by them beforehand. Wherefore, since we love your honor and advancement with the whole force of our mind and wish you to begin nothing of this kind unless compelled by reasonable cause, we urge your highness by these letters, first to examine and ponder the needs of the area with the aid of the princes of that realm, and carefully seek out the will both of its Church and of its princes and people, and take their advice, as is fitting. If, when you have done this, you see that the region is in immediate need, and its Church advises it, and the princes of the area have themselves also requested your highness's aid and given their advice, you can then go forward in the matter according to their request and advice, and fulfil your laudable desire, supported by divine protection. . . .)

(c) Sane discretio tua et nostram dissuasionem, quam rationabiliter credimus fecisse, provida deliberatione consideret, atque alia, per quae ad illud iter tam festinanter aspiras, inspiciat et attendat. . . .

(Indeed, your discretion should with prudent deliberation ponder our counter advice, which has been given, we believe, for sound reasons, and also ponder and consider other ways by which you may as speedily approach that path. . . .)

It is my contention that the original *Laudabiliter* said something very similar to Henry II in 1155–56. Following a flattering *arenga* and commendation of the king's laudable scheme for the improvement of the Irish people, Adrian advised that Henry take no action until the Irish Church, princes, and people requested his intervention. With the inclusion of such material, the bull might have read something like this:

(1) Laudabiliter et satis . . . principium acceperunt.
(Laudably and profitably . . . and conclusion.)

(3) Significasti siquidem nobis . . . et integra conseruare,
(Inasmuch as you have indicated . . . and unimpaired,)

(4) Nos itaque pium . . . denarii pensione.
(We therefore . . . from every household.)

(2) Sane Hiberniam et omnes insulas . . . exigendum
(Indeed there is no doubt . . . so to do.)

(a) Verum cum excellentia . . . plurimum esse festinata.
(But yet, although your excellency . . . exploit.)

(b) Accedit ad hoc quod alienam terram . . . adimplere.
(Add to this, that to enter another land . . . protection.)

(c) Sane discretio tua . . . inspiciat et attendat.
(Indeed, your discretion . . . approach that path.)

(5) Si ergo quod concepisti animo . . . in seculis obtinere.
(Then, if you consider . . . for all ages.)[136]

Or: 1, 3, 4, 2, 5, *a, b, c.*

Twelfth-century papal letters were constructed from a series of independent clauses that could be inserted, transposed, or omitted according to need, so that it was a simple matter to change the order or even omit whole passages without creating an obvious lacuna or dislocation of the text. In this case, it would have been a simple matter to transpose one paragraph and excise the conclusion; and this, I suggest, is precisely what Gerald did. To fit *Laudabiliter* into the five justifications for Henry's Irish lordship, Gerald placed the papal assertion of jurisdiction over islands immediately after the *arenga*, thus inverting the natural order of the letter, in which reference to the king's petition (*narratio*) would have followed the grandiloquent opening;[137] and he omitted Adrian IV's carefully phrased advice to seek advance approval and support from the Irish

---

[136] Below, Appendix I and II for Latin text and translation.

[137] *The Letters of Pope Innocent III (1198–1216) concerning England and Wales,* ed. C. R. Cheney and Mary G. Cheney (Oxford, 1967), xviii: "If a letter calls for any *narratio* or statement of the case, it usually follows in that section the words of the enquiry or the petition to which the answer is given." It is significant that Roger of Wendover, followed by Matthew Paris, re-established the true order of the letter by transposing the *Sane Hiberniam* clause to after segment [4].

Church, princes, and people. He thus created a seriously falsified, though not forged, text.

Paradoxically, the presence of such advisory clauses in the genuine *Laudabiliter* would explain the great care that Henry II took to secure recognition of his lordship by all interested parties as fully and publicly as he could *before* seeking Alexander III's approbation. Henry's actions in 1171–72 seem to be following Adrian's instructions to the letter. Immediately after landing near Waterford on October 17, 1171, Henry II spent two days in the company of Christian î Conairche, the Cistercian bishop of Lismore (1151–79), who was at that moment one of the most influential ecclesiastics in the island. Aubrey Gwynn suggested that Christian had been forewarned of Henry's arrival, and that he had willingly collaborated with him.[138] In the sequel, it was he, as papal legate, who presided at the second council of Cashel (1172), which ratified Henry's lordship; and it was his name that headed the list of Irish prelates who reported Ireland's recognition of Henry II to the pope.[139] This is the likely context in which *Laudabiliter* was employed by Henry II, not as papal validation, for Adrian was long dead, but as a blueprint for creating the grounds upon which unambiguous papal approval could be sought from the present pope. The suppressed sections supplied the political strategy (acknowledgment by the Church and princes of the land); the remainder of the text provided the argument of moral crusade; and both feature strongly in the three letters that Pope Alexander issued in September 1172.

Adrian's *Laudabiliter* had been designed to dissuade Henry from invading Irish territory; but since no pope could prevent the powerful English king from doing what he was resolved to do and strident prohibition

---

[138] Christian, indeed, was only the latest in a line of native Irish ecclesiastical reformers who had close links with external movements: see esp. Bethell, "English Monks and Irish Reform"; Martin, "Diarmait Mac Murchada and the Coming of the Anglo-Normans," esp. pp. 51–55.

[139] Gwynn, *The Irish Church*, pp. 304–5; Watt, *Church and Two Nations*, p. 39. Indeed, Christian may have done more than "report." Dr. Flanagan suspects that he created the illusion of Irish episcopal unanimity: "Henry II," pp. 186–87, 205, and esp. 209: "The episcopal consensus which Gilla Críst [Christian], as papal legate, may have presented both to Henry II and to Pope Alexander III may not have reflected reality"; that the Council of Cashel may have been far less representative than generally thought (the archbishop of Armagh, for example, may not have been present (p. 205); and that Christian probably supported Diarmait Mac Murchada, who had appealed to Henry II in the first place (p. 205).

would have been counterproductive, he employed all the rhetorical powers of his *dictatores* to persuade against the proposed action. At the same
time, however—almost in the same breath—he set out a series of prerequisites intended to safeguard the rights of the indigenous Church and
people, supported by an assertion of papal authority over islands. Only
if these prerequisites were met—that is, if Henry had consulted the will
of the Irish Church, princes, and people, if "the region [was] in immediate need," and its Church advised it, and if "the princes of the area
. . . requested [his] aid and [gave] their advice"—was he authorized to
"go forward in the matter," which might lead to his acknowledgement as
lord by "the people of that land." Adrian did not grant or give Ireland to
King Henry, but he laid down parameters within which the king might
lawfully obtain its lordship, and, according to John of Salisbury, he sent
an emerald ring that could be used to symbolize that lordship if it were
obtained in the future. Rings, of course, were commonplace symbols of
authority, mostly spiritual and ecclesiastical: bishops and abbots and
sometimes even archdeacons wore rings. But they also featured among
the high-status gifts exchanged between eminent persons. In May 1198,
for example, Innocent III sent four gold rings to Richard I, each one set
with a different precious stone (emerald, sapphire, garnet, and topaz),
representing faith, hope, charity, and good works, while the gold itself
represented wisdom, the greatest of gifts, with which Solomon had ruled
his people; and in 1206, Philip II of France received a sapphire.[140] It is
possible that Adrian's emerald ring symbolized not lordship over the
island of Ireland, but faith and wisdom. No matter how conditional, however, Adrian's carefully modulated letter could be interpreted as a weak
and flickering amber light, which John of Salisbury, followed by Gerald,
chose to record as a clear and unambiguous green.

Yet even as Gerald presented it, *Laudabiliter* did not make Henry
lord, still less king of Ireland: there is no mention of "hereditary right,"
or indeed any other kind of "right," that the king is to exercise there.
After commending Henry's laudable aims to extend his own fame on
earth,[141] "to enlarge the boundaries of the Church; to reveal the truth of

---

[140] *PL*, ccxiv, 179–80 no. 206; cf. Brenda M. Bolton, "Innocent III's Gift List," in
Pope Innocent III and His World, ed. John C. Moore (Aldershot, 1999), pp. 113–40
at 137–38.

[141] Giraldus and Diceto read "glorioso nomine ([the *or* your] glorious name),"
which Martin translated as "the glorious name of Christ"; but Roger of Wendover

the Christian faith to peoples still untaught and barbarous, and to root out the weeds of vice from the Lord's field," the pope declared it "pleasing and acceptable" that the king should enter the island for the good purposes stated and that "the people of that land receive you honourably and respect you as their lord *(et illius terre populus honorifice te recipiat et sicut dominum ueneretur)*," "on condition that the rights of the churches remain intact and unimpaired, and without prejudice to the payment to St. Peter and the holy Roman church of an annual tax of one penny from every household." The whole paragraph, of course, was expressed in the subjunctive voice and implied no directive that the Irish people *should* accept Henry's lordship, although the pope would not be displeased if they did. Not only is the highly conditional nature of the document glossed over in Gerald's presentation, but the spurious Alexandrine letter was concocted to "confirm" what it called "[Pope Adrian's] concession regarding the grant to you of dominion over the Irish realm *(concessionem eiusdem super Hibernici regni dominio vobis indulto)*." *Laudabiliter,* of course, said nothing of the sort; but the juxtaposition of the two letters, the one falsified *(Laudabiliter)* and the other forged *(Quoniam ea)*, supported by the apparently unimpeachable witness of John of Salisbury, created a plausible myth.

Laudabiliter as an Instrument of Protest

Despite official silence about Pope Adrian's "privilege" for at least a century, the letter somehow surfaced in Hiberno-English disputes in the mid- to late thirteenth century, during which it acquired an authority and significance that it did not have in its own time. There are three, what one may call official, versions surviving from the late thirteenth–early fourteenth century: one in the Carew manuscripts in Lambeth Palace

---

and Matthew Paris, perhaps correctly, appended "tuo" to the phrase, making it unambiguously "your glorious name." Support for this reading is provided by the concluding sentence, which balances earthly honor with heavenly happiness; and this pairing is found also in Adrian IV's letter to the German bishops, written after the Besançon incident (late 1157), in which he called on them to remind Frederick I that he could "lay up for himself both honour on earth and blessedness in heaven *(et honorem in terris et felicitatem in celis sibi poterit cumulare)*" by following the example of "Justinian and other Catholic emperors": *Adrian IV*, ed. Bolton and Duggan, pp. 254–55.

Library;[142] one in the National Archives (formerly the Public Record Office),[143] and another, inserted into the so-called Book of Leinster in the early fourteenth century.[144] In addition, there is evidence that copies were sent to Rome, Vienne, and Avignon by Irish or Anglo-Irish prelates between 1256 and 1327, of which one was enclosed with John XXII's admonition (May 30, 1318) to Edward II to mend the ways of his administration in Ireland;[145] and the text was available to John Darcy, the Irish justiciar, for whom Andrea Sapiti, King Edward's Roman agent, drew up a petition to Pope John XXII between 1323 and 1327, seeking the proclamation of a crusade against malcontents in Ireland.[146]

The earliest non-chronicle copy (L) occurs at the foot of a single parchment sheet, transcribed in a good administrative hand, datable to the second half of the thirteenth century. Its survival among the extensive collection of materials relating to Irish History assembled by the Elizabethan nobleman George Carew in the late sixteenth and early seventeenth

---

[142] London, Lambeth Palace, Carew MS 619, fol. 206; cf. J. S. Brewer and William Bullen, *Calendar of the Carew Manuscripts Preserved in the Archiepiscopal Library at Lambeth* (= *Carew Manuscripts*), 6 vols. (London, 1867–73), [vi] (1871), p. 464; cf. Watt, "*Laudabiliter* in Medieval Diplomacy," p. 424.

[143] SC 8/177 no. 8818.

[144] Dublin, Trinity College MS H. 2. 18, cat. 1339, p. 342 (*olim* fol. 40v).

[145] Watt, "*Laudabiliter* in Medieval Diplomacy," pp. 423–32; see below, at n. 157.

[146] Biblioteca Apostolica Vaticana, MS Barb. Lat. 2126, fol. 125rv; cf. J. A. Watt, "Negotiations between Edward II and John XXII concerning Ireland," *Irish Historical Studies* 10, no. 37 (1956), 1–20, at 18–20. A more accurate text will appear in Barbara Bombi's edition of Andrea Sapiti's Register. It is her dating (between 1323 and 1327) that is followed here, in preference to Watt's suggested 1327–34. The petition's reference to the heresy of Adam Duff O'Toole implies that he had not been apprehended at the time of writing, but he was condemned in 1327. Four of its phrases, "pro dilatandis ecclesie terminis, pro vitiorum restringendo decursum," "pro corrigendis moribus et virtutibus inserendis et pro christiane religionis augmento," "ut tam per ipsum regem quam per alios, quos ad hoc fide, verbo, et vita ydoneos esse prospexerit," and "decoretur ibi ecclesia, plantetur et crescat fidei christiane religio," echo the words of *Laudabiliter* very closely. Insofar as any conclusions can be drawn from this evidence, Sapiti's petition is closer to the "protest" than to the Chronicle tradition, as one would expect: it adds "et" before "pro Christiane" (as *PR*); and reads "alios" (as *LS*).

centuries confirms its Irish provenance.[147] The surviving text begins, "Cum ab Adriano quondam apostolice sedis episcopo illustri Anglorum regi Henrico secundo iam pridem fuisset indultum ut Hybernie regnum ingrediens sub conditione subscripta populum suo subiugaret imperio . . . ," but it lacks all marks of authorship, date, or address, and the copy of *Laudabiliter*, which is written after a space of four lines, is equally bereft of date.[148] As it stands, the document reads like the core of a petition submitted to the English king or to the pope.[149]

The second, and most important, survivor—a single leaf bound up with a bundle of miscellaneous documents, including petitions, in the National Archives, formerly the Public Record Office (*P*)—is equally puzzling. Maurice Sheehy thought (rightly, I think) that it was a "re-cast" version of the text transmitted by the chroniclers (Gerald and Diceto), but he did not include its variant readings in his *apparatus criticus*, and he offered no explanation for its appearance among survivals from royal archives. Michael Richter, in contrast, did study *P*, together with the related version in the "Book of Leinster" (*R*), and he concluded not only that they were derived from a source independent of the chronicles but that they confirmed the bull's authenticity.[150] Neither argument is conclusive. The numerous variants (see Appendix) are better explained by the scribal slips and adjustments common in the transmission of medieval texts than by the suggestion that *P* and *R* derived from a different and better source independently of the chronicles; and although *P* is written in a good administrative hand and survives among official documents, it lacks all chronological marks, and appears without any kind of identification or endorsement.

---

[147] George, Baron Carew, Earl of Totnes (1555–1629), whose family claimed descent from Robert FitzStephen (see above, at n. 102), one of the first conquerors of Ireland: *Carew Manuscripts,* [i] (1867), pp. vii–lxiii, esp. vii–ix; *ODNB*, x (2004), pp. 46–48.

[148] London, Lambeth Palace, Carew MS 619, fol. 206; cf. *Carew Manuscripts,* [vi] (1871), p. 464. The text is printed by M. P. Sheehy, "English Law in Medieval Ireland. Two Illustrative Documents," *Archivium Hibernicum* 23 (1960), 167–75 at 174–75; cf. Watt, *Church and Two Nations,* p. 121 and n. 2, 123–24; Watt, "*Laudabiliter* in Medieval Diplomacy," p. 424, where tentatively dated *c.* 1291.

[149] This is the view of Watt, *Church and Two Nations,* pp. 123–24.

[150] "Giraldiana," p. 431: "It is no longer permissible to doubt the authenticity of *Laudabiliter.*"

These omissions are a major stumbling block to the suggestion that it derived from an official source independent of the literary transmission discussed above. It is almost inconceivable that in the circumstances of the late thirteenth or early fourteenth century, an official copy of an important papal document would have omitted its dating clause. *P*'s source is therefore unlikely to have been the "original" in the royal archives. The most likely explanation of its survival in the dossier of materials and petitions from the late thirteenth and fourteenth centuries is that it issued from Irish protests against abuse of ecclesiastical rights in the island. Its accomplished script places it within the period *c.* 1300–20,[151] and the triangular placement of three dots (∴) before the opening "Adrianus" suggests that the transcript was originally enclosed within another document, in which the reference to *Laudabiliter* was so marked, either interlineally or in the margin. Such *signes de renvoi* were commonplace features of contemporary manuscripts, where passages in the main text were linked to marginal or supplementary matter by the paired use of distinctive symbols.[152]

A strong case has been made for linking *P* to the "Advice," drafted in French, addressed to Edward II by *Lestat Dirlande*, the "middling people" of (Anglo-) Ireland in 1317–19, which does indeed refer to Adrian's bull.[153]

---

[151] For this precise dating, I have to thank Miss Helen Watt and Dr. Jonathan Mackman from the E 179 project at the National Archives. I am also very grateful to Dr. Paul Dryburgh and Dr. Louise Wilkinson for their advice and comment. Dr. Haren ("*Laudabiliter*: Text and Context," p. 160), dates the copy to the late thirteenth century.

[152] M. B. Parkes, *Pause and Effect. An Introduction to the History of Punctuation in the West* (Berkeley/Los Angeles, 1993), p. 307.

[153] *Documents on the Affairs of Ireland Before the King's Council*, ed. G. O. Sayles, Irish Manuscripts Commission (Dublin, 1979/80), 99–101 no. 136, at 99: "Mᶜmurwoth, roi de Leynestiere, qi fust enchacez, vint au roi Henri en temps seint Thomas de Canterbiry, et li pria qil vousist entremettre a conquere la terre par eide de li, et li conta comment homicides et prochez abominables resuerent en la terre. Sor quei le roi manda a la Postoil Adrian la suggestion Mᶜmurwoth et pria qil pust cele tere entre a souzmettre la poeple a lei et les enfourmer en virtu et les termes de seinte esglise eslargir. . . . Lapostoile de la mauvoite des Irois par ses delegaz acertez, granta par sa bulle au roi qe por souzmettre les Ireis a lei et enfourmer les en vertu et les termes de seinte eglise eslargir qil cel isle entrast (Mac Murchada, king of Leinster, who had been driven out, went to King Henry in the time of St. Thomas of Canterbury, and begged that he would undertake the conquest of the land with his assistance, and told him that murders and abominable deeds were springing up in the land. Upon

The two texts occur nearby, nos. 8818 (*Laudabiliter*) and 8820 ("Advice"), in a sequence of four original documents, nos. 8817–20, which a modern archivist marked a–d, in the dossier of ancient petitions in London, National Archives, SC 8/177. Both have filing holes and evidence of stitching along the left margin, but there is no visible *signe de renvoi* in the "Advice," no reference to an enclosure, and its eight needle marks[154] seem to match those of no. 8817 (a petition from the mayor and commonalty of Dublin in 1317)[155] more closely than the seven along the left edge of *P*.[156]

---

which the king sent Mac Murchada's proposal to Pope Adrian and begged that he could enter that land to subject the people to the law and instruct them in virtue and extend the boundaries of Holy Church. [...] The pope, being assured by his legates of the wickedness of the Irish, granted by his bull that the king could enter that island to subject the Irish to the law and instruct them in virtue and enlarge the boundaries of Holy Church)"; cf. J. R. S. Phillips (citing Dr Philomena Connolly), "The Remonstrance of 1317: An International Perspective," *Irish Historical Studies* 27, no. 106 (1990), 112–29, at 118, n. 22; Phillips, "The Remonstrance Revisited: England and Ireland in the Early Fourteenth Century," in *Men, Women and War*, ed. T. B. Fraser and K. Jeffrey, Historical Studies, 18 (Dublin, 1993), pp. 13–27, esp. 7 and 24 n. 42.

154 At 7, 13, 23, 34, 45, 56, 66/7, and 72 mm from the top, although the eighth, at 72 mm, is obscured by a horizontal cut or tear in the parchment. Examination of the punctures is rendered difficult by the way in which these documents were bound into a single volume. About 110 mm below this cut, there are a further three small punctures arranged vertically down the left margin at 184, 191/2 and 200 mm, and these exactly match the three needle marks on the left side of no. 8819 (at 6/7, 14/15, and 22/23 mm), the four-line petition (in French) that the coast of Wales be well guarded against Thomas Dun and other Scottish felons who may cross from Ireland to Wales.

155 The Dubliners asked that the king should reserve to himself the release of the earl of Ulster and all felons: *Affairs of Ireland*, ed. Sayles, pp. 85–86 no. 111.

156 At 13, 23, 34, 46, 57, 67, and 73 mm. There are similar needle marks, varying between three and twelve, along the left margins of National Archives, SC 8/177 nos. 8803, 8813, 8828–29, 8830–31, 8835. Cf. also SC 7/16/17, a small sealed *cedula*, which Pope Gregory X had sent in May 1274 to Edward I, together with the *littera patens* (SC 7/16/20), to which it refers. Although three prominent puncture marks along its left margin show that the *cedula* was once sewn to something else, its companion *littera patens* is unblemished: the two were not sewn together in the royal archives. For a discussion of the diplomatic form of these two documents, see C. Egger, "*Littera patens, littera clausa, cedula interclusa*. Beobachtungen zu Formen urkundlicher Mitteilungen im 12. und 13. Jahrhundert," in *Wege zur Urkunde. Wege der Urkunde. Wege der Forschung. Beiträge zur europäischen Diplomatik des Mittelalters*, ed. K. Hruza and P. Herold (Vienna, 2005), pp. 41–64, at 61–62; cf. *Original Papal Documents*, ed. Sayers, nos. 760–61.

An alternative possibility is that *P* was the copy sent by the Irish princes to Pope John XXII in late 1317, together with their "Remonstrance," both of which were enclosed in the admonition that the pope sent to Edward II in May 1318.[157] Physical examination reveals that *P* had been folded into a small square or oblong package, measuring roughly 3¼ × 3⅛ ins (84 × 79 mm) or 3¼ x 6⅛ ins (84 × 156 mm), which could easily have been enclosed within another folded document.[158] It is thus possible that *P*'s presence among files of petitions to the crown is explained by this curious circumstance—that it was attached to the complaint of the Irish princes, which John XXII had referred to Edward II. Indeed, Professor Phillips has suggested that the papal letter, with its enclosures, was discussed by the royal council in August 1318, for envoys of the two cardinals who had been engaged in the affair were allowed to travel to Ireland on August 18, and the king's response to the papal admonition was issued on the 25th of the same month.[159] John XXII's letter, the Irish protest, and *P* may have been stitched together and filed with current Irish material, although no trace of the papal letter or of the Irish princes' appeal has been found in the royal archives.[160]

---

[157] Phillips, "The Remonstrance of 1317," p. 128. The application of the term "remonstrance" to the prince's appeal has no ancient authority (p. 117). For the pope's letter, see *Vetera monumenta Hibernorum et Scotorum historiam illustrantia quae ex Vaticani, Neappolis ac Florentiae tabulariis deprompsit . . . Ab Honorio III usque ad Paulum III. 1216–1547*, ed. Augustin Theiner (Vatican City, 1864), p. 201 no. 422: "Ut autem de predictis gravaminibus et querelis, quibus predicti innituntur Ybernici, tuis sensibus innotescat ad plenum, prescriptas litteras [the "Remonstrance"] missas cardinalibus antedictis [Gaucelin d'Eauze, cardinal priest of SS. Marcellino e Pietro and Luke Fieschi, cardinal deacon of S. Maria in Via Lata: they were nuntios—*nuntii*—not legates—*legati*], cum anima (*sic*) formam litterarum, quas predictus Adrianus, predecessor noster, eidem Henrico regi Anglie de terra Ybernia concessisse dicitur, continente, tue magnitudine mittimus presentibus interclusas (So that you should be fully informed of the aforesaid grievances and complaints on which the aforesaid Irish rely, we send to your magnificence, enclosed with these, the said letters [Remonstrance] sent to the aforesaid cardinals, containing a form of the letter that the aforesaid Adrian, our predecessor, is said to have granted to the same Henry, king of England, concerning the land of Ireland)." The resulting package must have been quite bulky!

[158] Parchment leaf, measuring 267 x 158 mm,

[159] Phillips, "The Remonstrance of 1317," p. 128.

[160] Ibid., p. 115.

The third non-chronicle copy *(R)* neatly complements the other two. Although contained in the late twelfth- and early thirteenth-century compilation of Irish materials made by the Irish priest Áed and commonly but improperly known as the "Book of Leinster," it formed no part of the original work and was for that reason omitted from the modern printed edition.[161] Its transcription, on the *verso* of the second (half) leaf of a *bifolium* inserted into the manuscript in the early fourteenth century, links it not with Henry II's assertion of lordship (of which there is no mention in the "Book") but with the construction of anti-English protests more than one hundred years later.[162]

These three tantalizing transcriptions point to circulation in official Anglo-Irish circles from the second half of the thirteenth century onwards, but how soon did the letter make its way into public debate? In what is the most authoritative study on the subject, Jack Watt suggested that the first unambiguous citation of *Laudabiliter* in a politico-diplomatic context occurred in Henry III's defence of the actions of the English government in Ireland on the grounds of fulfilment of the "mandatum pape," to which Honorius III responded on March 19, 1221.[163] But the phrase suggests Alexander III's *Celebri fama* of September 20, 1172,[164] rather than Adrian's supposed *Laudabiliter*, for *Laudabiliter* contains no mandatory language, whereas *Celebri fama* enjoined reform of specific moral abuses among the Irish people "in remissionem . . . peccatorum"; and we know that a copy was to hand in the *Black Book of the Exchequer.*[165] Equally, there is not the merest whiff of *Laudabiliter* in the three documents relating to the complaints addressed respectively to Henry III and Pope Alexander IV by Archbishop Florence Mac Floinn of Tuam

---

[161] *The Book of Leinster*, ed. R. I. Best, O. Bergin, and M. A. O'Brien, 6 vols. (Dublin, 1954–83).

[162] The "Book of Leinster" is available in the original manuscript through Internet Access from ISOS (Irish Script on Screen; cf. Trinity College Dublin, MS 1339), although the half leaf on which *Laudabiliter* is written (p. 342) is so damaged by damp that it is virtually unreadable on screen; but there is an excellent facsimile version, *The Book of Leinster*, ed. Robert Atkinson (Dublin, 1880), p. 342. For the dating, see W. O'Sullivan, "Notes on the Script and Make-up of the Book of Leinster," *Celtica* 7 (1966), 1–31, esp. 29; Haren, *Laudabiliter*: Text and Context," p. 160, dates it somewhat earlier: late thirteenth century.

[163] Watt, *"Laudabiliter* in Medieval Diplomacy," p. 422.

[164] *Pontificia Hibernica (i)*, pp. 21–22 no. 6.

[165] Above, at n. 131.

and others in 1255–56,[166] which Watt cites as evidence of its influence in the middle years of the century.[167] The chief objections raised against the king's government in Ireland related to abuse or denial of the judicial and inheritance rights of the Irish Church and people, and nowhere is there any reference to the authority by which the king ruled the island. And the same is true of the report of the inquisition into the king's government in Ireland (1285–92). Its key clause—"Because it is conceded to the kings of England by the Apostolic See that the Irish Church should be regulated and subjected to the kingly dignity in the premises [= rights over bishoprics during vacancies] as is the English Church (*Quia indultum est Regibus Angliae per sedem apostolicam quod ecclesia Hiberniae sit regulate et dignitati regie subjecta in premissis ut est ecclesia Anglicana)*"[168]—could not have been based on the text of *Laudabiliter*, which said nothing of the kind; but it may echo a lost papal recognition of the royal right to episcopal temporalities during vacancies, or even represent a misinterpretation of the references in Giraldus Cambrensis to the introduction of English customs into the Irish Church.[169] Nor did the confederation of mutual defense made by the four archbishops of Ireland and their suffragans (led by Nicholas Mac Maol Iosa, archbishop of Armagh) and recorded in the Register of John Swayne, September 23, 1291, make any specific reference to *Laudabiliter*.[170]

On the other hand, some time between 1247 and 1274, *Laudabiliter* was cited in a memorandum drawn up to demonstrate the lawfulness of

---

[166] *Calendar of Documents, relating to Ireland, preserved in Her Majesty's Public Record Office*, ed. H. S. Sweetman, 5 vols. (London, 1875–86), 2:1252–84 (1977), 74–75 no. 460, 78–79 no. 480, 82–83 no. 503. A late thirteenth-century copy of Alexander's response, addressed to Henry III in 1256, is in London, Lambeth Palace, Carew MS 619, fol. 207; cf. *Carew Manuscripts*, [vi] (1871), p. 464 no. 3.

[167] Watt, "*Laudabiliter* in Medieval Diplomacy," p. 423.

[168] Ibid., p. 424; cf. *Calendar of Documents . . . Ireland*, 3:1285–92 (1879), 1–15 no. 2, at 9–10.

[169] *Expugnatio* (ed. Scott and Martin), p. 100. The English customs cited referred only to liturgical practice (*omnia divina*), but a wider application might have been deduced by an inattentive reader.

[170] *The Register of John Swayne, Archbishop of Armagh and Primate of Ireland, 1418–1439, and Some Entries of Earlier and Later Archbishops*, ed. D. A. Chart (Belfast, 1935), p. 3.

the English king's dominion of Ireland;[171] and another memorandum, from 1277, preserved among the Chancery Miscellanea, refers to the unfulfilled requirement to pay Peter's Pence in conformity with "la charte postoille Adrian."[172] It is also possible that Nicholas IV's marriage dispensation (1290) for Simon de Ianville (son of Geoffrey de Geneville, lord of Ludlow and Trim), which recited the petitioner's reference to Henry II's armed invasion of Ireland "with the approval of the Apostolic See" (*de voluntate sedis ipsius*), implied knowledge of *Laudabiliter*, as Watt thought (though the emphasis on armed force suggests derivation from Roger of Wendover),[173] and also that it lay behind the reference to the *licentia papae* that had ordered respect for the Irish and Roman Churches, contained in the *Gravamina* of the Irish Church *(Ecclesia Hibernica)* presented at the Council of Vienne, 1311–12.[174]

The first of the surviving free-standing copies *(L)*, in fact, fits into a mid- to late thirteenth-century context very well. The only datable reference, a complaint about the actions of a former justiciar of Ireland, John FitzGeoffrey (1245–56), would seem to place it in the context of protests being made in the 1260s and '70s,[175] a dating supported by its position in the Carew collection, where it is followed by documents that can be dated 1275–81 and 1256 respectively.[176] The second free-standing copy *(P)*

---

[171] Phillips, "The Remonstrance of 1317," p. 120, citing Cambridge, University Library, MS Ii.IV.5. fols. 76–77 and Cambridge, Trinity College, MS B.15.11, fol. 55r; cf. Ullmann, "Influence of Geoffrey of Monmouth," part III.

[172] PRO Chancery Miscellanea 10/13/18, for which see: *Affairs of Ireland*, ed. Sayles, pp. 14–16 no. 19 at 16; cf. Seymour (J. R. S.) Phillips, "David MacCarwell and the Proposal to Purchase English Law, c. 1273–c. 1280," *Peritia: Journal of the Medieval Academy of Ireland* 10 (1996), 253–73, at 265.

[173] *Vetera monumenta*, ed. Theiner, 151 no. 331, dated Rome, S. Maria Maggiore, May 12 (1290): "clare memoriae Henricus olim Rex Anglorum de voluntate sedis ipsius [= apostolice] armata manu terram predictam intravit"; cf. Watt, "*Laudabiliter* in Medieval Diplomacy," p. 424. Roger of Wendover (above, n. 46), used the phrase, "insulam hostiliter intrare."

[174] *Proceedings of the Royal Irish Academy*, 27 Section C (1926), pp. 141–48; cf. Watt, "*Laudabiliter* in Medieval Diplomacy," p. 426.

[175] Listed and discussed by Watt, *Church and Two Nations*, pp. 121–29.

[176] The petition is followed, on a separate folio (207), by a memorandum, in French, of the proffer of 10,000 marks by the Irish episcopate, to have the Common Law extended to native inhabitants of Ireland (which can be dated by one of its proposers, Bishop David O'Cusby of Emly (1275–81), and a copy of Pope Alexander

almost certainly comes from the same context, though somewhat later, *c.* 1317; and the third "detached" version *(R)*, written in a skilled clerical hand of the early fourteenth century, belongs to the same environment. The so-called "Book of Leinster" had been compiled by an Irish priest at Oughavall in County Leix in the late twelfth century, where it remained as a precious monument of native Irish history until the fourteenth century. The parish of Oughavall (now Stradbally), however, passed to the Anglo-Norman priory of Great Connell, which had been colonized by Meiler FitzHenry with Augustinian canons from Llanthony Secunda in Monmouthshire, and it was thus brought into the circle of Anglo-Irish influence, for the priors of Great Connell were members of the Irish parliament.[177] The copy of *Laudabiliter* that was inserted into Oughavall's ancient book was certainly seen as vindication of Irish criticisms of the English government's abuse of native rights. The heading supplied by the Anglo-Irish scribe reads, "Bulla concessa regi Anglie super collatione Hybernie in qua nichil derogat iuri Hybernicorum sicut in serie verborum patet (Bull granted to the king of England relating to the invasion of Ireland, in which nothing derogates from the right of the Irish, as is demonstrated by the sequence of words)." Moreover, *R*'s close textual affinities with *P*, and to a lesser extent with *L* and with the text in the *Scotichronicon* (to be discussed below), confirms its association with the protest movement.

Although *Laudabiliter* may have been known to the framers of late thirteenth-century protests, its first unambiguous appearance in Hiberno-English-Papal relations was in the "Remonstrance" of the Irish princes, led by Domnall O'Neill, king of Tir Eoghain (Tyrone), which was laid before Pope John XXII in 1318.[178] Not only did the "Remonstrance" cite or echo the words of "the bull" five times, it enclosed a transcription of the text, which was transmitted as an appendix to the princes' protest in Walter Bower's mid-fifteenth-century *Scotichronicon*, a work that incor-

---

IV's letter to Henry III in January 1256, in the wake of protests by the archbishop of Armagh and the bishop of Killala: cf. *Carew Manuscripts,* [vi] (1871), p. 464 nos. 2 (wrongly dated "temp. Henry II. [?]") and 3.

[177] O'Sullivan, "Notes on . . . the Book of Leinster," pp. 2–3.

[178] For the very interesting suggestion that Michael Mac Lochlainn, OFM, later bishop of Derry 1319–49, whose election to Armagh had been quashed in 1303 and who may have been a relation of Domnall O'Neill, was the author of the "Remonstrance," see Phillips, "The Remonstrance Revisited," pp. 19–20.

porated materials assembled by John of Fordun in the mid-fourteenth century.[179] Collation reveals a clear affinity with the texts in the National Archives *(P)* and the "Book of Leinster" *(R)*, and to a lesser extent with the Carew text *(L)*;[180] and the manner in which reference to the bull was introduced into the princes' argument suggests that its ultimate source was Gerald's *Expugnatio*. The Irish set Adrian's grant in the context of Becket's murder, and dated it 1170 "in the year of the Lord MCLXX, at the false and wicked representation of King Henry, under whom and perhaps by whom St. Thomas of Canterbury, as you know, in that very year suffered death for justice and defence of the church, Pope Adrian, your predecessor, an Englishman not so much by birth as by feeling and character, did in fact, but unfairly, confer upon that same Henry . . . this lordship of ours by a certain form of words, the course of justice entirely disregarded and the moral vision of that great pontiff, blinded, alas! by his English proclivities."[181] In response to this denunciation of English

---

[179] *Scotichronicon by Walter Bower: in Latin and English,* ed. D. E. R. Watt, et al., 9 vols. (Aberdeen, 1987–98), vol. 6 (1991), ed. N. F. Shead, W. B. Stevenson, and D. E. R. Watt, xii. 27–33: 384–405, at 402–5; cf. pp. 481–83 (commentary). For a full description of Bower's "working text" (Cambridge, Corpus Christi College, MS 171), see 9:148–92. John of Fordun (d. 1384), a priest attached to the cathedral in Aberdeen, had travelled widely between 1363 and 1384 in his search for materials. Fordun and Bower transmitted the Irish Remonstrance in full because it concluded with a formal withdrawal of allegiance from Edward II and recognition of Edward Bruce (brother of the famous Robert Bruce, victor of Bannockburn in 1314) as king of Ireland (see Watt, *Church and Two Nations,* pp. 183–84, 186–88; Phillips, "The Remonstrance Revisited," p. 16); but it was also seen as an object lesson for the Scots: "I have carefully inserted the foregoing remarks about the Irish in this work so that the Scots may learn never to be willing to be subject to the tyranny or the insufferable rule of the English" (*Scotichronicon,* 6:405). For further copies of the "Remonstrance," with or without the attached *Laudabiliter,* see Phillips, "The Remonstrance of 1317," pp. 114–17.

[180] See Appendix.

[181] Domnall O'Neill to John XXII (1317): *Scotichronicon,* pp. 386–87 (Latin, with English translation); cf. *Irish Historical Documents,* ed. Curtis and McDowell, p. 39: This garbled sequence of events might have been deduced from Giraldus, whose *Expugnatio* is not overburdened with chronological markers. The alleged letter from the same Domnall to Fineem MacCarthy (H. Wood, "Letter from Domnall O'Neill to Fineem MacCarthy, 1317," *Proceedings of the Royal Irish Academy* 37 C [1926], 141–48) has been revealed as "nothing but a commonplace eighteenth-century forgery": Diarmuid O Murchadha, "Is the O'Neill–MacCarthy Letter a Forgery?," *Irish Historical Studies* 23 (1982), 61–67, at 67.

government in Ireland, John XXII sent letters of admonition to Edward II, enclosing the Irish protest and the copy of the letter, "quas predictus Adrianus, predecessor noster, eidem Henrico Regi Anglie de terra Ybernie concessisse dicitur (which the aforesaid Adrian, our predecessor, is said to have granted to the same Henry, king of England, concerning the land of Ireland)."[182] The pope's employment of the word *dicitur* ("is said") is significant, for it implies some hesitation on the part of the Curia about the authenticity of the bull; and that hesitation is evident also in the mandate sent at the same time to the papal ambassadors in England.[183] John's letter is certainly not an acknowledgement of the bull's authenticity; and Jack Watt found no evidence of any subsequent papal confirmation.[184]

Thereafter, *Laudabiliter* became a stock-in-trade of both sides in the Anglo-Irish debate,[185] but its later use is irrelevant to the question being debated here. What is significant is the absence of *Laudabiliter* from royal, papal, or Irish sources in the hundred years from its supposed issue in 1156 to its reappearance in the 1260–70s, as evidenced by *L*. And the context of its reappearance suggests derivation, not from the alleged original lodged in the royal treasury at Winchester, but from the version

---

[182] *Vetera monumenta*, ed. Theiner, 201 no. 422, dated Avignon, May 30, [1318]. For a discussion of this practice, see Egger, *"Littera patens, littera clausa, cedula interclusa,"* pp. 56–58.

[183] *Vetera monumenta*, ed. Theiner, *pp.* 201–2 no. 423.

[184] Watt, *"Laudabiliter* in Medieval Diplomacy," pp. 431–32.

[185] For both sides it became a useful propaganda instrument that could be used to challenge the actuality of royal government in Ireland. Having become a *mandatum papae,* both sides could appeal to it: one for authority, the other for grounds for complaint: see Watt, *"Laudabiliter* in Medieval Diplomacy," pp. 431–32. Cf. for example, *Statute Rolls of the Parliament of Ireland, First to the Twelfth Years of the Reign of King Edward the Fourth,* ed. Henry F. Berry (Dublin, 1914), pp. 436–39, c. 8. "whereas our most holy father, Adrian, formerly Pope of Rome, was possessed of all the seignory of this land of Ireland, in his demesne as of fee, in the right of his Church of Rome, which seignory, to the intent that vices should be subdued and virtues increased, he alienated to the King of England the said land, for a certain rent to be received in England. . . ." (translated from the French). See also the puzzling transcript made in the late fifteenth century of earlier royal mandates relating to English absenteeism in Ireland, to which is appended a somewhat defective copy of *Laudabiliter,* supplied with the fictitious date "Dat. anno domini m^o c^o liiij^o": PRO, C47/10/30, last item. That date, however, suggests knowledge of Diceto's *Ymagines,* which transmitted the text *sub anno* 1154 (above, at n. 30).

disseminated through the narrative account of Giraldus Cambrensis. Had any of the free-standing transcripts *(LPR)*, or the text attached to the Irish "Remonstrance" in the *Scotichronicon (S)*, been derived from the "original," one would expect the dating clause to have been included. But *P* has no final protocol; *L* and *R* transmit an incongruous "Valete" in place of the absent date; and *S* appended an authentic-looking "Dat', c." (for "Dat', etc."), which could have been supplied by anyone. The date of Adrian's letter would have read, "Dat. Beneuenti," followed by the day of the month according to the Roman calendar, as in the mandate sent to the archbishop of Sens and the bishop of Auxerre in December 1155, which is dated "Dat. Beneuenti .xiiii. kal. Ianuarii."[186] That Gerald's *Expugnatio* is the source of the text is supported not only by the allusion to Becket's murder in the Irish "Remonstrance," but also by the petition of the "middling people," that declared that the defeated king of Leinster had sought the aid of King Henry in the time of St. Thomas of Canterbury, and that Henry had transmitted Mac Murchada's suggestion to Pope Adrian and asked if he could enter this land to subject the people to the law, etc.[187] This confused and inaccurate juxtaposition reflects the way in which Gerald introduced *Laudabiliter* into the story of the Conquest: after Mac Murchada's appeal and the murder of Thomas Becket.

Conclusion

There remains the problem of explaining Gerald's "factional" record of the papal confirmation of Henry II's "conquest" of Ireland. Since he was very well informed about Henry's embassy to Alexander III in 1172 and the king's publication of the papal approval for the Irish venture that he had been so careful to obtain, publicize, and preserve in the royal archives,[188] why did Gerald substitute one redundant (and falsified) and one certainly fake papal bull for Alexander's genuine "September letters"? These three bulls, addressed respectively to the archbishops and

---

[186] *Decretales ineditae saeculi XII*, ed. and revised S. Chodorow and C. Duggan, Monumenta Iuris Canonici, 4 (Città del Vaticano, 1982), pp. 7–9 no. 4, esp. 9.

[187] Above, n. 153.

[188] See above, at n. 128.

bishops of Ireland, Henry II, and the kings and princes of Ireland,[189] had been drawn up on the basis of written submissions from the island's prelates, amplified by the oral testimony of the king's own envoy, Archdeacon Ralph of Llandaff;[190] and they could not have been more explicit about the grounds upon which the pope accepted and applauded the *fait accompli* of Henry's lordship.[191] But those letters did not confirm *Laudabiliter* or grant the lordship of Ireland to Henry II; so, Gerald concocted one which did.[192] Having forged one papal letter, it did not take much audacity to tinker with another; and it would have been a simple matter to suppress Adrian's restrictive clauses. Thus modified, *Laudabiliter*, supported by the forged *Quoniam ea*, produced the desired justification of Henry II's assumption of the lordship of Ireland.

Gerald's version of events was constructed to demonstrate the prophetic nature of Norman dominion both in Ireland and in Wales (and, for that matter, in England). He called his history of the conquest *Vaticinalis Historia* ("Prophetic History"), and although his second recension (if it *is* from his hand) played down the prophetic element and suppressed some of the prophecies (and also *Quoniam ea*), the work was originally conceived in that form. The *Expugnatio* is therefore a work of art: not

---

[189] *Pontificia Hibernica (i)*, pp. 19–23 nos. 5–7.

[190] As the pope stated in his letter to the king, "sicut venerabiles fratres nostri Christianus Lesmoriensis episcopus apostolice sedis legatus, archiepiscopi et episcopi terre suis nobis litteris intimarunt, dilectus filius noster R[adulfus] Landavensis archidiaconus, vir prudens et discretus et regie magnitudini vinculo precipue devotionis astrictus…viva voce tam solicite quam prudenter exposuit . . . sicut eisdem archiepiscopis et episcopis significantibus et prefato archidiacono plenius et expressius nobis referente comperimus. . . .": *Pontificia Hibernica (i)*, p. 21.

[191] Cf. the letter to the Irish kings and princes: "communi fama et certa relatione nobis innotuit quod vos karissimum in Christo filium nostrum H[enricum] regem Anglie illustrem in vestrum regem et dominum suscepistis et ei fidelitatem iurastis. . . . (it has become known to us by general rumour and reliable report, that you have received our dearest son in Christ H[enry], illustrious king of England, as your king and lord, and that you have sworn fealty to him. . . .)": *Pontificia Hibernica (i)*, p. 23.

[192] Flanagan, "Henry II," p. 190: "Indeed, Gerald of Wales found Alexander III's letter to Henry so deficient in respect of Henry's lordship of Ireland, that he felt obliged to forge one in Alexander's name, explicitly granting to Henry *dominiun Hibernici regni.*"

fiction, indeed, but generously enlivened with creative and imaginative reconstructions. His immediate purpose in introducing the papal letters was to establish the legitimacy of Henry II's rule. The two texts are followed immediately by a chapter (ii. 6) on the fivefold right of the English king, "two of long standing and three of recent origin." The ancient justifications were derived from Geoffrey of Monmouth's accounts of early Britain: the story of Gurguit's (Gurguintius's) grant of Ireland to the ancestors of the Irish (who had been expelled from Spain) and King Arthur's subsequent conquest of the island;[193] the three recent ones were Henry's possession of Bayonne, "the chief city of the Basques from which the Irish originally came," the submission by which the princes of Ireland 'freely bound themselves,'" and "the added weight of the authority of the supreme pontiffs, who have responsibility for all islands by reason of their own peculiar rights, and of the princes and rulers of all Christendom."[194] Wholly secular interests had drawn Henry into Ireland in late 1171, although he was able to clothe the venture, *post factum*, in a religious aura;[195] but Gerald, writing at the end of Henry's reign, when a new political and religious settlement had come into being, contrived to

---

[193] Geoffrey of Monmouth, *Historia regum Britanniae*, iii. 12, ix. 10, 12 (ed. Acton Griscom [London, 1929]), pp. 292, 445, 451–52; Lewis Thorpe, trans., *The History of the Kings of Britain* (London, 1966), pp. 100–101, 221–22, 225–28, esp. 227. Cf. Giraldus, *Expugnatio*, ii. 6 (ed. Scott and Martin, pp. 148–49). Giraldus also owed much of his own conceptualization of the prophetic nature of the Cambro-Norman conquest of Ireland to Geoffrey's *Prophetiae* (in *Historia*, vii). For a general overview of Geoffrey's influence, see Leckie, *The Passage of Dominion*.

[194] *Expugnatio*, ii. 6 (ed. Scott and Martin, pp. 148–49).

[195] As succinctly argued by Watt, *Church and Two Nations*, pp. 36–38. The counter view, proposed by Warren, Richter, and Flanagan (above, n. 54) does not persuade. Ullmann ("Alexander III and the Conquest of Ireland," p. 381, n. 40) found Warren's version of the "Canterbury plot" theory unconvincing, although he accepted both the authenticity of *Laudabiliter* and *Quoniam ea* as well as Warren's interpretation of *Laudabiliter* (p. 385 n. 59). O'Doherty (above n. 54) argued trenchantly for the Canterbury plot theory, but he saw no connection between *Laudabiliter* and Henry's actions in 1171–73: "St. Laurence O'Toole and the Anglo-Norman Invasion," pp. 600–601.

turn Henry's intervention into a kind of crusade to civilize the Irish,[196] for which the falsified *Laudabiliter* provided the justification.[197]

---

[196] For the creation of Norman/English attitudes of cultural superiority to the Celts, see John Gillingham, "The Beginnings of English Imperialism," *Journal of Historical Sociology* 5 (1992), 392–409.

[197] Gerald, of course, was not alone in concocting materials to support a case. Not only had Battle Abbey commissioned a whole series of forged royal charters purporting to be from Kings William I and Henry I in the 1150s, the anonymous author of its famous *Chronicle* has recently been described as "a forger on a very grand scale," and his work as an example of "the fictitious manipulation of narrative history": Nicholas Vincent, "King Henry II and the Monks of Battle: the Battle Chronicle unmasked," in *Belief and Culture in the Middle Ages: Studies Presented to Henry Mayr-Harting*, ed. Richard Gameson and Henrietta Leyser (Oxford, 2001), pp. 264–85, at 265. For what might be called "industrial strength forgery" at Rochester, see Martin Brett, "Forgery at Rochester," *Fälschungen in Mittelalter, MGH Schriften* 33 (1988), 4:397–412.

Appendix I

The textual transmission of Laudabiliter

Maurice Sheehy's text for *Hibernia Pontificia* was based exclusively on the copies transmitted by Giraldus Cambrensis and Ralph de Diceto, since he considered that the single leaf copy in the National Archives *(P)* was "a re-cast version of the bull" (*Pontificia Hibernica*, i, 15–16 and n. *e)*. For Professor Richter, however, the existence of *P* and of the closely related insertion in the "Book of Leinster" *(R)*, with their numerous variants from the Cambrensis-Diceto tradition, was evidence of independent derivation from the original bull and therefore virtually conclusive proof of its authenticity. The textual argument is not, however, as strong as it appears, especially when the variants are examined in detail, and the two additional members of the "protest tradition" *(L* and *S)* are brought into the picture.

Collation of Laudabiliter, *based on the following witnesses:*
1. The Giraldus–Diceto version:
   A   early recensions of Giraldus Cambrensis, *Expugnatio Hibernica*: London, BL, MSS, Royal 13 B. viii (*c.* 1200), fols. 56va–57ra (*A¹*); Royal 14 C. xiii (early 14th cent.), fol. 182r–v (*A²*); cases of agreement are marked *A*
   D   Ralph de Diceto, *Ymagines Historiarum*: London, BL, MS, Royal 13 E. vi, fol. 55rb–va (*D¹*); London, BL MS, Cotton Claudius E. iii, fol. 65va–66ra (*D²*); cases of agreement are marked *D*
2. The "protest tradition"
   L   London, Lambeth Palace, Carew MS 619, fol. 206
   P   London, National Archives (formerly the Public Record Office), SC 8/177 no. 8818
   R   Dublin, Trinity College, MS H. 2. 18 (cat. 1339), p. 342 (*olim* fol. 40v)
   S   Cambridge, Corpus Christi College, MS 171B, fol. 269r–v (cf. *Scotichronicon by Walter Bower: In Latin and English*, ed. D. E. R. Watt, et al., 9 vols. (Aberdeen, 1987–98), 6:402–4 (xii. 33)

3. The Wendover-Paris version
(significant additions, omissions, and rearrangements only are noted in parentheses)
W   Roger of Wendover, *Flores historiarum*, 1:11–13
M   Matthew Paris, *Chronica Majora*, 2:210–11

Adrianus episcopus seruus seruorum Dei, carissimo[1] in Christo filio[2] [3]illustri Anglorum regi[3] salutem et apostolicam benedictionem.

(1)   Laudabiliter et satis[4] fructuose de glorioso nomine [tuo *add.* WM] propagando in terris et eterne felicitatis[5] premio cumulando in celis tua magnificencia cogitat, dum ad dilatandos ecclesie terminos,[6] ad declarandam indoctis et rudibus populis Christiane fidei ueritatem et uiciorum plantaria[7] de agro Dominico extirpanda,[8] sicut [9]catholicus princeps[9] intendis, et[10] ad id conueniencius exequendum consilium [11]apostolice sedis[11] exigis et fauorem. In quo facto quanto altiori consilio et maiori discrecione procedis tanto in eo feliciorem progressum [12]te, prestante Domino,[12] confidimus habiturum,[13] eo quod ad [14]bonum exitum semper[15] et finem[14] soleant[16] attingere[17] que de[18] ardore fidei et

---

[1] karissimo *ADR*

[2] nostro *add. S*

[3-3] illustri Anglie regi *D²*; illustri regi Angl' *H. L*; illustri regi Anglorum Henrico (Henr. *R*) *PR*; Henrico illustri regi Anglie *S*

[4] *om. AL*; et satis (*marked for correction to* satis et) *D¹*

[5] salutis *PR*

[6] et *add. PR*

[7] plantia (!) *L*; plantas *S*

[8] exstirpanda *D¹R*; extirpandas *S*

[9-9] princeps catholicus *L*; in *P, a filing hole cuts through the ending of* catholi[cus]

[10] *om. A²*

[11-11] apostolicum *PR*

[12-12] prestante Domino te *L*; te *S*

[13] *om. R*

[14-14] bonum finem et exitum semper *L*; finem bonum et exitum semper *S*

[15] *om. PR*

[16] solent *S*

[17] pertingere *D²PR*

[18] ex *S*

religionis amore principium acceperunt. [eo quod . . . acceperunt *om. WM*]

(2) Sane Hiberniam[19] et omnes insulas quibus sol iusticie Christus[20] illuxit, et[21] que documenta[22] fidei [23]Christiane ceperunt,[23] ad ius beati Petri[24] et sacrosancte Romane ecclesie, quod tua[25] etiam[26] nobilitas[27] recognoscit,[28] non est dubium pertinere. Unde[29] tanto[30] in[31] eis libencius [32]plantacionem fidelem[32] et germen gratum Deo[33] inserimus quanto[34] id[35] a nobis[36] interno[37] examine districtius prospicimus exigendum.

[Sane Hiberniam . . . pertinere (*om.* Unde . . . exigendum) *trans. to after* pensione *WM*]

(3) Significasti [38]siquidem nobis,[38] [39]fili[40] in Christo carissime,[39] te Hibernie[41] insulam ad subdendum [42]illum populum[42] legibus [Christianis *add. WM*] et [43]uiciorum plantaria inde[43] extirpanda[44] uelle intrare, et de singulis domibus annuam [45]unius denarii beato

---

[19] Hyberniam *A¹D¹R*; Yberniam *A²*

[20] *om. LS*

[21] *om. PR*

[22] documentum *S*

[23-23] Christiane receperunt *D*; perceperunt *PR*; acceperunt *S*

[24] apostoli *add. PRS*

[25] *om. L*

[26] *om. PRS*

[27] uoluntas *P(after correction);R*

[28] cognoscit *L*

[29] Ut in (*reading uncertain*) *L*; et *S*

[30] *om. PR*

[31] tantam *marked for correction to* tanto *D²*; *om. S*

[32-32] plantacionem fidei *PR*; fidei plantacionem *S*

[33] Deo gratum *D*; gratum *L*

[34] quando (*with t superscript, post medieval?*) *D²*; quando *P*; [. . .]to *R*

[35] *om. S*

[36] in *add. LPRS*

[37] uero *L*; extremo *S*

[38-38] nobis siquidem *LPRS*

[39-39] in Christo fili karissime *S*; [39/2] karissime *DR*

[40] *interlin. P*

[41] Hybernie *A¹R*; Ybernie *A²*; Hyberniam *L*

[42-42] populum illum *LPRS*

[43-43] inde uiciorum plantaria *PR*, inde *om. S*

[44] extyrpanda *A¹*; exstirpanda *R*; extirpandum *S*

Petro[45] uelle[46] soluere pensionem, et iura ecclesiarum illius terre illibata[47] et integra conseruare,

(4) Nos itaque[48] pium et laudabile desiderium tuum[49] cum[50] fauore congruo prosequentes, et peticioni tue benignum[51] impendentes assensum, gratum et acceptum habemus ut pro dilatandis ecclesie terminis, pro[52] uiciorum restringendo decursu,[53] pro corrigendis moribus et uirtutibus inserendis,[54] pro Christiane[55] religionis augmento, insulam illam[56] ingrediaris et que ad honorem Dei[57] et[58] salutem [59]illius terre[59] spectauerint[60] exequaris, et illius terre populus [61]honorifice [honorifice om. WM] te[61] recipiat[62] et sicut dominum uenereretur;[63] iure nimirum ecclesiarum illibato et integro permanente et[64] salua[65] beato[66] Petro[67] et sacrosancte Romane ecclesie [et sacrosancte . . . ecclesie om. WM] de singulis domibus [68]annua unius denarii[68] pensione.
[Sane Hiberniam . . . pertinere ins. here WM]

45-45 beato Petro unius denarii PR
46 om. PR
47 illabata male P
48 autem tam S
49 om. R
50 om. DPRS
51 benign' D; benigne LPR
52 om. S
53 recursu R; discursum S
54 et add. PR
55 Christiano A²
56 Hibernie S
57 om. A²
58 ad add. L
59-59 terre illius PR
60 fuerint S
61-61 te honorifice S
62 respiciat P
63 reuereatur S
64 om. L
65 saluo D¹ (before correction); LP(reading uncertain)
66 beata D (before correction)
67 apostolo add. PR
68-68 eiusdem L, unius denarii annua PR; om. S

(5) Si ergo quod [69]concepisti animo[69] effectu[70] duxeris prosequente
complendum, stude[71] gentem illam [72]bonis moribus[72] informare, et
agas[73] tam per te quam per illos[74] quos ad hoc fide,[75] uerbo et uita
idoneos[76] esse prospexeris,[77] ut decoretur ibi ecclesia, plantetur et
crescat fidei Christiane[78] religio, et que ad honorem Dei et salutem
pertinent[79] animarum taliter ordinentur ut[80] a Deo sempiterne mercedis cumulum consequi merearis, [81]et in terris gloriosum nomen
ualeas in seculis obtinere.[81]

The above collation confirms Professor Richter's opinion of the close
affinity between *P* and *R* in comparison with the versions transmitted by
Giraldus ($A^{1,2}$) and Diceto *(D)*, but the variants are not, to my mind, of
such a kind as to prove ultimate derivation from a different and/or better
source. To anyone acquainted with the manner in which papal decretals
were handled by decretal scribes, there is nothing very surprising about
the changes that crept into the text of *Laudabiliter* when controversialists
began to use it as ammunition in their attacks on English abuses. Moreover, *L* and *S*, which derive from the same protest tradition of the text, but
which Richter did not discuss, are in fact closer to Giraldus-Diceto than
to *PR*, although they share some significant peculiarities with *PR*.

The cumulative number of variants of all kinds (eighty-one) at first
sight appears significant, but only thirty-one occur in more than one
non-chronicle source: twenty-nine are shared by *PR* (the exceptions are

---

[69-69] cepisti animo A^2L, animo incepisti *P*, animo concepisti *R*, incepisti animo *S*

[70] affectu A^2PR; effectuque *S*

[71] studeas *PRS*

[72-72] moribus bonis *L*

[73] eam *add. L*

[74] alios *LS*

[75] *om.* A^2S, et *add. PR*

[76] ydoneos *R*

[77] perspexeris D^1S

[78] Christiane fidei A^2

[79] pertinet *S*

[80] et *add. D*

[81-81] in terris et gloriosum nomen in celis valeas obtinere. Valete *L*, et in terris
gloriosum nomen ualeas et in celis obtinere *PR* (optinere *R*; Valete *add. R*), in celis
(*interlin. above* terris, *which is deleted*) et gloriosum nomen valeas in terris optinere,
Dat', c. *S* $8^{1/2}$ optinere *D2*

20 and 74); five (24, 26, 32, 49, 71) by *PRS*; one (51) by *LPR*; two by *LS* (20, 74); and only four (3, 36, 38, 42) by all four non-chronicle sources.

A. *Variants in more than one non-chronicle source (the* Scotichronicon
    *is included with the "non-chronicle" witnesses because it transmitted
    the version that was attached to the Irish princes' Remonstrance)*

3.	illustri Anglorum regi	illustri Anglie regi *D²*; illustri regi Angl' H. *L*; illustri regi Anglorum Henrico *PR*; Henrico regi Anglie illustri *S*
5.	felicitatis	salutis *PR*
6.	terminos	et *add. PR*
11.	apostolice sedis	apostolicum *PR*
15.	semper	*om. PR*
17.	attingere	pertingere *D²PR*
20.	Christus	*om. LS*
21.	et	*om. PR*
23.	Christiane ceperunt	Christiane receperunt *D*, perceperunt *PR*, acceperunt *S*
24.	Petri	*add.* apostoli *PRS*
26.	etiam	*om. PRS*
27.	nobilitas	uoluntas *PR*
30.	tanto	*om. PR*
32.	plantacionem fidelem	plantacionem fidei *PR;* fidei plantacionem *S*
36.	nobis	in *add. LPRS*
38.	siquidem nobis	nobis siquidem *LPRS*
42.	illum populum	populum illum *LPRS*
43.	uiciorum plantaria inde	inde uiciorum plantaria *PR* , uiciorum plantaria *S*
45.	unius denarii beato Petro	beato Petro unius denarii *PR*
46.	uelle	*om. PR*
50.	cum	*om. DPRS*

51.	benignum	benign' *D*; benigne *LPR*
54.	inserendis	et *add. PR*
59.	illius terre	terre illius *PR*
67.	Petro	apostolo *add. PR*
68.	annua unius denarii	eiusdem *L*, unius denarii annua *PR*; *om. S*
70.	effectu	affectu *A²PR*; effectuque *S*
71.	stude	studeas *PRS*
74.	illos	alios *LS*
75.	fide	*om. A²S*; et *add. PR*
81.	et in terris gloriosum nomen ualeas in seculis obtinere	in terris et gloriosum nomen in celis valeas obtinere. Valete *L* et in terris gloriosum nomen ualeas et in celis obtinere *PR* (Valete *add. R*) in celis (*interlin. above* terris, *which is deleted*) et gloriosum nomen valeas in terris optinere, Dat', c. *S*

The closest affinity is between *P* and *R*, that is, between the early four-teenth-century transcript preserved among petitions in the National Archives and the copy inserted into the "Book of Leinster" in the same period, which came from the same environment. While the high number of their common readings confirms their own textual affinity, it does not prove dependence on a more authentic text. Twelve of the variants are simple changes in word order or minor single-word omissions (15, 21, 27, 30, 38, 42, 43, 45, 46, 50, 59, 68), and four are trivial additions of "et" or "in" (6, 36, 54, 75). Only thirteen add or change words (3, 5, 11, 17, 23, 24, 27, 32, 51, 67, 70, 71, 81), and all can be ascribed either to carelessness or to scribal emendation, whether conscious or uncon-scious. The addition of Henry's name in the protocol did not need access to the "original," which would, presumably, have transmitted the king's name, "Henrico" (3); the addition of "apostoli" or "apostolo" to St. Peter's name would have come naturally to fourteenth-century scribes (24, 67); "plantacionem fidei" would have appeared better than the more unusual "plantacionem fidelem (true cutting)" (32), as would "salutis" for "felicita-tis" (5). The readings "uoluntas" for "nobilitas," and "affectu" for "effectu" are probably misreadings (27, 70); so too is "perceperunt" for "Christiane ceperunt" (23)—given that "Christiane" would have been abbreviated "xpe," and "alios" for "illos" (74).

This process of elimination leaves only five readings (11, 17, 51, 71, and 81), which might represent better readings derived from an *authenticum*, although, equally significantly, not even one is shared by all "protest" witnesses.

B. Significant variants

11.	apostolice sedis	apostolicum *PR*
17.	attingere	pertingere *D²PR*
51.	benignum	benign' *D*; benigne *LPR*
71.	stude	studeas *PRS*
81.	et in terris glorio- sum nomen ualeas in seculis obtinere	in terris et gloriosum nomen in celis valeas obtinere. Valete *L* et in terris gloriosum nomen ualeas et in celis obtinere *PR (*Valete *add. R)* in celis (*interlin. above* terris, *which is deleted)* et gloriosum nomen valeas in terris optinere, Dat', c. *S*

Of these, the first, "apostolicum," in the phrase "consilium apostolicum," was so commonplace that its substitution for "consilium apostolice sedis" (11) needed no special knowledge; nor did the substitution of the adverbial "benigne" for the adjectival "benignum" (51), which could, in any case, have been derived from the abbreviated form *benign,'* which occurs in Diceto, as does "pertingere" for "attingere" (17). Only "studeas," the present subjunctive, which balances "agas," in the same tense and mood, might be argued to be a better reading than the imperative "stude" (71) transmitted by Giraldus–Diceto, but that could be the result of emendation in the "protest tradition."

The treatment of the last sentence (81) seems to point not to independent derivation from a more accurate (and authentic) text but to corruption of what had been received from the narrative source(s). In Giraldus–Diceto the passage reads, "ut a Deo sempiterne mercedis cumulum consequi merearis, et in terris gloriosum nomen ualeas in seculis obtinere (that from God you deserve to receive the crown of everlasting reward, and on earth obtain a name renowned for all ages.),'" which *PR* rendered as "ut a Deo sempiterne mercedis cumulum consequi merearis, et in terris gloriosum nomen ualeas et in celis obtinere (optinere) (that from God you may deserve to attain the crown of everlasting reward, and earn a glorious name on earth and in heaven)" (to which *R* added a wholly inappropriate "Valete").[82] This reading can hardly be considered better or more authentic than Giraldus–Diceto. Rather, it seems to have been produced, either by misreading "celis" for "seculis" in the penultimate word, or by unconscious substitution of "celis" in order to balance the preceding "terris." *L*, derived from *PR*'s source, made matters worse by omitting the first "et," so that Henry's eternal reward would be "in terris" and his "glorious name" "in celis": "ut a Deo sempiterne mercedis cumulum consequi merearis in terris et gloriosum nomen in celis valeas obtinere (that from God you may deserve to attain the crown of everlasting reward on earth, and earn a glorious name in heaven)" (followed, as in *R*, by the redundant "Valete"). A similar blunder was made, and rectified, by Walter Bower, in the primary manuscript of his *Scotichronicon* (Cambridge, Corpus Christi College, MS 171b). The scribe first wrote "ut a Deo sempiterne mercedis cumulum consequi merearis in *terris*, et gloriosum nomen valeas in terris optinere" (followed by "Dat', c."), but he subsequently deleted *terris* and inserted "celis" as an interlinear correction. This made better sense, since Henry's eternal reward is more properly associated with heaven than earth, and his "glorious name" carries terrestrial rather than celestial implications. But Walter Bower's source, John of Fordun's *Chronica gentis Scotorum*, was itself confused at this point,[83] and the insertion of "celis" may have been an intelligent correction made by Bower as he checked his text, rather than a better tradition. What the treatment of the concluding passage shows, however, is that none of the "official" texts can be used to prove the existence of an authentic *Laudabiliter* separate from the Giraldus–Diceto text. Two of the four versions *(LR)* filled the lacuna created by the missing dating clause not with a better derivation but with the commonplace "Valete," which,

---

[82] Haren, "*Laudabiliter*: Text and Context," p. 147, agrees that "it is to be judged in all probablility a misplaced scribal addition," but he did not know that it appears also in *L*.

[83] Johannus de Fordun, *Chronica gentis Scotorum*, ed. William F. Skene, *The Historians of Scotland*, 1–2 (Edinburgh, 1871), 2:908 at n. 4.

apart from its plural form following a letter quite properly addressed to the king in the second person singular, would never have been appended to a formal papal letter; and the third *(S)* supplied a short abbreviation *(Dat' c.)*, which proves no more than that somewhere along the line, some copyist realized that there should be some kind of date. Similar emendation may explain what may indeed be a better reading in *S* and its source, John of Fordun. Where *A, D, W,* and *M* read *interno examine, L* reads *uero, PR* read *in interno examine,* and *S* reads *in extremo examine* ("in the last judgment").[84] The insertion of this correction would transform the awkward *quanto id a nobis interno examine districtius prospicimus exigendum* ("as we realize from the scrutiny of our own conscience that it is strictly required of us") into *quanto id a nobis in extremo examine districtius prospicimus exigendum* ("as we foresee that it will be strictly required of us in the last judgment")—which seems eminently preferable. The insertion of *in* before *interno examine* in *P* and *R* may record an intermediate stage, either in the correction of an earlier error or in the transformation of the less usual "in the scrutiny of our own conscience" into the more commonplace "in the last judgment."

---

[84] Above, nn. 34 and 35; cf. John of Fordun, 2:907.

Appendix II

English translation of the original Laudabiliter:

(1) Laudably and profitably enough does your magnificence contemplate extending [your?] glorious name on earth and laying up a reward of eternal bliss in heaven, as you strive, as a Catholic prince should, to enlarge the boundaries of the Church, to reveal the truth of the Christian faith to peoples still untaught and barbarous, and to root out the weeds of vice from the Lord's field; and the more expeditiously to achieve this end, you seek the counsel and favor of the Apostolic See. The higher the resolve and the greater the discretion with which you go forward in this action, the more successful, we believe, with God's help, will be your progress in it, since enterprises which have their beginning in ardent faith and love of religion are wont always to attain a good outcome and conclusion.

(3) Inasmuch as you have indicated to us, very dearly beloved son in Christ, that you wish to enter the island of Ireland to make that people obedient to the laws and to root out from there the weeds of vices, and that you are willing to pay St. Peter an annual tax of one penny from every household, and to preserve the rights of the churches of that land intact and unimpaired,

(4) We therefore, supporting your pious and praiseworthy intention with the favor it deserves and granting our benevolent consent to your petition, deem it pleasing and acceptable that, to enlarge the boundaries of the church, to check the downward course of wickedness, to correct morals and implant virtues, to encourage the growth of the Christian religion, you should enter that island and pursue policies directed towards the honor of God and the wellbeing of that land, and that the people of that land receive you honorably and respect you as their lord, on condition that the rights of the churches remain intact and unimpaired, and without prejudice to the payment to St. Peter and the holy Roman church of an annual tax of one penny from every household.

(2) Indeed there is no doubt, as your nobility also recognizes, that Ireland, and indeed all islands on which Christ, the sun of justice, has

shed His rays, and which have received the teachings of the Christian faith, belong to the jurisdiction of blessed Peter and the holy Roman church. Hence we are all the more eager to establish in them a transplant of the faith, an offshoot pleasing to God, as we realize that an examination of our own heart sternly requires us so to do.

(a)   But yet, although your excellency . . . particular exploit.

(b)   Add to this, that it would seem to be neither wise . . . protection.

(c)   Indeed, your discretion should with prudent . . . that path.[1]

(5)   Then, if you consider it proper to complete in effect what you have conceived in your mind, take particular care to instruct that people in right behavior and, both in person, and acting through those whom you consider well-suited for this purpose by reason of their faith, eloquence and manner of life, strive to ensure that the church there may be enhanced, that the Christian religion may be planted and grow, and that everything pertaining to the honor of God and the salvation of souls may be so ordered that you may deserve to attain the crown of everlasting reward from God, and on earth, earn a name renowned for all ages.

---

[1] Above, pp. 138–39 for sections (a)–(c).

Middle Eastern Apocalyptic Traditions in Dante's *La Divina Commedia* and Mohammed's *Mi^craj* or Night Journey

Brenda Deen Schildgen
University of California, Davis

TWO TEXTS IN the Koran refer to a vision in which Mohammed receives a divine messenger (81:19–25 and 53:12–18). Also, Koran 17:1, "Praised be he who traveled by night with his servant from the sacred mosque to the farthest sanctuary," has been interpreted in each of the following ways: 1) it refers to Mohammed's ascension to heaven; 2) it refers to a night journey to Jerusalem; 3) it refers to the prophet's vision of the other world.[1] This night journey, "isra," through the heavens, has inspired a

---

Some of the material in this essay has been discussed in a different context in my book *Dante and the Orient* (Urbana, 2002) and in another essay, "Allegory, Time, and Space in the *Mi^craj* and its Commentary Tradition," *Allegorica* 22 (2001), 31–46.

[1] See "*Mi^craj*," in *The Encyclopaedia of Islam*, new edition, 7 (MIF–NAZ), ed. C. E. Bosworth, E. van Donzel, W. P. Heinrichs and Ch. Pellat (London, 1993), pp. 97–105; also, for an overview of *mi^craj* and its influence on Islamic culture, see Annemarie Schimmel, *And Muhammad Is His Messenger: The Veneration of the Prophet in Islamic Piety* (Chapel Hill, 1985), especially "The Prophet's Night Journey and Ascension," pp. 159–75; Étienne Renaud, "Le Récit du *Mi^crâj*: Une version Arabe de l'ascension du prophète, dans le *Tafsîr* de Tabarî," in *Apocalypses et Voyages dans l'Au-Delà*, ed. Claude Kappler (Paris, 1987), pp. 267–90; and Angelo M. Piemontese,

---

number of texts called *mi'raj*, meaning ladder, describing Mohammed's ascent to the heavens. The *mi'raj* tradition can be considered a commentary or expansion on Sura 17:1 in the Koran, in which, with God speaking, Mohammed is described as going by night from the Sacred Temple (Mecca) to the Farther Temple (Jerusalem). Widely dispersed in many different versions, the *mi'raj* is a combination of both the night journey and the vision of heaven. In this vision, one night as Mohammed was sleeping in Mecca, he was awakened by the angel Gabriel, who lifted him onto an exotic mount, a winged animal named Buraq.[2] Accompanied by Gabriel, Mohammed made a night journey in which he traveled through the seven heavens, saw the marvels of heaven and punishments of hell, met all the former prophets, and climbing the heavenly ladder, had an encounter with God.

Like other apocalyptic texts,[3] the multiple versions of the *mi'raj*, or *Book of the Ladder*,[4] possess many parallels with Dante's *Divina*

"Le Voyage de Mahomet au Paradis et en Enfer: Une Version Persane du *Mi'raj*," in *Apocalypses et Voyages*, ed. Kappler, pp. 293–320.

[2] For "Al burak," see R. Paret's entry in *Encyclopedia of Islam*, new edition, 1, pp. 1310–11. In the *Mi'raj*, Buraq is described as an animal larger than an ass but smaller than a mule with a man's face; its hair was made of pearls, the mane of emeralds, and the tail of rubies; its feet and hooves were like a camel's; and its color was pure light.

[3] For a discussion of apocalyptic literature in the ancient and medieval Middle East, see James C. Vanderkam, "Apocalyptic Literature," in *The Cambridge Companion to Biblical Interpretation* (Cambridge, 1998), pp. 305–22; for a discussion that includes medieval apocalyptic literature, see "Apocalypses des Religions du Livre," in *Apocalypses et Voyages*, ed. Kappler, pp. 183–374. With specific reference to the *Mi'raj*, see Brooke Olson Vuckovic, *Heavenly Journeys, Earthly Concerns: The Legacy of the Mi'raj in the Formation of Islam* (New York, 2005).

[4] The Latin and French versions of the *mi'raj* are printed in Enrico Cerulli, *Il "Libro della Scala" e La Questione delle Fonti Arabo-Spagnole della Divina Commedia* (Vatican City, 1949), pp. 24–247. See also *Le Livre de l' Échelle de Mahomet*, a dual-language Latin text and modern French translation, translated and edited by Gisèle Besson and Michèle Brossard-Dandré (Paris, 1991). It is the Latin text used here, and is referred to as *Livre de l'Échelle*; English translations are mine. E. Blochet, *Les Sources orientales de la Divine Comédie* (Paris, 1901; rpt., 1969) deals with parallels between the *mi'raj*, which he traces to Persian origins, and the *Commedia*. See also Vicente Cantarino, "Dante and Islam: History and Analysis of a Controversy," in *A Dante Symposium in Commemoration of the 700th Anniversary of the Poet's Birth (1265-1965)*, ed. William de Sua and Gino Rizzo (Chapel Hill, 1965), pp. 175–98, which includes a lengthy and annotated bibliography of the work on the subject up to that date.

Commedia. The first-person narrator that the *Commedia* and the *miʿraj* share connects each text to the apocalyptic genres of the ancient and medieval Near East (whether canonical works, such as Ezekiel, Daniel, and the Apocalypse of John, or noncanonical, such as the Apocalypse of Paul) and the *miʿraj* traditions as they appear in Sufi writings.[5] Putting the works side by side as popular narratives also highlights the apocalyptic prophetic traditions shared by Christianity and Islam and represented in these contemporary heavenly journeys. In this essay, I maintain that both the *Commedia* and the *miʿraj* share a common literary tradition in that they adopt the genre of apocalyptic,[6] which has its sources in Middle Eastern literary traditions, whether biblical, apocryphal, or Koranic. But although they share a common matrix in sacred or apocryphal apocalyptic writings, a parallel reception in popular and high culture milieu in their respective parts of the world (images from the works appear in cartoons as well as in major works of art and illuminated manuscripts [in the West for Dante], and decorations for trucks and cars or exceptional illuminated manuscripts [in Islamic-dominated regions]), the works nonetheless are also very different. Dante's is a poetic work, following the precedents of ancient Roman poetry, which the poet transforms according to his own needs; it is profoundly biblical; it is steeped in patristic and medieval Christian theology; and it recounts the journey of a sinful man, Dante, as typological new Adam. The *miʿraj,* at least in the versions that were translated for Western readers in the Middle Ages, is, in contrast to the *Commedia,* a prose work, told in the voice of the prophet of Islam, and although it is a religious work that reinforces Islamic faith profession and practices with repeated references to the Koran, it lacks the extensive literary-theological apparatus that characterizes Dante's poem. The expansive theological and mystical apparatus one finds in Dante's

---

5 Theodore Silverstein and Anthony Hilhorst, *Apocalypse of Paul: A New Critical Edition of Three Long Latin Versions* (Geneva, 1997). Quotations of the "Visio Pauli" in this essay come from the Paris text. For a translation of the Latin "Apocalypse of Paul," see Edgar Hennecke and Wilhelm Schneemelcher, *New Testament Apocrypha,* vol. 2 (Philadelphia, 1963), pp. 759–98. For translations of various heavenly and infernal visions that include these apocryphal texts, see Eileen Gardiner, ed., *Visions of Heaven and Hell Before Dante* (New York, 1989).

6 For apocalyptic in Dante, see Raoul Manselli, "Apocalisse," in *Enciclopedia Dantesca,* vol. 1, pp. 315–17. See also Nicolo Mineo, *Profetismo e apocalittica in Dante: strutture e temi profetico-apocalittici in Dante dalla Vita nuova alla Divina commedia* (Catania, 1968).

poem, however, was central to the numerous versions and commentaries on the *miᶜraj* written by Islamic philosophers and mystics in Arabic and Persian.

To observe Dante's interest in a popular apocalyptic literary tradition does not prove influence. Neither does it necessarily demonstrate the practice of "Orientalism," that is, the invention of the East by Western scholars and writers, from Homer to the nineteenth century, as Edward Said ardently argued in *Orientalism*.[7] Rather, it demonstrates a shared eschatology in the works and the cultures from which they emanate: otherworldly visions above all embrace God's judicial role, and both works, while following their own cultural and religious convictions, assign absolute justice to the divinity. Whether a projection of utopian desire or the product of a harsh unforgiving spirit, apocalyptic writing inevitably calls humans to account for their transgressions. Both works employ codes of ethics based on biblical or Koranic precedents, with the *miᶜraj* also functioning as a means for reinforcing Islamic communal identity.[8] In linking the works to apocalyptic traditions, thus, this essay seeks to emphasize common convictions of Islam and Christianity that characterize the two texts, even in the medieval context of crusade that brought Christian and Islamic civilization into open warfare. Thus, the *miᶜraj*, as one of the texts that for Dante belong to what Wolfgang Iser has called a literary repertoire,[9] shows that the poet shares his apocalyptic visionary mode with the *miᶜraj* text he may have encountered and that he could recognize in it a common system of divine justice and punishment.

Both the commentary tradition on the *miᶜraj* texts and the various versions highlight the diverse approaches taken to interpreting its visionary

---

[7] Edward Said, *Orientalism* (New York, 1979). Said's views have been critically scrutinized and questioned from their first appearance and have recently come under severe attack. See, for example, Robert Irwin's review of *Orientalism*, "Writing about Islam and the Arabs: A Review of E. W. Said, *Orientalism*," in *Ideology and Consciousness* 9 (Winter, 1981/2); Aijaz Ahmad, *In Theory: Classes, Nations, Literatures* (New York, 1992), pp. 159–219, and recently Robert Irwin, *Dangerous Knowledge: Orientalism and Its Discontents* (Woodstock and New York, 2006). The factual questions these authors raise, however, have not prevented the spawning of imitations that apply Said's polemical position blithely to an array of medieval and other European texts.

[8] Vuckovic, *Heavenly Journeys*, p. 97.

[9] Wolfgang Iser, *The Act of Reading: A Theory of Aesthetic Response* (Baltimore, 1978), p. 79.

meaning. For some, like Abu-Bakr, this journey was literally true. For the Sufi masters and mystical writers, like Bistami (d. ca. 261 AH), al Hallaj (d. 309 AH), al-Qushayri (d. 465 AH), Al-Ghazali (450–505 AH), and Ibn Arabi (d. 638 AH), besides being a model for ecstatic experience, the *mi'raj* is an allegory about a journey to God and the knowledge that accrues from such a journey.[10] A version of the *mi'raj* attributed to Avicenna (370–428 AH) and written in Persian allegorized and philosophized the journey narrative and all that the pilgrim had seen. Avicenna's text tells of Mohammed's ascent into heaven, but the commentary, which is the central purpose of his work, follows Islamic traditions of allegory, intellectualizing the elements of the text that do not make sense according to rational apprehension. Avicenna specifically uses a kind of allegory to rationalize the eschatology in the literal level of the text. He writes, "A friend of ours has continually inquired about the meaning of the Ascension, desiring it explained in a rational way."[11] Thus, by making the text a philosophical allegory, Avicenna's commentary radically alters its temporal and spatial dimension. Allegorizing the text enables him to turn the duration and locations of the journey into abstractions; furthermore, turning an ostensible material experience into an allegory allows him to focus on the ontological implications of the metaphorical journey. He thus eliminates both the *mi'raj* text's eschatology and its materialism in favor of its philosophical relevance.[12]

Eighty years ago Western medieval scholars first began to argue that a version of the *mi'raj* was a major Islamic source for the *Divina Commedia*.[13] Miguel Asín Palacios's 1919 and 1927 studies had argued that the

[10] For introductory material, see Michael A. Sells, trans. and ed., *Early Islamic Mysticism: Sufi, Qur'an, Mi'raj, Poetic and Theological Writings* (New York, 1996), pp. 47–61. See also Vuckovic, *Heavenly Journeys*, p. 125.

[11] Peter Heath, *Allegory and Philosophy in Avicenna (Ibn Sina), With a Translation of the Book of the Prophet Muhammad's Ascent to Heaven* (Philadelphia, 1992), p. 111.

[12] Heath, *Allegory and Philosophy in Avicenna.* See also "Allegory, Time, and Space in the *Mi'raj*" for a discussion of Avicenna's technique for finessing the irrational elements in the narrative.

[13] Besides Blochet, Cerulli, and Miguel Asín Palacios, *La escatología musulmana en la Divina Comedia* (Madrid, 1919; rpt. 1943) and *Dante y El Islam* (Madrid, 1927), others who have written on the Islamic influences on the *Divine Comedy* include Leonardo Olschki, "Dante e l'Oriente," *Il Giornale dantesco* 39 (1938), pp. 65–90; Olschki argues, not surprisingly, that a fatal schism divided the "Occident"

texts that circulated about Mohammed's night journey had influenced Dante's major poem, although in fact Dante did not know Arabic and many of Palacios's sources had not been translated from Arabic into any European languages. Around the middle of the twentieth century, Enrico Cerulli explored and sought to demonstrate concrete links between Dante's poem and Mohammed's night journey.[14] Cerulli provided innumerable other testimonies to the widespread diffusion of the narrative(s) including the remains of the Castilian manuscript, the texts, told in the voice of Mohammed, in the *Primera Cronica General*,[15] undertaken at the court of Alfonso X, and those of Ramon Lull. Palacios and Cerulli's work led scholars to recognize that Islamic eschatology was known and described in a number of Western Latin and vernacular texts and that ample evidence showed various versions of the *mi^{c}raj* were circulating in Western Europe by the thirteenth century.

"Orientalists" in the tradition of nineteenth-century literary scholars (as described by Edward Said), Palacios and Cerulli were deeply trained in languages,[16] particularly Arabic and Persian—(Cerulli was the Italian ambassador to Persia). They belong to an earlier school of literary study, one in which the researcher sought primarily to track down sources, sometimes to prove dependency and sometimes to demote the status of the receiving author whose originality was therefore suspect. In addition, in the case of Dante, another intellectual purpose was underway, for to locate Dante's sources outside the Latin Western literary tradition would identify his masterpiece with more than just another of his many sources. To locate a source in the popular eschatological traditions of Islam was to link Dante with popular culture, with Islam, and potentially with heterodoxy.

---

from the "Orient" in Dante's time; René Guénon, *L'Esoterismo di Dante* (Rome, 1951); F. Gabrieli, "Dante e l'Islam," *Cultura e Scuola* 13–14 (1965), pp. 194–97. Rosa Trillo Clough, "Gli studi intorno alle fonti islamiche in Dante e nelle poesie della scuola del *Dolce Stil Nuovo*," *L'Alighieri* 9, no. 2 (1968), pp. 66–73.

    [14] See Cerulli, *"Libro della Scala"*; Enrico Cerulli, *Nuove ricerche sul Libro della Scala e la conoscenza dell'Islam in Occidente* (Vatican City, 1972).

    [15] See Ramón Menéndez Pidal, ed., *Primera Crónica General de España*, 2 vols. (Madrid, 1978), 1: 270–72.

    [16] See Said, *Orientalism*, for a discussion of the training of European "orientalists" in the nineteenth century, pp. 95–105.

Of course, the medieval period also had its learned "Orientalists," in the Said sense, beginning from at least the twelfth century. When Peter the Venerable visited the Cluniac monasteries in Spain in the twelfth century, he was astonished by the intensity of learned activity spurred by the Arab presence in Iberia. The first to recognize the necessity of dialogue with Islam, even while believing that Islam was "an enemy of the Cross of Christ," Peter recommended peaceful efforts at conversion rather than belligerent confrontation. Peter studied Islam, its texts, and its prophet, and he commissioned a series of translations from Arabic, including the Latin translation of the Koran. His studies led him to conclude that Islam was a Christian heresy that grew while the Roman Empire was declining and, as a religious-political movement, could occupy by arms most of Asia, all of Africa, and a part of Spain.[17] Another twelfth-century scholar of the East, William of Tyre (b. 1130, Jerusalem; bishop of Tyre from 1175–84/85, chancellor of the kingdom of Jerusalem from 1174) produced the *Chronicon*, a history of the Middle East up to the imminent conquest of Jerusalem by Saladin in 1170. Jacques de Vitry (b. 1160–70; d. 1240), a French monk who became bishop of Acre in 1217 and later bishop of Jerusalem, reproduced a version of William's *Chronicon*.[18] Both circulated in the Latin West.

A thirteenth-century Florentine, Frate Ricoldo da Montecroce (1234–1320), who had entered the Dominican order in 1267 and who lectured at Santa Maria Novella intermittently until he left for Asia in 1288, brings Dante directly into contact with a scholar of Islam. In Baghdad for twelve years, Ricoldo stayed even after Acre fell in 1291, returning to Florence in 1300. So, it is likely that Dante encountered him, especially since the poet frequented the Dominican *studium* at Santa Maria Novella. In Baghdad, where Ricoldo studied Arabic, he preached and disputed religious beliefs with Arab scholars. He knew Arabic well enough to preach Christianity on the streets in Baghdad, but when he returned to Florence in 1300, he did not teach it. Scholars have argued that Dante did know Ricoldo, but

---

[17] See *"Liber Contra Sectam,"* in James Kritzeck, *Peter the Venerable and Islam* (Princeton, 1964), introduction, pp. 220–91, particularly pp. 220–26.

[18] William, Archbishop of Tyre. *A History of Deeds Done Beyond the Sea* in 2 vols., Emily Atwater Babcock and A. C. Krey, trans. and annotated (New York, 1976); *Chronicon* in 2 vols., ed R. B. C. Huygens, with notes and dates by H. E. Mayer and G. Rösch in *CCSL* Continuatio Mediaevalis 63 and 63A (Turnhout, 1986). Jacques de Vitry, *La Traduction de l'Historia Orientalis*, ed. Claude Buridant (Paris, 1986).

that he did not immerse himself in Arabic studies as some have maintained, even though he clearly respected Arabic philosophy.[19] Ricoldo is the author of an *Itinerarium*,[20] a guide for crusaders and pilgrims that describes the holy places, for which there is a fourteenth-century Italian translation,[21] of the *Confutatio Alcorani*, and of the *Libellus contra errores Judaeorum*.

These works were disseminated in Florence, where Ricoldo produced his major work, *Contra Legem Sarracenorum*, a polemic that shows a sophisticated understanding of the religious beliefs and practices of Islam, even though the author clearly scorns Mohammed, the Koran (which he argues is a disordered law), and Islamic beliefs.[22] This treatise includes a version and a commentary on what Ricoldo calls "the ridiculous vision of Mohammed" that is based on one of the circulating versions of the *mi'raj*.[23] Ricoldo tells the story of Mohammed's night journey, but he seems intent on proving its unreliability. About Buraq, Mohammed's famous steed on which he rode from Mecca to Jerusalem in the vision, a very common iconographic representation of Mohammed to this day, he asks, "Why would he have needed an ass to go from Mecca to Jerusalem when he went to the ends of the heavens without a steed?"[24] As if to demonstrate the falsity of the story, he reports that after Mohammed told people about it, sixty thousand men denounced his law. According to Ricoldo, and in the tradition of his fellow Dominican, Thomas Aquinas, Mohammed could not perform miracles. For Ricoldo, the vision story

---

[19] For Ricoldo's history, see Ricoldo da Montecroce, *I Saraceni: Contra Legem Sarracenorum*, ed. Giuseppe Rizzardi (Florence, 1992), pp. 7–24. For Ricoldo, see also Ugo Monneret de Villard, *Il Libro della Peregrinazione nelle Parti d'Oriente di Frate Ricoldo da Montecroce* (Rome, 1948), pp. 84, 104–18. For Dante and Ricoldo, see Gabrieli, "Dante e l'Islam." For Santa Maria Novella and Dante, see Charles T. Davis, "The Florentine Studia and Dante's 'Library,'" in *The Divine Comedy and the Encyclopedia of Arts and Sciences*, ed. Giuseppe Di Scipio and Aldo Scaglione (Amsterdam, 1988), pp. 339–66.

[20] Ricoldo da Monte Croce, *Pérégrination en Terre Sainte et au Proche Orient*, Latin text and French translation (Paris, 1997).

[21] *Viaggio in Terra Santa di fra Ricoldo da Monte di Croce*, volgarizzamento del secolo XIV (Siena, 1964).

[22] Ricoldo, *I Saraceni: Contra Legem Sarracenorum*, pp. 7–24.

[23] Ricoldo, *I Saraceni*, the section on the vision, pp. 149–53; Enrico de Cerulli, *Il "Libro della Scala,"* pp. 346–57.

[24] Ricoldo, *I Saraceni*, p. 152.

proves Mohammed holds the objectionable view that God and the angels occupy a physical space. Ricoldo's concerns bear similarities to those that led Avicenna to rationalize the visionary elements of the *mi'raj*.[25]

Demonstrating scholarly engagement with Islam and Islamic beliefs in the twelfth and thirteenth centuries in Western Europe, nonetheless, these works defend the Christian dispensation and argue against Islamic popular belief. Ricoldo, in particular, writing after the recent defeat of the Christians and their final retreat from Acre, defends Christianity against what he perceives as the violence, falsities, and hedonism of Islam and its prophet, "questo Maometto [che] perseguitò la legge di Dio più di tutti quelli che la perseguitarono e la perseguiteranno" [this Mohammed who persecuted the law of God more than any who have persecuted it or will persecute it].[26]

Thus we might see some similarities between twelfth- to thirteenth-century and nineteenth-century "Orientalisms," in that deep immersion in knowing the "other" culture led these scholars to learn the languages, read central texts of that "other," and foster translations into European languages, in the earlier time, primarily Latin. But here the similarities end. While Peter the Venerable clearly saw Islam as a challenge to Christianity, he, like William of Tyre and Ricoldo, became interested in Islam and the cultures that grew up in and around it because they desired knowledge of this "other" to bolster Christianity against its intellectual, military, and cultural challenges. They were not colonialists intent on intellectual conquest or supporters of colonial projects; rather they were in a defensive position, upholding Christianity and what they believed were Christian truths against what they perceived, rightly or wrongly, as a dangerous threat.

More recently, with the advent of postcolonial theory, Dante's attitudes toward Islam have been scrutinized through the lens of postcolonial "Orientalist" eyes, and since he condemned Mohammed and his nephew, Ali, to Hell as schismatics (*Inferno* 28, 28–36), Said concluded, "Dante's poetic grasp of Islam [is] an instance of the schematic, almost cosmological inevitability with which Islam and its designated representatives are creatures of Western geographical, historical, and above all, moral apprehension."[27] Dante's position is not radically different from the

---

[25] Ricoldo, *I Saraceni*, pp. 151–52. See "Allegory, Time, and Space in the *Mi'raj*."

[26] See Ricoldo da Montecroce, *I Saraceni*, p. 57; English translations are mine.

[27] Said, *Orientalism*, p. 69.

attitudes expressed in Peter the Venerable, Thomas Aquinas, or Ricoldo da Montecroce. Thomas wrote in the *Summa Contra Gentiles:*

> . . . mahumeto, qui carnalium voluptatum promissis, ad quorum desiderium carnalis concupiscentia instigat, populos illexit . . . sed dixit se in armorum potentia missum, quae signa etiam latronibus et tyrannis non desunt. . . . homines bestiales in desertis morantes [crediderunt], omnis doctrinae divinae prorsus ignari, per quorum multitudinem alios armorum violentia in suam legem coegit.

> [Mohammed . . . seduced the people by promises of carnal pleasure to which the concupiscence of the flesh goads us . . . Mohammed said that he was sent in the power of his arms—which are signs not lacking even to robbers and tyrants. . . . Those who believed in him were brutal men and desert wanderers, utterly ignorant of all divine teaching, through whose numbers Mohammed forced others to become his followers by the violence of his arms.][28]

Thomas's concerns highlight the Christian position that Islam was a schism from Christianity and that it had spread not by "divine teaching" but by force of arms, and Dante shows he adheres to the accepted medieval Christian learned position on Islam and its prophet.

But Dante's attitudes were broader than this widespread medieval Christian view of Islam. He found spaces for Averroës and Avicenna, domiciled with Plato, Socrates, and Aristotle in Limbo (*Inferno* 4, 143–44) and also for Saladin (*Inferno* 4, 129).[29] Furthermore, he overlooked the crisis of orthodoxy at the University of Paris in the 1270s to find a place for the Averroist Siger of Brabant in *Paradiso* (10, 136). Dante gives special dispensation to Averroës, Avicenna, and Saladin, finding places for them among the moral pagans in Limbo, even though they lived after the time of the Incarnation and therefore could have become Christians. Averroës, in

---

[28] Thomas Aquinas, *Summa Contra Gentiles,* vol. 2, in *S. Thomae Aquinatis Opera Omnia,* ed. Roberto Busa, S.J. (Stuttgart, 1980), Bk. I, ch. 6; for the trans., see Anton C. Pegis, trans. and ed., *On the Truth of the Catholic Faith: Summa Contra Gentiles* (New York, 1955), p. 73.

[29] All quotations whether in Italian or English come from *The Divine Comedy,* trans. and commentary by Charles S. Singleton (Princeton, 1970–76).

fact, "che 'l gran comento feo" (who made the great Commentary [144]),[30] receives special attention for his learned accomplishment. This apparent inconsistency in Dante's condemnation of Mohammed and his son-in-law, the Caliph Ali, and his reverence for famed Islamic scholars stems from the poet's willingness to distinguish learned activity—particularly that which informed the theological work of Albert the Great and Thomas Aquinas,[31] whose own work was so indebted to the Islamic philosophers and commentators on Aristotle—from political activity. Casting Mohammed and Ali to hell among the schismatics while settling Averroës and Avicenna in Limbo's garden of repose follows the same distinction the poet makes in dividing Ancient Greek learning from Ancient Greek politics. His aversion to Ulysses and Diomedes provides a vivid contrast with his respect for Plato, Socrates, and Aristotle, who await final judgment with Averroës and Avicenna in Limbo. This is a common division in medieval Christian learned traditions. Both Albert and Thomas were engaged intellectually with Averroism because of Averroës's translations and commentaries on Aristotle's works, many of which came to them first in Arabic versions. In allowing this dispensation, Dante seems to adopt Augustine's distinction between the useful and the enjoyable ("uti" and "frui" in *De Doctrina Christiana*)[32] when he judges all the "lights" in Limbo, for their works proved useful; their writings contributed to Christian conversion and theology, even though those who inhabit Limbo were not recipients of this illuminating and enjoyable end. Furthermore, the special status of Saladin, the Islamic leader who recaptured Jerusalem in 1187,[33] provides a radical contrast with Frederick II, last Roman emperor, whom Dante

---

[30] Averroës was known in the Middle Ages as "the commentator" because he wrote commentaries or summaries of all of Aristotle's major works. For his works, see Harry Austryn Wolfson et al., eds., *Corpus Commentariorum Averrois in Aristotelem*, Medieval Academy of America, 54 (Cambridge, Mass., 1953–56).

[31] See, for example, Albert the Great, *De Anima*, ed. A. Borgnet (Paris, 1890), pp. 117–443, and *De Natura loci*, where he points out the differences in Ptolemy's and Averroës's cosmographical theories. For Christian theological differences with the works of Averroës and Avicenna, see Thomas Aquinas, *Summa Contra Gentiles*.

[32] Augustine, *De Doctrina Christiana*, in *CCSL* 32 (Turnhout, 1962), pp. 1–167.

[33] See Américo Castro, "The Presence of the Sultan Saladin in the Romance Literatures," in *An Idea of History: Selected Essays of Américo Castro 1954*, trans. and ed. Stephen Gilman and Edmund L. King (Columbus, OH, 1977; rpt. "Présence du Sultan Saladin dans les littératures romaines," *Diogènes* 8 [1954], 1–23), pp. 241–69.

condemns to Hell for his reputed epicurean and Islamic cultural indulgences and for his failure in his duty as emperor to unify the Latin world. But in keeping with medieval Latin convention, Dante's Saladin is a model Islamic leader, and thus he receives the same deferential treatment from the poet as other ancient luminaries.

Unlike Saladin's conquest of Jerusalem, Mohammed's schism, according to Dante's view, splintered the Christian world and its geopolitical territory, or erstwhile Roman imperial boundaries. Like all schisms, it was doomed to create further schism, just as all the other examples of civil disruption the poet presents in *Inferno* 28 (whether their settings were ancient Greece or Rome, whether they were religious disruptions, contemporary ones, or occurred in Italy, or someplace else in Europe).

In recent years, critics interested in Dante and Islam have shifted their focus from locating Dante's sources to assessing how the poet has incorporated Islamic texts or ideas into his major work. Maria Rosa Menocal has argued that Dante wrote the *Commedia* as a direct answer to the Islamic version of the other world circulating in one of the versions of the *mi'raj* texts.[34] Maria Corti, on the other hand, took up the influence of Averroës and Averroism on Dante.[35] While Dante's encyclopedic reading no doubt led him to a version of the *mi'raj* text,[36] translated into Latin or French, nonetheless it still remains as one among many of the poet's sources.

Originally written in Arabic in many different versions, the *mi'raj* was translated from Arabic into Castilian by Abraham Alfaquin, a Jewish physician at the court of Alfonso X el Sabio (d. 1284). Thence, also in the second half of the thirteenth century, it was retranslated under the king's patronage into Latin by Bonaventure of Siena, a friend of Brunetto Latini's (*Inferno* 15, 24–124), who was in exile from Florence at the court of Alfonso X, along with a number of other Florentines, and then into French as early as 1264. In fact, Bonaventure of Siena actually explains this history of transmission through languages in his introduction to his own translation.[37] Besides various Arabic and Persian versions, Latin, Old

[34] Maria Rosa Menocal, *The Arabic Role in Medieval Literary History: A Forgotten Heritage* (Philadelphia, 1987). See ch. 5, pp. 115–35.

[35] Maria Corti, *Percorsi dell' invenzione: Il linguaggio poetico e Dante* (Turin, 1993).

[36] See "Libro della Scala," in *Enciclopedia Dantesca*, vol. 2 (Rome, 1973).

[37] See *Livre de l' Échelle de Mahomet*, pp. 78–80. For the history of the translations in the Latin Middle Ages, see Reginald White, *The Prophet of Islam in Old*

French, and Castilian versions still survive. Once translated into Latin and French, one might argue, the *mi'raj* joined a community of European texts, even while it retained its evident links to its Islamic origins as well as to earlier apocalyptic textual traditions. With all these global connections in the *mi'raj* tradition of many versions, even if not of a particular text, we might see it as belonging to a typical economy of medieval letters in which borrowing and exchange flourish while territorial, cultural, and linguistic specifics are overcome in favor of literary adaptation.[38]

Connecting the *mi'raj* tradition with Dante's poem through this apocalyptic dimension is not intended to undermine what I take to be its most evident relationship to Augustine's *Confessions*, to the Latin classics, to the Bible, and to Western philosophy and theology. These connections link Dante's poem to a vast repertoire of long-revered textual traditions, which indeed cannot be said of the *mi'raj*, although ancient apocalyptic texts have conversion as their rhetorical purpose, which they share with Dante's poem. Like the *Confessions,* Dante's poem is a personal drama and also a judgment of history like the *Aeneid*. In addressing this apocalyptic element, I am not trying to reduce Dante to a single-minded follower of the Joachimite movement. As M. Barbi wrote many years ago, "*La Divina Commedia* è una profezia, una rivelazione, nessun dubbio. Ma Dante non ebbe bisogno perciò d'ispirarsi né ai sogni del monaco calabrese né a quelli dei seminatori di discordia nell' ordine francescano . . . ebbe più sincere fonti d'ispirazione nei profeti veri."[39] [*The Divine Comedy* is a prophecy, a revelation, no doubt. But Dante had neither the need to inspire himself with the dreams of the Calabrian monk nor with the sowers of discord in the Franciscan order . . . he had purer sources of inspiration in true prophets.] It is these sources of inspiration in the "true prophets" that both Dante's poem and the *mi'raj* texts share. Dante adopts the voice of biblical prophets and apocalyptic texts to declare that personal failures and triumphs, along with the violence and

---

French: *The Romance of Muhammad (1258) and the Book of Muhammad's Ladder (1264)* (Leiden, 1997), pp. 19–25.

[38] Pascale Casanova, *The World Republic of Letters*, trans. M. B. DeBevoise (Cambridge, Mass., 2004). For the discussion of the role of translation in conferring literary value, see pp. 133–37, where Casanova writes, "Translation is the foremost example of a particular type of consecration in the literary world" (133).

[39] M. Barbi, "Il gioachimismo francescano e I Veltro," in *Studi Danteschi* 18 (1934), pp. 209–11; my translation.

redemption of history, will be judged in the beyond.[40] This last feature ties Dante's work with the *mi'raj* and with Middle Eastern apocalyptic literary traditions.[41]

The genre of apocalyptic has been a controversial topic, some scholars going so far as to insist that it cannot be classified as a literary genre.[42] Indeed, the fact that most apocalyptic literature is not in the biblical canon itself provides persuasive evidence of the Church Fathers' original resistance to it when they debated what would be included in the canon.[43] Christian scholars also resist recognizing the role of apocalyptic in Christian literature even though, as John Collins highlights, numerous examples from the ancient Middle East include Jewish, ancient and Rabbinic, Greek and Latin, Gnostic, and Persian, as well as Christian apocalypses.[44] In a study of the ancient Jewish apocalypses, Collins later

---

[40] See Bruno Nardi, "Dante Profeta," in *Dante e la cultura medievale* (Bari, 1949), pp. 258–334; André Pézard, "Daniel et Dante ou les vengeances de Dieu," *Studi Danteschi* 50 (1973), pp. 1–96, for a discussion of Dante's use of Daniel from the beginning of the poem.

[41] For Middle Eastern Apocalyptic traditions, see John J. Collins, *The Apocalyptic Imagination: An Introduction to the Jewish matrix of Christianity* (New York, 1984); D. Hellholm, *Apocalypticism in the Mediterranean World and the Near East* (Tübingen, 1983).

[42] See Gerhard von Rad, *Theologie des Alten Testaments* (Munich, 1978–80), vol. 2, 330. An excellent overview of the status of work on ancient apocalyptic writing is provided in Bernard McGinn, "Early Apocalypticism: The Ongoing Debate," in *The Apocalypse in English Renaissance Thought and Literature*, ed. C. A. Patrides and Joseph Wittreich (Manchester, 1984), pp. 2–39.

[43] Evidence for canon formation survives in the records of the Council of Hippo (393), repeated at Carthage (397), which lists the book canon of the New Testament as it is today. The Council of Hippo records read: "The canonical books of the New Testament are the four books of the evangelists, the acts of the apostles, thirteen letters of Paul, one letter to the Hebrews, two letters of Peter, three of John, one of James, one of Jude and the Apocalypse of John," in Charles Joseph Hefele, *Histoire des Conciles* Tome II (Paris, 1908), p. 89; William R. Farmer and Denis M. Farkasfalvy, *The Formation of the New Testament Canon* (New York, 1983); Henry Y. Gamble, *The New Testament Canon* (Philadelphia, 1985); and Bruce M. Metzger, *The Canon of the New Testament* (Oxford, 1987), pp. 211–12, 235, and 237 discuss canon formation.

[44] In an issue of *Semeia*, a journal of biblical studies, published in 1979, John Collins, editor of the volume, attempted to make a detailed study of the various examples of apocalypse. He defined it as a "genre of revelatory literature with a narrative framework, in which revelation is mediated by an otherworldly being to a human recipient, disclosing a transcendent reality which is both temporal, insofar as

noted that not all apocalypses share the same features, but one feature they all have in common is the theme of judgment and destruction of the wicked.[45] Absence of this feature would exclude otherworldly visits as found in the ancient epics like the *Aeneid*, which lacks the eschatological dimension, even though Virgil does provide us a supernatural world. Also, Augustine's *Confessions*, though it presupposes a transcendent reality that will adjudicate salvation or damnation, does not present an encounter with that world mediated by an otherworldly figure. In contrast, for both Dante and the *mi'raj* texts, the other world is presented as a visionary experience through which supernatural or no longer living humans guide the first-person narrator.

What do the *mi'raj* traditions and the *Commedia* have in common? Both are vernacular—and therefore popular—apocalyptic religious-literary works, written in the first person and describing judgment after death. The *mi'raj* and the *Commedia* present their narratives as real journeys, in which the pilgrims have visionary experiences, mediated by a guide, Gabriel in the former case, and Virgil, Beatrice, and St. Bernard in the latter. On the journey, the pilgrim learns what humans must do to achieve salvation, and he hears prophecies about and is a witness to eternal judgment. These features characterize apocalypse. Like the *Commedia*, the *mi'raj* is a first-person journey narrative describing the joys of Heaven and the punishments of Hell. Hell in both works houses mythical creatures (*L'Échelle de Mahomet*, ch. 57; *Inferno*, 3, 82–111; 5, 4–24; 6, 13–33, *passim*), serpents (*L'Échelle de Mahomet*, ch. 58; *Inferno* 24, 85–108; 25, 4–9), and a chained devil (*L'Échelle de Mahomet*, ch. 60; *Inferno* 34, 28–51). In addition, there are many eschatological similarities between the two works, including the symbolic treatment of light (*L'Échelle de Mahomet*, ch. 32; 34, *passim*; *Paradiso, passim*), precious stones floating in the heavens (*L'Échelle de Mahomet*, ch. 6; 34; 36, *passim*; *Purgatorio* 1, 13; 7, 73–78; 29, 124–25; 31, 116; *Paradiso*, 2, 33–34; 3, 14; 6, 127; 10, 71; 15, 22; 18, 115 and 117; 19, 4; 20, 17; 22, 29; 30, 66), ascent and descent through parallel hierarchies of Heaven and Hell (*L'Échelle de Mahomet*, ch. 72, *passim*), and a common use of the inexpressibility *topos* to highlight the impossibility of describing such a visionary experience (*L'Échelle de Mahomet*, ch. 45; 48, *passim*; *Paradiso* 1, 70–72; 33, 121–23, *passim*).

---

it envisages eschatological salvation, and spatial, insofar as it involves another supernatural world." See "Apocalypse: the Morphology of a Genre," *Semeia* 14 (1979), p. 9.

[45] Collins, *The Apocalyptic Imagination*, p. 6.

On the other hand, *mi^craj* is a revelation that takes the prophet from Mecca to Jerusalem in a move that traverses the holy sites of Islam, whereas Dante's poem, I would argue, in the tradition of Jerome and Augustine, suppresses interest in the historic Jerusalem in favor of a metaphorical city where Christ was crucified, and a redeemed Rome becomes the center of Dante's political and religious aspiration, as most cogently argued in the *Monarchia* and repeatedly emphasized in the *Commedia*.[46] Furthermore, in terms of the legacy of both works, while Dante's poem embraces Christian-Roman thought, the poem cannot be considered central to the formation of Roman Catholic consciousness, since its primary reception has been as a literary and poetic work. The *mi^craj*, on the other hand, both in its tradition as learned commentary and in its popular reception played a significant role in the formation of Islamic identity, practice, and belief.[47] The *mi^craj*, like the *Commedia*, is theological and steeped in mystical traditions and inflected by Neoplatonic philosophy. But the *mi^craj*, unlike the *Commedia*, installs central features of the profession and practice of Islamic faith, as in the order from God that Mohammed's people fast seventy days a year and pray fifty times a day (chapter 20), or when God gives the Koran to Mohammed (chapter 49), or where the question of how many days of fasting and how many prayers per day is once again discussed, with a reduction of daily prayers to five (chapter 50). Dante's poem, in contrast, brings human history and its major typological actors (whether mythical, literary, sacred, or historical) to court to be judged as malicious, forgivable, or sanctified. Dante makes the writing of his poem the central purpose of his journey when he has his great-great grandfather Cacciaguida commission him to write the *Commedia* in *Paradiso* 17 and to tell all that he has seen; in contrast, Mohammed in the *mi^craj* is charged to install religious and cultic practices.

Still, one important feature the two works do share is that, like other prophetic or apocalyptic texts from the biblical, apocryphal, and Koranic

---

[46] On Dante's politics, see, among others, Charles T. Davis, "Dante's Vision of History," in *Dante's Italy and Other Essays* (Philadelphia, 1984), pp. 23–41; Charles T. Davis, *Dante and the Idea of Rome* (Oxford, 1957); A. P. Entrèves, *Dante as a Political Thinker* (Oxford, 1952); Joan M. Ferrante, *The Political Vision of the Divine Comedy* (Princeton, 1984); Francesco Mazzoni, "Teoresi e prassi in Dante politico," intro. to *Dante Alighieri, Monarchia, Epistole politiche* (Turin, 1966), pp. 9–111; Bruno Nardi, "Il concetto dell'Impero nello svolgimento del pensiero dantesco," in *Saggi di filosofia dantesca* (Florence, 1967; 1st edition 1930), pp. 215–75.

[47] Vuckovic, *Heavenly Journeys*.

traditions, in which the pilgrim witnesses the justice of God, they adopt the first person as the narrative voice, and it is this feature that ties them together as popular vision narrative. Indeed, a remarkable fact of the study of the relationship between the two works is that the use of the first-person narrator has not been addressed. Despite Dante's clear dependence on the Greco-Roman epic tradition, he did not adopt its third-person narrative mode. Rather, in the tradition of biblical prophets and the Koran, and like Augustine in the *Confessions* and the *mi^craj*, he tells his story in the first person. Of course, besides Augustine's *Confessions*, Dante had other models of first-person narrative. Macrobius's *Commentary on the Dream of Scipio*[48] and Boethius's *Consolation of Philosophy*,[49] both visionary works, come to mind immediately. In the vernacular, Guillaume de Lorris and Jean de Meun's *Le Roman de la Rose* also offered another visionary model.[50] But none of these are apocalyptic in the manner of the *Commedia*, the Bible's apocalyptic texts, the *mi^craj*, or other Islamic visionary texts. *The Remembrance of Death and the Afterlife*, where Al-Ghazzali (d. 764 AH) addresses the state of souls after death, also adopts the first person. Al-Ghazzali describes the other world in ways remarkably similar to Dante's and shares with the Italian poet a parallel interest in philosophy and theology.[51]

In addition to the use of the first person, many features of apocalyptic appear in the *Commedia* that find sources in canonical biblical visions such as the Book of Daniel or the Apocalypse of John, apocryphal apocalyptic texts such as the two books of Enoch, the Apocalypse of Ezra, or of Abraham, and the noncanonical "Apocalypse of Paul."[52] Establishing the shared texts between the two seems unnecessary because both Dante

---

[48] Macrobius, *Commentarium in Somnium Scipionis*, ed. J. Willis (Leipzig, 1970).

[49] Boethius, *De Philosophiae consolatione*, ed. L. Bieler, *CCSL* 94 (Turnhout, 1957).

[50] Guillaume de Lorris and Jean de Meun's *Le Roman de la Rose*, ed. Armand Strubel (Paris, 1992).

[51] Al-Ghazali, *The Remembrance of Death and the Afterlife. Kitab dhikr al-mawt wa-ma ba dahu. Book XL of the Revival of the Religious Sciences, Ihya' ulum al-din*, trans. with intro. T. J. Winter (Cambridge, 1989).

[52] For texts of the Coptic "Apocalypse of Paul," "First Apocalypse of James" and "Second Apocalypse of James," and "The Apocalypse of Adam," see *The Nag Hammadi Library*, ed. James M. Robinson (San Francisco, 1978), pp. 256–86; for the "Book of Enoch," "The Apocalypse of Baruch," "The Apocalypse of Ezra," and "The Apocalypse of Peter," see *The Other Bible*, ed. Willis Barnstone (San Francisco, 1984), pp. 487–500, 509–11, 515–16, and 532–36.

and the *mi⁶raj* traditions have access to the Bible's apocalyptic texts, to the Koran,[53] and to other apocryphal apocalyptic texts.

Dante adhered to an orthodox or canonical visionary tradition. As Ronald Herzman puts it in discussing Dante and the Apocalypse of John, "To say that the Apocalypse has influenced Dante's *Commedia* must lie somewhere between a commonplace and an understatement."[54] He goes on to argue persuasively that in addition to the fact that the *Commedia* is a conversion narrative, Dante also assumed the role of *scriba dei*, for "Dante saw himself writing in imitation of the Bible."[55] In addition to the visionary mode of the *Commedia*, Dante also makes direct references to the Apocalypse of John. For example, the description of the beast Geryon, "Ecco la fiera con la coda aguzza" (Behold the beast with the pointed tail [*Inferno* 17, 1]) and "La faccia sua era faccia d'uom giusto" (His face was the face of a just man [*Inferno* 17, 10]) seems to echo Apocalypse 9:7, 10: "et facies earum sicut facies hominum . . . et habebant caudas similes scorpionum" (and their faces were like human faces . . . and they had tails like scorpions).[56]

The imagery in *Inferno* 19 where the simoniac popes are condemned also adopts the language of the Apocalypse (17:1, 3, 7, 9, 12, 18), as Dante indicts the shepherds for "puttaneggiar coi regi" (committing fornication with the kings [*Inferno* 19, 108]).[57] There are other allusions, as for example, "sigillum sextum" (sixth seal) or "alterum angelum ascendentem ab ortu solis/habentem signum Dei" (another angel rising from the east, carrying the seal of God [Apocalypse 7:2]) and Francis's rising in the east and receiving "l'ultimo sigillo" (the last seal [*Paradiso* 11, 50, 107]). The "magno volume" (great volume) read by Cacciaguida (*Paradiso* 15, 50) recalls the "libro *vitae*" of Apocalypse 3:5, 20:12–15, 21:27, and 22:9, where the names of the saved are inscribed. Dante's river of light in *Paradiso* 30, 61–69 adopts language from the river of the water of life of Apocalypse 22:1: "et ostendit mihi fluvium aquae vitae splendidum tamquam

---

[53] We have to recall that Peter the Venerable sponsored the twelfth-century translation of the Koran into Latin. See Kritzeck, *Peter the Venerable and Islam*.

[54] Ronald B. Herzman, "Dante and the Apocalypse," in *The Apocalypse in the Middle Ages*, ed. Richard K. Emmerson and Bernard McGinn (Ithaca, NY, 1992), pp. 398–413.

[55] Herzman, "Dante and the Apocalypse," p. 413.

[56] Biblical quotations are from *Biblia Sacra Iuxta Vulgatam Versionem* I and II (Stuttgart, 1969). Translations are mine.

[57] Herzman, "Dante and the Apocalypse," p. 409.

cristallum precedentem de sede Dei" (and [the angel] showed me the river of the water of life, sparkling like crystal coming from the seat of God).

A cursory look at the *mi'raj* also reveals the influence of the Apocalypse of John, or a version of it. In chapter 21 of the Latin *Livre de l'Echelle*, the visionary describes the angels who carry the throne of God, each with four faces, a man's, an eagle's, a lion's and a bull's. This is a direct reference to Apocalypse of John 4:7, and of course to Ezekiel 1:10, the four creatures usually associated with the four evangelists. Also in chapter 21, there is a long quotation that seems inspired by the very next verse in the Apocalypse of John in which the angels praise God, "Sanctus, sanctus, sanctus, Dominus Deus omnipotens, qui erat, et qui est, et qui venturis est" (Apocalypse of John 4:8); "Sanctus, sanctus, sanctus Deus, cuius Gloria sunt celi et terra pleni" (*Livre de l'Echelle*, ch. 21, 158). Here, too, one suspects that the original translator of the *mi'raj* from Arabic to Latin has imposed a Christian liturgical prayer to replace a similar Koranic formula. The mention of Gog and Magog in chapter 26 also finds a source in Apocalypse 20:7, though, of course, there are many provenances for this reference. Both the *Commedia* and the *Livre de l'Echelle* include versions of the Apocalypse's (22:1) river of light:

> e vidi lume in forma di rivera
> fulvido di fulgore, intra due rive
>
> dipinte di mirabil primavera.
> Di tal fiumana uscian faville vive,
> e d'ogne parte si mettien ne' fiori,
>
> quasi rubin che oro circunscrive. (*Paradiso* 30, 61–69)

[And I saw a light in form of a river glowing tawny between two banks painted with marvelous spring. From out this river issued living sparks and dropped on every side into the blossoms, like rubies set in gold.]

Arena quoque huius fluminis tota erat de lapidibus preciosis qui omnium manerierum erant que possint ab homine cogitari. . . . Et hoc flumen totum est plenum angelis qui, stantes super pedes suos erecti, in multis maneriebus eundo ac veniendo continue Deum laudant (*Le Livre de l'Échelle*, ch. 25).

[The gravel of the river consists entirely of precious gems of every kind that a man can imagine. . . . This river is quite full of angels who all remain standing, coming and going in many ways, while they praise God.]

Transfiguring nature, both texts describe luminous rivers full of angels, precious stones, and a translucent brightness. There are important differences here also. Both descriptions evoke a symbolic environment, and they use the same images of rivers, precious stones, and light. But Dante's version is beyond representation—"lume in forma di rivera" (light in the form of a river), and this was "dipinte di mirabil primvera" (painted with marvelous spring), and the "faville vive" (living sparks) are "quasi rubin" (like rubies). In keeping with his mode in *Paradiso*, the poet transfigures nature to employ imagery that removes what is being described to the realm of pure metaphor, as he strains the mimetic capacity of language.[58] In contrast, the *Livre de l'Échelle* version, while featuring what is seen as incommensurable, nonetheless identifies the sight as a river (not in the form of), where angels stand and praise God. This is one feature that distinguishes Dante's approach to describing Paradise from the *mi'raj*; Dante pushes language to its limit and in so doing emphasizes the impossibility of imagining a material heaven. On the other hand, in *Inferno*, as in the *mi'raj's* descriptions of hell, mimesis is the dominant literary mode. This can be no more evident than in the representation of Lucifer in Canto 34 or the terrifying beast of *Livre de l'Échelle*, chapter 73.

Another apocalypse that both works seem to have in common as a source is the "Apocalypse of Paul" (*Visio Pauli*), a Greek text probably originating in Egypt and dated before the fourth century that circulated widely in the Middle East and the Latin West.[59] Texts of the "Apocalypse of Paul" in Greek, Latin, Syriac, Armenian, Old Russian, Slavonic, Ethiopic, and Coptic testify to its widespread diffusion. By the seventh century, it was known throughout the Mediterranean world. There are fifty extant manuscripts in Latin dating from the eighth to the fifteenth

---

[58] For Dante's straining of the capacity of language in *Paradiso*, see John Freccero, "An Introduction to the *Paradiso*," in *Dante: Poetics of Conversion*, ed. Rachel Jacoff (Cambridge, Mass, 1986), pp. 209–20.

[59] See "Introduction," Silverstein and Hilhorst, *Apocalypse of Paul*.

centuries, persuasive testimony to how widespread it was.[60] Led by an angel who appears in the night (like the angel in Mohammed's night vision), Paul journeys to the other world and recounts a first-person narrative that describes the bitter suffering of the damned and the joys of the saved. Theodore Silverstein argued nearly seventy years ago that Dante knew the "Apocalypse of Paul,"[61] his argument partly resting on the fact that in 2 Corinthians 12:2, Paul does not refer to a descent but to an ascent to Paradise. The morally neutral residents of *Inferno* 3 (34–42) have parallels in the *Livre de l'Échelle* (chapter 54), and both likewise echo the "Apocalypse of Paul": "Neque calidi neque frigidi sunt, quia neque in numero iustorum inuenti sunt neque in numero impiorum" (These are neither hot nor cold, for they are not among the just or the impious [31, 25–27]). The Apocalypse of John (3:15–16) also refers to the lukewarm in very similar terms, making common sources likely. All three texts detail the sufferings of the damned. Here, predictably, we find darkness and gloom: in *Visio Pauli*, "there was no light in that place, but only darkness and sorrow. . ." (non erat lumen in illo loco, sed tenebre et tristicia . . . [31.16–18; 32.15; 34.10; 35.26; 36.1; *passim*; *Livre de l'Échelle*, ch. 56, *Inferno*, 5–34). In addition all three texts include a sea, desert, or "river of fire burning with heat" (illic fluvium ignis ferventem [*Visio Pauli*, 31:18]); and there is a sea of fire ("et est ibi eciam mare quoddam igneum " [*Livre de l'Échelle*, ch. 54]); so did the eternal burning descend there, and the sand was kindled by it like tinder under the flint, to redouble the pain ("tale scendeva l'etternale ardore; / onde la rena s'accendea, com 'esca / sotto focile, a doppiar lo dolore" [*Inferno* 14, 28–39]). Nasty snakes also appear in all three texts (*Livre de l'Échelle*, ch. 57; *Inferno* 25; *Visio Pauli*, 37.4; 42.2). The *Visio Pauli* describes a "locum glacie" (39.12), while the *miᶜraj*'s seventh region, the devil's seat and realm, is a place of intense cold, where we find the shackled monstrously large devil (and his army) (chapter 60), just as in *Inferno* 34.

---

[60] See Giovanni Fallani, "Paolo," in *Enciclopedia Dantesca*, vol. 4, pp. 271–75, at p. 272.

[61] Theodore Silverstein, "Did Dante Know the Vision of St. Paul?" *Harvard Studies and Notes in Philology and Literature* 19 (1937), pp. 231–47; see also Theodore Silverstein, *Visio Pauli: The History of the Apocalypse in Latin Together with Nine Texts* (London, 1935); see Theodore Silverstein, "Dante and the *Visio Pauli*," *Modern Language Notes* 47 (1932), pp. 397–99, for *Inferno* 9, 3–13, and the "Visio Pauli."

These parallels, echoes, allusions, and citations from this amalga-mation of apocalyptic texts, whether canonical, apocryphal, or Islamic, demonstrate the compendiousness of Dante's literary repertoire. To describe his poem as an epic in the tradition of Virgil, as an extended lyric as some have done, as a medieval *Confessions*, or as a prophetic text cannot reduce the poem's generic categories. To see parallels between the *mi^craj* versions and the *Commedia* is to emphasize that as orthodox as the poem is in such elements as its adoption of a common vernacular language, its interest in vernacular literary traditions, and its inclusion of apocryphal biblical narratives, its poet explored a broad repertoire of literary antecedents. Furthermore, to show that the poem shares a matrix with the *mi^craj* is to emphasize the common roots and concerns of Islam and Christianity in the late Middle Ages. But, just as contrasts between Virgil's *Aeneid* and Dante's poem highlight the different purposes and political visions of the two poems, despite Dante's obvious allegiance to his Roman source, the contrast between the *mi^craj* and the *Commedia* draws out the distinctions between the literary-cultural purposes of the two otherworld works.

Enrico Cerulli and Asín Palacios sought to identify Dante's sources and to show his indebtedness to the *mi^craj* traditions. But Brian Stock and others' idea of "communities of texts" advances the notion that cer-tain texts may be in continuity or collaboration with each other.[62] Writ-ing about the "repertoire of a literary text," Wolfgang Iser recognizes a syncretic quality in literary allusion as the writer frees him or herself to incorporate diverse sources, thus remaking the original in the terms of the individual aesthetic product.[63] Incorporating references from apocalyp-tic texts common to both religious traditions demonstrates how literary works emerge from a vast interplay or fusion of diverse cultural phenom-ena that do not belong to any one people, religion, society, or nation. Wai

---

[62] See Brian Stock, *The Implications of Literacy: Written Language and Models of Interpretation in the Eleventh and Twelfth Centuries* (Princeton, 1983), pp. 522–31; Jacob Neusner, *Canon and Connection: Intertextuality in Judaism* (Lanham, MD, 1987), pp. 147–59.

[63] See Wolfgang Iser, *The Act of Reading: A Theory of Aesthetic Response* (Baltimore, 1978), p. 79.

Chee Dimock's idea of "literature as a continuum,"[64] like Stock's idea of "communities of texts," suggests a different approach to literary relationships. Seeing the relationship among this "family of texts," despite differences and similarities, agreements and disagreements, contributes to understanding how they belong to a dynamic republic of letters with its own conversations, systems, laws, rules, and commitments. Breaking away from the "tendency to isolate texts from one another" allows us to see, as Pascale Casanova recently argues "the entirety of the configuration to which all texts belong; that is the totality of texts and literary aesthetic debates with which a particular work of literature enters into a relation and resonance, and which forms the basis for its singularity, its real originality."[65]

This idea of cultural continuum and familial relationship, applied to the *miʿraj* and the *Commedia*, demonstrates that the two works share more than parallel references to the punishments and rewards of the afterworld. In other words, when we examine the literary repertoire of both texts, we discover indeed that the style of writing differs, and that their literary repertoires both overlap and radically diverge because of the difference in the purposes of the works, which of course forms the basis for the singularity of the *Commedia* and the *miʿraj* traditions. However, what they share is a common conviction about the absolute justice of God and the proposition that humans will be called to account for their unjust actions, which both works render in apocalyptic prophetic first-person voices.

---

[64] See Wai Chee Dimock, "Literature for the Planet," *PMLA* 116, no. 1 (2001), p. 174.

[65] Casanova, *World Republic of Letters*, p. 3.

Praying by Numbers

Rachel Fulton
University of Chicago

FEW ASPECTS OF late medieval devotional practice have been as consistently ridiculed as the systematic counting of prayer. Whether priests
in their chantries, pious laypeople at their books and beads, flagellants in
the town squares, or monks and nuns in their choirs, all, it seems, were
susceptible to this "fantastical pursuit of numbers" in piling up prayers.
So many Our Fathers per Hail Marys of the rosary, so many cracks of the
whip per psalm, so many genuflections per Mass, so many souls saved
per tear shed in prayer, all according to the logic that the number, as
much, if not more so than the actual words of the prayers, was itself of
pressing significance.[1] So, for example, in reciting the rosary, or so Alain

---

This article was first presented in an earlier form as the Burkitt Foundation
Lecture on Christian Thought at Rice University, March 2004. I would like to thank
William Parsons and the Department of Religious Studies for the opportunity to
speak, and Werner Kelber for his continuing inspiration and encouragement. I am
also grateful to Roger Dahood and the reader for *Studies in Medieval and Renaissance History* for their attentive criticism and suggestions for improvement. The
article is dedicated to my father, Dr. Robert L. Fulton (d. March 10, 2005), for sharing with me his lifelong love of numbers and for teaching me to ask the one question
that really matters: "Why?"

[1] For these and similar criticisms, see Thomas Lentes, "Counting Piety in the
Late Middle Ages," in *Ordering Medieval Society: Perspectives on Intellectual and*

---

de la Roche (1428–75) advised the members of his prayer confraternity, one should say fifteen sets of ten Hail Marys each, each set of Hail Marys punctuated by a single Our Father, because the fifteen Our Fathers recall the fifteen moments of the Passion and the 150 Hail Marys recall the 150 Psalms. Further, the fifteen sets of ten Hail Marys themselves recall, on the one hand, the 150 *habitudines morales* or moral habits, the product of multiplying the Ten Commandments by the fifteen virtues (three Theological, four Cardinal, seven Capital, plus Religion and Penitence, minus one, since the cardinal virtue of Temperance corresponds to the capital virtue of Abstinence); and, on the other, the 150 *habitudines naturales* or natural habits, the product of multiplying the eleven heavenly spheres plus the four elements by the ten Aristotelian categories.[2] As the great Dutch historian Johan Huizinga (1872–1945), one of the most famous critics of this numerical style of devotion, once put it, here above all, it would seem, we see Christian symbolism in its decline, "petrified," "parasitic," "purely mechanical," "a disease of thought" given over to "[hopelessly degenerate] play," "a superficial fantasizing on a simple association of ideas" called forth by "mere correspondence in number."[3]

For many modern scholars following Huizinga, one of the most suspect, if not downright puzzling, of these "grotesquely statistical" devotions has been that centered on the numbering of the wounds Christ suffered at the crucifixion: 6,666 according to some; 5,475 according to others.[4] This latter accounting, by far the best known, had purportedly

---

Practical Modes of Shaping Social Relations, ed. Bernhard Jussen, trans. Pamela Selwyn (Philadelphia, 2001), pp. 55–91.

[2] Alain de la Roche = Alanus de Rupe, *Beatus Alanus redivivus*, ed. J. A. Coppenstein (Naples, 1642), passim; cited by Johan Huizinga, *The Autumn of the Middle Ages*, trans. Rodney J. Payton and Ulrich Mammitzsch (Chicago, 1996), p. 241.

[3] Huizinga, *Autumn*, pp. 240–42.

[4] On these numberings, see Caroline Walker Bynum, "Violent Imagery in Late Medieval Piety," *Bulletin of the German Historical Institute* 30 (Spring 2002), 3–36, at p. 5; Lentes, "Counting Prayers," pp. 58–59; David S. Areford, "The Passion Measured: A Late-Medieval Diagram of the Body of Christ," in *The Broken Body: Passion Devotion in Late-Medieval Culture*, ed. A. A. MacDonald, H. N. B. Ridderbos, and R. M. Schlusemann (Groningen, 1998), pp. 211–38, at p. 217; John B. Friedman, *Northern English Books, Owners, and Makers in the Late Middle Ages* (Syracuse, N.Y., 1995), pp. 162–64; Andrew Breeze, "The Number of Christ's Wounds," *The Bulletin of the Board of Celtic Studies* 32 (1985), 84–91; Cameron Louis, ed., *The Commonplace Book of Robert Reynes of Acle: An Edition of Tanner MS 407*, Garland Medieval Texts 1

been revealed to a certain pious recluse by none other than the Lord Jesus Christ himself, who spoke to her and said: "Say every day for a whole year fifteen Our Fathers and fifteen Hail Marys, and at the year's end you shall have worshipped every wound and fulfilled the number of the same."[5] In similar fashion, so it was told, one hundred Our Fathers said daily over the course of fifteen years would yield the number of drops of blood Christ shed from his wounds. As one popular fifteenth-century jingle put it: "The novmbre of thes dropes all / I wyll reherse in generall. / VC ml. for to tell, / And xlvii ml. weell, / VC also gret and small. / Here is the nombre of hem alle"[6]—i.e., 547,500, or 100 times the number of Christ's wounds.

No less fantastic, at least to most modern expectations about prayer, were the promised effects of such prayerful reiterations. For every year of praying the fifteen Our Fathers and fifteen Hail Marys, Christ promised the recluse and her imitators release from the pains of Purgatory for the souls of fifteen family members and continuing good life for fifteen of their living kin.[7] According to some versions of the same legend, the ones

---

(New York, 1980), pp. 369–72; Thomas W. Ross, "Five Fifteenth-Century 'Emblem' Verses from Brit. Mus. Addit. MS. 37049," *Speculum* 32, no. 2 (1957), 274–82, at p. 275; and Carleton Brown, *Religious Lyrics of the Fifteenth Century* (Oxford, 1939), pp. 322–23. For the numbering 6,666, see Sixten Ringbom, *Icon to Narrative: The Rise of the Dramatic Close-Up in Fifteenth-Century Devotional Painting*, 2nd ed. (Doornspijk, The Netherlands, 1984), p. 26, n. 21. "Grotesquely statistical" is from Douglas Gray, *Themes and Images in the Medieval English Religious Lyric* (London, 1972), p. 133. On the wounds generally, see also Douglas Gray, "The Five Wounds of Our Lord," *Notes and Queries* 208 (1963), 50–51, 82–89, 127–34, and 162–68. I thank Marlene Hennessy for advice on these devotions and for sharing work from her unpublished dissertation with me. See Hennessy, "Morbid Devotions: Reading the Passion of Christ in a Late Medieval Miscellany, London, British Library, Additional MS 37049" (PhD diss., Columbia University, 2001), chap. 2.

[5] *Commonplace Book of Robert Reynes*, ed. Louis, no. 84, p. 264; trans. John Shinners, in *Medieval Popular Religion 1000–1500: A Reader*, ed. John Shinners, Readings in Medieval Civilizations and Cultures 2 (Peterborough, Ontario, 1997), p. 366.

[6] *Commonplace Book of Robert Reynes*, ed. Louis, no. 15, p. 152; trans. Shinners, in *Medieval Popular Religion*, ed. Shinners, p. 335: "The number of these drops all / I will rehearse in general: / 500 thousand for to tell, / Plus 47,000 as well / 500 also great and small / Here is the number of them all." A version of the same jingle appears in BL Add. MS 37049, fol. 24r. See Hennessy, "Morbid Devotions," fig. 2.

[7] *Commonplace Book of Robert Reynes*, ed. Louis, no. 84, pp. 264–65; trans. Shinners, in *Medieval Popular Religion*, ed. Shinners, p. 366. For discussion and context, see Louis, *Commonplace Book of Robert Reynes*, pp. 463–65.

praying might accrue even further benefit by adding to their daily recita-tions a series of meditations on the Passion, the so-called "Fifteen Oes." As the Lord explained to the recluse (often identified in this context as St. Bridget of Sweden [ca. 1303–73]):

> He who says these prayers in the prescribed form fifteen days before his death shall see my holy body and receive it, and thereby be deliv-ered from everlasting hunger. I shall give him my blood to drink so that he shall never have thirst. And I shall set before him the sign of my victorious Passion as a subsidy and defense against all his enemies. And before his death, I shall come with my own dear Mother and take his soul and lead it into everlasting joy. And when I have brought it there, I shall give him a sip from the chalice of my godhead.[8]

Perhaps criticism of such extravagant claims for the power of prayer is to be expected. And yet, it is surely curious that, however elaborate or symbolically freighted they may have been, what has been criticized most about the prayers like those on Christ's wounds or the Hail Marys of the rosary is above all the fact that they were so carefully counted. At best, it would seem, such accountings as, for example, of the prayers and psalms said by the priests of the chantries, "appear to give a high, almost magical, value to mere repetition of formulae, reminiscent of the scribes of [Christ's own] day, who thought to be heard for their much speaking."[9] At worst, or so Huizinga and others would have it, these accountings devolve into "the excesses of decadent sentimentalism," thereby reducing Christian symbolism to "nothing more than arithmetical exercises."[10] Indeed, even

---

[8] *Commonplace Book of Robert Reynes*, ed. Louis, no. 84, p. 265; trans. Shinners, in *Medieval Popular Religion*, ed. Shinners, p. 366. On these meditations, see also Rebecca Krug, "The Fifteen Oes," in *Cultures of Piety: Medieval English Devotional Literature in Translation*, ed. Anne Clark Bartlett and Thomas H. Bestul (Ithaca, N.Y., 1999), pp. 107–12; and Eamon Duffy, *The Stripping of the Altars: Traditional Religion in England 1400–1580* (New Haven, 1992), pp. 248–56.

[9] K. L. Wood-Legh, *Perpetual Chantries in Britain* (Cambridge, 1965), p. 312. See also Francis Oakley, *The Western Church in the Later Middle Ages* (Ithaca, N.Y., 1979), p. 118.

[10] Ross, "Five Fifteenth-Century 'Emblem' Verses," p. 275, citing Johan Huizinga, *The Waning of the Middle Ages: A Study of the Forms of Life, Thought, and Art in France and the Netherlands in the Fourteenth and Fifteenth Centuries*, trans. Frederik

readers as sympathetic as Caroline Walker Bynum to such late medieval symbolic "excesses" as the enumeration of Christ's wounds have found it difficult not to be put off by the "obsessive and quantitative nature of such spirituality."[11] The more typical response has been either to ignore or to dismiss it as (in Rosemary Woolf's words) "scarcely poetical material." In Woolf's estimation, even the otherwise fine "Dollorus complant of oure lorde Apoune þe croce Crucifyit" is "only marred once, by the following weak stanza: 'ffor þe, man, þou sall understande, / In body, heid, fute and hande, / ffyve hundreth woundis, and fyve thousande, / And þairto sexty / And fyftene, / Was taulde and sene / On my body'. . . . From the poetical point of view [i.e., Woolf's], the point is sufficiently made in the first line of the next stanza: 'Behalde, on me nocht hale was left'."[12]

The source of at least a part of this antipathy is not far to seek. Counting prayers, it has often been argued, whether Masses or decades of a rosary, Our Fathers, or the "Fifteen Oes," appealed to late medieval Christians because it made praying easier by reducing the otherwise all-too-complicated effort of communication with the Divine to a straight-forward matter of bookkeeping: so many prayers said over so many days, neatly totted up to some nominal and prearranged sum, all under the (of course) mistaken assumption that something as precious as the presence of God or the salvation of one's soul could be purchased with anything less than the whole of creation or grace.[13] This is the way, most recently, Thomas Lentes has described the phenomenon: "prayer [in the later Middle Ages] became, in effect, a currency" with which the faithful paid for not only the joys of paradise, but also, if almost surreally, "various parts of the furnishings of heaven": clothing and crowns for the saints, garlands of roses for the Virgin Mary, necklaces, mantle fasteners, and

---

Hopman (London, 1924), p. 185. Cf. Huizinga, *Autumn*, trans. Payton and Mammitzsch, p. 240: "Whole perspectives of symbolic contact arise, particularly when the symbolic contact comes from a mere correspondence in number. Symbolizing becomes simply the use of arithmetical tables."

[11] Bynum, "Violent Imagery," p. 5.

[12] Rosemary Woolf, *The English Religious Lyric in the Middle Ages* (Oxford, 1968), p. 204. For the full text of this "Dollorus complant of oure lorde Apoune þe croce Crucifyit," see Brown, *Religious Lyrics of the Fifteenth Century*, no. 102, pp. 151–56.

[13] For a recent example of this argument, see Arnold Angenandt, Thomas Braucks, Rolf Busch, and Hubertus Lutterbach, "Counting Piety in the Early and High Middle Ages," in *Ordering Medieval Society*, ed. Jussen, pp. 15–53.

even gardens.[14] So, for example, the going rate at the convent of Colmar for a damask mantle for the Virgin was 30,000 Hail Marys; for the silk thread with which to sew it, 1,000 Magnificats; and for the golden stars to ornament it, "12 times all their sequences, which comes to 3180 verses."[15] Why the simple act of counting should necessarily be equated with such a commercial exchange Lentes tends to assume more than he explains, but the assumption is hardly his alone. Max Weber (1864–1920), after all, suggested much the same thing: the origins of the ascetic rationalism of the Protestant ethic and its attendant "spirit of capitalism" can be most clearly seen in the systematized and methodical (i.e., calculated) structures of medieval monasticism, above all in their schedules of prayer.[16] Commercial profit, in other words, was a direct, if unintended, consequence of calculated, reckoned prayer. For Lentes as for Weber, it would seem, it is little wonder, then, if the prayers themselves so carefully calculated should be taken as a way of reckoning spiritual profit or purchasing spiritual goods. This was "a piety trapped in a commercial mentality," "an arithmetical art . . . tied to excessive promises of grace."[17]

Whether as "hopelessly degenerate play" (in Huizinga's words), "mere repetition of formulae" accorded "almost magical value" (as K. L. Wood-Legh would have it), or proto-capitalist calculations of grace (in Weber's and Lentes's account), the late medieval practice of counting prayers clearly falls short of what most modern historians of Christianity tend to recognize as "real" prayer, that "spontaneous emotional discharge" through which the one praying seeks "intimate intercourse with God."[18] Some things, it would seem, are worth counting; others, including the

---

[14] Lentes, "Counting Piety," pp. 55–56, 63. See also Lentes, "Die Gewänder der Heiligen: Ein Diskussionsbeitrag zum Verhältnis von Gebet, Bild und Imagination," in *Hagiographie und Kunst: Der Heiligenkult in Schrift, Bild und Architektur*, ed. Gottfried Kerscher (Berlin, 1993), pp. 120–51.

[15] Colmar, Bibliothèque municipale, MS 267bis, fol. 68r; cited by Lentes, "Counting Piety," p. 56.

[16] For Weber's use of monasticism in the development of his sociological view of religion, see Lutz Kaelber, *Schools of Asceticism: Ideology and Organization in Medieval Religious Communities* (University Park, Pa., 1998), pp. 13–21.

[17] Lentes, "Counting Piety," pp. 57, 67.

[18] Friedrich Heiler, *Prayer: A Study in the History and Psychology of Religion* (Oxford, 1932), p. 65. But see now Philip Zaleski and Carol Zaleski, *Prayer: A History* (Boston, 2005), pp. 128–57, for a more sympathetic discussion of devotional, routinized prayer.

injuries that Christ suffered for the salvation of humanity or the numbers of souls even a single prayer might release from their pain, are not. Indeed, or so most modern accounts of the late medieval enumeration of Christ's wounds or the tallying of Hail Marys in the rosary would suggest, counting things that should not be counted, such as prayers, borders at once on the obsessive, decadent, and grotesque, not to mention the Pharisaical, the commercial, and the poetically inept.

The problem is not so much whether such criticisms are fair as whether they have defined their target correctly. Historians, like the objects of their study, are creatures of their times; we judge according to the yardsticks accepted in our day. Rather, the question, as always, is whether we are applying the right yardsticks and, if not, whether we are conscious of our resistance to applying others than those we consider least naïve or most profound. In our early twenty-first-century world, for example, we count things because we want to buy and sell them; we count the money that we use to buy and sell the things that we count; we count money as a measure of our success and status. Money, for us, is salvation. We even sometimes think of salvation in terms of something we can buy or, at least, worry that others think about salvation in this way. But money is not the only thing that we count. We count calories; we count populations; we count years of our lives. To be sure, some of the things that we count, we count in exchange for money: hours of our days, pieces of work completed. Other things are more difficult to exchange for money, and yet, still we count: repetitions of an exercise for a skill that we are trying to learn, points scored in a competition, stitches completed in a knitting pattern, pages of a book. Counting does more than simply assign reciprocal value to the things that we count; it is both a method of discipline and a method of ordering. Counting, in other words, may be qualitative as well as quantitative in its purposes. We count things that we care about; if something "does not count," we mean, quite literally, that it does not matter, regardless of its price.[19]

Why count prayers? Hitherto, historians, particularly those inclined, like Weber, to prefer material explanations for religious behavior, have tended to answer this question in terms of changes in the social and economic makeup of late medieval Europe and the cultural dominance of

---

[19] Cf. Thomas Crump, *The Anthropology of Numbers* (Cambridge, 1990), for further reflections on the effects of counting.

metaphors of commercial exchange. And, indeed, it is arguable, given the commercial development that Europe experienced from the turn of the first millennium, that there were medieval Christians who conceptualized their relationship with God through monetary or mercantile metaphors. Moreover, as we shall see, even at the time there were those who criticized above all the calculations of prayers as penances in precisely these terms. Nevertheless, then as now, there were things to count other than money or its equivalents and reasons for counting other than commerce or exchange.

To understand why devotions to the numbering of Christ's wounds or the recitation of the fifteen decades of the rosary achieved the popularity that they did in late medieval Christianity, we need to lay aside for a moment our conviction that what counts most is how much something costs, and likewise our sense that counting things other than consumers or commodities (e.g., calories, trains spotted, miles run, wounds suffered by God) is somehow unbalanced or diseased. Number as symbol matters in this context, as Huizinga noted with a certain degree of chagrin, but so does practice, prayers being after all not things, but sayings and actions. From a commercial perspective, thirty thousand Hail Marys for a damask mantle for the Virgin might seem inflationary; calculated as threads or stitches in a luxurious piece of cloth, however, such a number is entirely reasonable. Considered as exercises, one might begin to wonder whether even thirty thousand repetitions of the prayer could be enough, when, as recent studies in the acquisition of cognitive and motor expertise have shown and as athletes, musicians, and martial artists know all too well, it takes upwards of ten thousand repetitions of even the simplest action to begin to perform it correctly, never mind comprehend its meaning.[20]

---

[20] Niklaus Suino, *Practice Drills for Japanese Swordsmanship* (New York, 1995), p. 4: "Only through practice does one develop skill. After the first ten thousand repetitions, the student may begin to think he understands the meaning of the drills, while after one hundred thousand, he will begin to realize the road to mastery is a very long one. The rare swordsman who cuts one million times with the sword, and who is also very lucky, will develop a very unusual kind of perception that few other people ever experience." On the importance of such long-term deliberate practice for the development of expert cognitive and motor skills, see Philip E. Ross, "The Expert Mind," *Scientific American* 295, no. 2 (August 2006), 64–71; and K. Anders Ericsson, "The Acquisition of Expert Performance: An Introduction to Some of the Issues," in *The Road to Excellence: The Acquisition of Expert Performance in the Arts and Sciences, Sports, and Games*, ed. K. Anders Ericsson (Mahwah, N.J., 1996), pp. 1–50.

Symbolically speaking, the stakes could be even higher, if, as St. Augustine of Hippo (354–430) argued in his reading of Wisdom 11:21 ("You have ordered all things in measure, number and weight"), it was number by which God had effected the whole of creation. Unpoetical, obsessive, or mechanical as such calculations might seem to us, number in this context was far from accidental to the success of a prayer; "how many times?" was as critical a question as "what should I say?"

Why Count Prayers? Penance, Profit and the Arithmetic of Salvation

As we have already seen, some of the benefits associated with counted prayers in the later Middle Ages were, if highly desirable, nevertheless themselves somewhat difficult to count; for example, the reception of communion fifteen days before death or the sight of Christ at one's deathbed for the regular recitation of the "Fifteen Oes." Others, however, were clearly desirable only insofar as they could be counted, and not only counted, but added up. This is the reckoning given by one late medieval lay confraternity of the prayers accumulated by its participants: "290 secular persons at Zurich provided our little ship well with spiritual interest and annuities [*mit geistlichen zynßen vnd renten*]; namely, they gave 436,700 Paternosters and Ave Marias and 200,800 Ave Marias, 1,574 rosaries, 14,357 Salve, 676 Miserere, 200,982 Credo in deum, 12 Magnificat, 12,100 Gloria Patri, 12 Nunc Dimittis, 1,000 Veni sancte, 30 vigils, 86 masses, and another 13,000 Paternoster and Ave Maria, and many pilgrimages with other blessed works and prayers." Why the need for so many prayers? According to the confraternity's own statutes, to pay the ferryman into the hereafter the "wage and shipping fee" for the confraternity's patrons, St. Ursula and her eleven thousand martyred companions, of course. And if one failed somehow to tot up the necessary amount? The confraternity itself would make up the difference out of the spiritual treasury (*thesaurus*) its members had so diligently filled.[21]

According to Ericsson, it takes on average some ten years to achieve excellence in a particular performance domain, but only if one is practicing under conditions of high relevance, concentrated effort, and attention for some four hours per day, seven days per week.

[21] André Schnyder, *Die Ursulabruderschaften des Spätmittelalters. Ein Beitrag zur Erforschung der deutschsprachigen religiösen Literatur des 15. Jahrhunderts,*

"Shipping fees" for the saints were only a part of the expenses that the faithful hoped to cover with their prayers. As every late medieval Christian knew, however much he or she had assisted in the work of outfitting the saints, the total of these carefully enumerated prayers would ultimately be reckoned against an even more stringent account: that owed to the Judge in compensation for humanity's sins. By the later Middle Ages, there were a number of ways one might settle one's own part of this judicial accounting: with fasting, typically on bread and water for a certain number of days per year; with alms-giving or other "good works," including going on pilgrimage; or with prayer. There were, to be sure, certain qualifications, as every good confessor would feel obliged to point out. Strictly speaking, all of these methods were forms not of payment for sin but of "satisfaction" or punishment, contrition and confession having wiped away the actual guilt. Moreover, although there were general guidelines—for example, seven years' fasting for serious sins like adultery, perjury, fornication, and murder; two weeks' fasting and so many Our Fathers for having been "wanton" with one's wife on Good Friday—it was the responsibility of the confessor to set the appropriate severity and duration of penance to cover one's account.[22] Nevertheless, the idea of an exchange, penances for punishment, was a fairly straightforward one, as long as one confessed fully, with contrition.

So far, so good. But what if, or so many parishioners most certainly asked, one's confessor got one's punishment wrong and made it too light or too heavy; would it still count? Even worse, what if it was right and yet one died before it was finished? Would one still be absolved of one's sins? The answer to the last question is, yes, of course; absolution of guilt follows immediately upon confession. But to satisfy God's justice the punishment must not only be right (thus the burden on the confessors to know the appropriate penances), but also completed even if one died before one's penance was finished, and for this, from the twelfth century at the latest, there was Purgatory.[23] Now, Purgatory, to be sure,

---

Sprache und Dichtung, n.s. 34 (Bern and Stuttgart, 1986), p. 233; trans. Lentes, "Counting Piety," pp. 62–63. On this confraternity, see also Lentes, "Gewänder der Heiligen," pp. 141–43.

[22] Thomas N. Tentler, *Sin and Confession on the Eve of the Reformation* (Princeton, 1977), pp. 318–27.

[23] For what follows on Purgatory, indulgences, and penance generally, see Bernard Hamilton, *Religion in the Medieval West*, 2nd ed. (London, 2003), pp. 84, 91–95,

was almost certainly a better place to spend some time than was Hell, but most people still hoped that they would be able to spend as little time there as possible (only the saints would go directly to Heaven). Short of dying immediately after baptism, however, it was difficult to see how one could avoid altogether a certain degree of exposure to the fires of Purgatory. Perhaps the safest option was to give up the world entirely and enter a monastery, but by the later Middle Ages, at least, there were other, arguably more appealing, options: taking the cross, for example, or going on pilgrimage to Rome. Admittedly, these pious exercises, while potentially grueling, could of themselves no more guarantee one's immediate passage to Heaven than could any other penance. Nevertheless, coupled with the promise of a plenary indulgence from the pope, as such exercises, particularly pilgrimage to Jerusalem for the sake of the cross, had from 1096 started to be, they were, or so it was fervently believed, the next best thing to dying without ever having sinned.

It is with the introduction of indulgences into the equation that things start to get trickier and where, at least for most modern scholars, the counting of prayer starts to look more and more like a process of bargaining or purchase and less and less like an exercise of humility or devotion, despite the fact that not all counted prayers were indulgenced (although some of the most famous, for example, the rosary, were) and not all indulgences involved counted prayers. They are not the only ones to express this concern. The reformer Martin Luther (1483–1546) had something to say about this, as did Meister Eckhart (ca. 1260–1327 or 1328) some two hundred years before him.

As Luther saw it, counting prayer at all, never mind, as with certain indulgenced prayers, itemizing its efficacy according to precise reckonings of days or years, was perilously akin to believing that there was something—anything—one could do to settle one's debt with the Creator other than repent and believe. True prayer is a matter not of piecemeal accounting for one's sins, but of asking God for what we need out of obedience to God's commandment to pray. As Luther explained in his *Larger Catechism*, "To pray, as the Second Commandment teaches, is to call

97–98, 105–9; R. N. Swanson, *Religion and Devotion in Europe, c. 1215–c.1515* (Cambridge, 1995), pp. 191–234; Duffy, *Stripping of the Altars*, pp. 338–76; Jacques Le Goff, *The Birth of Purgatory*, trans. Arthur Goldhammer (Chicago, 1984); and Tentler, *Sin and Confession*, pp. 318–40.

upon God in every need. . . . What we shall pray, and for what, we should regard as demanded by God and done in obedience to him."[24] Our needs being what they are (i.e., continuous), "upright Christians pray without ceasing, though they pray not always with their mouths." Indeed, "the [very] sigh of a true Christian is a prayer." Given that the Lord himself told us what to say when we do use words as we pray, what need, Luther would insist, for words endlessly multiplied as, for example, in the recitation of the rosary? True Christians "pray continually" in their hearts, "sleeping and waking," much as they carry the cross, "though [they] feel it not always."[25]

Meister Eckhart was, if anything, even more pointed in his criticisms of counted prayer. As he saw it: "Just as, in the words of Augustine, 'the single prayer of an obedient man,' however short, 'is better than ten thousand prayers of a scoffer,' a single deed performed out of greater love is better than all the deeds in the world if the love therein be less—for number, size, length, breadth, height, and depth add nothing to goodness and merit."[26] "Even one *Ave Maria* said in this spirit, when a man has gone out of himself, is of more value than reading a thousand psalters without it. In fact a single step with it would be better than crossing the

---

[24] Luther, *Deudsch Catechismus*, pt. 3 (Wittenberg, 1529), fol. 58r–v; trans. Robert H. Fischer, as *The Large Catechism* (Philadelphia, 1959), pp. 65–66. For Luther's views on prayer more generally, see Roland H. Bainton, *Here I Stand: A Life of Martin Luther* (New York, 1955), pp. 43, 280–81.

[25] *Colloquia, oder, Christliche nützliche Tischreden Doctoris Martini Luthers . . .*, ed. Johann Aurifaber, chap. 17 (1566; rev. ed. Jena, 1591), fol. 215r; ed. and trans. William Hazlitt, as *The Table-talk of Martin Luther*, chap. 337, rev. ed. with a Memoir by Alexander Chalmers (London, 1890), p. 159; cf. Luther, *Werke: Kritische Gesammtausgabe. Tischreden, 1531–46*, vol. 3, *Tischreden aus den dreiziger Jahren*, no. 2918, ed. Ernst Kroker, Karl Drescher, and Oskar Brenner (Weimar, 1914), p. 79: "Christianus semper orat, sive dormiat sive vigilet. Cor enim eius orat semper, et suspirium est magna et fortis oratio. Sic enim dicit: Propter gemitum pauperum nunc exurgam, Esaiae 11 [Psalm 12:6]. Sic christianus semper fert crucem, licet non semper eam sentiat." For the history of this ideal, see Fabio Giardini, "Unceasing Prayer," *Angelicum* 72, no. 2 (1995), 281–312.

[26] Eckhart, *Expositio Libri Genesis*, 1:31, n. 130, ed. Konrad Weiß, in *Meister Eckhart. Die lateinischen Werke*, vol. 1 (Stuttgart, 1964), p. 284; trans. Lentes, "Counting Piety," p. 68. For Eckhart's views on prayer more generally, see Bernard McGinn, *The Mystical Thought of Meister Eckhart: The Man from Whom God Hid Nothing* (New York, 2001), pp. 130–31.

sea without it."[27] Indeed, in Eckhart's view, those who sought to increase their worth in God's estimation by performing such carefully enumerated good works as "fasting, vigils, praying, and the like . . . so that our Lord may give them something in return or do something that would please them" were "merchants," who, in giving something to God in the hope of receiving something in return were, quite simply, "cheated in such an exchange,"[28] for "God regards not what the works are, but only what love and devotion and what kind of a spirit is in the works. For He is little concerned with our works, but only with our state of mind in all our works, that we love Him alone in all things."[29] How much the more, one wants to say tragic, but in Eckhart's terms the better adjective is probably foolish, to suppose that saying a certain number of prayers might have any effect at all on one's relationship to God's justice simply because the number itself was purportedly correct? It would almost be better to abandon oneself entirely to sin than to presume so to circumscribe penitence, never mind God's justice, with numbers.

And yet, some would argue, this is exactly what the system of indulgences did.[30] For our purposes, there are three important things to know about indulgences. One, although often misunderstood, both in their heyday and since, as payments for sin, they were, like penances, technically satisfactions only for the punishment owing to God following the absolution of one's sins. Two, by the later Middle Ages, many of them could be acquired by way of alms-giving for particular projects, for example, the financing of a crusade or the construction of a bridge; hence, arguably, the frequent confusion between making a donation of money and receiving pardon for one's sins. And three, like money and other countable, transferable but abstract things, indulgences, too, were subject to inflation, perhaps

---

27 Eckhart, *Die rede der underscheidunge*, chap. 11, ed. Josef Quint, in *Meister Eckhart. Die deutschen Werke*, vol. 5, *Traktate* (Stuttgart, 1963), p. 227; trans. and ed. M. O'C. Walshe, as "The Talks of Instruction," in *Sermons and Treatises*, 3 vols. (Shaftesbury, Dorset, 1987), 3:27.

28 Eckhart, Sermon 1, ed. Josef Quint, in *Meister Eckhart. Die deutschen Werke*, vol. 2 (Stuttgart, 1971), pp. 153–54; trans. Lentes, "Counting Piety," p. 69.

29 Eckhart, *Die rede der underscheidunge*, chap. 16, ed. Quint, p. 247; trans. Walshe, *Sermons and Treatises*, 3:34.

30 For the standard version of this argument, see Henry Charles Lea, *A History of Auricular Confession and Indulgences in the Latin Church*, vol. 3, *Indulgences* (Philadelphia, 1896). For more recent discussions of the system of indulgences, see above, n. 23.

even more so than money, since it was often unclear what exactly it was (if anything) that they could buy. Perhaps all too predictably—Eckhart and Luther certainly would not have been surprised—when coupled with prayers, particularly counted prayers, the rate of inflation only tended to increase.[31] The problem is whether, as scholars like Lentes and others have argued, this susceptibility to enumeration and inflation meant that indulgenced prayers, like other prayers associated with numbers were, in effect, metaphorically (if not also actually) equated with money; that, in fact, as Joel Kaye has put it, there was a "sense that everything was for sale, that all ancient values and structures had a price attached to them," including penitential satisfaction through prayer.[32]

To answer this criticism of counting and its effect on counted prayers fully, we need to know a little more about the way in which indulgences were calculated and how, exactly, they tended to increase. Prior to the mid-fourteenth century, most genuine indulgences granted by the popes and other officials of the ecclesiastical hierarchy were for "quarantines" or periods of forty days, sometimes accumulative for up to seven years, the recommended penance for most mortal sins. After the ravages of the plague years of 1347–48 and the success of the Roman Jubilee in 1350, however, the periods of remission offered tended to multiply, so that by the early fifteenth century, pilgrims to Rome might earn (or so the notices posted outside its doors promised) no less than seven thousand years and seven thousand quarantines daily for a visit to the church of St. Lawrence plus two thousand years for praying on the spot where Christ

---

[31] Images like the Veronica were particularly susceptible to such inflationary claims. See Ringbom, *Icon to Narrative*, pp. 23–30. On the multiplicative tendencies of the Veronica itself, see Jeffrey Hamburger, "Vision and the Veronica," in *The Visual and the Visionary: Art and Female Spirituality in Late Medieval Germany* (New York, 1998), pp. 317–82, 558–68.

[32] Joel Kaye, *Economy and Nature in the Fourteenth Century: Money, Market Exchange, and the Emergence of Scientific Thought* (Cambridge, 1998), p. 168: "By the beginning of the fourteenth century (1308), monetization and rationalized price measurement had so invaded the realm of official theology that the proportion of payment to reward in indulgence could be officially fixed by Clement V at one penny of Tours for each year of pardon conferred. The repercussions of this commoditization, the sense that everything was for sale, that all ancient values and structures had a price attached to them, was profoundly experienced in every European society of this period."

had once appeared to St. Peter.[33] Guidebooks to the city promised even greater rewards, particularly for those pilgrims who took the time not only to visit the churches on the route, but also to pray. Accordingly, for every hour that a pilgrim gazed upon the image of Christ at the altar of the Veronica in St. Peter's, he would receive—or so the Augustinian prior Leopold of Vienna reported on the basis of one such *Liber indulgentiarum* that he had consulted for a pilgrimage he made in 1377—an indulgence of three thousand years if he were a Roman, nine thousand years if an Italian, and an impressive twelve thousand years if he were a foreigner. Leopold calculated that he had spent a total of eighty-one hours in prayer before the image, earning in all an indulgence of 972,000 years—if, that is, his accounting of hours was correct.[34]

Even more impressive were the years of pardon (or so the fifteenth-century publishers of the woodcuts and devotional primers promised their purchasers) that one could accrue by staying home and reciting relatively simple cycles of prayer. One popular woodcut circulating in England promised "to them that before this ymage of pyte [the Man of Sorrows] devoutly say fyve Pater noster fyve Aveys & a Crede" no less than 32,755 years of pardon.[35] Another circulating in Germany with images of the *Arma Christi* (or "Arms of Christ") promised "as many days of indulgence as our Lord Jesus Christ received in wounds for our sins" for reciting devoutly but a single prayer.[36] The examples, much like

---

[33] Jonathan Sumption, *Pilgrimage: An Image of Medieval Religion* (Totowa, N.J., 1975), pp. 243–44. On the general inflation of indulgences following the Black Death, see Swanson, *Religion and Devotion*, pp. 220–22. According to Swanson, the indulgences offered prior to the 1350 Roman Jubilee, including those offered for the Roman Jubilee of 1300, were much more modest. For the link as the fifteenth-century Dominican professor Michael Francisci de Insulis saw it between the Jubilee of 1350 and the symbolic importance of counted prayers, see below, p. 225.

[34] Sumption, *Pilgrimage*, p. 242, citing Philip, *Liber de Terra Sancta* (1377), ed. J. Haupt, *Oesterreichische Vierteljahresschrift für katholische Theologie* 10 (1871), 511–40, at pp. 519–20.

[35] Duffy, *Stripping of the Altars*, pp. 214, 238–39, and fig. 85. On the different printed versions of this image, see Henry Bradshaw, "On the Earliest English Engravings of the Indulgence Known as the 'Image of Pity,'" in *Collected Papers of Henry Bradshaw* (Cambridge, 1889), pp. 84–100. For the details of its iconography, see Gabriele Finaldi, *The Image of Christ: Catalogue of the Exhibition* Seeing Salvation, The National Gallery, London, 26 February–7 May 2000 (London, 2000), pp. 154–55.

[36] Ringbom, *Icon to Narrative*, p. 26, n. 21, citing W. L. Schreiber, *Handbuch der Holz- und Metallschnitte des XV. Jahrhunderts*, 2nd ed., 7 vols. (Leipzig, 1926–29), no. 876.

the prayers, could be easily multiplied: eighty thousand years for praying three prayers (one in Flemish; two, a Pater Noster and an Ave Maria, in Latin) before a woodblock image of Christ on the cross; fourteen thousand years for "[seeing] and [reflecting] on Our Lord's weapons, the weapons by which He suffered and with which He was lamentably tortured by the ignorant Jews, and then kneeling and [saying] three Our Fathers and three Hail Marys and [repenting one's] sins"; thirty-three thousand years for reciting "The Seven Prayers of St. Gregory" before an image of Pope Gregory's Mass.[37] The possibility of saying additional, perhaps even daily, repetitions of such ostensibly well-indulgenced prayers must have been, to say the least, tempting, particularly for those who had purchased their own copies of the available woodcuts.

But what, exactly, did earning 32,755 years of pardon for saying five Pater Nosters, five Ave Marias and a Credo mean? On the one hand, one might want to apply the years of pardon directly to the time that one might expect to have to spend in Purgatory oneself. On the other, a more generous, arguably more Christian option would be to apply the years not to one's own punishment or suffering, but to that of one's loved ones and other Christian souls, either in expectation of the time that they would have to spend in Purgatory for any penances that they had not yet completed or against the time that they had already spent in Purgatory if they were already dead. Pious women in particular were often remarked for the numbers of souls that their prayers had been able to release from bondage to their sins. The German nun Christina Ebner (1277–1356) alone accounted for the redemption of 23,710,200 souls through her prayers; her monastic sister Adelheid of Langmann (1306–75) was credited with an additional 30,000.[38] According to the legends, St. Bridget of Sweden (ca. 1303–73) released so many souls from their torment with her "Fifteen

---

[37] Flemish woodblock of Christ on the Cross (ca. 1450): Swanson, *Religion and Devotion*, fig. 5; *Mass of St. Gregory* (ca. 1460): Henk van Os, with Hans Nieuwdorp, Bernhard Ridderbos, and Eugène Honée, *The Art of Devotion in the Late Middle Ages in Europe, 1300–1500*, trans. Michael Hoyle (Princeton, 1994), p. 112 (transcription) and plate 34; "The Seven Prayers of St. Gregory": Ringbom, *Icon to Narrative*, p. 25.

[38] Siegfried Ringler, *Viten- und Offenbarungsliteratur in Frauenklöstern des Mittelalters. Quellen und Studien*, Münchener Texte und Untersuchungen zur deutschen Literatur des Mittelalters 72 (Munich and Zurich, 1980), p. 197 (Christina Ebner); and *Die Offenbarungen der Margaretha Ebner und der Adelheid Langmann*, ed. Philipp Strauch, trans. Josef Prestel and Mystiker des Abendlandes (Weimar, 1939), p. 116 (Adelheid); cited by Lentes, "Counting Piety," p. 57.

Oes" that the fiends of Hell themselves started to worry.[39] And even Margery Kempe (ca. 1373–1438), albeit a laywoman, received assurance from Christ that her prayers would be credited to her fellow Christians as she requested: "half to Master R. to the increase of his merit, as if he did these [good works] himself. And the other half . . . on [behalf of Christ's] friends and enemies and [her] friends and enemies, for," Margery explained to Christ, "I will have only yourself for my reward."[40] The theologically more sophisticated (which, arguably, Margery at least was not) might protest that such bargaining and enumeration of souls saved per prayers said were necessarily somewhat by the by, given that Purgatory itself is a timeless state and so no authentically promulgated indulgence, including a plenary, would ever be granted for more years than one could reasonably expect to live and therefore spend doing an earthly penance. Our question here is whether what Margery and her fellow daughters of God were doing in accumulating souls for prayers much as their contemporaries piled up years of indulgence through their pilgrimages and devotions is best described as making some sort of commercial or, more properly, mercantile exchange.

The visionary Gertrude of Helfta (1256–1301 or 1302), for one, thought that the prayers she and her sisters said were gifts, which she then saw Christ distributing "for the relief of souls who were present and yet were quite invisible to her." Later in the same vision she saw her prayers as a medicine: "a little river, pure as crystal, issuing from the Lord's breast and flowing into the heart of the person for whom she was praying." And when she asked the Lord what else he would like her to add to her prayers for the souls suffering in Purgatory, he replied: "Confidence alone is sufficient to obtain everything easily; but if in your devotion you really desire to add something over and above, then recite the psalm 'O praise the Lord all ye nations' [Psalm 116] three hundred and sixty-five times to make up for any negligence of theirs in my divine praise." It is surely significant that the one thing, at least in this context, Gertrude thought her prayers were most definitely not was a payment, any more than Christ's gifts to her might be considered a wage and she simply a hireling to whom

---

[39] *Commonplace Book of Robert Reynes*, ed. Louis, no. 84, pp. 267–68; trans. Shinners, in *Medieval Popular Religion*, ed. Shinners, p. 367.

[40] Margery Kempe, *The Book of Margery Kempe*, bk. 1, chap. 8, ed. Sanford Brown Meech and Hope Emily Allen, Early English Text Society, o.s. 212 (London, 1940), pp. 20–21; trans. B. A. Windeatt (Harmondsworth, 1985), p. 55.

he deigned to show his secrets for the price of her faith. As Christ himself chided her for doubting the great condescension of his love, "Remember how often you have despised yourself, thinking yourself utterly unworthy of the gifts of my grace, and even thinking that you have been given them as an incentive, like a hireling who serves for wages, almost as though you could not be faithful to me without this gift?"[41]

Nor is it as easy as modern scholars like Lentes have tended to suggest to find a direct equation between the prayers tallied up daily by late medieval laypeople in their devotions to Christ, his Mother, and his wounds and any expectation that these prayers, simply by virtue of being counted, could be reckoned in some sense as a payment for sin. One might buy a woodcut or a string of rosary beads, but, as the instructions included on the images themselves made clear, it was still necessary to say the prayers devoutly and with contrition for the possession of these objects to have its intended effect. Performance, including the number of repetitions, mattered as much, if not more so, than purchase for the efficacy of these devotions. The history of the devotion to the rosary, Huizinga's favored example of the degeneracy of late medieval religious practice into the fantastical arithmetic of a petrified symbolism, is here a case in point.

Although its precise lines of development are still somewhat unclear, "bidding one's beads" was a practice that by the later Middle Ages was becoming increasingly popular among laity and clergy alike, so much so that in the last decades of the fifteenth century the prayer clubs or confraternities founded by preachers like the Dominican Alain de la Roche (1428–75) attracted tens of thousands of members throughout Europe. We know this because the confraternities themselves kept lists of their membership; indeed, to be listed in the book of the confraternity was one of the principle attractions of membership, for to be so enrolled was to benefit from the accumulation of the confraternity's likewise carefully inscribed prayers.[42] And, of course, to add to the appeal of saying the prayer there

---

[41] Gertrude of Helfta, *Legatus divinae pietatis*, bk. 3, chap. 9, ed. Pierre Doyère, as *Oeuvres spirituelles III: Le Héraut (Livre III)*, Sources chrétiennes 143 (Paris, 1968), pp. 34–42; trans. Margaret Winkworth, as *The Herald of Divine Love* (New York, 1993), pp. 161–64.

[42] On these confraternity lists, see Anne Winston-Allen, *Stories of the Rose: The Making of the Rosary in the Middle Ages* (University Park, Pa., 1997), pp. 116–17; Jean-Claude Schmitt, "La Confrérie du rosaire de Colmar (1485): Textes de fondation, 'Exempla' en allemand d'Alain de la Roche, listes des Prêcheurs et des Soeurs

were indulgences: seven years and seven quarantines according to a bull of Pope Sixtus IV (reigned 1471–84) issued in 1478, five years and five quarantines according to one issued in 1479.[43] As with other indulgenced prayers, expectations of benefit tended rapidly to multiply. As one promotional ditty (*Ein new lied von dem Rosenkrantz vnd bruderschafft Marie*) put it: "If you will pray the holy rosary / every day through for a week, / indeed, the indulgence amounts to / one hundred thousand and five thousand days / plus fifteen, I tell you / In Jesus's name."[44]

Whether spiritual or economic, profit alone cannot, however, be the reason that so many thousands took up the recitation of this prayer, nor can it explain why the prayer was so enthusiastically promoted by so many ecclesiastical authorities. The Church itself (if we may speak so monolithically of such a temporally and regionally contingent institution) earned little if any money directly from the confraternities. Indeed, the statutes of the brotherhoods stipulate as much, "for," as the confraternity handbook printed at Ulm in 1483 put it, "this is not a brotherhood of earthly riches but of the spirit and of the achievements of virtues and of all spirituality."[45] Even more to the point: "No one," or so the great Dominican theological master Jakob Sprenger (ca. 1436–94) insisted in the charter for the confraternity he founded at Cologne in 1475, "of any status or condition should be excluded; rich, poor, religious, or secular— all should be received."[46]

Neither was it the confraternities' purpose to enforce one or another particular method of saying the prayer. As we have seen, Alain de la

---

dominicaines," *Archivum fratrum praedicatorum* 40 (1970), 97–124, at pp. 101–2, 118–24; and Jakob Hubert Schütz, *Die Geschichte des Rosenkranzes unter Berücksichtigung der Rosenkranz-Geheimnisse und der Marien-Litaneien* (Paderborn, 1909), p. 26 (Cologne statutes). Cf. Lentes, "Counting Piety," pp. 62–65, on the process and effects of recording prayers. On the rosary as practice, see Eithne Wilkins, *The Rose-Garden Game: The Symbolic Background to the European Prayer-beads* (London, 1969).

[43] For the text of the bulls of 1478 and 1479 as recorded in the book of the Cologne confraternity, see Schütz, *Geschichte des Rosenkranzes*, pp. 33–36.

[44] Philipp Wackernagel, *Das deutsche Kirchenlied von der ältesten Zeit bis zu Anfang des 17. Jahrhunderts*, 5 vols. (Leipzig, 1864–77), 2:862, no. 1064, stanza 12; trans. Winston-Allen, *Stories of the Rose*, p. 127.

[45] *Vnser lieben Frauen Psalter*, attributed to Alain de la Roche (Alanus de Rupe) (Ulm, 1483), fols. A6r–A7r; cited by Winston-Allen, *Stories of the Rose*, p. 119.

[46] Schütz, *Geschichte des Rosenkranzes*, p. 24: "Nullos cujuscumque status vel conditionis excludit, divites pauperes religiosos seculares recipit."

Roche recommended the recitation of 150 Hail Marys by analogy with the 150 psalms (in Alain's view, the proper name for the prayer was not *rosarium* or chaplet, but *psalterium* or psalter), each set of 150 to be said daily "in remembrance of the 150 joys that [Mary] had from heaven from her sweet baby Jesus." The fifteen Our Fathers accompanying the Hail Marys, likewise said daily over the course of the year, were to recall "all the wounds of our redeemer Jesus" (15 times 365, equaling 5,475 Our Fathers per year).[47] In contrast, for Jakob Sprenger, it was enough if the members of the brotherhood should recite three *rosaria*—again, 150 Hail Marys (or "white roses") and 15 Our Fathers (or "red roses") each—but once a week.[48] Other confraternities and prayer books recommended somewhat different groupings of prayers and meditations, some with only five repetitions of the ten Hail Marys (as, for example, that founded at Colmar in 1485), others with as many as twenty.[49] One popular handbook, *Von dem psalter vnnd Rosenkrancz vnser lieben frauen*, which was reprinted in seven editions between 1483 and 1502 and attributed to Alain de la Roche, suggested as many as six different ways of praying the psalter (here, three rosaries). "However," it advised its readers, "if none of the six above-mentioned ways pleases you, or if you should have greater devotion by another method, take it for your own, only [and this was the main point] let this praiseworthy prayer be spoken with diligence and devotion according as it is possible and proper for each person."[50] Jakob Sprenger had suggested much the same thing in justifying the monetary requirements (i.e., none) for membership in his brotherhood. Although, Sprenger felt it necessary to point out, the prayers said by the poor were the more pleasing (*behäglicher*) and agreeable (*gefälliger*) to God, the point was for both the rich and the poor to say the prayers as well as they could, not for them somehow to pay for them.[51]

---

[47] *Livre et ordonannce de la devote confrarie du psaultier de la glorieuse vierge Marie* (1475–1476), ed. Gilles Gerard Meersseman, *Ordo Fraternitatis: Confraternite e pieta dei laici nel medioevo*, 3 vols., Italia Sacra 24–26 (Rome, 1977), 3:1164–69, at p. 1165. The same document also refers the 150 Hail Marys to the 150 prophecies, joys, and pains of Mary.

[48] Schütz, *Geschichte des Rosenkranzes*, p. 26.

[49] Schmitt, "La Confrérie du rosaire de Colmar," p. 106; Winston-Allen, *Stories of the Rose*, p. 25.

[50] *Von dem psalter vnnd Rosenkrancz vnser lieben frauen* (Augsburg, 1492), fol. B7r; cited by Winston-Allen, *Stories of the Rose*, p. 25.

[51] Schütz, *Geschichte des Rosenkranzes*, p. 26.

So, it would seem, counted prayer was not or, at least, not only about buying one's way into heaven. It was also about doing—we might even say, making—something that one then might give to God, perhaps as a payment, but more properly, as Gertrude learned in her visions, as a gift. Nor were such gifts given always in expectation of reciprocal temporal or eternal returns as critics like Eckhart and Luther so caustically charged. *Pace* those who would insist along with Henry Charles Lea (1825–1909) that even the indulgences promulgated in support of such spiritual works as attendance at the Office for a particular feast or the daily recitation of a prayer were more often than not simply "enormous bribe[s],"[52] thousands of indulgenced prayers were said daily by the members of the various confraternities for free; i.e., with no profit whatsoever to the Church other than, presumably, the spiritual health of the devotees. Indeed, barring the price of a woodcut or a set of beads, such prayers were also materially as well as spiritually free to their practitioners. Anybody, as Jakob Sprenger insisted, could say the prayers of the rosary. Indeed, as miracle stories promoting the Hail Mary had long pointed out, such prayers said devoutly by even the humblest of the Virgin's lovers were more pleasing to the Lady than the most elaborate devotions of the rich.[53]

Likewise, simply because they were counted did not of itself make such prayers an inflation-prone currency to be hoarded up against the threat of damnation nor the indulgences that they earned bribes. If for the confraternity of St. Ursula and her companions the prayers that its members accumulated were imagined as shipping fees to the hereafter, for the nuns of Colmar they were counted as golden stars and silken threads. Far from reflecting a desire to accumulate prayers, as it were, indiscriminately ("just in case") so as to cover any residual penances left

---

[52] Lea, *Indulgences*, pp. 184–88.

[53] For these stories, see *Miracula sanctae virginis Mariae*, ed. Elise F. Dexter, University of Wisconsin Studies in the Social Sciences and History 12 (Madison: University of Wisconsin Press, 1927), pp. 17–18; Evelyn Faye Wilson, *The* Stella maris *of John of Garland* (Cambridge, Mass., 1946), pp. 178–79; Gonzalo de Berceo, *Miracles of Our Lady*, trans. Richard Terry Mount and Annette Grant Cash (Lexington, Ky., 1997), pp. 32–35; Johannes Herolt, *Miracles of the Blessed Virgin Mary*, trans. C. C. Swinton Bland (London, 1928), pp. 76–77, 100; Henry Adams, *Mont Saint Michel and Chartres* (Harmondsworth, 1986), pp. 249–50; R. W. Southern, *The Making of the Middle Ages* (New Haven, 1953), pp. 248–49; and Rachel Fulton, *From Judgment to Passion: Devotion to Christ and the Virgin Mary, 800–1200* (New York, 2002), pp. 253–54.

unaccounted for on one's balance-sheet of sins, such reckonings suggest not only the concreteness but also the boundedness of the things prayed for or, perhaps more accurately, imagined by the ones praying. The whole point of the rosary was not, as critics of the indulgenced versions of this prayer have been tempted to suggest, simply to say "lots" of prayers or "as many as possible because you never know," but rather to make a daily practice of saying a carefully calculated number of prayers. If, for Huizinga, such calculations were an obvious symptom of symbolic thinking gone mad, the mysteries of holiness trivialized because reduced to mere arithmetical exercises, for Alain de la Roche they were what gave the rosary its structure and purpose as a *psalterium* (by definition, a cycle of 150 psalms) and thus as a prayer.

They were also, as we shall see, what gave it its power as an imaginative practice. Shipping fees, golden stars, and silk threads were not, after all, the only things that late medieval Christians sought to make through their prayers. There were also, as Alain explained in his justification of the numbers of the rosary, itemized remembrances of Mary's sorrows and her joys, not to mention the enumerations of Christ's wounds. Hard as it has been for most modern scholars to acknowledge, number in this context was far more than just a tool for making sure one said the necessary quota of prayers. Rather, or so philosophers, theologians, and exegetes since antiquity had insisted, it was the very ground of spatiotemporal, material being; it was number through which God had brought the world into being. If, for Eckhart, number was something, therefore, to be avoided in thinking about God, for theologians such as Augustine and preachers such as Alain de la Roche, it was that which made it possible to think about God at all. Moreover, as miracle story after miracle story on the efficacy of the recitation of the rosary sought to make clear, it was through number—specifically, numbered prayers—that the faithful might themselves participate in this work of creation by weaving for God's Mother garlands of roses, damask mantles, and sleeves.

Number and Creation: Worship and Making

It is a truism easy to forget, if nevertheless one to which those, like Eckhart, steeped in the mystical numerology of pseudo-Dionysian Neoplatonism could not help but be sensitive: whether said badly or well, piously or with ill-will, prayers are enumerable; i.e., susceptible to counting, for the very simple reason that they, like money, flowers, articles of clothing, wounds, drops of blood, and sins, are things made in both space (because material or performable by virtue of having a living body) and time.[54] They are countable because, unlike God (a.k.a. the One), they are creatures, and so, as Eckhart put it, "[they fall] outside the One and into number and division." In falling outside the One, they are, again in Eckhart's words, "imperfect," "inferior and corruptible" things, because "number and division always belong to imperfect things and come from imperfection. In itself number is an imperfection, because it is a falling away or lapse outside the One that is convertible with being. This is the reason why only inferior and corruptible beings are numbered and divided under a single species." [55] For Eckhart, these "inferior and corruptible beings" included not only God's first two creations (heaven and earth) of which he is speaking here, but also that distinction of self from God experienced by those who, when they pray, think to ask anything of God in expectation of some return.[56] As the bull of condemnation posthumously issued against Eckhart by Pope John XXII (reigned 1316–34) excerpted Eckhart's position, "He who prays for anything particular [*hoc aut hoc*] prays badly and for something that is bad, because he is praying for the negation of good and the negation of God, and he begs that God be denied to him."[57]

Others, like Augustine, likewise influenced by the tradition of Neoplatonism, were inclined to see number and enumerable things (such as particularized prayers) somewhat more positively, particularly the capacity of number to point God's creatures to the truth about his Word and its creation. Augustine himself put it perhaps most succinctly in his *De doctrina Christiana*. In his words: "It is perfectly clear to the most stupid

---

[54] On Eckhart's knowledge of Neoplatonism, see McGinn, *Mystical Thought*, pp. 92–93. For the Neoplatonic sources of late medieval Dominican mysticism more generally, see Bernard McGinn, *The Harvest of Mysticism in Medieval Germany* (New York, 2005), pp. 39–47.

[55] Eckhart, *Liber parabolarum Genesis*, nos. 11, 17, ed. J. Koch, in *Meister Eckhart: Die lateinischen Werke*, vol. 1; trans. Edmund Colledge, as "Book of the Parables of Genesis," in *Meister Eckhart. The Essential Sermons, Commentaries, Treatises and Defense* (New York, 1981), pp. 97, 99.

[56] McGinn, *Mystical Thought*, pp. 130–31.

[57] "In agro dominico" (March 27, 1329), ed. M.-H. Laurent, "Autour du procès de Maître Eckhart. Les documents des Archives Vaticanes," *Divus Thomas* (Piacenza), Ser. 3, 13 (1936), 435–46; trans. Colledge, in *The Essential Sermons*, p. 78. I have been unable to verify this edition.

person that . . . numbers have immutable rules not instituted by men but discovered through the sagacity of the more ingenious." Thus, he contended, it should be obvious to all "studious and intelligent youths" that numbers cannot be neglected when interpreting Scripture and other matters of doctrine. According to Augustine, these rules include not only such operational regularities as "three threes [making] nine [and] geometrically [producing] a square figure,"[58] but also such symbolic truths as may be gleaned from the "legitimate" numbers commended by Scripture, as, for example, seven, ten, and twelve.[59]

"Legitimately" speaking, according to this way of thinking, seven is "perfect" because it is made up of three and four, three being "the first odd whole number" and four being "the first whole even number."[60] The reasoning here is geometric, more properly, (Neo-)Pythagorean: one or the monad is not a number but rather "the beginning, font, and origin of numbers."[61] Likewise, two or the dyad is not a whole or real number, but rather the beginning of otherness, "the source and foundation of the diversity of numbers," while itself remaining without form because it is only a line.[62] Three is the first real or whole number because it has extension in space (three points designate a triangle) and time (beginning, middle, and end).[63] And four is likewise real because four points describe the first solid (a pyramid) and thus "the limit of corporeality and three-

---

[58] Augustine, *De doctrina christiana*, bk. 2, chaps. 38–39, paragrs. 56–58, ed. Joseph Martin, CCSL 32 (Turnhout, 1962), pp. 71–72; trans. D. W. Robertson, as *On Christian Doctrine* (New York, 1958), pp. 72–73.

[59] Augustine, *De doctrina christiana*, bk. 3, chap. 35, paragrs. 50–51, ed. Martin, pp. 110–11; trans. Robertson, *On Christian Doctrine*, pp. 112–13.

[60] Augustine, *De civitate Dei*, bk. 11, chap. 31, ed. Bernardus Dombart and Alfonsus Kalb, 2 vols., CCSL 47–48 (Turnhout, 1955), 2:351; trans. Henry Bettenson, as *Concerning the City of God Against the Pagans* (Harmondsworth, 1972, 1984), pp. 465–66.

[61] Henri de Lubac, *Exégèse médiévale: Les quatre sens de l'Écriture*. 2 vols. in 4. Théologie: Études publiées sous la direction de la Faculté de Théologie S.J. de Lyon-Fourvière 41.1–2, 42, and 59 (Paris, 1959–64), 4:13, n. 4, citing Isidore of Seville and Boethius.

[62] Iamblichus (attributed to), *The Theology of Arithmetic: On the Mystical, Mathematical and Cosmological Symbolism of the First Ten Numbers*, trans. Robin Waterfield (Grand Rapids, Mich., 1988), p. 41.

[63] Augustine, *De musica*, bk. 1, chap. 12, n. 20, ed. J.-P. Migne, PL 32 (Paris, 1845), col. 1095.

dimensionality."[64] More particularly, four is the number of the material or corporeal creation, thus the four winds, four elements, four seasons, and four bodily humors; while three, the sum of the monad and the dyad, is the number of the spirit and of the soul, itself created in the image and likeness of the Trinity.

By this reasoning, hardly original to Augustine and yet still current in Alain de la Roche's day, seven as the sum of three and four designates the totality of creation in both space and time, and thus God rested on the seventh day; while ten, the sum of three and seven, signifies the unity of the Trinity of the Creator with the hebdomad of his creation.[65] Twelve, the product of three and four, points to the end of things and the twelve thrones on which the judges of the twelve tribes of Israel will sit with the Son of Man (Matthew 19:28).[66] Fifteen, like three, six, and ten, a triangular number, is the sum of seven, the number of universality, and eight, the number of eternity and resurrection, because Christ rose again to life on the eighth day, the day after the Sabbath, and eight is the cube of two.[67] Fifty is the sum of seven times seven plus one and so the number of the eternal rest (the rest of God times the day of the Sabbath) plus the union with God in contemplation; it is accordingly associated with the coming of the Spirit at Pentecost.[68] One hundred as the square of ten is the number of totality and perfection (note the correspondences with seven and ten), and one hundred fifty is appropriately the number of the Psalms—

---

[64] Iamblichus, *Theology of Arithmetic*, trans. Waterfield, p. 55.

[65] On these correspondences, see Heinz Meyer, *Die Zahlenallegorese im Mittelalter: Methode und Gebrauch*, Münstersche Mittelalter-Schriften 25 (Munich, 1975), pp. 133–39 (on seven), 142–45 (on ten); de Lubac, *Exégèse médiévale*, 4:15–17, 21–30; and Vincent Foster Hopper, *Medieval Number Symbolism: Its Sources, Meaning, and Influence on Thought and Expression* (New York, 1938), pp. 83–85. For exhaustive treatment of all of these numerological allegories, see Heinz Meyer and Rudolf Suntrup, *Lexikon der Mittelalterlichen Zahlenbedeutungen*, Münstersche Mittelalter-Schriften 56 (Munich, 1987). For further references on medieval number symbolism, see below, n. 71.

[66] Augustine, *De civitate Dei*, bk. 20, chap. 5, ed. Dombart and Kalb, 2:704; trans. Bettenson, *City of God*, p. 901.

[67] Meyer, *Zahlenallegorese*, p. 150–51; and Hopper, *Medieval Number Symbolism*, pp. 43–44, 77–81, 101.

[68] Augustine, *De doctrina christiana*, bk. 2, chap. 16, paragr. 25, ed. Martin, p. 51; trans. Robertson, *On Christian Doctrine*, p. 52. See also Meyer, *Zahlenallegorese*, pp. 164–66; and Hopper, *Medieval Number Symbolism*, p. 81.

here, following the popular early twelfth-century commentator Honorius Augustodunensis—because it is the sum of one hundred (perfection) and fifty (eternal joy).[69]

It would be easy to go on—Augustine's exposition of the 153 fish of John 21:11 is particularly neat, 150 being the sum of three fifties plus the three of the Trinity as well as the triangular sum of the numbers from one to seventeen[70]—but the pattern is doubtless now clear. In philosophical as well as exegetical terms, counting, whether divisions of time, bodily humors, days of creation, thrones, psalms, or fish, was never just counting. Rather, it was a meditation on the very nature of existence, whether created, and therefore, numerable, or uncreated, and so radically Other than number but nevertheless its source.[71] This is the way Augustine understood this existential capacity of number (the passage, worth citing in full, is from his treatise *De libero arbitrio*):

> Look on earth and sky and sea, and whatsoever things are in them or shine from above or creep beneath or fly or swim; they have forms because they have numbers: take these away, they will be nothing.

---

[69] Augustine, *De civitate Dei*, bk. 20, chap. 7, eds. Dombart and Kalb, 2:710; trans. Bettenson, *City of God*, p. 908; and Honorius Augustodunensis, *Expositio in psalmos*, Psalm 150, ed. J.-P. Migne, PL 172 (Paris, 1854), cols. 305–6. See also Meyer, *Zahlenallegorese*, pp. 177–78, 183–84.

[70] Augustine, *De doctrina christiana*, bk. 2, chap. 16, paragr. 25, ed. Martin, p. 51; trans. Robertson, *On Christian Doctrine*, p. 52. See also Meyer, *Zahlenallegorese*, pp. 184–85.

[71] For discussion, see Edward I. Condren, *The Numerical Universe of the Gawain-Pearl Poet* (Gainsville, Fla., 2002); Lawrence P. Schrenk, "God as Monad: The Philosophical Basis of Medieval Theological Numerology," in *Medieval Numerology: A Book of Essays*, ed. Robert L. Surles, Garland Medieval Casebooks 7 (New York, 1993), pp. 3–10; Annemarie Schimmel, *The Mystery of Numbers* (New York and Oxford, 1993), pp. 19–25; Gillian R. Evans, "Number-Symbolism and the Theory of Signification in Odo of Morimond and Some of His Successors," *Cîteaux* 34 (1983), 111–20; Russell A. Peck, "Number as Cosmic Language," in *Essays in the Numerical Criticism of Medieval Literature*, ed. Caroline D. Eckhardt (Lewisburg, Pa., 1980), pp. 15–64; Donald W. Fritz, "*The Pearl*: The Sacredness of Numbers," *The American Benedictine Review* 31, no. 2 (June 1980), 314–34; Walter Horn, "On the Selective Use of Sacred Numbers and the Creation in Carolingian Architecture of a New Aesthetic Based on Modular Concepts," *Viator* 6 (1975), 351–90; Christopher Butler, *Number Symbolism* (New York, 1970), pp. 22–46; and Edmund Reiss, "Number Symbolism and Medieval Literature," *Medievalia et Humanistica: Studies in Medieval and Renaissance Culture*, n.s. 1, ed. Paul Maurice Clogan (Cleveland, 1970), pp. 161–74.

From what then are they, if not from number, seeing that they have being only in so far as they have number?

And even human artificers, makers of all corporeal forms, have numbers in their art to which they fit their works; and they move their hands and tools in the fashioning till that which is formed outside, carried back to the light of numbers which is within, so far as may be attains perfection, and through the mediating sense pleases the inner judge looking upon the heavenly numbers.

Then seek what moves the limbs of the artificer himself: it will be number; for they too are moved in the rhythm of numbers. And if you take away the work from the hands, and from the mind the intention of making something, and that motion is directed towards pleasure, you will have a dance. Seek then what it is that gives pleasure in a dance; number will answer, "Behold, it is I."

Look now upon the beauty of the formed body; numbers are held in space. Examine the beauty of mobility in the body; numbers move around in time. Go into the art whence these proceed, seek in it time and place: never will it be, nowhere will it be; yet number lives in it, nor is its region of spaces, nor its age of days; and yet when they who would be artists apply themselves to learning the art, they move their bodies through space and time, and even their mind through time—[and] with the passing of time . . . they become more skillful. Transcend, therefore, the artist's mind also, to see the sempiternal number. Now wisdom will flash forth to you from her innermost throne, and from the very sanctuary of truth. If she dazzles and blinds your as yet too feeble vision, turn back the eye of the mind into that path where she showed herself joyfully; but remember then that you have put off the vision which, when you are stronger and sounder, you may seek again.[72]

---

[72] Augustine, *De libero arbitrio*, bk. 2, chap. 16, paragr. 42, ed. William M. Green, CCSL 29 (Turnhout, 1970), pp. 265–66; trans. C. M. Sparrow, as *De libero arbitrio voluntatis; St. Augustine on Free Will*, University of Virginia Studies 4 (Charlottesville, 1947), repr. in Vernon J. Bourke, *The Essential Augustine*, 2nd ed. (Indianapolis, 1974), pp. 126–27.

This, as Augustine and his fellow exegetes would have it, is what the author of Wisdom meant when he said in praise of God (Wisdom 11:21): "You have ordered all things in measure, number and weight."[73] Without number, there would be no creation. Neither, and this is the crux of the matter for prayer, would there be any way to apprehend the Creator or, rather, if there were, very few could follow it. As the great Franciscan St. Bonaventure Bagnoregio (ca. 1217–74) explained, citing Boethius (ca. 470 or 475–524): "'Number is the principal exemplar in the mind of the Creator,' and in creatures it is the principal vestige leading to wisdom. Since number is most evident to all and is closest to God, it leads us very close to God by its seven-fold distinction; and it makes God known in all bodily and sensible things when we become aware of numerical realities, when we take delight in numerical proportions, and when we come to make irrefutable judgments by means of the laws of numerical proportions."[74] Number, in short, brings us, by way of creation, to God.

Esoteric (not to mention, risible) as such numerological speculation may seem to us, it was arguably as familiar to the devout of the rosary's late medieval heyday as the passion for statistics of all sorts (sporting, actuarial, nutritional, demographic, financial) is to most Americans today. Indeed, long before Alain applied his symbolic calipers to the Hail Marys of the rosary, the ninth-century laywoman Dhuoda (m. 824, d. after 843) instructed her son William in the numerological mysteries contained in the single word, "God" (*Deus*), so that he should know how not only to praise and love God as "he who *laid the foundations of the earth* and *the measures thereof*," but also to pray (Job 38:4–5).[75] By the

---

[73] Cited by Augustine, *De civitate Dei*, bk. 11, chap. 30, eds. Dombart and Kalb, 2:350; trans. Bettenson, *City of God*, p. 465.

[74] Bonaventure, *Itinerarium mentis in Deum*, chap. 2., paragr. 10, ed. PP. Collegii a S. Bonaventura, trans. Zachary Hayes with Introduction and Commentary by Philotheus Boehner, in *Works of St. Bonaventure*, vol. 2 (Saint Bonaventure, N.Y., 2002), pp. 76–77.

[75] Dhuoda, *Liber manualis*, bk. 1, ed. Pierre Riché, as *Manuel pour mon fils*, Sources chrétiennes 225a, 2nd ed. (Paris, 1991), p. 104; trans. Carol Neel, as *Handbook for William: A Carolingian Woman's Counsel for Her Son* (Washington, D.C., 1991), p. 10: "Our *D*, with which the name of God begins, is called *delta* by the Greeks. Thus it signifies four, the number of perfection, in Greek numerals; according to the Latin language, the same *D* expands to contain the great number 500. Nor is this empty of holy mystery." Dhuoda dedicates the whole of her ninth book to the symbolism of number.

later Middle Ages, such numerate mysteries had acquired not only existential but also performative significance, as we have already seen with Alain's own defense of the 150 Hail Marys of his confraternity's *psalterium*.[76] Alain's contemporary, the Dominican Michael Francisci de Insulis (ca. 1435–1502), professor of theology at the university in Cologne and supporter of Jakob Sprenger's efforts to popularize the practice of the rosary prayer, concurred—and said so publicly in a series of lectures he gave at Cologne in 1475 and published thereafter at Sprenger's behest.[77] "The confraternity of the Blessed Virgin," Francisci de Insulis proposed to demonstrate, "is founded upon a certain number of salutations and Our Fathers (*sub certo salutationum et orationum dominicalium numero institute*). Which number, indeed, is not lacking in mystery (*Qui quidem numerus . . . non caret misterio*)."[78] In proper scholastic fashion, the demonstration hinged upon five proofs: one, that there are certain numbers that pertain to the worship of God, the Blessed Virgin, and of the saints (*ad Dei et beate virginis et sanctorum cultum pertinent uti certo numero*); two, that the number fifty is not lacking in mystery for the salutations to the Virgin; three, that the number 150 has significance as both the number of the psalms and the salutations of the rosary; four, that the number

---

[76] On the importance of this number symbolism for the practice of the rosary, see also Lorenzo Francisco Candelaria, "The 'Rosary Cantorales' of Early Modern Spain: An Interdisciplinary Study in Attribution" (PhD diss., Yale University, 2001), pp. 104–27. For the performative importance of such symbolism more generally, see Craig Wright, "Dufay's *Nuper rosarum flores*, King Solomon's Temple, and the Veneration of the Virgin," *Journal of the American Musicological Society* 47, no. 3 (1994): 395–441; and Wright, *The Maze and The Warrior: Symbols in Architecture, Theology and Music* (Cambridge, Mass., 2001), passim.

[77] The lectures appeared in two editions, the first under the title *Determinatio quodlibetalis facta colonie* (1476), the second as *Quodlibet de veritate fraternitatis rosarii seu psalterii beate Marie virginis conventus Coloniensis ordinis Predicatorum* (1480). See Winston-Allen, *Stories of the Rose*, p. 67. Candelaria, "Rosary Cantorales," pp. 123–24, notes the popularity of these lectures in the first half of the sixteenth century in Spain.

[78] Michael Francisci de Insulis, *Quodlibet de veritate fraternitatis rosarii seu psalterii beate Marie virginis conventus Coloniensis ordinis Predicatorum* (Cologne, 1480), pp. 16, 36; consulted online at Verteilte Digitale Inkunabelbibliothek, http://inkunabeln.ub.uni-koeln.de/ (accessed August 6, 2006). The same argument appears in a shorter form in the first edition of Francisci's lectures: *Determinatio quodlibetalis facta colonie* [Basel: Bernhard Richel (?), after 10 March, 1476], fols. 6–7; cited by Candelaria, "Rosary Cantorales," pp. 124–27.

of Our Fathers contains a mystery; and five, that it is not an accident that the rosary should be said by the fraternity only once a week and not daily or as often as one pleased.[79] The proofs that follow would make exegetes from Augustine to Alain proud.

Primum, that there are numbers pertinent to God and his worship, may be shown first through the eternal law according to which God, three persons but one essential unity, ordained that there should be produced certain numbers of creatures, human beings, and angels predestined to worship him in eternity. This, Francisci de Insulis averred, is as it says in Wisdom 11: "Et breviter omnia in pondere numero et mensura fecit, ut per Sapientia 11."[80] Further proof of the pertinence of number to God and his worship might be found in the institutions of the old law, for example, in the number of angels (three) who appeared to Abraham by the oaks of Mamre and for whom Abraham prepared a tender calf (Genesis 18); in the numbers of offerings, sacrifices, and days of service specified for the priests in Exodus, Leviticus, and Numbers; in the number of gifts offered by the princes of the people as per Numbers 7; and in the number of singers and gatekeepers David established for the service of the Lord throughout his villages according to 1 Chronicles 9. Similar evidence might be found in the institutions of the new law, for example, in the fact that Christ willed to be circumcised and baptized, rise from the dead, and ascend into heaven after a specified amount of time; that he had a certain number of apostles and disciples and fed a certain number of people with five loaves and two fish; that there are seven sacraments, seven gifts of the Holy Spirit, twelve articles of faith, seven petitions in the Our Father, and seven works of spiritual and corporal mercy by which God is to be worshiped and honored; that there are seven canonical hours of the liturgical day as per Psalm 118:164. And, again, there are proofs in the institutions of the law still to come, in the nine orders of angels and the chorus of 144,000 singing a new song before the Lamb.[81]

Accordingly, or so Francisci de Insulis continued, that there are mysteries in the numbers fifty (*secundum*), one hundred fifty (*tertium*), and fifteen (*quartum*) for the Hail Marys and Our Fathers of the rosary should come as no surprise. This significance can be seen for the number fifty

---

[79] Michael Francisci de Insulis, *Quodlibet de veritate fraternitatis*, p. 36.
[80] Ibid., pp. 36–37.
[81] Ibid., pp. 37–38.

above all in the provision of the old law for observing every fiftieth year as a jubilee during which all possessions were to be restored, all debts forgiven, and all captives set free, as in Leviticus 25. "It is not without significance (*misterio*)," Francisci de Insulis argued, "that we should therefore honor by this number that one through whom was restored to us that which Eve took away." The fifty curtain loops and gold clasps of the tabernacle of Moses (Exodus 26), the greatness of David's sin and of God's mercy as confessed in the fiftieth psalm ("Miserere mei Deus"), the coming of the Holy Spirit on the fiftieth day after the resurrection, the jubilee year proclaimed in 1350 by Pope Clement VI (reigned 1342–52) for the remission of sins— all point to the appropriateness of praising with this number the Virgin through whom we were redeemed.[82] Likewise, the 150 psalms aptly figure the 150 Hail Marys of the rosary, because in them David prophesied not only concerning Christ, but also concerning the Virgin Mary. This numerate mystery may also be seen in the dimensions of the Solomonic House of the Forest of Lebanon (100 cubits long and 50 cubits wide; cf. 3 Kings 7:2), by its width signifying the Virgin's love, which extends over all the earth, and by its length, her mercy, which extends to the end of time (*in novissimum diem*).[83] And just as the 150 Hail Marys recall the joys and sorrows of the Virgin (Francisci de Insulis references here "magister Alanus;" i.e., Alain de la Roche), so the fifteen Our Fathers recall the number of Christ's wounds "which he bore on the body which he took from the Virgin and by which he washed us in his blood for our sins."[84] Francisci de Insulis's *quintum* is somewhat more practical than figurative, albeit still focused on the importance of number to worship: saying the rosary once a week rather than daily makes it a practice accessible to all, regardless of occupation or status. It also, by the by, follows the ancient practice of the Church more closely of saying the Davidic psalter in honor of Christ only once a week.[85]

Whether because they found such exegetical enumerations too difficult to follow or simply beside the point, then as now, not everyone was necessarily convinced. For those still skeptical of the power of number and its importance for the proper worship of God and his Mother, accordingly,

---

[82] Ibid., p. 39.
[83] Ibid., pp. 40–41.
[84] Ibid., pp. 41–42.
[85] Ibid., pp. 42–43.

there were miracles, some of which, by Francisci de Insulis's time, had been circulating for well over a hundred years. Appropriately, given what not only Augustine but also Bonaventure had said about the importance of number for God's work of creation, one such story had to do with Mary's sleeves. This is the way that Chaucer's friend Thomas Hoccleve (ca. 1366–1426) told it: Some time ago, possibly but not necessarily in the days of St. Dominic, there was a rich and worthy man specially devoted to Mary the Mother of Christ who taught his son to say every day fifty Hail Marys in honor of the Virgin. At his father's will, this young man later became a monk, who, returning one day to visit his father's house, went to pray in the family chapel. As he was praying, suddenly the Virgin Mary appeared to him wearing a beautiful dress with no sleeves. Marveling at her garment, the monk asked her why she had no sleeves, and she answered him:

> . . . This clothynge
> Thow hast me yoven, for thow every day,
> Fifty sythe 'Ave Maria' seyynge,
> Honured hast me. Hens foorth, I the pray,
> Use to treble that by any way,
> And to every tenth 'Ave' joyne also
> A 'Pater Noster,' do thow evene so.

When a week later, having trebled his devotions as instructed, the monk came to pray in the chapel, the Virgin appeared to him now fully clothed, saying:

> . . . Beholde now
> How good clothing and how fresh apparaille
> That this wyke to me yoven hast thow.
> Sleeves to my clothynge now nat faille:
> Thee thanke I, and ful wel for thy travaille.

The Virgin went on to advise the monk that if he returned to his abbey and instructed "the covent and the peple" there in the recitation of her "psalter," he could expect a blissful reception into Heaven at his death. [86]

---

[86] Thomas Hoccleve, "The Monk and Our Lady's Sleeves," ed. Beverly Boyd, *The Middle English Miracles of the Virgin* (San Marino, Calif., 1964), pp. 50–55.

Clearly, while the 50 Hail Marys that the monk's father had taught him to say were good, the 150 plus the 15 Our Fathers that Mary, now fully clothed, had taught him were even better. This same story was picked up later in the fifteenth century as part of Alain de la Roche's campaign (of which Michael Francisci de Insulis was a supporter) to promote the recitation of the proper "Dominican" Marian psalter of 150 Hail Marys, as opposed to the shorter Carthusian rosary of only 50 Hail Marys already popular in his day.[87] While fifty repetitions of the angel's salutation were sufficient to supply the body of a dress, the story made clear, additional repetitions were necessary to make its sleeves. Indeed, in Hoccleve's words, the monk's prayer was a labor ("travaille"); i.e., a work of making bounded, like God's, according to the measure, weight, and number of the things to be made.

Dresses and sleeves were not the only things that properly enumerated prayers to Mary could make; flowers and jewelry were popular, too.[88] Nor, to judge at least from the quantity of prayers enjoined upon the nuns at Colmar, were all things equally labor-intensive to make. Damask mantles, silk threads, and golden stars required greater handiwork than straightforward sleeves. Roses, on the other hand, could be made one prayer at a time, or so the robbers who sought to disturb one pious brother's prayers learned when they came upon him in the forest kneeling beside his horse and saying his customary Aves. "But," as one late fifteenth-century rosary handbook tells the story, "as they approached [the monk], [the robbers] saw from a distance a wonderfully beautiful maiden standing by him, who, every little while, took from his mouth

---

Hoccleve's version appears in Huntington Library, MS 744, fols. 36r–39v, but an earlier version under the title "Coment le sauter Noustre Dame fu primes contrové" appears in Oxford, Bodleian Library, MS Digby 86 (ca. 1275), fols. 130r–132r; and Edinburgh, National Library of Scotland, Advocates MS 19.2.1 (The Auchinleck Manuscript; ca. 1330–40), fols. 259rb–260vb. See Boyd, pp. 8–9, 119. For the Auchinleck manuscript version, see *The Auchenlick Manuscript,* eds. David Burnley and Alison Wiggins, Version 1.1 (The National Library of Scotland, July 3, 2003), http://www.nls.uk/auchinleck/mss/saute.html (accessed July 25, 2006). Cf. also the version told of the Dominican nun Beli von Lütisbach of Töss, cited by Lentes, "Counting Piety," pp. 55–56.

[87] Winston-Allen, *Stories of the Rose,* pp. 66–67.

[88] Winston-Allen, *Stories of the Rose,* p. 103; Lentes, "Gewänder der Heiligen"; and Eugène Honée, "Image and Imagination in the Medieval Culture of Prayer: A Historical Perspective," in van Os, *Art of Devotion,* pp. 170–72.

a beautiful rose and added it to a chaplet that she was making. When the rose chaplet was complete, she placed it on her head and flew off to heaven." Leaving off their plans to relieve the monk of his horse, the robbers ran to him and asked who the maiden was that they had seen taking the roses out of his mouth, to which the monk replied: "I did not have any maiden with me. I have only been reciting fifty Ave Marias as a chaplet for Queen Mary, as I was instructed. And that is all I know." The brother was, understandably, delighted when the robbers told him what they had seen "and from that day forward made a spiritual rose chaplet of fifty Ave Marias for Queen Mary daily and instructed other good people in the practice." [89]

In addition to flowers and clothing, one could also make scenes, for example, of the angel bringing his greetings to Mary, or of Mary giving birth to her Son, or, still following Hoccleve's poem on the monk and Mary's sleeves, of Mary's coronation in heaven with her Son. As Anne-Winston Allen has shown, arguably even more so than the miracle stories used by the Dominicans to promote the practice, such image-centered creations (the more typical term is "meditations") played an important role in the development of the 150-Aves rosary prayer in use by the end of the fifteenth century. Following what would become one of the more standard schemes, for every rosary, the orant would accordingly say five sets of ten Aves to enable meditation on the Joys of the Virgin (the Annunciation, the Visitation, the Nativity, the Presentation, and the Finding of Jesus in the Temple); five sets of the same in meditation on Mary's Sorrows (the Agony in the Garden, the Scourging, the Crowning with Thorns, the Carrying of the Cross, and the Crucifixion); and, finally, five sets again in meditation on the Glories (the Resurrection, the Ascension, the Descent of the Holy Spirit on the Apostles, Mary's Assumption into Heaven, and the Last Judgment),[90] each set punctuated by an Our Father for a total of 150 plus 15 prayers (the Creed was added in the late

---

[89] "Wie der rosenkrantze ist funden: Daz erste exempel by dem Rosenkrantze," Cologne, Historisches Archiv der Stadt, MS GBf 47, fol. 50, ed. Karl Joseph Klinkhammer, *Adolf von Essen und seine Werke: Der Rosenkranz in der geschichtlichen Situation seiner Entstehung und in seinem bleibenden Anliegen: Eine Quellenforschung,* Frankfurter Theologische Studien 13 (Frankfurt am Main, 1972), pp. 173–74; trans. Winston-Allen, *Stories of the Rose,* pp. 100–101.

[90] Winston-Allen, *Stories of the Rose,* p. 3, 65–80, esp. pp. 74–75: "Table 1: Elaboration of Meditations."

fifteenth century, the Gloria during the sixteenth). [91] Rosary handbooks and confraternity manuals printed at this time often included woodcut images to help in this work of meditative numbering along with instructions on how many Aves and Paters to say per illustration: ten Aves for an image of the angel Gabriel bringing his greeting to the Virgin, one Pater Noster as Christ sweat drops of blood on the Mount of Olives, ten more Aves for Mary's meeting with her cousin Elizabeth, one Pater Noster as Christ suffered at the flagellation, ten Aves for the joy Mary experienced when she gave birth to Our Lord, one Pater Noster as Christ suffered from the crown of thorns, ten Aves for the joy that Mary felt on finding her son sitting in the Temple in the midst of the learned doctors, one Pater Noster for the sufferings Christ experienced on the way to the crucifixion, ten Aves for the joy that Mary had at her death and assumption, one Pater Noster "to the suffering, the pain, and the bitter death that [Christ] endured on the cross."[92] The more devoutly and attentively one

---

[91] Following Huizinga, more recent studies of the rosary including Winston-Allen, *Stories of the Rose*, make relatively little of the numbering of the meditations, emphasizing rather the narrative aspect of the prayer. See also Anne Winston, "Tracing the Origins of the Rosary: German Vernacular Texts," *Speculum* 68, no. 3 (1993), 619–36. Carol M. Schuler, "The Seven Sorrows of the Virgin: Popular Culture and Cultic Imagery in Pre-Reformation Europe," *Simiolus* 21 (1992), 5–28, notes the importance of numbered devotions of Mary's sorrows as a way of distinguishing devotions to Mary from devotions to Christ. She does not, however, explore the significance of the numbering itself beyond the fact that (p. 16), "while five and especially seven remained the most frequent counts [of Mary's sorrows], some texts relate even more elaborate lists of up to 12, 13, 15, 16, 27, 50, and even 150 sorrows, each with varying selections of torments." On the numbering of Mary's Joys and Sorrows more generally, see Kathryn A. Smith, *Art, Identity and Devotion in Fourteenth-Century England: Three Women and Their Books of Hours* (Toronto, 2003), pp. 184–85; Fulton, *From Judgment to Passion*, pp. 231–32; Carol Monica Schuler, "The Sword of Compassion: Images of the Sorrowing Virgin in Late Medieval and Renaissance Art" (PhD diss., Columbia University, 1987), pp. 233–71; Woolf, *English Religious Lyric*, pp. 134–43, 268–72, 297–302; and André Wilmart, *Auteurs spirituels et textes dévots du moyen age latin: Études d'histoire littéraire* (Paris, 1932; repr. 1971), pp. 326–36, 505–36.

[92] Winston-Allen, *Stories of the Rose*, pp. 31–64. Cf. the meditation in Schmitt, ed., "La Confrérie du rosaire de Colmar," p. 106; trans. Winston-Allen, *Stories of the Rose*, p. 173, n. 15. On the method and content of these rosary meditations, see also Jeffrey Hamburger, *Nuns as Artists: The Visual Culture of a Medieval Convent* (Berkeley, 1997), pp. 66–80.

prayed, the more vivid or, rather, well made one's own mental images of these scenes would presumably become.

There is, as Francisci de Insulis sought to show in his carefully enumerated proof and his fellow Augustinian exegetes would most likely agree, a deep significance in the number of Hail Marys of the rosary that goes beyond simple parallelism with the Davidic psalter straight to the heart of prayer. To paraphrase Francisci de Insulis, "Numbers are not lacking in mystery for the worship of God, Mary and the saints." Given what we have learned about the numbered practices promoted by the authors of the miracle stories and rosary handbooks, we might think a moment longer about why this should be. Meditation, like prayer, requires focus, thus, it is often said, the usefulness of painted or sculpted images, at least, in monastic terms, for those less able to close out the distractions of the world simply by concentrating on a word ("Jesus") or words ("*Ave Maria, gratia plena, dominus tecum*") or a mental image, say, of Christ on the cross.[93] And yet, it would seem, meditations like those accompanying the late medieval rosary also require number, otherwise the focus (a word, a picture, a mental image) would be enough. Why isn't it enough? Perhaps—or so Augustine himself might insist in encouraging us to think experientially as well as symbolically about number—because there is more to meditation than focus and more to counted prayer than simply the devotional or ecstatic surrender oft-cited in more recent accounts as the experiential goal of cyclical, repetitive, yet unbounded (i.e., uncounted) prayer.[94]

Uncounted prayer, idealized by Eckhart and Luther, themselves following Paul (1 Thess. 5:17), as prayer "without ceasing," might, to be sure, lead one more immediately to the experience and understanding of the One. But counted prayer, to put it in Augustinian terms, might,

---

[93] On the importance of such images for monastic meditational practice, see Rachel Fulton, "The Virgin in the Garden, or Why Flowers Make Better Prayers," *Spiritus* 4 (2004), 1–23; Mary Carruthers, *The Craft of Thought: Meditation, Rhetoric, and the Making of Images, 400–1200* (Cambridge, 1998), pp. 116–70; Jeffrey Hamburger, "The Visual and the Visionary: The Image in Late Medieval Monastic Devotions," in *The Visual and the Visionary*, pp. 111–48, 502–10; and Karl F. Morrison, *History as a Visual Art in the Twelfth-Century Renaissance* (Princeton, 1990), pp. 48–91.

[94] On these effects of uncounted prayer, see Zaleski and Zaleski, *Prayer*, pp. 128–57; and Wilkins, *Rose-Garden Game*, pp. 64–79.

by contrast, make one more conscious of oneself at once as a creature (differentiated from the One by the act of creation) and as a maker (of images, prayers, roses, and sleeves), made in the image and likeness of the One who created the Many. From this perspective, counted prayer might better be seen as a recognition of prayer as a work, not simply of attention or surrender (like other meditational practices), but also of art.[95] And art, like God's act of creation, requires number because, as Augustine averred, it is number that gives everything other than God its potential for being. Eckhart might still insist that the only perfect prayer is that which proceeds from an empty spirit, utterly detached from all saying and doing in the realization of its nothingness with respect to the One.[96] Augustine would rather remind us, "It is a marvelous gift, granted to few persons, to go beyond all that can be measured and see the Measure without measure, to go beyond all that can be numbered and see the Number without number, and to go beyond all that can be weighed and see the Weight without weight."[97] More prosaically, human beings, like all God's creatures, are beings of space and time; we exist bounded by number, weight, and measure. Take these away, as Augustine would say, and we are nothing. The irony, at least for Augustine, is that it is above all in boundedness that we as creatures but also as embodied minds come to the experience of "Measure without measure," "Weight without weight," "Number without number"; that is to say, God.

---

[95] For prayer as an art of making and the one praying as an artisan, see Peter the Chanter, *De oratione et speciebus illius*, ed. Richard C. Trexler, *The Christian at Prayer: An Illustrated Prayer Manual Attributed to Peter the Chanter (d. 1197)*, Medieval and Renaissance Texts and Studies 44 (Binghamton, N.Y., 1987), p. 179: "Materia orationis sunt littere et sillabe, dictiones et orationes. Artifex est orator, cui necessaria est scientia, que instruat eum esse orandum aliquot septem dicendorum modorum."

[96] Eckhart, *Die rede der underscheidunge*, chaps. 2 and 6, ed. Quint, pp. 190–91 and 201–6; trans. Walshe, *Sermons and Treatises*, 3:12–13, 16–18. See also McGinn, *Mystical Thought of Meister Eckhart*, pp. 130–31.

[97] Augustine, *De Genesi ad litteram*, bk. 4, chap. 3, trans. John Hammond Taylor, as *The Literal Meaning of Genesis*, 2 vols., Ancient Christian Writers 41–42 (New York, 1982), 1:108.

On Boundedness and Prayer as a Skill

Does this mean that Eckhart and Luther were wrong to insist that the goal of the Christian should be not counted but rather unceasing prayer? Ironically or, perhaps more accurately, tragically, given the social and political cataclysm that was to follow on Luther's bitter critique of such practices as the counted rosary prayer, not to mention the consequent inability of more recent scholars to accept that such counting may have had a stimulus other than pathological obsession or models of commercial exchange, no.[98] It is rather a case, as Eckhart himself would be the first to agree, of confusing method (counting) with goal (unceasing prayer). Spiritual advisors know the symptoms all too well. This is the way that Eckhart described the phenomenon:

> It is just like learning to write: truly if a man has to acquire this art, he must apply himself and practise hard, however heavy and bitter a task it seems to him, and however impossible. If he is prepared to practice diligently and often, he will learn and master the art. Of course, at first he has to remember every letter and fix it firmly in his mind. Later on, when he has acquired the art, he will be completely free of the image and will not have to stop and think but will write fluently and freely—and the same with playing the fiddle or any other task that requires skill. All he needs to know is that he intends to exercise his skill, and even if he is not paying full attention, wherever his thoughts may stray, he will do the job because he has the skill. Thus a man should be pervaded with God's presence, transformed with the form of his beloved God, and made essential by Him, so that God's presence shines for him without any effort; rather he will find emptiness in all things and be totally free of things. But first there must be thought and attentive study, just as with a pupil in any art.[99]

---

[98] Relating to his brethren one day at table the story of the monk saved from robbers by his recitation of the Hail Mary, Martin Luther is reported to have exclaimed (*Werke: Kritische Gesammtausgabe. Tischreden, 1531–46*, vol. 5, *Tischreden aus den Jahren 1540–44*, no. 6476, ed. Karl Drescher, Oskar Brenner, and Ernst Kroker [Weimar, 1919], pp. 683–84): "Ach, lieber Herrgott, was haben wir doch nicht durffen gleuben!"

[99] Eckhart, *Die rede der underscheidunge*, chap. 6, ed. Quint, pp. 207–9; trans. Walshe, *Sermons and Treatises*, 3:19.

Numerous more recent studies on the psychological and physiological effects of practice and the acquisition of skill, most particularly the work of psychologist Mihaly Csikzentmihalyi on the experience of happiness or, in his terms, "flow," would bear Eckhart out: fluency and thus the experience of being "utterly detached," even "pervaded with God's presence," come not from abandoning art ("just going with the flow"), but rather from diligence, for example, in counting repetitions of a letter form or recitations of a prayer.[100] The problems come when students of a particular art want instant results (e.g., ecstasy) and do not have the patience to bear with the training and so become discouraged and blame either their teachers or the methods they have been taught. Conversely, and this is the problem that Eckhart himself saw in his contemporaries, they fix on the method (so many repetitions per day, so many exercises per week) as itself the goal and so lose sight of the reasons that the method (e.g., counting) was introduced in the first place. But if, as Eckhart explained, they can bear with their practice no matter how heavy and bitter it may seem, eventually, they will find themselves able to dispense with the method ("be completely free of the image") and simply exercise their skill ("find emptiness in all things and be totally free of things"; in Augustine's words, "go beyond all that can be numbered and see the Number without number"). This, at least, among other things, is what one modern Orthodox Russian spiritual seeker learned (or, perhaps more accurately, is said to have learned) when he set out to follow Paul's injunction to the Thessalonians on how to pray. [101]

---

[100] Mihaly Csikszentmihalyi, *Flow: The Psychology of Happiness* (London, 1992); and *Finding Flow: The Psychology of Engagement with Everyday Life* (New York, 1997).

[101] On the pilgrim's almost picaresque story as a consciously crafted prayer manual rather than an actual historical account, see Zaleski and Zaleski, *Prayer*, p. 140: "Historians have long puzzled over how to reconcile the author's polished style with his reported poverty, which would seem to preclude a literary education. In recent years, consensus has been reached that the book is likely a pious fabrication. If so, it is fiction born of truth and this in two senses: it conveys spiritual verities with admirable insight; and the origins of the tale may lie in a firsthand narrative written in 1859 by Orthodox priest Mikhail Koslov (1826–84), to which the prayer experiences of generations of monks have accreted."

The story as narrated in the oft-translated *The Way of a Pilgrim* is a familiar one, almost hagiographic in its motifs.[102] One autumn, on the twenty-fourth Sunday after Pentecost sometime in the mid-1800s, the pilgrim entered a church to say his prayers, where he heard the following verse from Paul's first letter to the Thessalonians read out during the liturgy: "Pray without ceasing" (1 Thess. 5:17). At once he began to wonder how this might be possible, "since a man has to concern himself with other things also in order to make a living. . . . I thought and thought, but knew not what to make of it." Going the rounds of various churches, the pilgrim heard numerous "very fine sermons on prayer; what prayer is, how much we need it, and what its fruits are; but no one," he lamented, "said how one could succeed in prayer [or] how it was to be done." Nor could any of the other potential spiritual teachers the pilgrim encountered do any more than encourage him to "pray more, and pray more fervently."[103]

At long last, the pilgrim came upon an old monk who taught him the words to the Jesus Prayer ("Lord Jesus Christ, have mercy on me") and how to practice it as recommended in the writings of the great patristic and medieval fathers of the Orthodox Church published collectively in the late eighteenth century as the *Philokalia*: "Sit down alone and in silence. Lower your head, shut your eyes, breathe out gently and imagine yourself looking into your own heart. Carry your mind, i.e., your thoughts, from your head to your heart. As you breathe out, say 'Lord Jesus Christ, have mercy on me.' Say it moving your lips gently, or simply say it in your mind. Try to put all other thoughts aside. Be calm, be patient, and repeat the process very frequently."[104] Encouraged by this advice, the

---

[102] First published in Russian in 1884 as *Otkrovennye rasskazy strannika dukhovnomu svoemu ottsu* and translated into English in 1930 as *The Way of a Pilgrim*, the text has become something of a best-seller since it was popularized by J. D. Salinger in his story collection *Franny and Zooey* in 1961. For the original publication date, see *The Way of a Pilgrim and The Pilgrim Continues His Way*, trans. R. M. French (London, 1954), p. viii. French notes (p. vii) that a more literal translation of the original title would be "Candid Narratives of a Pilgrim to His Spiritual Father."

[103] *The Way of a Pilgrim*, trans. French, pp. 1–4. I have also consulted the newer translation by Olga Savin (Boston, 2001).

[104] *The Way of a Pilgrim*, trans. French, p. 10. For the fuller version of this instruction traditionally attributed to St. Symeon the New Theologian, see St. Nikodimos of the Holy Mountain and St. Makarios of Corinth, *The Philokalia: The Complete Text*, vol. 4, trans. and ed. G. E. H. Palmer, Philip Sherrard, and Kallistos

pilgrim found himself a "little thatched hut" in which he could live alone and begin to practice this prayer continuously, as the fathers themselves said one should. Although things started well, they quickly deteriorated, much to the pilgrim's frustration: "I felt lazy and bored and overwhelmingly sleepy, and a cloud of all sorts of other thoughts closed around me. I went in distress to my *starets* [i.e., the old monk, his spiritual elder] and told him the state I was in." The *starets* reassured the pilgrim that such assaults by "the kingdom of darkness" were to be expected whenever one set out to enter into the place of the heart. "It is too soon," he explained, "for your unmeasured zeal to approach the loftiest entrance to the heart. You might fall into spiritual covetousness."[105]

As a defense against this impatience and spiritual avarice, the *starets* gave the pilgrim the following instructions: "Here is a rosary [lit. *chotki*, or prayer rope, typically "beaded" with one hundred knots]. Take it, and to start with say the Prayer three thousand times a day. . . . Say it quietly and without hurry, but without fail exactly three thousand times a day without deliberately increasing or diminishing the number. God will help you and by this means you will reach also the unceasing activity of the heart."[106] The results of this counted practice surprised even the pilgrim. Whereas for the first two days, he found the going "rather difficult," by the third day the practice had become "easy and likable," so much so, indeed, that when he stopped saying the Prayer he "felt a sort of need to go on," and did so "freely and willingly, not forcing [himself] to it as before."[107]

Ware (London, 1995), pp. 72–73. For the history of the Jesus Prayer, see Kallistos Ware, "The Origins of the Jesus Prayer: Diadochus, Gaza, Sinai," in *The Study of Spirituality*, ed. Cheslyn Jones, Geoffrey Wainwright, and Edward Yarnold (London, 1986), pp. 175–84; Robert E. Sinkewicz, "An Early Byzantine Commentary on the Jesus Prayer: Introduction and Edition," *Mediaeval Studies* 49 (1987), 208–20; and Irénée Hausherr, *The Name of Jesus*, trans. Charles Cummings, Cistercian Studies Series 44 (Kalamazoo, Mich., 1978), pp. 265–324.

[105] *The Way of a Pilgrim*, trans. French, pp. 8–9, 11–12; cf. trans. Savin, 7, 9–10.

[106] *The Way of a Pilgrim*, trans. French, pp. 12–13; cf. trans. Savin, p. 10: "Take this *chotki* and use it while you repeat the prayer, at least three thousand times a day to begin with. . . . Do not be loud or rush the prayer, but without fail repeat it three thousand times each day, neither increasing nor decreasing this number on your own. Through this exercise God will help you to attain to the unceasing prayer of the heart."

[107] *The Way of a Pilgrim*, trans. French, p. 13.

The next week, the *starets* increased the number of repetitions to six thousand a day; ten days later, he told the pilgrim to up the number to twelve, and the pilgrim did as he bade:

> The first day I scarcely succeeded in finishing my task of saying twelve thousand prayers by late evening. The second day I did it easily and contentedly. . . . For five days I did my set number of twelve thousand prayers, and as I formed the habit I found at the same time pleasure and satisfaction in it.

> Early one morning the Prayer woke me up as it were. I started to say my usual morning prayers, but my tongue refused to say them easily or exactly. My whole desire was fixed upon one thing only—to say the Prayer of Jesus, and as soon as I went on with it I was filled with joy and relief. It was as though my lips and my tongue pronounced the words entirely of themselves without any urging from me. I spent the whole day in a state of the greatest contentment, . . . and I easily finished my twelve thousand prayers by the early evening. I felt very much like still going on with them, but I did not dare to go beyond the number my *starets* had set me.[108]

After two weeks of this practice, the pilgrim went once again to the *starets* and reported on his success. To which accounting the *starets* replied: "Thank God that the ease and desire for prayer have been manifested in you. This is a natural consequence that comes from frequent practice and great effort. . . . I now give you leave to repeat the prayer as much as you desire and as frequently as possible."[109] Which, according to the pilgrim, is what he did: "I grew so used to the Prayer that I went on with it all the time. In the end I felt it going on of its own accord within my mind and in the depths of my heart, without any urging on my part. Not only when I was awake, but even during sleep just the same thing went on. Nothing broke into it and it never stopped even for a single moment, whatever I

---

[108] Ibid., pp. 14–15.

[109] *The Way of a Pilgrim*, trans. Savin, p. 12; cf. trans. French, p. 15: "Be thankful to God that this desire for the Prayer and this facility in it have been manifested in you. It is a natural consequence which follows constant effort and spiritual achievement."

might be doing. My soul was always giving thanks to God and my heart melted away with unceasing happiness."[110]

As the pilgrim discovered to his lifelong joy, counting, far from being a barrier to authentic spiritual practice, may as often as not be the secret to its success. Perfection, with prayer as with any other skill, as Eckhart himself pointed out, takes practice and time, and it does not do, as the pilgrim did initially, to start at the end, with the goal. As the medieval Orthodox fathers themselves cautioned all those who would take up the Jesus Prayer and attempt to pray without ceasing, such expectations of ability to perform effortlessly from the start lead only to frustration, boredom, anxiety, and doubt (in their terms, attacks by demons who cause such thoughts to arise when one attends to the demons' deceptions rather than to the prayer).[111] Better, instead, to start small and build up gradually from there. Nor, spiritual teachers like the modern pilgrim's *starets* would most likely insist, does it help, in these early stages, to listen overmuch to the experts at a particular skill, like Luther for prayer, who might insist that practice so incrementalized can never amount to the desired whole. In the fathers' terms, such experts might be said to have fallen victim to the sin of pride, "for when the demons see the soul freed from passions and temptations through the indwelling of grace and the resulting state of peace, they attack it through such thoughts."[112] We might rather say that they have simply forgotten the experience of learning or, perhaps more likely, failed to see the link between the frustration, anxiety, boredom, and doubt they experienced as beginners and the apparently gratuitous facility they enjoy in exercising their skill now.[113]

---

[110] *The Way of a Pilgrim*, trans. French, p. 42.

[111] On the attacks of the demons, see *The Philokalia,* vol. 4, ed. Palmer, Sherrard, and Ware, pp. 56, 68, 74, 104–5, 127–28, 224–25, 242–45, 249–50, 270–71, 282–83, and passim.

[112] St. Symeon the New Theologian, "One Hundred and Fifty-three Practical and Theological Texts," in *The Philokalia,* vol. 4, ed. Palmer, Sherrard, and Ware, p. 56.

[113] As is well known, Luther was himself a great itemizer in his youth, not only of his prayers, but also of his sins, as his confessor Johann von Staupitz knew all too well. In Luther's own words: "I was a good monk, and I kept the rule of my order so strictly that I may say that if ever a monk got to heaven by his monkery it was I" ("Die kleine antwort auff H. Georgen nehestes buch," in *Werke: Kritische Gesammtausgabe,* vol. 38, ed. Karl Drescher (Weimar, 1912), p. 143; trans. Bainton, *Here I Stand,* p. 34). "How I tormented myself with those *Horae canonicae* [the canonical Hours of the monastic Office] before the Gospel came," Luther told his students later in life,

To be fair, this failure on the part of experts like Luther to acknowledge the usefulness of such bounded preliminaries may not be entirely their fault, as recent psychological studies on the experience of such absorptive states as the pilgrim's once he had mastered the Prayer have shown. Rather, if there is a fault, it is one to which even the most self-aware among us are prone, whenever, for example, we see someone struggling with a complex task that we find easy and tell him or her, with the best intentions in the world, that it would be easier if he or she would simply "relax!" or "just do it!" Surely we do not mean that our anxious struggler should be able to play that Rachmaninov prelude without practicing the fingering for hours a day, week after week; or apply just the right blue to the Virgin's mantle in that icon without practicing for years in the mixing of paint; or experience the unceasing happiness of the pilgrim without praying thousands of prayers with perfect attention for days, weeks, months, or years on end. No, what we are charitably, if more often than not ineffectually, attempting to impart is rather the paradoxical feeling that we have when we are able to do something difficult well: of surrender ("Relax! Don't think so much!") but also of control ("Just do it!"), of being able to act or think in exactly the way that we intend ("Just do it!") while at the same time of being unable to explain, after the fact, how exactly we did it ("Relax!").

Athletes often refer to this state as "being in the zone." Mystics following Augustine might speak rather of "ecstasy."[114] Psychologist Mihaly Csikzentmihalyi has coined the term "flow" to refer to such states.[115] Historian and critic of the symbolic elaboration of counted prayer Johan

---

"I cannot express. On the Saturdays, I used to lock myself up in my cell, and accomplish [in the one day] what the whole week I had neglected." For Luther, looking back on his time as a monk, these dreaded Hours epitomized the "mere tongue-threshing (*Plappern und Wortgewäsch*)" of prayer "in Popedom . . . the howling and babbling in cells and monasteries, where they read and sing the psalms and collects, without any spiritual devotion, understanding neither the words, sentences, nor meaning" (*Colloquia*, ed. Aurifaber, chap. 17, fol. 221v; trans. Hazlitt, *Table-talk*, chap. 330, p. 157; cf. Luther, *Tischreden*, vol. 3, ed. Kroker et al., no. 3651, p. 486). Seen as exercises during which Luther honed the skills necessary to sustain himself perpetually in prayer, these "tongue-threshing" *Horae* take on a rather different complexion, however.

[114] For Augustine's use of this term (*ecstasis*), see Bernard McGinn, *The Foundations of Mysticism: Origins to the Fifth Century* (New York, 1991), pp. 253–54.

[115] Csikszentmihalyi, *Flow*, pp. 48–70; and *Finding Flow*, pp. 28–34.

Huizinga would speak rather of "play."[116] Phenomenologically, such bliss-ful, focused yet effortless states would appear to be culturally universal. For our purposes in understanding the appeal of the late medieval prac-tice of counted prayer, what is most important, however, is under what circumstances they most typically occur. In Huizinga's terms, play, like prayer, is distinguishable from other kinds of activities by being volun-tary, not forced, standing outside the wants and appetites of "ordinary" life (i.e., physiological survival), "connected with no material interest . . . but at the same time absorbing the player intensely and utterly."[117] It takes place at times and in spaces specifically marked off for play, which themselves are distinguished as forbidden spots and moments in which no other activities should take place (the stadium, the pool table, the church, the stage, the dojo, the court of justice; the bowl, the tournament, the Mass, the play, the practice, the trial).[118] Above all, however, play has rules. Such rules are "absolutely binding and allow no doubt"; if the rules are broken, the game ends, and "the whole play-world collapses." It is the rules—i.e., boundedness—that make the game a game and not "ordinary life"; hence the punishments exacted on the "spoil-sports, apostates, her-etics, innovators, prophets" who "break the magic world" by refusing to acknowledge those rules.[119]

Csikzentmihalyi, too, has noted the importance of rules for the occur-rence of such absorptive, "optimal" states, when time stands still and one's whole being is absorbed fully in the present, one's attention focused, one's perceptions clear, and all of one's actions effortless and exact. Occa-sionally, to be sure, such moments simply come to us, when we catch sight of a particularly beautiful flower or hear a particularly haunting bar of music (Swann and Odette's "little phrase"). For the most part, how-ever, they are, or so Csikzentmihalyi has repeatedly found, most likely to occur not when we are passively relaxing (e.g., when watching television), but rather when we are concentrating on challenging tasks that, on the one hand, require the use of particular physical or mental skills and, on the other, provide clear goals and immediate feedback as to how well we

---

[116] Johan Huizinga, *Homo ludens: A Study of the Play-Element in Culture* (Boston, 1950).

[117] Huizinga, *Homo ludens*, pp. 1–13.

[118] Ibid., p. 10.

[119] Ibid., pp. 11–12.

are doing.[120] As with play, so with flow, what sets these activities apart from everyday life is precisely the fact that they are "[bounded by] rules for action that make it possible for the player to act without questioning what should be done, and how."[121]

Rules—monks might say "*regulae*"—do more than simply tell us what to do: for example, "To start with, say the Prayer three thousand times a day." They also, as Csikzentmihalyi himself has pointed out and Eckhart would doubtless agree, make it possible for us to learn. Although applicable to all skilled, playlike activities (Huizinga includes law, war, philosophy, poetry, and art), the developmental necessity of rules is perhaps most evident for those activities involving immediate physical or, as the pilgrim discovered when he set out to learn the unceasing prayer of the heart, psychospiritual risk. Csikzentmihalyi gives various examples: hang gliding, spelunking, rock climbing, race-car driving, deep-sea diving. The medieval hesychast fathers (i.e., those, like the latter-day pilgrim, practicing stillness) would include sitting with attention, head bowed toward the navel, and restraining the breath while repeating the Jesus Prayer.[122] Csikzentmihalyi notes: "It is usual to explain the motivation of those who enjoy dangerous activities as some sort of pathological need: they are trying to exorcise a deep-seated fear, they are compensating, they are compulsively reenacting an Oedipal fixation, they are 'sensation seekers.'"[123] Critics of the hesychasts' practice made analogous accusations in their own day. Barlaam the Calabrian, most famously, called them *omphalopsychoi* or "navel-psychics," mocking them for attempting to draw their intellects and, therefore, their souls into their bodies rather than, as he contended they should, shunning the body as a trap for the soul.[124]

Such criticisms, both Csikzentmihalyi and Barlaam's antagonist St. Gregory Palamas (1296–1359) would aver, miss the point. Far from inviting danger, whether, as with the mountain climber, of falling from the

---

[120] Csikszentmihalyi, *Flow*, pp. 49–59. Examples of such activities are easy to give: playing chess, knitting a sweater, running a marathon, playing a musical instrument, counting prayers.

[121] Csikszentmihalyi, *Flow*, p. 49; *Finding Flow*, p. 29.

[122] On this posture, see St. Gregory of Sinai, "On Stillness: Fifteen Texts," in *The Philokalia*, vol. 4, ed. Palmer, Sherrard, and Ware, p. 264.

[123] Csikszentmihalyi, *Flow*, p. 60.

[124] For these accusations, see *The Philokalia*, vol. 4, ed. Palmer, Sherrard, and Ware, pp. 288, 290, 331–32.

mountain or, with the hesychasts, of succumbing to attacks from the "kingdom of darkness" and the temptations of the spirit and the flesh, such "specialists in risk" (in Csikzentmihalyi's phrase) do everything in their power to minimize the risk, most notably by acquiring through practice the necessary skills. The mountain climber who does not have the muscular strength to lift his body to the next foothold or the mental strength to fix his attention on the task at hand will die; the hesychast who fails to keep the correct posture or allows himself to be distracted by the images with which the prince of the abyss and his demons seek to fill his mind risks possession, madness, and death.[125] Nevertheless, contrary to expectations, it is not the danger itself, or so Csikzentmihalyi has found, but rather the ability to contain it that contributes most to the experience of flow: "what people enjoy is not the sense of *being* in control, but the sense of *exercising* control in difficult situations."[126]

Risk is necessary here—unless one attempts the mountain or goes into the wilderness to seek out the demons, how will one know whether he or she can stay in control?—but so, too, are rules, for it is the rules—"Sitting from dawn on a seat about nine inches high, compel your intellect to descend from your head into your heart, and retain it there. Keeping your head forcibly bent downwards, and suffering acute pain in your chest, shoulders and neck, persevere in repeating noetically or in

---

[125] According to "The Three Methods of Prayer" attributed to St. Symeon the New Theologian, standing with arms raised and eyes lifted to heaven was the most dangerous posture one could take: "Some [of those who adopt this method of prayer] have become completely possessed by demons and wander from place to place in their madness. . . . Still others, incited by the devil, have committed suicide, throwing themselves over a precipice or hanging themselves" (*The Philokalia,* vol. 4, ed. Palmer, Sherrard, and Ware, p. 68). The demons could be quite terrifying, even taking bestial forms: pigs, donkeys, and stallions for desire; lions for wrath; wolves and leopards for greed; snakes, vipers, and foxes for malice; dogs for shamelessness; cats for listlessness; snakes, crows, and jackdaws for lechery; birds for carnal-mindedness. As St. Gregory of Sinai explained (*The Philokalia,* vol. 4, ed. Palmer, Sherrard, and Ware, pp. 224–25): "The demons fill our minds with images; or, rather, they clothe themselves in images that correspond to the character of the most dominant and active passion in our soul, and in this way they provoke us to give our assent to that passion. . . . Our fantasy transmutes the images of the demons in a threefold manner corresponding to the tripartite nature of the soul: into birds, wild animals and domestic animals, that correspond respectively to the desiring, incensive and intelligent aspect of the soul."

[126] Csikzentmihalyi, *Flow*, p. 61.

your soul, 'Lord Jesus Christ, have mercy'"—that enable one to develop the skills that make it possible to exercise control.[127] In Eckhart's words, "first there must be thought and attentive study, just as with a pupil in any art."[128] Numbering prayers is one such rule, likewise adhering to a schedule for one's day. This is the schedule St. Gregory of Sinai (ca. 1265–1346) suggested: "From early morning the hesychast must devote himself to the remembrance of God through prayer and stillness of heart, praying diligently in the first hour, reading in the second, chanting psalms in the third, praying in the fourth, reading in the fifth, chanting psalms in the sixth, praying in the seventh, reading in the eighth, chanting psalms in the ninth, eating in the tenth, sleeping in the eleventh, if need be, and reciting vespers in the twelfth hour."[129] As the Russian pilgrim learned some five hundred years later, it was discipline such as this, and this alone, that made it possible for him to withstand the rigors of saying the Jesus Prayer "unceasingly" throughout the day, "aware only of the fact that I [was] saying my Prayer."[130]

And then came the moment of surrender: "After no great lapse of time," the pilgrim recounted,

> I had the feeling that the Prayer had, so to speak, by its own action passed from my lips to my heart. That is to say, it seemed as though my heart in its ordinary beating began to say the words of the Prayer within at each beat. Thus for example, *one*, "Lord," *two*, "Jesus," *three*, "Christ," and so on. I gave up saying the Prayer with my lips. I simply listened carefully to what my heart was saying. . . . Sometimes my heart would feel as though it were bubbling with joy, such lightness, freedom and consolation were in it. Sometimes I felt a burning love for Jesus Christ and for all God's creatures. Sometimes my eyes brimmed over with tears of thankfulness to God, who was

---

[127] St. Gregory of Sinai, "On Stillness," in *The Philokalia*, vol. 4, ed. Palmer, Sherrard, and Ware, p. 264.

[128] See above, n. 99.

[129] St. Gregory of Sinai, "On Commandments and Doctrines, Warnings and Promises; on Thoughts, Passions and Virtues, and also on Stillness and Prayer: One Hundred and Thirty-Seven Texts," no. 99, in *The Philokalia*, vol. 4, ed. Palmer, Sherrard, and Ware, p. 233.

[130] *The Way of a Pilgrim*, trans. French, pp. 17–18; cf. trans. Savin, p. 14: "The prayer alone filled my consciousness."

so merciful to me, a wretched sinner. Sometimes my understanding, which had been so stupid before, was given so much light that I could easily grasp and dwell upon matters of which up to now I had not been able even to think at all. Sometimes that sense of a warm gladness in my heart spread throughout my whole being and I was deeply moved as the fact of the presence of God everywhere was brought home to me. Sometimes by calling upon the Name of Jesus I was overwhelmed with bliss, and now I knew the meaning of the words, "*The Kingdom of God is within you.*"[131]

This, as spiritual teachers like Augustine, Eckhart, and the Gregorys have known for centuries although they might not put it in precisely these terms, is the paradox of goal-directed, rule-bounded, risk-taking flow: in the moment of performance, so rapt is one's attention on the necessity of acting, speaking, or thinking correctly—i.e., according to the rules— that there is no space anymore in one's consciousness for an ego or "I." One's whole being is absorbed in the activity itself, leaving (in Csikzentmihalyi's words) "no room for self-scrutiny" or preoccupation with self.[132] In the pilgrim's experience, this absorption even excluded sensations of bodily pain (hunger, cold, rheumatism, or other symptom of illness).[133] Others report a sense of being "out of time," either of time "standing still" while they are engaged in their performance or of a heightened capacity to keep track of time, sometimes even down to a hundredth of a second.[134] That this should be the case when we so focus our attention on something other than ourselves would appear to have something to do, in neurological terms, with the way in which our capacity for consciousness evolved.[135] In spiritual terms, this experience of unboundedness—of no longer being conscious of oneself or the fact that one is doing anything

---

131 *The Way of a Pilgrim*, trans. French, pp. 19–20, 41. In fact, the pilgrim's prayer practice continued to develop over the course of his travels; I am here eliding two separate stages of the process. Diligent practitioners are encouraged to study his narrative in full.

132 Csikszentmihalyi, *Flow*, p. 63.

133 *The Way of a Pilgrim*, trans. French, p. 18.

134 Csikszentmihalyi, *Flow*, pp. 66–67.

135 Jonathan Haidt, *The Happiness Hypothesis: Finding Modern Truth in Ancient Wisdom* (New York, 2006), pp. 1–22.

in the midst of concentrated, challenging activity—is what many would call "true prayer."[136]

The convert and mystic Simone Weil (1909–43) perhaps put this relationship between attention, boundedness (as, for example, by an academic subject), learning, and prayer best in her "Reflections on the Right Use of School Studies with a View to the Love of God":

> The key to a Christian conception of studies is the realization that prayer consists of attention. It is the orientation of all the attention of which the soul is capable toward God. The quality of the attention counts for much in the quality of the prayer. Warmth of heart cannot make up for it. . . . School children and students who love God should never say: "For my part I like mathematics"; "I like French"; "I like Greek." They should learn to like all these subjects, because all of them develop that faculty of attention which, directed toward God, is the very substance of prayer. . . . If we concentrate our attention on trying to solve a problem of geometry, and if at the end of an hour we are no nearer to doing so than at the beginning, we have nevertheless been making progress each minute of that hour in another more mysterious dimension. Without our knowing or feeling it, this apparently barren effort has brought more light into the soul. The result will one day be discovered in prayer.[137]

It is attention, as Weil would put it, that is our treasure, the kingdom of God that is within us. The capacity to focus our attention is the pearl beyond price for which we should give up everything that we have (cf. Matt. 13:45): our possessions, our self-consciousness, our time. Nor is it, Weil would go on, only the love of God that has "attention for its substance; the love of our neighbor, which we know to be the same love, is made of this same substance." To love someone other than ourselves is to be able to pay attention to him or her; moreover, this "capacity to give one's attention to [another] is a very rare and difficult thing; it is almost a

---

[136] Cassian, *Conlationes* 9.31, ed. and trans. into French by E. Pichery, as *Conférences VIII–XVII*, Sources chrétiennes 54 (Paris, 1958), p. 66; trans. Colm Luibheid, as *Conferences* (New York, 1985), p. 120: "Prayer is not perfect when the monk is conscious of himself and of the fact that he is actually praying."

[137] Simone Weil, *Waiting for God*, trans. Emma Craufurd (New York, 1951; repr., 2001), pp. 57–58. I thank Barbara Newman for bringing this essay to my attention.

miracle; it *is* a miracle. . . . This way of looking is first of all attentive. The soul empties itself of all its own contents in order to receive into itself the being it is looking at, just as he is, in all his truth. Only he who is capable of attention can do this."[138]

Gertrude of Helfta would understand; so, likewise, her contemporaries, Eckhart and the Orthodox hesychasts.[139] As we have already seen, the prayers that Gertrude said were not only for her own sake, but also, and much more importantly in her mind, for the sake of others.[140] But, as both Weil and Gertrude realized, it was Gertrude's attention to others that made her prayers (what she said and thought) prayer (attention to God). As Gertrude recalled one year at the feast of the Purification during the midnight Mass (here she is speaking to her Beloved, the Lord), "making some effort to recollect myself, so as to warm you gently with my loving caresses, I seemed to be making little progress until I started to pray for sinners, for souls in purgatory, and for other afflicted souls. I soon felt the effects of my prayer, particularly one evening when I

---

[138] Weil, *Waiting for God*, pp. 64–65.

[139] For the possibility of a connection between the hesychasts' prayer practice and that of the Latin West, see Kallistos Ware, "The Holy Name of Jesus in East and West: The Hesychasts and Richard Rolle," *Sobornost* 4, no. 2 (1982), 163–84. For the contemporary devotion to the Holy Name in the West, see Denis Renevey, "Name above Names: The Devotion to the Name of Jesus from Richard Rolle to Walter Hilton's *Scale of Perfection I*," in *The Medieval Mystical Tradition: England, Ireland and Wales. Exeter Symposium VI*, ed. Marion Glasscoe (Cambridge, 1999), pp. 103–21. On the corollary importance of Eastern exempla for the development of late medieval devotional art, see Maryan W. Ainsworth, "'À la façon grèce': The Encounter of Northern Renaissance Artists with Byzantine Icons," in *Byzantium: Faith and Power (1261-1557)*, ed. Helen C. Evans (New York and New Haven, 2004), pp. 545–93.

[140] On the importance of the nuns' communal liturgy for Gertrude's spirituality generally, see Miriam Schmitt, "Gertrude of Helfta: Her Monastic Milieu and Her Spirituality," in *Hidden Springs: Cistercian Monastic Women*, Medieval Religious Women 3, Bk. 1, ed. John A. Nichols and Lillian Thomas Shank, Cistercian Studies Series 113 (Kalamazoo, Mich., 1995), pp. 471–96; and Cyprian Vagaggini, *Theological Dimensions of the Liturgy: A General Treatise on the Theology of the Liturgy*, trans. Leonard J. Doyle and W. A. Jurgens (Collegeville, Minn., 1976), pp. 740–803. On the importance of community for the account of her visions, see Anna E. Harrison and Caroline Walker Bynum, "Gertrude, Gender, and the Composition of the *Herald of Divine Love*," in *Freiheit des Herzens: Mystik bei Gertrud von Hefta*, ed. Michael Bangert, Mystik und Mediävistik 2 (Münster, 2004), pp. 57–76, at p. 65: "Gertrude depicts herself as representative of a community that encompasses all humanity; she also writes as if she is a model for that community on pilgrimage toward paradise."

proposed to pray for all souls." Like a schoolgirl, Gertrude found, it was above all when she was "exerting all [her] powers to sing and fixing [her] attention (*intentionem*) on [her Beloved] at each note, like a singer who has not yet learned the melody and follows it carefully in the book" that he was "sweetly affected" by her prayers.[141] "Give your attention to me alone (*Intende mihi soli*)," he assured her one Sunday when she and her sisters were praying for the souls in Purgatory, "and enjoy the sweetness of my grace."[142]

Nevertheless, as for the hesychasts, so for Gertrude, there were risks, a lapse of attention carrying the possibility of not only madness, demonic possession, or physical death but also that second death, the death of the soul, as Gertrude herself learned one day when she was saying the Canonical Hours "with less attention (*minus intente*)" than usual. Suddenly, she had a vision of "the ancient enemy of mankind" standing by her side and keeping careful count of every stumble and slip of her tongue. "You can make eloquent discourses on any subject whenever you want," the devil chided her, "but when you speak to [your creator, your savior and your lover] your words are so hasty and careless that just now in this psalm you left out this number of letters, this number of syllables, and this number of words." No schoolchild was ever more soundly reprimanded for her mistakes, but then, as Gertrude and her sisters understood it, "if this wily enemy had counted so exactly the letters and syllables, it was so that after death he could bring grave accusations against those who tend to say the Hours of the Divine Office in a hurry and without attention (*sine intentione*)."[143] When, however, she found herself able, through practice

---

[141] Gertrude, *Legatus divinae pietatis*, bk. 2, chap. 16, ed. Pierre Doyère, as *Oeuvres spirituelles II: Le Héraut (Livres I et II)*, Sources chrétiennes 139 (Paris, 1968), p. 292; trans. Winkworth, pp. 115–16.

[142] Gertrude, *Legatus divinae pietatis*, bk. 3, chap. 9, ed. Doyère, p. 36; trans. Winkworth, p. 162.

[143] Gertrude, *Legatus divinae pietatis*, bk. 3, chap. 32, ed. Doyère, p. 170; trans. Winkworth, p. 205, with slight changes. For a similar concern with lapses of attention while praying the psalms, see Nikitas Stithatos (fl. 11th century), "On the Inner Nature of Things and on the Purification of the Intellect: One Hundred Texts," in *The Philokalia*, vol. 4, ed. Palmer, Sherrard, and Ware, pp. 126–27: "As you pray and sing psalms to the Lord, watch out for the guile of the demons. Either they deceive us into saying one thing instead of another, snatching the soul's attention and turning the verses of the psalms into blasphemies, so that we say things that we should not say; or, when we have started with a psalm, they cause us to skip to the end of

and grace, to concentrate her attention on her Beloved alone, then "she understood the admirable and ineffable condescension of God's love, sometimes coming down to man and generously and copiously flooding him with grace, and yet sometimes refusing him lesser favors in order to preserve humility, the fundamental grace which preserves all the others; and how in both these ways the Lord makes everything work together unto God for loving souls."[144]

"Prayer," as the hesychast Theoliptos of Philadelphia (ca. 1250–1322) put it, "is the mind's dialogue with God, in which words of petition are uttered with the intellect riveted wholly on God. For when the mind unceasingly repeats the name of the Lord and the intellect gives its full attention to the invocation of the divine name, the light of the knowledge of God overshadows the entire soul like a luminous cloud."[145] Surely the opportunity to surrender to such an overshadowing is worth the three thousand, six thousand, or even twelve thousand repetitions a day it would take to become skilled enough, grace permitting, to experience it.

Why count prayers? *Pace* the critics from Luther to Lentes, there are a number of reasons, only some of them having to do with mere repetition of formulae, obsessive accounting, or metaphors of money.

1) Because it takes practice to pray, to focus one's attention unceasingly on God. This is why, at least when one is a beginner, as most of those who are not veteran monks or nuns are, it helps to count. Counting allows the possibility of success, and not only success, but improvement; as today I pray ten rosaries, perhaps tomorrow or the next week I will be able to pray twenty, the currency here being not that of transferable value

---

it, distracting the intellect from what lies between; or else they make us return time and again to the same verse, through absent-mindedness preventing us from going on to what comes next; or, when we are in the middle of a psalm, they suddenly blank out the intellect's memory of the sequence of the verses, so that we cannot even remember what verse of the psalm it was that we were saying, and thus we repeat it once more. This they do to make us neglectful and listless, and to deprive us of the fruits of our prayer."

[144] Gertrude, *Legatus divinae pietatis*, bk. 3, chap. 9, ed. Doyère, p. 38; trans. Winkworth, pp. 162–63. This is the same vision in which Gertrude sees the Lord distributing her and her sisters' gifts of prayer and recommends to her the counted recitation of Psalm 116.

[145] Theoliptos, "On Inner Work in Christ and the Monastic Profession," in *The Philokalia,* vol. 4, ed. Palmer, Sherrard, and Ware, p. 181.

but that of the increase in skills over time as measured against the challenges in practice one is able to meet. Anyone who has pushed him- or herself to "go the extra mile," "do one more repetition," "read one more page" will understand the allure, and therefore the importance, of this bounded incrementalism. There is no need to look to analogies with money to make sense of such developmental trajectories. They are rather a function of getting better—i.e., more skilled—at what we do.

2) Because counting prayers reminds us that human beings are creatures, if not (or, not only) of a Creator, then (or, but also) of experience and art, our skills, like our future creations, dependent on that which we have done in the past. Practically put, this means that the novice or the amateur (alias *layperson*) may not at this moment or, indeed, ever be able to achieve the expert's (alias, *monk's* or *nun's*) level of performance. This is not to say that the experience of flow will be less intense for the one than for the other, only the degree of challenge necessary to push against the limits of one's skill. It is to say, however, that we get better with practice and so should expect the more practiced to require greater challenges in order to experience the sweetness we associate with success. Beginners might start with fifteen Hail Marys and fifteen Our Fathers a day, but the more practiced would want to say all 150 Hail Marys of the rosary, while the experts, like Gertrude of Helfta or Christina Ebner, would be unlikely to be content with even the weekly recitation of all 150 scriptural psalms prescribed by their monastic rule. The point is to have a rule—a bounded space of expectations within which to practice one's skills—as well as a goal to give their exercise meaning.

3) Because, as St. Benedict of Nursia (ca. 480–ca. 547) explained in the prologue to his "little rule for beginners" (i.e., the rule against which the monks and nuns of Christian Europe would measure themselves for centuries), human beings have so little time as creatures on this earth. We are mortal and everything that we do is bounded by the expectation of our deaths. Our mortality is that which makes our lives meaningful; it is the boundedness against which we strive as we "run . . . in the light of life" to "accomplish all these things"—Benedict has been speaking of the instructions the Lord has given those who would "dwell in his tent"— "while there is still time"; i.e., before our death.[146] Prayer looks always

---

[146] Benedict, *Regula*, prologus, 39–44; ed. and trans. Timothy Fry et al., *RB 1980: The Rule of St. Benedict in Latin and English with Notes* (Collegeville, MN, 1981), p. 165.

to the ultimate boundary ("The hour of our death") and to the end of counting that death will inevitably bring. Souls in Purgatory only suffer; they cannot count up prayers (thus the need to pray for them), while souls in heaven (we may assume, if Eckhart was correct about detached souls) have gone beyond number, weight, and measure to oneness with the Number without number, God.

4) Because it is much as Augustine said: moving through space and time, like artists or athletes—and we may recall here that monks and nuns, the prayer professionals of medieval Europe, considered themselves not only soldiers, but athletes of Christ—we as creatures are bounded by numbers, and yet it is the light of the sempiternal numbers within that gives form and purpose to what we do. More to the point, without number, our activities of making, saying, moving, and being would have no beginning or end and therefore, at least experientially, no apparent meaning or purpose, not to mention little possibility of success. As St. Isidore of Seville (ca. 560–636) put it, "Through number, indeed, we are instructed in order not to be confounded. Take number from all things and all things perish. Take calculation from the world and all is enveloped in ignorance."[147] Number guarantees the existence and meaningfulness of the creaturely world.

5) Because it is only in counting that Christians, if not also historians, may come to appreciate the magnitude of the suffering that Christ endured in becoming bounded; i.e., incarnate as a human being, the Maker of Number become a creature of number and so subject to limitation in space and time. From this perspective, it is not enough simply to say, as Christians meditate on Christ's wounds, "Behalde, on me nocht hale was left." We (that is, those who would say the prayers effectively) must number them all—pay attention to them all—down to the very last drop of blood. Only thus, or so countless medieval Christians might arguably have insisted, can we as human beings come to appreciate what it meant for the prophet to say of the extent of Christ's suffering (Isaiah 1:6): "From the sole of the foot unto the top of the head, there is no soundness therein; [only] wounds and bruises and swelling sores." Perhaps, in the end, Christians like Alain and Gertrude and Leopold and the author, whoever he or she may have been, of the "Fifteen Oes," were not so "fantastical" in their

---

[147] Isidore, *Etymologiae*, bk. 3, chap. 4, paragr. 3, ed. J.-P. Migne, PL 82 (Paris, 1850), col. 156; trans. Hopper, *Medieval Number Symbolism*, p. 113 (with changes).

pursuit of numbers after all as they prayed in the words of the second of the "Fifteen Oes":

> O blessed Jesus, creator of the entire world, you whose measure may not be taken by a man, you who hold the whole earth in your hand, remember your bitter sorrow. First, the Jews fastened your blessed hands to the cross with blunt nails. Then, to increase your pain because you would not conform to their will, they added sorrow upon sorrow to your bitter wounds by piercing your blessed, tender, and sweet feet. They stretched your blessed body to match the length and breadth of the cross with such cruelty that all the joints of your limbs were dislocated and broken apart. Mindful of your blessed Passion, I beseech you, merciful Jesus, give me grace to keep myself in both your love and your dread. Amen. Our Father. Hail Mary.[148]

Repeat.

---

[148] "The Fifteen Oes," trans. Krug, in *Cultures of Piety*, p. 113.

Agnes Bowker's Cat, the Rabbit Woman of Godalming, and the Shifting Nature of Portents in Early Modern Europe

Philip M. Soergel
University of Maryland, College Park

IN THE BLEAK midwinter of 1568–69, Agnes Bowker bore a monster in the English village of Market Harborough in the County of Leicestershire. In the days that followed this remarkable delivery, someone rushed to publicize the event by printing a sensationalistic pamphlet about the birth. Unfortunately, that document is now lost, but its fantastic overtones quickly prompted an investigation. A local clergyman, Anthony Anderson, was entrusted with conducting an inquiry into the incident, an inquiry that turned up evidence that still proves remarkable today. On close interrogation, Bowker, a local, admitted to having had sex with a schoolmaster, after which she had been dismissed from her position as a serving maid. In the itinerant days that followed, she claimed to have had intercourse with another servant as well as a succession of demons that took the shapes of animals, including one that appeared to her in the forms of a greyhound and a cat. During one of these encounters Bowker said she promised her soul to the devil and renounced her Christian faith. She became pregnant, although her term lasted far longer than the normal nine months. In an attempt to find some relief from this endless pregnancy, she scoured the countryside looking for a midwife that might successfully deliver her. Eventually, she turned up back in Harborough, where one Elizabeth Harrison succeeded in bringing forth from her a frightening "cat-monster." Upon closer questioning, Agnes Bowker said she had not seen the child after it emerged from her womb, although she trusted her midwife who told her about the monster.

These were the bare bones of the story that Bowker first told, and the incredible testimony soon prompted Anderson to deepen his investigations. He demanded to see Bowker's "cat-monster." The creature, he found, looked very much like a common household cat without fur, except that when he inspected it he discovered that the animal had already been disemboweled. Apparently, the locals had been somewhat suspicious of Bowker's story too. In the hours following her strange birth, the local innkeeper had opened up the animal's stomach to discover food and straw. Anderson's curiosity was now piqued, even more so when he found that a local cat had gone missing shortly before the "monstrous birth." He soon devised an experiment. He had a cat flayed and plunged into boiling water, and when the animal was removed he discovered that it looked exactly like Agnes Bowker's progeny. Thus what had begun as an investigation intended to unearth the circumstances surrounding the birth of a monster, an event of undeniable moral, religious, and political significance, now devolved into a case of fraud. Although it seems likely that Bowker had been delivered of a child sometime before and that she was using the cover of "monstrous birth" to hide her infanticide, the clergyman Anderson was never able to untangle the web of deception that had been spun at Harborough. Eventually, he bound up all his testimony together with an image he had drawn of Agnes Bowker's cat and forwarded it to the Queen's man in Leicestershire, who sent it on to William Cecil, Elizabeth I's chief minister. To come to terms with the case, Cecil elicited the opinion of the Bishop of London, who, although he deliberated on the matter for several weeks, proved as incapable of untying Harborough's Gordian knot as Anderson had. The bishop pronounced the incident a fraud, to be sure, but remained uncertain of just who was guilty. Thus Agnes Bowker's strange case came to be entertained in the highest echelons of Tudor power before fading into a centuries-long obscurity. There it languished until the English historian David

Cressy recently rediscovered it and explored its many implications for understanding politics and society in the Tudor era.[1]

The tale of Agnes Bowker transports us back to a very different time, in which the mechanics of political commentary functioned according to rules different from those in a modern "mass media" society. Certainly, similar cases of strangely deformed births and other seemingly fantastic events still fascinate the modern tabloid press and occasionally elicit apocalyptic pronouncements. But such events are no longer, in the West at least, subjects for official government inquiry, and so the question remains: why did this strange and ultimately fraudulent case of deformed birth come to involve some of England's brightest lights? The answer to such a question lies in the vitally political yet often equivocal role the portent played in sixteenth-century Europe. For centuries, frightening and highly unusual events revealed in nature had been interpreted as purposeful, awe-inspiring, and revelatory of greater secrets God had hidden in Creation.[2] At the same time medieval people had often dabbled in prophecy about such events, violating the famous prohibitions of Augustine and other early Church Fathers against divination.[3] Yet an undeniable shift in the ways in which such wonders were discussed and promoted began to occur at the end of the fifteenth century, as learned observers studied monsters, comets, and other curious and frightening natural events systematically for the clues they might reveal about the course of future events in the political and religious sphere.[4] As events like Agnes Bowker's strange birth became a central focal point of the cheap print culture that was emerging in sixteenth-century Europe, royal, territorial, and civic authorities frequently moved to exercise censorship over the purveyors and authors of such accounts. Everywhere, in other words, this new "portent press" attracted the attention of magistrates because of

---

[1] David Cressy, *Agnes Bowker's Cat: Travesties and Transgressions in Tudor and Stuart England* (Oxford, 2000), pp. 9–28.

[2] Caroline Bynum, "Wonder," *American Historical Review* 102 (1997), 1–26.

[3] Valerie Flint, *The Rise of Magic in Medieval Europe* (Oxford, 1991), pp. 88–92 and 116–21.

[4] A trend originally noted in Aby Warburg, *Heidnisch-antike Weissagung in Wort und Bild zu Luthers Zeiten* (Heidelberg, 1920).

the inherently destabilizing potential that reposed in commenting upon a natural sign.[5]

For those who investigated the controversy surrounding Agnes Bowker's strange birth, it was certainly not beyond the boundaries of believability that a woman might have delivered a feline monster, or, as such hybrids were known in the English of the day, a "moon-calf." A distinguished lineage of ancient and medieval authorities as well as contemporary experts confirmed that such cross-species progeny had often been verified, and the medical science of the age advanced a number of reasons for their occurrence.[6] But when such incidents happened at times of political and religious tension, they were, like Agnes Bowker's cat, particularly subject to heightened scrutiny.[7] Bowker's monstrous progeny had arrived at just one such moment of anxious expectation in England. Although Elizabeth I had ruled for more than a decade, her government was still struggling to make headway against its large Catholic minority, and Protestant religious practices were far from universally established throughout the country. In the north, Elizabeth's government faced a number of Catholic nobles, and the arrival of Mary Queen of Scots there in May of 1568 was raising fears of outright rebellion. A lineage of accounts of monstrous births, celestial apparitions, and other natural wonders published in broadsides and pamphlets throughout the 1560s had already set Tudor officials on edge at a time when they were facing considerable domestic and international opposition.[8] The debunking

---

[5] Bruno Weber, *Wunderzeichen und Winkeldrucker* (Zürich, 1972); Rudolf Schenda, "Die deutschen Prodigiensammlungen des 16. und 17. Jahrhunderts," *Archiv für Geschichte des Buchwesens* 4 (1963), 637–710 ; and Walter Strauss, *The German Single-Leaf Woodcut, 1550–1600*, 3 vols. (New York, 1976), 1:1-9.

[6] On the "long history" of monstrous birth and the roles that it had played in the intellectual discussions of medieval authorities, see Katherine Park and Lorraine Daston, *Wonders and the Order of Nature* (New York, 1998); and Jean Céard, *La nature et les prodiges: L'insolite au 16e siècle, en France* (Geneva, 1977).

[7] Park and Daston, *Wonders and the Order of Nature,* pp. 48–57 and 177–90; Céard, *Nature,* pp. 33–35; Lorraine Daston, "Marvellous Facts and Miraculous Evidence in Early Modern Europe," *Critical Inquiry* 18 (1991), 93–124; Dudley Wilson, *Signs and Portents: Monstrous Births from the Middle Ages to the Enlightenment* (London, 1993).

[8] Cressy, *Agnes Bowker's Cat,* p. 22; Christopher Hill, "The Many-Headed Monster in Late Tudor and Early Stuart Political Thinking," in *From the Renaissance to the Counter-Reformation,* ed. Charles H. Carter (New York, 1966), pp. 296–324;

of Agnes Bowker's misbirth insured that her feline fraud was not to be included within the catalogue of woes that seemed to portend an imminent end to Elizabeth's reign. Empirical observation and a healthy dose of skepticism thus became tools in the regime's efforts to combat the publicizing of that event as a prefiguration of political changes soon to unfold on the national scene.

By the 1560s, Europe had already experienced a number of "prophetic" moments similar to that which was unfolding in England during 1569. Such events grew increasingly common in early modern Europe, as the new patterns of communication fostered by the advent of cheap print opened up possibilities for the rapid broadcasting of natural disasters, wonders, and other oddities. While natural aberrations had long been included in historical chronicles, sermons, and natural philosophical texts, stories about these events came in the sixteenth century to circulate widely through cheap, printed accounts that satisfied the curiosity of a large readership for topical information. From their first appearance, prophecy about political and military developments played an important role in these texts. In Italy we can observe the first spurt of interest in "newsprint" about natural wonders developing, as a spate of dire warnings about the political importance of monstrous births, astral signs, and natural disasters appeared alongside the tense expectancy that accompanied the outbreak of the Italian Wars in 1494. In her masterful study of these themes, the Italian historian Ottavia Niccoli has shown how knowledge of these events—events like the famous monsters of Ravenna or Florence—circulated first in letters or through sermons before being exploited in print.[9] Printed accounts, in turn, tended to codify the visual attributes of a misbirth or a celestial sign, even as the circulation of wonders in print opened up a forum in which a lush variety of interpretation could be put forth for a certain wonder. Depending upon one's perspective, for instance, the monster of Ravenna—a fantastically deformed

---

Stephen Alford, *The Early Elizabethan Polity: William Cecil and the British Succession Crisis, 1558–1569* (Cambridge, 1998), pp. 182–208; and *Mr. Secretary Cecil and Queen Elizabeth* (New York, 1955), pp. 431–37.

[9] Ottavia Niccoli, *Prophecy and People in Renaissance Italy*, trans. Lydia G. Cochrane, (Princeton, 1990); and Niccoli, "'Menstruum quasi Monstruum': Monstrous Births and Menstrual Taboo in the Sixteenth Century," trans. Mary Gallucci, in *Sex and Gender in Historical Perspective*, ed. Edward Muir and Guido Ruggiero (Baltimore, 1990), pp. 1–25.

child born in that city in 1512—could signal coming catastrophe for the Ravennese or for the French, German, or Spanish combatants that were invading Italy at the time.[10]

The fashioning of highly specific political predictions about events like these did not preclude other kinds of interpretations, and often in the very same publication several different explanatory protocols appeared side by side. A general apocalyptic and eschatological sentiment figured prominently in many of the cheap printed accounts about these events, as did theories about these wonders' role in revealing God's Providence. The Hand of God, commentators often warned, was pitched, ready to strike, but a merciful Divinity was sending one last warning to try to encourage his children to flee sin. In addition, the specific contours of a monstrous infant's body or the shape of an apparition that had been witnessed in the night sky were "read," that is, they were subjected to complex allegorical patterns of elaboration and commentary. The monster of Ravenna, accounts warned, had been born without arms, and with a single claw-like foot that resembled a bird of prey. The child had been a hermaphrodite, too, and commentators who dissected its physical abnormalities thus related these physical facts to divine pronouncements on contemporary vices. The child's lack of arms thus became a condemnation of Italians' lack of charity. Its claw-like foot, an attribute of a bird of prey, was a statement about contemporary rapaciousness and avarice, and its status as a hermaphrodite pointed up the era's ripe sexual depravity.

Knowledge of momentous wonders like these spread quickly throughout Europe, and events like the Ravenna monster quickly began to acquire a mythic status. The child's image, for instance, reappeared in many "wonder books," printed in Europe during the sixteenth and seventeenth centuries, another genre that appeared as a result of the age's burgeoning interest in natural wonders and their prophetic divination.[11] In turn,

---

[10] Ottavia Niccoli, *Prophecy and People*, pp. 35–51; and Rudolf Schenda, "Das Monstrum von Ravenna: Eine Studie zur Prodigienliteratur," *Zeitschrift für Volkskunde* 56 (1960), 209–25.

[11] Rudolf Schenda, "Die deutschen Prodigiensammlungen des 16. und 17. Jahrhunderts," pp. 638–710; Schenda, *Die französischen Prodigiensammlungen in der zweiten Hälfte des 16. Jahrhunderts*, Münchener Romanististische Arbeiten, Heft 16 (Munich, 1961); Bernward Deneke, "Kaspar Goltwurm. Ein lutherischer Kompilator zweischen Überlieferung und Glaube," in *Volkserzählung und Reformation. Ein Handbuch zur Tradierung und Funktion von Erzählstoffen und Erzählliteratur im*

the publication of these "wonder books" and the many accounts that circulated in cheap newsprint operated in tandem to reinforce the notion that prodigious natural events were on the rise, and that collectively they were portents, signs of impending change on the political, religious, or social scene. In Germany, home to one of the most vigorous sixteenth-century discourses about these wonders, the exploitation of events similar to those broadcast in Italy had begun to heat up in the very same years that discussion was growing to the south. This fascination was inspired, in part, by the example of the humanist Sebastian Brant, who played a vital role in encouraging the prophetic "reading" of deviations throughout the empire at the time. Brant wrote several prophecies about natural wonders during the 1490s. His treatment of the Ensisheim meteorite, a 150-kilogram stone that fell to earth in an Alsatian village on November 7, 1492, helped establish certain conventions of interpretation among the German humanists of his day. Brant interpreted the Ensisheim meteorite at one and the same time as a terrifying event and also as a sign of divine favor, theorizing that the incident revealed Maximilian I's ultimate victory in his struggles against the Valois dynasty.[12] Several years later he spun a similar yarn in a poem he published concerning the birth of Siamese twins at Worms in 1495. While conjoined twins were usually taken as a fearsome occurrence, Brant dispensed with the twins' appearance in a more favorable way. The birth coincided with a meeting of the imperial diet to discuss the Turkish threat, and so as Brant considered the twins, he concentrated on the nature of their infirmity.[13] They had

---

Protestantismus, ed. Wolfgang Brückner (Berlin, 1974), pp. 124–78; Heinz Schilling, "Job Fincel und die Zeichen der Endzeit," in *Volkserzählung und Reformation*, pp. 325–93.

[12] Dieter Wuttke, "Sebastian Brant und Maximilian I: Eine Studie zu Brants Donnnerstein-Flugblatt des Jahres 1492," in *Die Humanisten in ihrer politischen und sozialen Umwelt*, ed. O. Herding and R. Stupperich (Boppard, 1976), pp. 141–76; and Wuttke, "Sebastian Brant Verhältnis zu Wunderdeutung und Astrologie," in *Studien zur deutschen Literatur und Sprache des Mittelalters: Festschrift für Hugo Moser zum 65. Geburtstag*, ed. Wolfgang Besch, et al., (Berlin, 1974).

[13] Dieter Wuttke, "Wunderdeutung und Politik: Zu den Auslegungen der sogenannten Wormser Zwillinge des Jahres 1495," in *Landesgeschichte und Geistesgeschichte: Festschrift für Otto Herding zum 65. Geburtstage*, ed. Kaspar Elm, Eberhard Gönner, and Eugen Hillenbrand (Stuttgart, 1977), pp. 217–44; and Irene Ewinkel, *De monstris: Deutung und Funktion von Wundergeburten auf Flugblättern im Deutschland des 16. Jahrhunderts* (Tübingen, 1995), pp. 102–18 and 227–37.

been joined at the forehead, and thus he concluded they signified coming European unification under the "headship" of the Holy Roman Emperor. The Strasbourg humanist's fascination with natural wonders soon proved infectious among northern Europeans, and in the first two decades of the sixteenth century, ancient divinatory texts, medieval prophecies, and works on historical reckoning came to be avidly studied by humanists, particularly in the circle of historians and court chroniclers that surrounded Maximilian I.[14]

Brant and other humanists may have found little to fear in natural wonders, yet the strains of interpretation that more often appeared in the cheap press of early modern Europe were usually more pessimistic and despairing. In the remainder of this paper, I would like to explore this fascination's implications for understanding early modern patterns of political communication. The journalistic genres that warned about these events and their roles as portents were particularly widespread and enduring in northern Europe throughout the sixteenth and seventeenth centuries, even as they began to disappear from the realm of public, journalistic discourse in the eighteenth. In the first part of this paper, I explore the emergence of a world of cheap newsprint in Europe and the patterns of political interpretation and publicity it granted to these events. These patterns were, by and large, inchoate; that is, although most commentators were convinced that the "terrifying" or "horrific" events they related were significant for the political order, they were rarely specific about just what changes were to follow these frightening events. Nor were those who commented upon natural wonders ever specific in recommending other types of polities to replace the current reality. Instead, the political order was interpreted as sacred and divinely established, and the ills that commentators identified in their treatments of natural wonders were the evils of social sins—lack of charity, avarice, pride, vanity, and other shortcomings.

The underlying mentality of these accounts most often viewed society and the body politic in terms of the human body, a tradition that stretched back to the medieval idea of the *corpus christianorum,* and which was in these texts an enduring conservative element that only occasionally led commentators to question the social order. At the same time political authorities feared cheap newsprints generally as a source of

---

[14] See the above-cited works by Wuttke (n. 13).

discontent, as the case of Agnes Bowker makes clear. The size and scope of this, Europe's first "Grub Street," was considerable. In almost every city of significance in northern Europe, the cheap press matured in the course of the sixteenth and seventeenth centuries to become an increasingly variegated industry that employed large numbers of producers and that satisfied a broad market of consumers. Often tightly regulated, the popularity of these organs of information helped develop the market that was to be exploited by the periodic newspapers and journals in the later seventeenth century. In both media—the cheap broadside press of the sixteenth century and the later, more cosmopolitan world of the *journals*—a taste for sensationalism and an enduring religious and political conservatism came to mingle side by side with the newer forces of empirical curiosity; that is, with a hunger for faithful, eyewitness accounts of what had been seen, heard, touched, and felt in the far corners of the world. Out of the interplay of these forces, the longstanding role that nature's disorders had played as signs and portents began to evaporate, and while such accounts survived, they were increasingly removed from the world of public, political debate, an event that helped to prepare the way for the vigorous, more secular-spirited political press that became common after the mid-eighteenth century.

Cheap Newsprint, Popular Piety, and the Political in the Early Modern World

During the early years of the Protestant Reformation, preexisting attention to natural wonders was quickly transformed to become a relatively permanent feature of the religious landscape and subject matter for frequent exploitation in the press. In this regard, the pronouncements of Martin Luther and Philipp Melanchthon were decisive in leading the way for the development of a truly popular press that was captivated by signs and portents. In 1524, both reformers published tracts on monsters; that is, at the same time as the controversies that their reforms and ideas were causing were heating up throughout Germany and northern Europe.[15]

---

[15] The two reformers' readings of the monsters are discussed briefly in Daston and Park, *Wonders*, pp. 187–88; and at greater length in R. W. Scribner, *For the Sake of Simple Folk: Popular Propaganda for the German Reformation*, 2nd ed. (Cambridge, 1997), pp. 127–32.

As knowledge of their texts spread, Luther's and Melanchthon's pronouncements came to exercise influence over many later interpreters of similar events. For his part, Luther treated the "Monk Calf of Freyberg," a deformed animal that observers said looked as if it were dressed in a religious habit, while Melanchthon exploited the case of the "Papal Ass," a fantastically concocted hybrid that had been little known in northern Europe to this point.[16] According to the legends that had circulated about it in Italy during the previous generation, the "Papal Ass" had been mysteriously pulled from the River Tiber near the papal Castel Sant'Angelo in 1495. Of these two treatments of monsters, Melanchthon's was the more explicitly prophetic, since he judged the strange animal to be a divine condemnation of the papacy as a force of Antichrist and argued that it was a sign of the nearness of the Last Judgment. Luther's treatment of the misshapen calf was more guarded. He intended his work above all to be a rejoinder to a recently published pamphlet that had broadcast the "Monk Calf'" as a divine condemnation of his reforming message. In his response, Luther refused to assume the mantle of the prophet, but he nevertheless theorized that the animal's birth might prefigure coming military catastrophe, even as he also hoped it might point to the nearness of the Last Judgment; the largest portion of his treatment explored the many highly specific meanings he sensed seemed to be revealed in the animal's abnormalities. In his hands, the calf became a microcosm of the degeneration sin had worked on the monastic estate throughout history, a commentary on the ills of church and society, and a likely portent of coming momentous change.

Like Italian commentators before him, Luther also conducted a kind of "sacred autopsy" on the Monk Calf. He roamed over the animal's body, relating the specific anomalies of the misbirth to contemporary religious, social, and political ills. His allegorical interpretation transformed the wonder into a highly specific mirror of sins, and in the years that followed many European commentators were to imitate his technique when

---

[16] Martin Luther and Philipp Melanchthon, *Deuttung der czwo grewlichen Figuren, Bapstesels czu Rom und Munchkalbs zu Freijberg ijnn Meijsszen funden*, in *D. Martin Luthers Werke*, 102 vols. (Weimar, 1883–), 11:370–85; reprinted (together with commentary and other controversial writings about the two monsters) in Konrad Lange, *Der Papstesel. Ein Beitrag zur Kultur- und Kunstgeschichte des Reformationszeitalters* (Göttingen, 1891).

they treated similar events. Throughout Germany, England, and France, accounts of monstrous births and dire warnings about other natural wonders were soon streaming from city presses, and a flood of broadsides, pamphlets, and historical chronicles of wonders (*Wunderzeichenbücher*) were satisfying the tastes of the age for these stories. At other levels of intellectual discussion, such events also captivated natural philosophers and theologians, and many impressive volumes on teratology (the science of monsters) as well as theological treatments of the subject of monstrosity appeared too. In the broadside press, this fascination reached its high-water mark in northern Europe during the second half of the sixteenth century, and in Germany, England, and France, the grim years of the 1560s and 1570s were particularly vigorous ones for the publication of prophecies about these events.[17] Like Luther and Melanchthon before them, the promoters of these accounts frequently warned that the bizarre events they reported pointed to the imminence of political or religious change. Yet the forces that inspired these accounts in each of these three regions were somewhat different. In England, the insecurities of Elizabeth's early reign were largely to blame for the rise in reporting, while in France, the developing Wars of Religion helped to sustain an anxious climate of commentary on portents as well. In Germany, by contrast, these accounts entered into the increasingly fierce competition that was developing between the emerging post-Reformation confessions, as well as the divided and bitterly contested debates that became common among Lutherans at the time. By any measure, the market for these prints was considerable. In France, for example, almost five hundred cheap canards survive that treat the subject of monstrous births alone from the years between 1529 and 1631.[18] Far more than that number have probably

---

[17] For further information on the development of this literature, see J.-P. Seguin, *L'Information en France avant le périodique* (Paris, 1964); Seguin, *L'Information en France de Louis XIII à Henri II* (Geneva, 1971); Bruno Weber, *Wunderzeichen und Winkeldrucker, 1543–1586*; Eugen Holländer, *Wunder, Wundergeburt und Wundergestalt: Einblattdrucke des fünfzehntnten bis achtzehnten Jahrhunderts* (Stuttgart, 1921); Lorraine Daston and Katherine Park, "Unnatural Conceptions: The Study of Monsters in Sixteenth- and Seventeenth-Century France and England," *Past and Present* 92 (1981), 20–54; and David Cressy, *Agnes Bowker's Cat*, pp. 29–50.

[18] J.-P. Seguin, *L'Information en France avant le périodique*, p. 14.

disappeared since that time, since these accounts were long considered "ephemera" and were only rarely collected and preserved.[19]

The popularity of these phenomena in the sixteenth-century press of northern Europe may have developed in part from the momentous changes that were occurring in the religious landscape of the time. Yet very soon, the fascination came to feed upon itself, and the rise in newsprints that reported monsters, celestial signs, and other natural disasters grew to become a "medium-induced" crisis. Early modern commentators, for instance, were convinced that their own time was witnessing a profound upswing in natural disasters and signs, and for evidence of this upswing they pointed to the many recent printed accounts that were circulating in their regions.[20] These accounts, in turn, satisfied a widespread desire for sensation, and printers seem to have been only too happy to oblige their customers with a steady stream of such accounts. At its most fundamental level, then, the fascination with prodigies and portents that developed at the time was a product of market forces, as the cheap printers that purveyed accounts of incidents similar to the Monk Calf of Freyberg kept their eyes and ears open to events that might be successfully and profitably exploited through cheap tracts and broadsides. This market, though, reveals far more than an upswing in mere sensationalistic journalism, for it shows the rise of a large and diverse readership that was interested in learning about contemporary events and the implications they might have for the course of the common weal.[21]

By any measure, the market in cheap newsprint seems to have been a formidable force in urban economies. During the century and a half that followed 1550, for example, more than fifty printers of cheap broadsides plied their trade in the city of Augsburg alone, one of Europe's most important early modern printing centers. At Augsburg, these modest

---

[19] One of the most famous exceptions being the large collection that was maintained by the Zürich pastor Johann Jakob Wick. See Bruno Weber, *Wunderzeichen und Winkeldrucker*; Matthias Senn, "Johann Jakob Wick (1522–1588) und seine Sammlung von Nachrichten zur Zeitgeschichte," (Diss. Zürich, 1974); and Franz Mauelshagen, "Wicks Wunderbücher. Enstehung- Überlieferung - Rezeption," (Diss. Zürich, 2000).

[20] See Daston and Park's discussion of this element of the discourse in *Wonders*, pp. 177–90.

[21] See esp. Weber, *Wunderzeichen und Winkeldrucker*; and Mauelshagen, "Wicks Wunderbücher."

printers formed the bottom rung of the city's considerable printing ladder, an industry that by the early eighteenth century employed 12 percent of the town's population.[22] As this industry developed in the sixteenth and seventeenth centuries, three-quarters of Augsburg's ranks of modest printers crowded their shops into just one of the city's suburbs, the St. James area just outside the town's walls, where many of Augsburg's poor artisans and shopkeepers lived, and where they might sell their wares not only to natives but to the many peddlers and merchants that visited the town.[23] Such producers operated in a world very different from the Frobens, Estiennes, and Garamonds of the day. Instead of treating issues of significance in the world of law, natural philosophy, or theology, they exploited topical themes, hawking their accounts of disasters, celestial signs, misbirths, and other "strange but true" stories to a broad readership that might pay their modest prices—four to six German pennies during the late sixteenth and early seventeenth centuries.[24] The accounts they churned out thus found a ready market, and printers at Augsburg, like those at Nuremberg, Strasbourg, Paris, London, and any of a number of European cities competed against one other to produce the stories that would generate the most sales among their local clientele.

In German cities, printers of these modest communications also helped to provide employment for a number of other categories of artisans, including *Briefmaler, Formschneider,* and *Patronirer. Briefmaler,* a category of minor artist, were responsible for producing illustrations on paper and were usually limited by guild regulations to working in watercolor and tempera. Besides coloring the illustrations of broadsides and producing modest images of the saints or biblical themes, they also were the chief producers of playing cards in central European cities. In the second half of the sixteenth century, many *Briefmaler* supplemented their incomes by painting the woodcut illustrations that adorned contemporary newsprints. *Formschneider,* on the other hand, produced the woodblocks from which these works' illustrations were made, while *Patronirer,* or stencilists, found employment, too, in cutting patterns for borders and other decorative elements used on the prints. The relationship between these

---

[22] H. Gier, "Buchdruck und Verlagswesen in Augsburg vom Dreißigjährigen Krieg bis zum Ende der Reichsstadt," in *Augsburger Buchdruck und Verlagswesen von den Anfängen bis zur Gegenwart,* ed. H. Gier and J. Janota (Wiesbaden, 1997).

[23] Walter L. Strauss, *The German Single-Leaf Woodcut, 1550–1600,* 1:1–9.

[24] Ibid.

various professions, though, was often more fluid than such neat distinctions might suggest, and *Briefmaler* and *Formschneider* were known to cross the line to become printers and purveyors of cheap broadsides, too.[25] Marx Anton Hannas (1610–76), one of Augsburg's most successful printers of broadsides and cheap pamphlets, was by trade a *Briefmaler* and *Formschneider* who rose to become one of the city's wealthiest publishers. He carved out a niche, not in publishing great elite works of law, theology, or natural philosophy, but by continuing to specialize in producing images of the saints, biblical characters, and the sensationalistic news broadsides favored at the time.[26] Hannas's career marked the successful rise of a minor artist into the ranks of highly successful Augsburg businessmen, but elsewhere, guilds frequently tried to stop the encroachment of *Formschneider, Briefmaler,* and other unlicensed printers on their market. In 1604, for instance, Frankfurt's printers brought suit against Balthasar Hoffmann for operating a press without a license; instead of submitting to the authority of Frankfurt's town council and its guild, Hoffman simply left the city, moving to nearby Darmstadt where his press survived until his death in 1622.[27] The German word *Winkeldrucker* (meaning literally "dark corner printer(s)") appeared at this time to refer to those like Hoffman who lacked official licenses to print—requirements for practicing the profession that were becoming more and more *de jure* at the time, not just in Germany, but everywhere in Europe where sizable contingents of cheap printers operated. Unsanctioned printers like these thus often worked in a shadowy world. Sometimes tolerated, they were often subjected to periodic attempts to put them out of business.[28]

In such a world, production values sometimes mattered little. The Strasbourg printer Thiebold Berger, for example, developed an ingenious method to keep his costs down. During the 1550s and 1560s, for instance, he used different blocks to depict his accounts of recent celestial apparitions: one that did not change and suggested a townscape in which the wonder had been observed, and another that he superimposed over top of it to suggest the precise nature of the celestial signs he recounted. He deployed his cityscape illustration in at least three separate reports of

---

[25] Dorothy Alexander and Walter Strauss, *The German Single-Leaf Woodcut 1600–1700*, 2 vols. (New York, 1977), 1:18.

[26] Ibid., 1:211–12.

[27] Ibid., 1:259.

[28] Weber, *Wunderzeichen und Winkeldrucker.*

apparitions: the first an event that had been witnessed in the skies over Ingolstadt, Regensburg, and Nuremberg in 1554; then, in an account of a celestial apparition in the town of Gengenbach near Strasbourg in 1563; and finally, in another report of a sign witnessed in the skies over the Black Forest in 1566.[29] By this time, however, his cityscape woodblock was showing clear signs of wear. Berger, at least, modulated his accounts by relying on a second block to suggest the precise contours of his "miracle." Other printers merely reused their illustrations over time, and in this way, a depiction of one recent wonder often did double duty for rendering another quite different event a few years later. By this time, though, most of the consumers who purchased these cheap prints may have long since forgotten that they had ever seen the illustration before. To fashion their illustration, too, printers relied on many of the more cultivated *Wunderzeichenbücher* being printed at the time for inspiration in depicting celestial signs, monsters, and other natural aberrations. In this regard, Conrad Wohlfahrt or Lycosthenes' *Prodigiorum ac ostentorum chronicon*, published at Basel in 1557, was among the most important works used by cheap printers and their *Formschneider*. Many printers seem to have kept a copy in their workshops. Its hundreds of illustrations of a broad array of natural wonders frequently were used as models for those anxious to exploit the news of recent phenomena, and its effect on the market can be seen, particularly in the second half of the sixteenth century in Germany and Switzerland. There it helped to produce a certain sameness in the illustrations used in the news press.[30]

Between 1550 and 1600 the contours of the New Tidings *(Neue Zeitungen)* treated by these cheap printers assumed the shape that they would continue to retain throughout much of the seventeenth century. Rather quickly, the accounts' structures became remarkably consistent, and they acquired the attributes typical of early journalism. Almost everywhere printers adopted a tripartite division of their prints to convey the "facts" about the events they related. The broadsides of the time came to have a long and complex title that described, often in great detail, the sensational event that was being retold. Usually a modest woodcut

---

[29] Strauss, *The German Single-Leaf Woodcut 1550–1600*, vol. 1, pp. 106, 109, and 115.

[30] Daston and Park, *Wonders*, pp. 182–87; Schilling, "Job Fincel und die Zeichen der Endzeit," pp. 380–84.

illustration appeared below this caption, although engravings were used, too, in more expensive single-leaf prints. Texts of varying length then set out the events that had been observed at a certain time. Often the data that was recorded was quite specific and included information about observers who had witnessed the event; the place, the date, and the time that it had occurred; and an interpretation of its underlying religious or political significance. The histories of these events were written in prose, in verse, or sometimes as ballads intended to be sung. In Germany, a study of the surviving accounts of comets from the period shows that about 70 percent of these texts were written in poetic form, while the remaining 30 percent were prose. This breakdown seems typical of accounts treating other themes, both in Germany and elsewhere in Europe.[31] Many works, though, included both prose and poetry, with a short poem sometimes used to begin or end a text otherwise written in prose.

Although the output of the genre was considerable and was for most of the sixteenth and seventeenth centuries consumed by readers from all walks of life, the theatrical sensationalism of this press was almost always viewed with unease by state and civic town authorities. At Nuremberg, one of the most fertile sixteenth-century centers of German broadside production, the town council introduced licensing requirements for all printers in 1571 and pledged to limit the number of printers, *Briefmaler,* and *Formschneider* who might practice in the city. Despite the council's intentions, the numbers of practitioners in all three professions rose over the next generation, so that at the end of the century there were two more printers, four more *Formschneider,* and ten more *Briefmaler* in the town than there had been a generation earlier. At Nuremberg, the flood of prints that warned of "strange," "horrifying," or "terrifying" events also prompted the town council to pass stringent censorship measures on numerous occasions after 1550. Those who printed these stories without first securing official permission were threatened with fines and expulsion, and several of the city's printers and *Briefmaler* were imprisoned on several occasions as the council tried to get the producers under control.[32]

---

[31] Alexander and Strauss, *The German Single-Leaf Woodcut 1600–1700,* vol. 1, p. 21.

[32] Ibid., p. 18.

Similar clashes between city authorities and printers occurred in almost every city where sizable contingents of these modest printers plied their trade. In London, home to one of the most precocious centers of cheap print production, the history of the broadside press displays many similarities to the somewhat later development of the Elizabethan theater. In 1520, London was already filled with purveyors of cheap print, whose ballads and newsy broadsides informed of the latest sensational events in England and on the Continent. Reams of broadsheets were sold at two or three a penny; a century later their price had doubled, but they were still cheap enough to be afforded by most of the city's population.[33] The cheap printers who produced this material crowded into the same stalls and shops that surrounded St. Paul's churchyard, the English capital's largest book market at the time. Here printers of cheap newsprints sold their wares side by side with those who retailed more elevated devotional, theological, and philosophical texts. During the course of the seventeenth century, London's marketplace was to become more geographically differentiated, with centers of sales and production developing in various quarters throughout the city, a phenomenon that anticipated the emergence of "Grub Street" around 1700, a recognizable urban district dominated by cheap booksellers, publishers, and literary hacks. While this phenomenon was late in arriving on London's scene, sixteenth-century royal and civic officials already recognized the cheap producers of newsprints as a subcategory within the greater community of printers and feared these producers as a source of dissent and disorder.[34]

Many cheap English broadsides were written in ballad form and set to the music of preexisting tunes, a style of production popular elsewhere in Europe, including France and Germany.[35] These texts were hawked in taverns and markets, and a sophisticated distribution network soon developed that sold such works in towns large and small throughout England. In 1533, Henry VIII decreed against the printing of "offensive" ballads in an attempt to rein in producers of exactly these kinds of broadsides. He repeated his condemnation in 1542, and his successors Edward I and Mary I also legislated against the activities of the news balladeers.[36]

---

[33] Watt, *Cheap Print and Popular Piety, 1550–1640* (Cambridge, 1991), p. 11.

[34] Ibid., pp. 75–78.

[35] Ibid., pp. 11–38.

[36] Cyprian Blagden, *The Stationers' Company: A History, 1403–1959* (Cambridge, Mass., 1960), see esp. chap. 1.

The topical creations of these printers concerning political and religious issues of the day were often perceived as a danger to public order, if not an outright vehicle for expressing dissent. Although Elizabeth I was generally more successful in controlling the broadside printers, the hard-fought battles of her government only gradually yielded results, as the furor surrounding the case of Agnes Bowker's cat reveals. During the 1560s and 1570s London's printers continued to churn out unsanctioned works, many of which Elizabeth's government feared as a source of dissent because of their prophetic expositions on recent events. Thus, even as church investigators were being sent to unearth the precise nature of Agnes Bowker's misbirth in the Elizabethan countryside, England's royal government was trying to tighten its control over its most sensationalistic urban printers. In an attempt to gain the upper hand, Elizabeth's officials relied on the Stationers' Company, a late-medieval institution that Mary I had granted a royal charter in 1557 for the purposes of awarding copyright and licensing the production of books, pamphlets, and broadsides. These regulations commanded that the texts of broadsides be submitted to the Archbishop of Canterbury or the Bishop of London for approval.[37] But despite such measures, as much as 40 percent of all the broadsides printed in the capital during Elizabeth's reign may never have been licensed. The failure to gain control over these small producers is all the more glaring when the size of the English broadside press is taken into account: as many as four million single-leaf prints may have been printed in London in the half-century that followed 1550.[38]

A consideration of these prints' subjects helps to explain the fears this sensationalistic press raised among political officialdom. Subject matter, of course, differed from region to region and changed over time, but natural disasters, signs seen in the nighttime skies, the deformed births of both animals and humans, and the discovery of strange new species of flora and fauna were everywhere common and enduring themes. Many accounts of natural disasters promoted in these news accounts traveled quite far. News of recent earthquakes, floods, and frightening conflagrations were exploited hundreds of miles from the points at which they

---

[37] W. W. Greg, *Some Aspects and Problems of London Publishing* (Oxford, 1956), esp. p. 6.

[38] Greg, *Some Aspects,* p. 7; and Watt, *Cheap Print and Popular Piety,* pp. 42–49.

occurred, often very quickly. Of all the categories of natural phenomenon treated, celestial phenomena like the aurora borealis, comets, and
other unusual "signs" seen in the evening skies were among the most
common, particularly in central Europe, where they were an enduring
staple of cheap printers throughout the seventeenth century. But an interest in celestial phenomena generally was one feature this cheap, ephem-
eral literature shared with elite natural philosophers and astronomers of
the day. In every country a category of "unbelievable, but true" events
was also to be found in the broadsides. Cases of women who survived
without food, instances of miracles revolving around communion or the
Host, wonders worked by images and statues, or strange tales about child
prophets—these were just a few of the many diverse kinds of tales that
found their way into the topical press.[39]

An enduring pessimism as well as a taste for marvels were thus two
features this "news" culture nourished in northern Europe in the first
century of its existence. These modest printers did not treat the inter-
nal workings of government or anything that modern sensibilities might
associate with the "political," because in most places open discussion of
state policies, royal intrigues, and court personalities would have resulted
in quick and Draconian suppression. Accounts of recent battles and sieges
were the closest the printers came to exploiting events of direct political
significance, and these often concentrated on the gruesome elements of
these encounters. If news broadsides generally avoided incidents of outright political significance, they were filled all the same with interpretive
strains that displayed the underlying political and religious mentalities of
those that consumed them. One of the striking things about such prints
was their relatively slight reliance on doctrinal or confessional formulae
and their great similarity across very different national boundaries. That
God punishes the wicked, that the actions of communities and populations had a direct bearing on the health and survival of states, and that
the world was like a gigantic book in which the Divinity was constantly
writing signs of warning—these were enduring themes that were as

---

[39] For Germany, more specific information concerning content is discussed
in the introductions to the Strauss editions of sixteenth- and seventeenth-century
woodcuts. See Walter L. Strauss, *The German Single-Leaf Woodcut, 1550–1600*, vol.
1, pp. 1–9; and Alexander and Strauss, *The German Single-Leaf Woodcut, 1600–1700*,
vol. 1:17–22. For England, see Tessa Watt, *Cheap Print and Popular Piety*; and for
France, the above-cited works by J.-P. Seguin.

common in Catholic France as they were in Lutheran Germany or Anglican England.[40] The world of newsprint, in other words, was often resistant to the attempts of Protestant or Catholic reformers and state officials at confessionalization, although its stock pieties continually included vigorous calls to repentance and amendment of readers' lives. The lessons that were drawn from a nighttime apparition, a comet, or a frightening birth were often the same, as promoters warned that these recent signs were visual sermons of repentance, phantasms produced by a God that longed to avoid using the far greater power at his disposal to wreak justice on human society and kingdoms. To the readers of this material, an enduring, truly popular Augustinianism interpreted deviations from the norm as proof of God's continuing intimacy with human affairs. Divine providence, in other words, was most often used as the dominant moral and interpretive framework to grant meaning to these events.

An Information Society

Despite the presence of a substratum of religious beliefs that gave shape to its interpretations, the world of cheap newsprint was not resistant to all change. Transformations had already begun to occur in this press in the years following 1600, and these transformations steadily intensified in the decades that followed. Although it is difficult to generalize about the literature because its tens of thousands of accounts were published across many different regional, national, and linguistic barriers, this journalism nevertheless came to display almost everywhere a steadily deepening attempt to satisfy audiences' demand for information and to shape readers' understanding of the extraordinary events the reports related. In these cheap newsprints, then, can be seen in microcosm the preparation of the seedbed for the development of a sphere of public, political journalism, a sphere that was to play a vital role in fashioning the processes of political communication that since the eighteenth century have been such an important part in modern societies. These forces, to be sure, are not evident in every account. Until the present, the press has continued to churn out sensationalistic stories that seem more at home in the

---

[40] See, in particular, the remarks of Tessa Watt in *Cheap Print and Popular Piety*, on pp. 324–32, concerning the religious conservatism of the English broadsides; Daston and Park, *Wonders*, pp. 177–90; and Jean Céard, *La Nature*.

sixteenth than in the twenty-first century. Yet inexorably, over the course of the early modern period, a deepening curiosity combined with skepticism akin to the critical eye the Elizabethan cleric Anthony Anderson trained on the young unfortunate Agnes Bowker grew more prevalent throughout northern Europe.

Curiosity mingled with religious sentiment had always existed just below the surface of the fascination with natural wonders, and since the explosion of cheap news accounts had begun to gather steam in the early sixteenth century, printers had attracted readers to their stories of natural wonders with sensational hyperbole. The events they related were styled as "gruesome," "terrifying," and "horrific." But beyond the printed page, a gawking inquisitiveness was an unavoidable fact of sixteenth- and seventeenth-century life. Since the first glimmer of macabre fascination with monsters, for instance, deformed infants had been preserved, set out for all to observe. Pilgrimages to places like the impact site of the Ensisheim meteorite became a common occurrence of the time. And the rock that had fallen from heaven there in 1492 soon had to be suspended from the ceiling of the local church to protect it from the chipping hammers of admirers. In this milieu, public display also offered a livelihood for the deformed who survived to adulthood, and many of these unfortunates even sold their own souvenir handbills so that their audiences might visually recall their numerous abnormalities when they had departed the scene. Beyond high streets, markets, and village squares, natural curiosities were collected; they were ensconced and catalogued in the "Wonder Cabinets" of sixteenth-century scholars and rulers. In this and other ways, nature's deviations could be possessed and compared, and over time the anxious force they exercised upon the early modern imagination came gradually to be disarmed.

A probing eye was thus an essential precondition for the entire enterprise of marketing cheap and sensational newsprint. Yet this same gaze held within it many of the very same sources that led to the extraordinary's evaporation. Thus, in the century and a half following 1550, it is possible for us to trace a history in northern Europe, a history in which wonder was undergoing a long process of "wearing out." We see evidence of this essential transformation in the publicity that was used to promote the careers of sixteenth- and seventeenth-century freaks. During the 1540s the Flemish unfortunate Hans de Moer embarked on a career displaying himself before crowds of paying onlookers. For more than twenty years he toured the continent, showing his deformity, a huge blue and red hemangioma that began at his ear and fell to his hips. De Moer could make this deformity take on the appearance of a Spanish hood, and even corral his tumor so that it looked like the gobbler of an American turkey. In the prints sold to commemorate his visits in German cities in the 1560s, de Moer's infirmities were intoned as a case of absolute incomprehensibility, a riddle whose "meaning is known only to God."[41]

A half-century later, though, a completely different set of sensibilities is evident among the audiences that consumed tales about the life and career of Magdalene Emohne, a maiden that accounts tell us had been born near Emden in East Frisia on September 12, 1596. Emohne survived to adulthood, and in the 1610s, she achieved great notoriety. She had been born without arms and ears and with only one leg. In defiance of these enormous handicaps, Emohne had managed to master four languages— French, German, Italian, and Dutch. She could, as the cheap printed accounts of her life broadcast, sing passably well, well enough to entertain kings and aristocrats. She managed to feed herself and even unlock trunks with her only foot. And despite being cut off from the world of human communication by her deafness, she had learned to read and was something of a scholar.[42] In the printed news accounts that circulated in central and western Europe about her life, she was usually shown surrounded by her books. The fearsome incomprehensibility so evident in the hawking used to advertise de Moer played little role in the publicity now accorded Emohne. Instead, the accounts that treated her life concentrated on the woman's exceptional achievements, achievements that were not incomprehensible but instead merely awe-inspiring. In the news stories that circulated about her, Emohne's life story became a testimony to what might be accomplished when human effort made use of the few remaining gifts God had left an unlucky woman. Rather than being a detestable spectacle, Emohne was a true prodigy whose life story excited no prophetic commentary on the course of nations or of future religious

---

[41] "Hans de Moer geboren aus Brabant" [incipit] (1566), reprinted in Wolfgang Harms, ed., *Die Sammlung der Herzog August Bibliothek in Wolfenbüttel*, 3 vols. (Tübingen, 1980–89), 1:230.

[42] "Eine rechte warhaffte Abcontrofactur unnd wunderbarlichen Geschöpf Von einer Jungfrawen welche in Ostfriessland dem 12. Novemb. 1596 geboren" (Prague, 1616), reprinted in Alexander and Strauss, *German Single-Leaf Woodcut 1600–1700*, 2:730.

predicaments. That narrative instead counseled readers to hard work, a redoubling of efforts against the forces of contingency and the realities of the environment.

The changes evident in Emohne's publicity can be seen elsewhere as well. The audience that hungered for tales of lives like hers and the printers that attempted to fill this demand were now concerned with a broader array of issues, issues that impinged on the precise context and the observable details that had been witnessed in tandem with one of nature's deviations. The consumers of Emohne's story demanded to know just how many languages she had mastered or how precisely she employed her one surviving limb despite the presence of only four toes. In this way they began to look past the traditional lenses of sin through which these events had long been viewed, and slowly began to disregard the longstanding interpretations that had stressed that such events were portents of significance to the body politic. In place of these discourses, they indulged an interest in nature's infinite complexities and possibilities and the multitude of human reactions that might be deployed to overcome the trials nature placed in one's way.

While one finds many accounts surviving throughout the seventeenth century that continued to decry nature as a mirror of human degeneracy and devolution, the tendency was undeniable all the same for these elements to shrink in cheap news accounts in favor of glimmers of a new confidence that argued that nature's secrets might be unlocked and comprehended. In the sixteenth century, writers of cheap newsprint had often fashioned allegorical interpretations for the phenomena they related. That world had clung tenaciously to traditional political metaphors that insisted that societies and nations were organized along principles analogous to the human body. The fashioners of prophetic commentary, from the first outburst of interest in natural anomalies in the press around 1500, had broadcasted their phenomena as emblems that laid bare the sins of society's various orders. Like Blake, the promoters of these events had seen "the world in a grain of sand," evidencing a fundamentally poetic and microcosmic mentality about nature and its importance for revealing the future course of political developments. Deformed infants, strange new species of flora and fauna, and even visions seen in the nighttime skies had been subjected to a persistent decoding that related these phenomena to the various parts that comprised the body social. The enormous folds of skin seen on a deformed infant could, in this way, be broadcast as condemnations of the wasteful *Pluderhosen,* or "Turkish trousers," popular among male peasants in contemporary village society, signs that appeared upon the legs of a deformed child because of the role the peasantry played as the foundation of society. In this way, too, the irregularities seen on a wildflower's corolla might point to the wasteful vanities of ruffs, the extravagant collars common to the patrician and commercial classes of late sixteenth-century cities.[43] Such jeremiads had linked the natural order, the political, and the moral together into a single inexorable discourse. But now as a second, more optimistic glance came to be directed at the external world, nature's moral and political messages grew less urgent.

A German account of a whale that beached on the Mediterranean near St. Tropez in 1640 points to this fledgling confidence. The discoveries of strange fishes, terrifying "sea-monsters," and enormous whales had been promoted in the sixteenth century as urgent eschatological signs, fearsome portents that many commentators argued revealed the growing instability of nature and of "momentous changes" about to occur. Such rhetoric had not died out by 1640, to be sure. In the broadside printed about the St. Tropez whale, the headline still coursed with the by-now obligatory rhetoric about the new discovery of a "terrifying sea monster." It began with a warning to readers of the consequences that might follow such a fearsome event. But once those stock pieties had been dispensed with, the commentator settled into a newsy relation of all the particulars. The account informed readers that the whale had been more than three hundred feet long and that it had had a thousand teeth. And in a nod to the rising commercial interests of the day, the whale's exploiters even told his readers just how much blubber had been rendered from the animal and the price it had fetched at market. Such an account dealt only peripherally with the animal's role in revealing human shortcomings, or in pointing to great transformations that might be on the horizon. At the text's conclusion, for instance, the author merely observed in a single sentence: "But the meaning of this fearsome sign is known only to God." The late-medieval and sixteenth-century fascination with allegorical explanation, with the attempt to see in the natural world a purposeful presentation of humankind's wickedness or a prefiguration

---

[43] Johannes Cuno, *Hoffarts Laster* (1590).

of political ills to come, was thus beginning to disappear here in favor of a new strain of empirical observation. This sensibility now stressed the human capability to know and understand nature through knowledge of all its particulars. Although the text's conclusion held out the possibility that the enormous whale might be a portent, the many different layers of information it presented about the animal tended all the same to submerge such rhetoric. The animal's meaning, in other words, lay in a different sphere, not in relating the Mediterranean whale to a cosmic drama of impiety and divine punishment or to impending political changes, but in the this-worldly circumstances that "more than a thousand" observers had witnessed on a Mediterranean beach some months before.[44]

A nature subjected to this kind of eye could become demystified, and in this process, a new sense that stressed that the natural world was merely an environment subject to human mastery might grow. Such a vision, to be sure, grew most quickly in learned society, where a new emphasis on natural law philosophy, the new science, an increasingly secular spirit, and greater technological mastery over the environment advanced quickly in the decades following 1650. But a key force that underpinned these changes and at the same time expressed the new spirit of the age lay in the periodic newspaper, a medium that had already begun to develop in the early seventeenth century in several German cities. During the course of the century periodic weeklies, fortnightlies, and monthlies were to spread to an increasing number of cities in northern Europe, helping to grant a more cosmopolitan flair to life in major towns. The cost of these publications may have been considerably higher than the single-leaf broadsides that had long been so important in the diffusion of information concerning recent spectacular events throughout northern Europe. And the readerships of these periodicals were often better educated. Yet complex, circuitous conduits came to disseminate the information reported in the new bourgeois journals to broad swaths of urban society, and the newspaper's youth was spent developing along other already established information organs.[45] One of the consumer products of the

---

[44] The text is reprinted in Alexander and Strauss, *German Single-Leaf Woodcut 1600–1700*, vol. 2, p. 781.

[45] Robert Darnton, "An Early Information Society: News and the Media in Eighteenth-Century Paris," *American Historical Review* 105, no. 1 (February 2000), 1–35.

seventeenth century, the newspaper soon became a sign of social distinction. In contrast to the older styles of "New Tidings" (*Neue Zeitungen*)
or "Relations" that still retained their popularity at the time, early newspapers did not treat a single extraordinary event but rather ranged over a
breadth of incidents recently reported in a geographical catchment, and
supplemented these stories with news from abroad. Despite its greater
breadth of subject matter, the early newspaper often expressed a similar taste for sensation. But alongside accounts of recent miracles, storms,
epidemics, gruesome murders, and so forth, they also presented news
of the court and accounts of other events that were significant to their
bourgeois readership. They pointed, in other words, to a rising political
consciousness and the growth of a sense of the interconnectedness of
developments. As they spread throughout northern Europe and matured
in the later seventeenth and early eighteenth centuries, these periodicals
came to be judged by the quality, depth, and extent of the information
they presented, although a taste for the exceptional still lingered.

By 1710, London was quickly becoming Europe's newspaper capital,
although the marketplace of print in the city remained extremely variegated and complex, with cheap broadsides, chapbooks, and a range of
other newsprint publications continuing to appear alongside the regularly published journals of the day. London's first periodic paper, the
London Gazette had, in fact, arrived rather late on the scene by continental European standards, appearing only in 1665. But during the reign of
Queen Anne, the city's papers multiplied quickly as a result of the party
politics of the era and because of the many *causes célèbres* that were soon
being exploited in the capital's papers. As readers began to evidence a
taste for this kind of news, the periodic newspaper of the capital took on
a prominent role in the city's coffee houses and bookshops, a role that it
was not to relinquish during the remainder of the eighteenth century. The
relationships that developed, in other words, between all these sources of
information dissemination—coffee house, newspapers, and bookshops
especially—became synergistic, with patrons visiting particular coffee
houses so that they might read and discuss the contents of the latest editions with their associates. London's coffee houses thus ranked among
the city's most important subscribers to the new journals, and as a conse-

quence, booksellers in and around London came to rely on the newspapers as an important outlet for advertising their latest books.[46]

One of the most visible components of the "information society" that was emerging in the English capital at the time was its lingering taste for the exceptional, an exceptional that might still be given religious and providential interpretations on the one hand, or which might just point up the infinite complexity and riddles that were to be solved in the world that lay outside the journals' boundaries. In the milieu that surrounded London's coffee house and the newspaper, monstrous prodigies, mineral oddities, and an incredibly diverse range of bizarre sensations continued to play a role on the popular entertainment scene, and private showings of these peculiarities were favorite pastimes in the drawing rooms of the rich. Among the many prodigies displayed in London in the early eighteenth century were hermaphrodites; Siamese twins; a "porcupine" boy covered with quills; "a boneless girl, eighteen inches tall, who had seven sets of teeth"; and a "Dutch boy who was born with the words 'Deus meus' inscribed on his right iris [and] 'Elohim' (in Hebrew characters) on his left."[47]

One of the most famous of the many strange figures to appear on the London scene at the time was the feral child, "Peter, the Wild Boy," a boy that turned up in the forests outside the Saxon town of Hameln in 1724, and who, it was alleged, had been raised by bears. Brought to England upon the orders of George I a year later, he became the subject of numerous newspaper accounts, broadsides, and pamphlets, even as he was soon being displayed at royal soirées and private showings throughout the capital. Some continued to see in Peter's appearance a portent, a divine condemnation of the ills of extravagance and corruption that surrounded

---

[46] Stephen Botein, Jack R. Censer, and Harriet Ritvo, "The Periodical Press in Eighteenth-Century English and French Society: A Cross-Cultural Approach," *Comparative Studies in Society and History* 23, no. 3 (July 1981), 464–90.

[47] Dennis Todd, *Imagining Monsters: Miscreations of the Self in Eighteenth-Century England* (Chicago, 1995), p. 5; Richard F. Altick, *The Shows of London* (Cambridge, Mass., 1978); and Aline Mackenzie Taylor, "Sights and Monsters and Gulliver's Voyage to Brobdingnag," *Tulane Studies in English* 7 (1957), 29–82.

the Hanoverian court.[48] Others found in his life, and in his continuing inability to acquire language, lessons that might be learned about the formative role of education and culture. And still others celebrated the young man, who continued to live in England for almost a half-century following his arrival, as noble savage. For Daniel Defoe, Jonathan Swift, and a host of other British luminaries who commented upon the child as he became toast of the town, Peter's life presented a puzzle to be solved, rather than a portent that might illuminate the course of future political developments. Yet even Defoe spent much of his efforts in pondering the precise character of Peter's soul: how, he wondered, was Peter able to speak to God and tend to the demands of his salvation without language? Was his nature without sin because he lacked the words to form intent? In the strange case of the feral Wild Boy, then, the old order of a nature that was sympathetic to human virtue and impiety came squarely face-to-face with the developing philosophical debates of the early Enlightenment.

While the appetite for freaks and monsters ran high, a fashion for persons who were born whole but who alleged to have experience of the most exotic surroundings became a defining feature of the age, too. From the arrival of the so-called Native of Formosa in England in 1703 until the discovery of Princess Caraboo of Javasu more than a century later in 1817, British society came to entertain the performances of a long line of fraudulent "exotics," figures that captivated society for a time, before being unmasked as tricksters. By the end of the eighteenth century, this trend had even given rise to its own term, the "hoax," a word coined from "hocus pocus" that encapsulated both the ineluctable fascination such tricksters exercised on their audiences and the skillful lies that lay at the heart of their deceptions. The allure these exotics had for English society was enormous, and reveals readers craving for "parts unknown." Yet even this fascination continued to partake of the longstanding desire to see in the natural order signs of God's providence, and here the brilliant performances of the Native of Formosa blazed a trail that numerous other charlatans and fakes were to follow. The Native's fascinating story, made

---

[48] Julia V. Douthwaite, "Homus Ferus: Between Monsters and Model," *Eighteenth-Century Life* 21, no. 2 (1997), 176–202, esp. pp. 179–81; Douthwaite, *The Wild Girl, Natural Man, and the Monster: Dangerous Experiments in the Age of Enlightenment* (Chicago, 2002); and Michael Newton, *Savage Girls and Wild Boys* (London, 2002).

up of numerous deftly crafted lies, has never been completely unraveled to this day.

The story began in 1700, when the Native, who was, in truth it seems, a Frenchman, enlisted in the army in Germany. Sometime soon afterward he began to impersonate a Japanese man, who could all the same speak fluent Latin. When posted to Holland, his prodigious feats and strange and exotic stories came to the attention of the Scottish chaplain William Innes. Innes quickly recognized that the man was a fraud when he asked him to translate Cicero into Japanese, but he soon became his accomplice in pawning off the deception on London society. Innes advised the man to refashion himself as a native of Formosa, an island society even less well known than Japan in England at the time, and when the pair arrived in London, Innes told the city's Bishop that he had successfully converted the man to Christianity. With his new Christian name, George Psalmanazar, the Native soon became a marvel on the capital's social scene, as men and women flocked to observe his strange customs. Psalmanazar slept sitting upright with lights burning; he ate raw meat that was heavily spiced; and in the history he wrote about his country and published in 1704, he spun a fascinating yarn about the bizarre customs of his island nation. Each year, the natives of his land were forced to sacrifice 18,000 boys to satisfy their gods' appetite for blood, his countrymen practiced polygamy, and they even performed their capital punishments by hanging men upside down and shooting arrows at them. In this vein, Psalmanazar kept English society entertained for several years and was even awarded a chair at Oxford as a translator and teacher of Formosan literature. Still questions inevitably began to arise. The Native was blonde, blue-eyed, and fair-skinned. Weren't Asians of a different complexion? Psalmanazar dismissed such charges by explaining that natives of his class kept their fair hair and skin because they were constantly shielded from the sun. The probing gaze did not subside, however, and the pressure upon the Native increased, especially when the French Jesuit Jean de Fontaney, a former missionary to China, published his rejoinder to the man's extraordinary claims and Psalmanazar was called before the Royal Society to answer charges. His response—that Fontaney was a Jesuit and that his statements therefore could not be trusted—dispelled the doubts of most members, and other more critical members such as William Halley came to be taken in by the even more complex lies that Psalmanazar spun to cover up his deception. In 1706, though, the Native of Formosa supposedly underwent a genuine conversion experience, and he soon revealed his trickery. After reforming his ways, he continued to live as an English subject, scraping by as a Grub Street translator and literary hack until the time of his death in 1763. During his long life, he eventually made the acquaintance of Samuel Johnson, who seems to have admired the mockery that Psalmanazar's great deception had made of his countrymen's credulity.[49]

Even in his posthumously published memoir, Psalmanazar refused to reveal his precise identity, and thus his identity has remained a mystery.[50] In his brief career as a London *cause célèbre* can certainly be gleaned the early glimmers of Orientalism, that fascination that was to give birth to many full blown racial and cultural theories in the nineteenth century about the differences between East and West. But Psalmanazar could already play upon the appetite for knowledge of the Other that was such a potent force in his own day, transforming his stories into a kind of performative art that captivated the "newsy" world of eighteenth-century London. The strange narratives the fraudulent Native constructed were avidly consumed at the time because they fit neatly within the growing empirical and environmental concerns of the seventeenth and early eighteenth centuries and into the attempt of the age to construct a verifiable, faithful portrait of the world through "eyewitness" accounts. In viewing Psalmanazar's story, in other words, we stand at a crucial juncture between the persistence of textual truth and the development of a more vital empiricism. His fantastic accounts were credible to many who consumed them because they were filled with the very same kind of seemingly faithful "eyewitness" details that readers had long craved. Like the promoters of sensational pulp journalism of the day, he filled his work with just the kind of information that an increasingly outward-looking, cosmopolitan, and commercial world desired. He even created out of whole cloth his own "Formosan" alphabet and a complete dictionary

---

[49] Jack Lynch, "Orientalism as Performance Art: The Strange Case of George Psalmanazar," paper delivered at the CUNY English Literature Seminar on January 29, 1999; Michael Keevak, *The Pretended Asian* (Detroit, 2004); Richard M. Swederski, *The False Formosan: George Psalmanazar and the Eighteenth-Century Experiment of Identity* (San Francisco, 1991); and Frederic J. Foley, *The Great Formosan Impostor* (Rome, 1968).

[50] *Memoirs of ****. Commonly known by the name of George Psalmanazar; a reputed native of Formosa* (London, 1765).

of the language, tools that he used to instruct his Oxford students in a completely concocted fiction for a time before he revealed his trickery. Yet the world that he fashioned in his narrative *Description of Formosa* (1704) seemed credible to many readers because it fit with the knowledge they had already gleaned of the world from other textual traditions.[51] Psalmanazar, to be sure, had cobbled that environment together out of the Utopian literature and travel accounts of the previous two hundred years. He set his imagined Chinese society on a far-off island similar to More's *Utopia* and then proceeded to construct for it a culture out of the bits and pieces that he knew about the Aztecs and Caribs of the New World. His accounts of his people's cannibalism seemed credible enough to his readers because they fit with his audience's understanding of what native peoples were like. The brilliant work of fictitious history and anthropology that he fashioned thus peopled this distant corner of the world with a strange people that had all the attributes long supposed of the "monstrous races": cannibalism, human sacrifice, and untold cruelty. Thus his vision fit with longstanding teratological and moral concerns, but his message was even more expertly modulated than this, for in the numerous jabs that he made in his work against Roman Catholicism and the Jesuits, Psalmanazar came to celebrate Protestant Christianity as testimony of God's mercy and providence. The Native's account was thus religious polemic, travel journal, and tribute to English exceptionalism all rolled into one.[52]

Clearly, the Native was a brilliant crafter of the good read, a polisher of a narrative so finely tuned to his audience's demands that we can now understand his friend Johnson's statement that the onetime fraudulent Formosan was "the best man he had ever known." Accounts like his were clearly the stuff of which London's newspapers were being crafted at the time. Yet the danger that lurked in their very falsity was that they might render the developing journalism of the time altogether irrelevant, a commercial enterprise destined to failure because readers might place no trust in the new medium's information. Thus, in the wake of the revelation that George Psalmanazar's story was nothing more than brilliant

---

[51] George Psalmanazar, *An Historical and Geographical Description of Formosa* (London, 1704).

[52] Frank Lestringant, "Travels in Eucharistia: Formosa and Ireland from George Psalmanaazar to Jonathan Swift," *Yale French Studies* 86 (1994), 109–25.

fiction, we find the many famous newspaper men of the London journal-istic world—figures as diverse as Richard Steele, Jonathan Swift, Daniel Defoe, and Joseph Addison among them—applying larger doses of skepticism in their gazettes, even as they simultaneously played upon the widespread taste for the extraordinary to craft numerous satires that poked fun at their countrymen's credulity. From the publication of Swift's own concocted prophecies as *A Vindication of Isaac Bickerstaff* (1709) through the same author's hilariously satirical white paper about a government study to raise Irish children for food, *A Modest Proposal* (1729), London's journalists saw their job, in part, as training readers to separate the wheat of truth from the chaff of fiction. Their satires, in other words, were the obverse side of their attempts to establish a press based upon credible news that was confirmed by men and women above reproach.

But searching for the "finger of God" still proved tempting to contemporaries, and despite the efforts of debunking journalists, controversies continued to erupt concerning the credibility of the "news." In this way the very drama that surrounded the establishing of empirical truth could become the raw material itself for journalists' fodder. In the famous case of Mary Toft, for instance, London's journalistic world entertained the capital's readers for several months with debates concerning this downtrodden woman's strange offspring. In October of 1726, Toft had been delivered of parts of a rabbit in the Surrey village of Godalming, and when news of her strange offspring soon came to the knowledge of the court, the Surgeon and Anatomist to the Royal Household, Nathanael St. André, traveled to inspect her.[53] Just as in the days of Agnes Bowker's deception, Hanoverian society had of late witnessed an increase in prophecies about strange events in the natural order, although in the intervening generations since that first deception, the promoters of portents and other signs were now far more definite in aiming their prophetic pronouncements at the halls of power. In place of erstwhile observations that natural wonders pointed to unnamed but "coming changes" in the worldly regiment, the prodigies and portents of the 1720s were now openly touted as revealing the corruption and decadence that surrounded King George I.[54]

---

[53] The narrative that follows is indebted to Dennis Todd, *Imagining Monsters*, pp. 1–37.

[54] Douthwaite, "Homus Ferus."

St. André's actions in seeking out the young, poverty-stricken woman seem to have been motivated less by his zeal to put such allegations to rest than they were by his own desires for professional advancement and self-promotion. After journeying to the young woman's birthing bed and retrieving bits and pieces of her strange offspring to study in his London laboratory, he pronounced the incident a legitimate monstrous birth, a verdict that soon set off a series of "medical examinations" by other figures in the realm. The parts that St. André found upon arriving in Surrey were, to be sure, from a rabbit, but his own investigations and those of others soon pointed to certain anomalies in identifying Toft's offspring as a monster. First of all, Mary Toft never seemed to produce any afterbirth or umbilical cord after her births. Then, the lungs of one of her rabbit babies had been shown to have drawn breath, a sure sign that it had been outside the womb before its alleged delivery. And finally, pellets had been found in one of the animal's intestines. Against the empirical evidence that these observations offered, St. André pronounced the woman's "monstrous birth" genuine, insisting that since the very birth was "preternatural" such criticisms, in fact, were invalid. As a "monstrous birth," in other words, normal standards of proof did not apply. Yet questions persisted, and King George I dispatched his household's private surgeon, Cyriacus Ahlers, to inspect Toft, who proved far less amenable to the young woman's deception. The dispute that quickly erupted between supporters of St. André's and Ahlers' conflicting judgments of the "miracle" were soon being waged in London's newspapers, where headlines such as "Rabbits or No Rabbits" expressed the deadlock that had developed between London's learned anatomists and medical authorities on the matter.

All the while, though, Mary Toft's monstrous progeny kept multiplying. In the days after her first birth she had been moved from her own village to the home of her surgeon John Howard in Guildford, and by the end of November, her "rabbit babies" numbered seventeen. On the 29th of that month, Nathanael St. André had her brought from Guildford to London, hoping to use her physical presence in the city to convince the town's medical establishment once and for all of the truth of his claims. He set her up in a rented room in the capital and invited the city's most influential male midwives, surgeons, and physicians to attend her, warning them that another delivery was imminent. In the days that followed the woman's room became choked with crowds, not only of medical men, but also of aristocrats and people of lower rank who flocked to witness the promised "monstrous birth." The street outside was also filled with a throng of onlookers, craning to get a glimpse of the woman. No birth, though, ever occurred. Surrounded by crowds, Mary Toft lacked the privacy to secret the animal parts into her vagina, as she had been doing all along. By this time, though, the serious fevers and convulsive fits that she was suffering as a result of this very behavior were all the same adding to the mood of tense expectancy that existed in Toft's make-shift birthing chamber. But despite the skepticism that grew when no more rabbits appeared, London's distinguished doctors could still not agree on whether the strange offspring the woman had already born were authentic. The evidence that came to incriminate Toft arrived not from the crowds of disagreeing medical authorities that surrounded her but from other quarters. In Surrey, the justice of the peace for Godalming had begun to ask questions of Mary Toft's neighbors and had found that her husband had all the while been buying up rabbits on the local market to feed his wife's deception. Soon the porter in the London building where Toft had been lodging also confessed that she had tried to cajole him into finding her a rabbit. Presented with such evidence of a fraud, one doctor now demanded she submit herself to surgical examination for the sake of science. Toft demurred, and instead confessed. She was imprisoned for a time, but soon released without a sentence. Although the scorn that was heaped upon her was enormous, it paled in comparison to what soon was poured upon the medical crowd that had rushed to her side, and which had been taken in for several months in varying degrees by her deception. Under questioning, Toft admitted that she had embarked upon her course to alleviate her family's poverty, and as with all such underdogs, the Rabbit of Godalming's trickery came to mean less to the audiences that consumed the tale than did the stupidity and credulity of the so-called experts. Mary Toft, in other words, had put one over on the establishment, and in the months that followed London's papers were to have a field day poking fun at the learned doctors for their inability to distinguish fact from fiction.

The "strange but true" case of Mary Toft admits, like that of Agnes Bowker a century and a half before, of many different readings. Historians of science, for example, have long pointed to Toft's fraud for the role that it played in producing reassessments of the learned medical notion of maternal impressions. Toft had explained the strange shapes of her offspring by recourse to this notion, crediting a fright she had received from a rabbit early in her pregnancy with the deformations of the offspring that occurred in her womb. In the months that followed the revelation of her trickery, the physician James Blondel was to publish his *Strength of Imagination in Pregnant Women Examin'd,* the first serious refutation of the notion of maternal impressions to appear in the eighteenth century, and the vigorous debate that it engendered subjected long-held beliefs about the power of a woman's mind to deform her unborn children to more serious scrutiny. Although the potency of maternal impressions as an explanation for birth defects survived into the early nineteenth century, Blondel's attack on the notion engaged a battle that continued to be waged in the years that followed. Eventually, the importance of the idea of maternal impressions began to shrink and survived into modern times, only as a folkloric, rather than as high science. In a recent book, Dennis Todd contends that the source of the very real anxieties that Mary Toft's rabbit babies produced lay not so much in their medical meaning but in the very epistemological dilemmas that the power of the imagination presented to the learned, literary figures of the age, men like Defoe, Swift, and Pope, who helped to feed the controversy with their satires about the event in the days and months that followed the unearthing of the deceit. In a world in which the power of the imagination was strong enough to deform, Todd has argued, the very stability of the mind to distinguish fact and fiction might be thrown into doubt and might threaten to distort every sense of reality. Toft's monstrous deceit was thus a direct challenge to these early Enlightenment thinkers' attempts to separate the act of literary production on the one hand from a world of faithfully recorded objective journalistic realities on the other.[55]

But still another source for the controversy that continued to boil concerning Mary Toft in the later 1720s lay in the longstanding tension this article has explored between two competing visions of the natural order. In Mary Toft's case can be seen the lingering tensions that existed in Europe between the attempt to present an observably accurate picture of nature and its disorders and the part that a moralized universe had long played in underpinning claims of political order and Christian theodicy. Among the many editorials, letters, and other communications printed in London's newspapers in the weeks that followed the Toft affair, an editorial from the Tory-sympathizing *Craftsman* in 1727 is particularly

---

[55] Todd, *Imagining Monsters,* see esp. chaps. 4–6.

telling in this regard. Mary Toft's case, the writer warned, presented an enormous danger to the public, a danger far greater than mere fraud, for her deception might undermine the age-old role that prodigies, portents, and omens had long played as a warning to the body politic. As in the days preceding the "Assassination of Julius Caesar and the great Duke of Buckingham," contemporary times were witnessing a slew of visual testimonies to the age's "notorious Infidelity and Libertinism. . . . Indeed the last year," the editorialist continued, "may be justly esteem'd a Year of wonders, not inferior to any recorded in History. . . . We have seen black Swans, Dogs, and dancing Elephants in abundance, which would have employed all the attention of ancient Oracles to Explain. . . . "[56] Mary Toft's deceit assaulted such venerable truths, and held out the possibility that in the future men and women might ignore the messages that nature and a beneficent Deity might send.

In many ways the *Craftsman's* zeal proved to be only too prescient. Cases of strange births continued to be reported in England during the remainder of the eighteenth and nineteenth centuries, but they never again managed to bubble up to be considered as significant to the body politic as Toft's case had been. Elsewhere in Europe, the battle against credulity similar to that evidenced in the Toft affair was to proceed apace in the eighteenth century, too. The extraordinary story of the Rabbit Woman and the reception and eventual dénouement of that story remind us of the long history by which the public world of political journalism came to be divested of the remaining vestiges of purposeful nature that had played such an important role in discussions of the body politic since the late Renaissance. That demystification of the public sphere had proceeded both from a steadily expanded curiosity that desired to discover a faithful, empirical portrait of the world. But it had also followed as a consequence from "fits and starts" like Agnes Bowker's cat or Mary Toft's rabbits. In the decades after the exposing of Toft, for example, no serious English intellectual ever came again to be drawn into the promotion of such a case, although a generation later the "Rabbit Woman of Godalming" was still prompting occasional comment. By then, Mary Toft had retired to a quiet life in her village, a life that seems only to have been interrupted once, when she was made to answer charges in 1740 that she had received stolen goods. Otherwise, she lived an unremarkable life,

---

[56] Editorial, *The Craftsman* (London, April 24–28, 1727).

occasionally being called to make an evening appearance as a conversation piece in the country house that the Duke of Richmond maintained in her village. Yet while the real Mary Toft faded from view, the role that her journalistic persona played in the mentality of the developing Enlightenment is perhaps nowhere better summarized than in William Hogarth's famous print of 1762, "Credulity, Superstition, and Fanaticism." Set inside a Methodist meeting house, a minister is shown ranting from his pulpit to a crowd of swooning enthusiasts, while around him swirl demons and even a witch flying on a broom. Below, prominently displayed in the print's left foreground, is the figure of Mary Toft, writhing in the pains of labor, with rabbits scurrying out from under her petticoats. Although Hogarth's print was soon controversial for the vitriol with which it attacked the Methodists, few now found any defense for the unfortunate "Rabbit Woman of Godalming." Her inclusion there was a reminder to the Augustan audience that a taste for marvels could find no place in the detached and less emotional body politic Hogarth longed might soon come to fruition. Her place, in other words, lay in the meeting house, and not the marketplace.

THE STATE OF THE SOUL AND THE SOUL OF THE STATE: RECONCILIATION IN THE TWO PARTS OF SHAKESPEARE'S *HENRY IV*

Charles R. Forker
Indiana University, Bloomington

I

THE THEME OF reconciliation pervades all three of the categories into which the First Folio divides Shakespeare's plays. Obviously, the comedies and tragedies figure prominently. In the first group, who can forget the scene of *Measure for Measure* in which Isabella pleads so eloquently for the forgiveness of her wronger or the miraculous reunion of Hermione and Leontes at the conclusion of *The Winter's Tale*? No less memorable among the tragedies is the powerful moment in *Julius Caesar* when Brutus and Cassius, friends of long standing, compose their painful quarrel with a handclasp and (in some productions) an embrace,[1] or in *King Lear* when the stricken monarch kneels in humility before Cordelia.

---

[1] James Blendick (Brutus) and Richard Bauer (Cassius) "embraced and wept together" in a 1974 production at the Arena Stage in Washington, D.C.; see B. S. Field, Jr., *Shakespeare's "Julius Caesar": A Production Collection; Comments by Eighteen Actors and Directors in Seven Different Productions, Illustrated with 101 Photographs* (Chicago, 1980), p. 121.

Studies in Medieval and Renaissance History, 3rd Series, Vol. 4 (2007)

Among the histories the theme of reconciliation comes to the fore in the two parts of *Henry IV*, powerfully salient in the twin scenes in which Prince Hal wins over his disapproving and suspicious father. The dual father-and-son episodes, positioned at crucial points in the structure of each drama, claim a special place in popular memory, perhaps because, in the first instance, Shakespeare parodies the serious confrontation in advance by giving us a Boar's Head version (the "play extempore" acted by Falstaff and the Prince), and, in the second case, by making the death-bed reconciliation prelusory to the rejection of the fat knight. The comedies and tragedies tend to handle forgiveness with a certain moral, even theological, clarity, since, however secular or pessimistic the context may be, the assumptions of a Christian *Weltanschauung* color the action and dialogue, even if, as in *Lear*, they may have to compete with more agnostic or nihilistic attitudes. When characters in these dramas experience reconciliation, wrongs are acknowledged, reparation, if possible, is implied, and healing takes place in an ethos of deepened consciousness, of renewed love, and even, in some cases, of spiritual grace. In the chronicle plays, however, the issue becomes more complex. Concerning rulers and commonwealths, reconciliation in the histories touches individuals and nations alike—kings and princes as well as their subjects. The state of the individual soul therefore becomes inextricably entwined with the soul of the state.

The intent of the present essay is to reexamine in fresh detail the complementary reconciliation episodes of the Henry IV plays and to argue that as Shakespeare evolved as a dramatist of chronicle history, he increasingly mingled the moral and theological aspects of personal forgiveness with dynastic and political issues that significantly complicate audience response. In the course of the discussion we shall have occasion to contrast *1* and *2 Henry IV* with *Richard III* to illustrate a shift that appears to have occurred in Shakespeare's treatment of the theme as he moved from the first to the second historical tetralogy.

It would have been unthinkable for any Elizabethan to treat reconciliation in depth without drawing, unconsciously or otherwise, upon the biblical, homiletic, and liturgical texts with which the culture had long been impregnated. The parable of the Prodigal Son (Luke 15:11–32), thrice alluded to in the Henry IV plays as well as frequently elsewhere in Shakespeare,[2] was probably the most familiar example of father-son reconciliation in the Bible and is clearly a leitmotif of the two chronicle dramas. The chief lesson of the parable, as everyone knows, is that even those who fall furthest from divine grace may be lavishly restored to it if they "come to themselves" (to use Luke's idiom) and, acknowledging their unworthiness, confess that they "have sinned against heaven and before" God.[3] The questionable relevance of the parable to Prince Hal's career may have been augmented tangentially in the dramatist's mind by its scriptural context—Jesus responding to scribes and Pharisees who object to his "receiv[ing] sinners, and eat[ing] with them" (Luke 15:2), disreputable types such as Falstaff and the Eastcheap ragtag. In addition, a theoretical link between the loving father of the parable and Shakespeare's Henry IV could be found in the common analogy between fathers as rulers over families and monarchs as heads of state. Thus Thomas Bilson in 1585, drawing obviously upon the concept of the king's two bodies,[4] could regard the "priuate familie" with its patrimonial hierarchy as "both a part and a paterne of the common-wealth."[5] The Church reinforced the importance of the Prodigal's acknowledgement of sin by incorporating the relevant sentence from St. Luke into the liturgies for

---

[2] See *1 Henry IV*, 3.3.79–80, 4.2.33–35; *2 Henry IV*, 2.1.144–45; see also *The Comedy of Errors*, 4.3.19; *The Merry Wives of Windsor*, 4.5.8; *The Merchant of Venice*, 2.6.14–17, 3.1.45; *The Winter's Tale*, 4.3.97. Unless otherwise noted, the text of Shakespeare used throughout is *The Riverside Shakespeare*, ed. G. Blakemore Evans (Boston, 1974).

[3] "Then he came to him selfe, and said, Howe manie hired servaunts at my Fathers have bread ynough, and I dye for hunger? I will rise and go to my father, and say unto hym, Father I have sinned against heaven, and before thee. And am no more worthie to be called thy sonne . . ." (Luke 15:17–19; Geneva version). Although Luke does not use the phrase "prodigal son," it became current because the Geneva translation featured it as a marginal heading. Future citations are to the Geneva Bible, the translation Shakespeare seems principally to have relied upon in the late 1590s.

[4] The classic discussion of this concept is Ernst H. Kantorowicz's important study, *The King's Two Bodies: A Study in Mediaeval Political Theology* (Princeton, 1957).

[5] Bilson, *The True Difference between Christian Subjection and Unchristian Rebellion* (Oxford, 1585), part 2, p. 249.

Matins and Evensong and by citing the parable in *An Homilie . . . of True Reconciliation unto God.*[6]

Even commoner in the consciences and consciousness of Shakespeare's contemporaries was the mandate to reconciliation in the "Our Father": "forgive us our trespasses, as we forgive them that trespass against us." This prayer had to be memorized by every confirmand, was invariably prayed in the Daily Offices as well as in the Baptismal and Eucharistic rites, and was followed in Matthew's gospel by the assurance that those who forgive will be forgiven by their "heavenlie Father" and the warning, "if ye do not forgive men their trespaces, no more wil your Father forgive you . . ." (6:14–15). The New Testament is replete with passages bearing upon reconciliation as a two-fold action—God's forgiveness of man by virtue of the Atonement (Christ's sacrifice on Calvary) and the duty of the already forgiven to imitate their Lord by forgiving each other. A well-known collect from the Sarum missal (a major source for the Anglican Prayer Book) refers to this truth as "the new covenant of reconciliation" established by the "Paschal mystery" of Christ's death and resurrection.[7]

But the *locus classicus* of the doctrine is enshrined in 2nd Corinthians where St. Paul links Christ's reconciling sacrifice for the sins of the world to the reconciling function of apostolic ministry:

> Therefore if anie man be in Christ, let him be a newe creature. Olde things are passed away: beholde, all things are become newe. And all things are of God, which hathe reconciled us unto him self by Jesus Christ, and hathe given unto us the ministerie of reconcilia-tion. For God was in Christ, and reconciled the worlde to him self, not imputing their sinnes unto them, and hathe committed to us the worde of reconciliation. Now then are we ambassadours for Christ: as thogh God did beseche you through us, we praye you in

---

[6] *The Book of Common Prayer, 1559: The Elizabethan Prayer Book*, ed. John E. Booty (Charlottesville, 1976), pp. 49–50; *Certaine Sermons or Homilies Appointed to be Read in Churches In the Time of Queen Elizabeth I*, ed. Mary Ellen Rickey and Thomas B. Stroup, 2 vols. in 1 (Gainesville, Fla., 1968), II, p. 257.

[7] In the *American Prayer Book of 1979* (p. 224), this collect is appointed for use at the Eucharist on the second Sunday of Easter; in the Sarum use it was to be said at Mass on the Friday of Easter week. See Marion J. Hatchett, *Commentary on the American Prayer Book* (New York, 1981), p. 180.

Christs stede, that ye be reconciled to God. For he hathe made him
to be sinne for us which knew no sinne, that we shulde be made the
righteousness of God in him.

(2 Corinthians 5:17–21)

Paul emphasizes that his ministry is a function of his having appropri-
ated God's reconciliation of the world to Himself—an appropriation to
be urged upon all Christians who may thereby be made "the righteousness of God" through the apostle's teaching. Given the Tudor doctrine
of the divinity that hedges kings, monarchs such as Henry IV could by
virtue of their anointing be thought of as models of divine reconciliation,
the quasi-priestly fathers of nations who in some sense mediate Christ's
Atonement not only to their sons and heirs but in a broader sense to the
entire body politic, conceived of as the body of Christ.

In the first play of Shakespeare's pair, Blunt speaks of King Henry's
"anointed majesty" (*1 Henry IV*, 4.3.40), and in the second, Prince John
refers to his father as God's "substitute" (*2 Henry IV*, 4.2.28). The problem, of course, as the dramatist presents it, is that Bolingbroke, despite
his sacramental anointing, is a usurper and a murderer who apparently
dies in a state of unabsolved sin, and whose reconciliation with Prince
Hal is rooted not in his righteous appropriation of Christ's sacrifice but
in his hope that he can pass on his ill-gotten crown with less "soil" (*2
Henry IV*, 4.5.189) than that by which it was achieved. Thus the play opens
up a rift between the sacral mysterium of Henry's political body and the
diseased corruption and moral frailty of his human one. The royal soul
has been sundered in some sense from the nation's soul, and whatever
grace may attend the King's deathbed reconciliation with his son is con-
taminated by the guilt of usurpation and the retrospect of a reign plagued
by the betrayal of former friends and the rebellion of subjects (including
an archbishop). Henry's physical debility has spread symbolically to his
"poor kingdom, sick with civil blows" (*2 Henry IV*, 4.5.133).

Reconciliation in its spiritual dimension inevitably implied confession. *The Elizabethan Prayer Book* specified that no one should "presume"
to receive Holy Communion (the mark of salvific unity between God and
man) "until he have openly declared himself to have truly repented and
amended his former naughty life," the priest being instructed to refuse
the Blessed Sacrament to "those betwixt whom he preceiveth malice and

hatred . . . until he know them to be reconciled."[8] The Eucharistic rite began with a rehearsal of the Decalogue, leading up (after the Epistle, Gospel, Creed, Offertory, and Prayer for the Whole State of Christ's Church) to an Exhortation to examine the conscience strictly and to a General Confession covering all transgressions. It was recited kneeling and preceded by an invitation to "earnestly repent," to "be in love and charity with [one's] neighbors," and to "intend to lead a new life, following the commandments of God."[9] After the bread and wine were consecrated and before their reception, the celebrant knelt before the "holy mysteries," praying on behalf of the congregation "that our sinful bodies may be made clean by [Christ's] body, and our souls washed through his most precious blood, and that we may evermore dwell in him, and he in us."[10] Shakespeare gives a sense of the tradition in *Richard II* where Mowbray acknowledges his former design upon Gaunt's life, a "trespass that doth vex my grieved soul": "But ere I last receiv'd the sacrament / I did confess it, and exactly begg'd / Your Grace's pardon, and I hope I had it" (1.1.138–41).

In addition to public confession at the Eucharist, Matins, and Evensong, private auricular confession, although not obligatory, was also enjoined, especially in time of sickness or of imminent death. The standard teaching among Anglicans regarding auricular confession is summed up in the famous statement (sometimes attributed to Queen Elizabeth herself) that "all may; none must: some should." Richard Hooker, the Thomas Aquinas of the Anglican settlement, defended auricular confession and was himself privately confessed on his deathbed.[11] A Prayer Book rubric in the Order for the Visitation of the Sick provided for a person to "make a special confession, if he feel his conscience troubled with any weighty matter" after which "the priest shall absolve him" by

---

[8] *Prayer Book*, ed. Booty, p. 247.

[9] Ibid., p. 259.

[10] Ibid., pp. 265, 263.

[11] See Izaak Walton, *The Life of Mr. Richard Hooker*, in *The Lives of John Donne, Sir Henry Wotton, Richard Hooker, George Herbert, and Robert Sanderson*, ed. George Saintsbury (London, 1927), p. 224. Like Hooker, Bishop Lancelot Andrewes was a strong believer in auricular confession; see Lee W. Gibbs, "Richard Hooker and Lancelot Andrewes on Priestly Absolution," in *Richard Hooker and the Construction of Christian Community*, ed. Arthur Stephen McGrade (Tempe, Ariz., 1997), pp. 261–74.

the sacerdotal authority derived from a passage in John's gospel in which Jesus in a post-Resurrection appearance breathed the Holy Spirit into His disciples, endowing them with the power to remit sins in His name.[12] An aspect of this rite with relevance to the deathbed scene in *2 Henry IV* is its speculation on the possible cause of illness in a particular case, "whether it be to try [the sufferer's] patience for the example of other[s]" or "be sent unto [him] to correct and amend in [him] whatsoever doth offend the eyes of our heavenly Father."[13]

According to rumors in the early fifteenth century, Henry IV was stricken with leprosy (Holinshed calls it "apoplexie")[14] in punishment either for his murder of Richard II or for his beheading of the holy, though rebellious, Archbishop of York.[15] But Shakespeare relates the King's illness to Prince Hal's defection from duty, to his supposed hostility to his father, and finally to the crown itself, which has "fed upon" and finally "eat[en its] bearer up" (*2 Henry IV*, 4.5.159–64). King Henry insinuates that God has used the wayward prince as a "revengement" and "scourge" to "punish [his] mistreadings" (*1 Henry IV*, 3.2.7–11). Later he insists that Harry's untimely removal of the crown from its pillow "conjoins with [his] disease," a "sickness" that has become the Prince's "friend" because it will hasten Henry V's accession (*2 Henry IV*, 4.5.63, 81). Henry IV calls for his sons during his final hours, but no confessor is present. He takes some comfort that his dying in a chamber named Jerusalem fulfills a prophecy that he should expire in the Holy Land, the destination of his unaccomplished crusade, and it may be that the ironic place name, taken from Holinshed, is intended as a figure for the New Jerusalem of his spiritual pilgrimage. Yet he clings to possession of the crown, "snatch'd with boist'rous hand" (4.5.191), at the same time praying, "How I came by the crown, O God forgive" (4.5.218). Perhaps he asks silently with Claudius, his fellow usurper, "May one be pardon'd and retain th' offense?" (*Hamlet*,

---

[12] *Prayer Book*, ed. Booty, p. 303. The passage in John (20:21–23) reads: "as my Father sent me, so send I you. And when he had sayd that, he breathed on them, and said unto them, Receive the holie Gost. Whosoevers sinnes ye remit, they are remitted unto them: and whosevers sinnes ye reteine, they are retained."

[13] *Prayer Book*, ed. Booty, p. 301.

[14] Raphael Holinshed, *The Chronicles of England, Scotland, and Ireland*, 2nd ed., 3 vols. in 2 (London, 1587), III, p. 541. See also Geoffrey Bullough, ed., *Narrative and Dramatic Sources of Shakespeare* (London, 1957–75), IV, p. 277 n. 4.

[15] See E. F. Jacob, *The Fifteenth Century, 1399–1485* (Oxford, 1961), p. 99.

3.3.56). The soteriological aspects of this scene remain, and are meant to remain, problematic, disturbing, ambiguous, perhaps even tragic.

By ancient tradition the reconciliation of a penitent or "shriving" (as Shakespeare normally terms it) was deemed to consist of five parts: examination of the conscience, contrition (together with the resolve to amend one's life), confession to a priest, absolution, and the performance, if practicable, of a symbolic penance. Although the words *shrive* and *shrift* appear regularly in the first historical tetralogy, their absence from *Henry IV* and indeed from the second sequence as a group hints at a new secular trend in the dramatization of history, or at least at a shift away from the traditionally Catholic and Anglican importance of reconciliation as a feature of one's ordinary Christian obligation. Bits of furniture remain from the orthodox belief system with its moral absolutes derived from the quest for salvation. The vocabulary of the miracle plays, the moralities, and the allegorical interludes shows up in the identification of Falstaff with Satan and the medieval Vice (the stage dagger of lath is mentioned), and also in references to characters attended by a good or evil angel, derived from plays utilizing the *psychomachia* such as *The Castle of Perseverance* and Marlowe's *Doctor Faustus*.[16] Textual remnants of Oldcastle, the Lollard martyr, account for elements of anti-Puritan satire that suffuse Falstaff's many references to scripture and his perpetual claims of intended reform. Two references to "amendment of life," a standard *Prayer Book* phrase associated with repentance, appear in the dialogue.[17] As for the Prince, however, the biblical model of the Prodigal, commonly invoked as a parallel, fits Shakespeare's character

---

[16] Cf. "Falstaff, that old white-bearded Sathan" (*1 Henry IV*, 2.4.463); "that reverent Vice, that grey Iniquity, that father ruffian, that vanity in years" (*1 Henry IV*, 2.4.453–54); "a dagger of lath" (*1 Henry IV*, 2.4.137); "good angel" (*1 Henry IV*, 3.3.177–78; *2 Henry IV*, 2.4.335); "ill angel" (*2 Henry IV*, 1.2.164–65).

[17] Prince Hal refers sarcastically to Falstaff's "good amendment of life" (*1 Henry IV*, 1.2.102); Falstaff jeers at Bardolph, "Do thou amend thy face, and I'll amend my life" (*1 Henry IV*, 3.3.24–25). The Geneva Bible uses such language in Matthew 3:8 and 3:11; Luke 15:7; and Acts 3:19, 26:20. *The Prayer Book*, however, is Shakespeare's more likely immediate source; cf. "Amend your lives, for the kingdom of God is at hand" (Morning and Evening Prayer, p. 49); "to amend our lives according to thy holy Word" (The Litany, p. 71); "confess yourselves . . . with full purpose of amendment of life" (Exhortation in Holy Communion, p. 257); "Amend your lives, and be in perfect charity with all men" (Exhortation in Holy Communion, p. 258).

imperfectly because the plays lay such scant emphasis on his sins. "Rather loose than wicked," as Dr. Johnson puts it,[18] Harry is more guilty of negligence and misdemeanors than of soul-endangering turpitude. And from his father's point of view, the Prince's forfeiting respect like Richard II's "Ming[ling] his royalty" and becoming "a companion to the common streets" (*1 Henry IV*, 3.2.63–68) is the prime offense.

The popular myth of Prince Henry reflected in Fabyan's chronicle and in other popular works was of a young man debauched, riotous, and given to "all vyce," who miraculously "became a newe man" at his accession.[19] Traces of this tradition survive in Shakespeare. We hear of Hal's violence, thievery, and wenching in *Richard II* (5.3.9–16); we witness his aggressive appropriation of Falstaff's booty at Gad's Hill in *1 Henry IV* (2.2.101–4); we learn of his assault upon the Lord Chief Justice and subsequent imprisonment in *2 Henry IV* (5.2.80–83); and we have the Archbishop of Canterbury's testimony in *Henry V* that, on becoming king, Hal suddenly "mortified" his former "wildness," embraced his reformation, which came upon him in "a flood," turned scholar of divinity, and allowed "Consideration, like an angel," to "whip . . . th' offending Adam out of him" (1.1.26–33). But, as Dover Wilson points out, Hal's repentance according to Shakespeare is "of the renaissance type, which transforms an idle and wayward prince into an excellent soldier and governor." Hal's sins are "not against God" so much as "against Chivalry, against Justice, against his father, against the interests of the crown," and against "England's political and social stability."[20]

Reconciliation, whether between subjects or between ruler and ruled, becomes a civic and political concern in *Henry IV* more than a religious one. The values suited to the education of a future king were *public* virtues such as valor, chivalry, prudence, justice, fortitude, temperance, courtesy, decorum, and munificence, all of them coalescing ideally in a figure who could balance his devotion to the Church against the imperatives of statecraft. Hal's self-conscious program of reform, famously announced in his early soliloquy, consists not merely in casting off the old man and putting on the new (to paraphrase Ephesians 4:22–25) but in recreating

---

[18] *Johnson on Shakespeare*, ed. Arthur Sherbo (New Haven, 1968), I, p. 523.

[19] Robert Fabyan, *Chronicle* (London, 1559), p. 389.

[20] J. Dover Wilson, *The Fortunes of Falstaff* (Cambridge, 1961), p. 24.

his official identity as a strategy of public relations.[21] Humanist writers
on princely formation such as Erasmus, Bodin, Elyot, Sidney, and Cas-
tiglione seem to have influenced Shakespeare's conception as undoubtedly did the realist Machiavelli, notorious for observing that "a ruler, and
especially a new ruler, cannot always act in ways that are considered good
because, in order to maintain his power, he is often forced to act treacherously, ruthlessly, or inhumanely, and disregard the precepts of religion."
Shakespeare gives us an obvious instance of Machiavelli's *Realpolitik* in
Prince John's duplicity at Gaultree Forest. It would seem that Hal's ice-
tempered brother, of whom the future monarch seems to approve, had
marked, learned, and inwardly digested Machiavelli's doctrine of strategic guile—to wit that rulers who have made their mark on history "have
set little store by keeping their word," honing their skills of cunning and
deceit, and thereby getting "the better of those who have relied on being
trustworthy."[22]

II

Some consideration of Shakespeare's earlier history, *Richard III*, may help
to sharpen our focus on reconciliation in *Henry IV* since interpretation of
the theme in that tragedy offers fewer challenges. Virtue and vice, salvation and policy, religion and anti-religion, naïve trust and Machiavellian
treachery are set starkly in contrast to each other, and the political chaos
of the play is ultimately resolved by the defeat of the tyrant protagonist (a
devil in human form) at the hands of Richmond (a spotless paragon who
can end England's nightmare of fear and bloodshed by reconciling the
Red Rose with the White). On the matter of reconciliation in the religious
sense the episode of Clarence's murder is instructive. Since his assassins
take him by surprise, the Duke has no opportunity to make confession to
a priest, but his eloquently narrated dream reveals the guilty state of his

---

[21] See D. J. Palmer, "Casting off the Old Man: History and St. Paul in *Henry IV*," *Critical Quarterly* 12 (1970), 267–83, especially 268–69. According to Naseeb Shaheen, *1* and *2 Henry IV* contain no fewer than ten allusions to Ephesians; see *Biblical References in Shakespeare's History Plays* (Newark: University of Delaware Press, 1989), p. 238.

[22] Niccolò Machiavelli, *The Prince*, ed. Quentin Skinner and Russell Price (Cambridge, 1988), Chapter 28, pp. 61–62.

soul and shows that, like anyone in his culture and situation, he would have wished to be shriven. Referring to himself as "a Christian faithful man" (*Richard III*, 1.4.4), Clarence dreams prophetically not only of his impending death but also of his damnation—of descending to a Senecan-style underworld, where the ghosts of those he has wronged accuse him terrifyingly. Weighing on his conscience are "perjury" (1.4.50), disloyalty, and murder. His betrayal and stabbing of his father-in-law Warwick are specifically mentioned; but audiences would remember also that this "quicksand of deceit," as Queen Margaret calls him in *3 Henry VI* (5.4.26), had selfishly abandoned his brother Edward IV, and had participated in the brutal slaying of the defenseless Prince of Wales, Lady Anne's husband.[23] Clarence is clearly penitent. Echoing words from the Prayer Book General Confession,[24] he moans,

> Ah, Keeper, Keeper, I have done those things
> (That now give evidence against my soul)
> For Edward's sake, and see how he requites me!
> O God! if my deep pray'rs cannot appease thee,
> But thou wilt be aveng'd on my misdeeds,
> Yet execute thy wrath on me alone!
> O, spare my guiltless wife and my poor children!
> (1.4.66–72)

After the two murderers enter, Shakespeare turns the scene into a morality playlet. While the First Murderer remains thuggishly resolute, his fellow, joking about "the great Judgment Day," responds to the promptings of conscience: it may be safe enough by worldly standards to slay the sleeping Clarence with Gloucester's "warrant" as protection, but no human document can "defend" a man against "be[ing] damn'd" (1.4.103–12). Mention of the promised fee banishes moral qualms for the moment, and the two set about their grisly errand only to be confronted by their waking victim, who appeals not merely to their sense of earthly justice but to their religion:

---

[23] See *3 Henry VI*, 4.1.61–64, 4.2.6–17, 5.1.81–102, and 5.5.32–40.

[24] Cf. "we have done those things which we ought not to have done" (*Prayer Book*, ed. Booty, p. 50).

> I charge you, as you hope to have redemption
> By Christ's dear blood shed for our grievous sins,
> That you depart, and lay no hands on me.
> The deed you undertake is damnable.
>
> (1.4.189–92).

Ignorant of Gloucester's malice, Clarence believes that King Edward, with whom he means to "be reconcil'd" (1.4.179), is the root cause of his danger; but when he reminds his assassins that to "do no murther" is a commandment of "the great King of kings," they respond by charging him with treacherously breaking his vow to defend Henry VI and with "Unrip[ping] the bowels of" Edward Plantagenet, the Lancastrian heir (1.4.195–207). Clarence argues that King Edward is as guilty of the prince's death as he, and thinks naïvely that Richard, his other brother, will intercede for his life. Then the shocking news that Gloucester rather than the King has sent the murderers and that one of his siblings has deceived the other prompts Clarence to recall that his father, speaking "from his soul," had once charged all three sons "to love each other" (1.4.237). Before striking the Duke down, one of the killers urges him to reconcile himself to heaven, a speech that causes Clarence to plead for his life:

> Have you that holy feeling in your souls
> To counsel me to make my peace with God,
> And are you yet to your own souls so blind
> That you will war with God by murd'ring me?
>
> (1.4.250–53)

Just before the fatal blow, the intended assassins move once again to opposite sides of the moral divide—the one toward pity and religious scruple, the other toward determined criminality. The Second Murderer warns Clarence suddenly to "Look behind [him]," but his mate stabs the Duke before he can resist and drags the wounded man offstage to be drowned "in the malmsey-butt," leaving the other to lament his complicity and to wish that, "like Pilate," he could "wash [his] hands" of "grievous murther" (1.4.268–73). A moment later the reluctant Second Murderer refuses to assist his partner in disposing of the corpse, repents "that the Duke is slain" (1.4.278), and refuses to accept money for the deed.

Especially notable about this highly didactic scene is its handling of family division and dynastic contention in a way that asks us to judge politics according to religious absolutes rather than by the more flexible standards of secular statecraft. The episode that immediately follows, in which the dying King Edward prepares to meet his maker by conducting a ceremony of reconciliation among his quarrelsome nobles, reinforces the religious morality of the play. For Edward, death will come as "an embassage / From [his] Redeemer," and he believes that his "soul shall part to heaven" with greater peace if he can make "peace on earth" among his peers (2.1.3–6). The elaborately staged ritual of reconciliation conducted between the parvenu members of the Queen's family and the established aristocracy with more venerable titles is conspicuously hollow, for their resentments and factionalism persist. But Edward wishes to die in a state of grace, having disburdened his conscience. He therefore warns Hastings and Rivers, two of the courtiers who shake hands and who will be sent to the block at a later point in the action, "Take heed you dally not before your king, / Lest He that is the supreme King of kings / Confound your hidden falsehood" (2.1.12–14).

Edward's moralistic words prove ominous. On the day of his execution, Hastings converses complacently and unwittingly with a priest on his way to a meeting at the Tower where he will be suddenly condemned. Buckingham jests with covert irony, "What, talking with a priest, Lord Chamberlain? . . . Your honor hath no shriving work in hand" (3.2.113–15). He adds that Hastings' enemy, Lord Rivers, already facing execution at Pomfret, is the one who now requires a confessor. But later the same day, Richard's henchman Ratcliffe will urge Hastings to "Make a short shrift" (3.4.95), and we will hear the condemned man himself acknowledge, "O now I need the priest that spake to me!" (3.4.87). Later on, Buckingham, Richard III's ambitious abettor in crime, meets his death on All Soul's Day, a day devoted in the liturgical calendar to prayers for the dead and by which he had falsely sworn. Now, facing the axe, he recognizes that the "high All-Seer, which I dallied with, / Hath turn'd my feigned prayer on my head" (5.1.20–21).

Richard III dramatizes political morality in a context of explicit Christian redemption. Men can only forgive and be forgiven by recognizing and trying to put themselves in tune with the Atonement, by acknowledging, in the familiar words of the Eucharist, Christ's "full, perfect, and sufficient sacrifice, oblation, and satisfaction for the sins of

the whole world."[25] The need for reconciliation and often its tragic failure to be realized pervade nearly all the political and social relationships
of *Richard III*—relationships between fellow murderers and between
murderers and their victims, between hostile peers, between widowed
queens, between lords spiritual and temporal, between kings and their
courts, between a usurper and his confederate, between citizens and their
manipulators, and ultimately between the Tudor deliverer and the nation
he frees from bondage. We are invited to view every aspect of the play's
action and characterization through the lens of a Christian metaphysic in
which the reconciliation of man with God and of neighbor with neighbor
is foundational and *a priori*.[26]

III

Henry IV contrasts markedly with *Richard III* in its embodiment of a
more secular and ambiguous ethic. The two reconciliation scenes resist
easy interpretation or consensus because the principal characters, the
King and his son, provoke such differing and mixed responses. In Part
I the interview between the two begins with other lords present, a sign
that the King mistrusts his son; and Henry soon accuses Hal of being his
"nearest and dearest enemy," a would-be traitor ready to "fight against"
him on the rebel side through "fear, / Base inclination, and . . . spleen"

---

[25] *Prayer Book*, ed. Booty, p. 263.

[26] *Richard III* is full of biblical echoes and Christian sentiments, many of them
delivered in mordantly ironic contexts. Rivers, for instance, failing to detect the
feigned piety, compliments Richard on praying for those who have supposedly been
the cause of Clarence's imprisonment: "A virtuous and a Christian-like conclusion —
/ To pray for them that have done scathe to us" (1.3.315–16). Later in the same scene
Richard soliloquizes comically on the thinly disguised hypocrisy of his methods;
after stirring up hatreds among his enemies, he boasts, "I sigh, and, with a piece of
scripture, / Tell them that God bids us do good for evil: / And thus I clothe my naked
villainy / With odd old ends stol'n forth of holy writ, / And seem a saint, when most I
play the devil" (1.3.333–37). The most prominent dramatization of religious humbug
in the play is Richard's appearance on the upper stage, prayer book in hand, between
two bishops—"Two props of virtue for a Christian prince, / To stay him from the fall
of vanity" (3.7.96–97).

(3.2.123–26).[27] In the version of this episode that appears in *The Famous Victories of Henry V* (a known source), the Prince enters his father's chamber *"with a dagger in his hand."* (line 539.1).[28] As for the King's attitude, we have already heard Hotspur speculate that he "loves [his son] not / And would be glad he met with some mischance" (1.3.231–32). Henry's accusation is clearly hyperbolic and unfair—a dramatization of the profound alienation and disappointment the father feels. But while he can tax the Prince with being "degenerate" (3.2.128), he is also capable of shedding tears for him, a "foolish tenderness" (3.2.91) he would never permit himself in public. Hal of course denies treasonable intentions, eventually altering his father's mindset by promising to defeat Hotspur in glorious battle, thus "scour[ing his] shame" (3.2.137). What worries the King most, however, is the bad public image Hal has projected by being "grafted to" "inordinate and low desires," "barren pleasures," "rude society," and "vulgar company"—behavior fatal to "the greatness of [his] blood" (3.2.12–16, 41) and the respect due to royalty. But his comparison of the Prince to Richard II, the "skipping King" who supposedly "profaned" his "great name" by keeping company with "shallow jesters," "cap'ring fools" and "gibing boys" (3.2.60–66), seems entirely to falsify the character of the royal martyr, at least as Shakespeare had recently presented him on the boards.

The painful tensions and misunderstandings that characterize this colloquy are exacerbated by evasiveness and indirection on both sides. The Prince kneels to his father, begging "pardon on my true submission," but his confession of "some things" wherein he had "faulty wand'red and irregular" is vaguely unspecific. Moreover he partly excuses his "offenses" by suggesting that flatterers and "base newsmongers" have exaggerated or misrepresented them for political advantage (3.2.19–28). For his part, the King also is at pains to minimize guilt, referring nebulously to "some

---

[27] Holinshed reports that enemies of Prince Henry at court "brought no small suspicion into the kings head, least his sonne would presume to usurpe the crowne" (III, p. 538).

[28] See Bullough, IV, p. 315. Cf. the King's words to Prince Hal in *2 Henry IV*: "Thou hid'st a thousand daggers in thy thoughts, / Whom thou hast whetted on thy stony heart / To stab at half an hour of my life" (4.5.106–08). In Holinshed the Prince clears himself of such suspicion by offering his dagger to the King and inviting him to slay him, not "wish[ing] to liue one daie with his displeasure" (III, p. 539).

displeasing service I have done" and to his usurpation as unnamed "mis-treadings" (3.2.5–11). Clearly the Prince wishes to rehabilitate himself in his father's eyes. He promises in the future to "Be more myself" (3.2.93), hoping that the King will "salve / The long-grown wounds of [his] intem-perance" (3.2.155–56). But he appears to feel little heartfelt contrition, mainly because he had deliberately cultivated his unseemly associations as part of an educational plan, "stud[ying] his companions" (2 Henry IV, 4.4.68), as Warwick later reports, rather than allowing himself to be cor-rupted by them. We have already learned from his own lips that he had assumed his "loose behavior" as a kind of disguise, "mak[ing his] offense a skill" so that "reformation," when it came," would "show more goodly and attract more eyes" (1.2.213–16) than if he had never frequented the Boar's Head in the first place. And even while converting his father from the spirit of blame to approval, he makes no vow to break immediately with Falstaff, for whom he will shortly procure a military commission and whom he will allow to steal the credit for slaying Hotspur. As he tells the old reprobate, "I am good friends with my father and may do any thing" (3.3.181–82).

Hal's character in the reconciliation scene needs of course to be set in the broader context of 1 Henry IV as a whole. We must balance Hotspur's dismissive epithet of the "nimble-footed madcap" against Vernon's glow-ing description of the Prince in arms as a "feathered Mercury" horsed upon his "fiery Pegasus" (4.1.95–109). Moreover, Prince Harry's gallantry at Shrewsbury proves him as good as his word—a knight who vindicates himself as a model of chivalry by defeating the rival whom the King had thought the better man and by saving his father from death at the hands of Douglas. Hal acknowledges before the battle that he has been "a truant . . . to chivalry" (5.1.94), and Vernon, whose choric voice carries weight because he is an enemy, cautions Hotspur that the Prince is "much misconstrued in his wantonness" (5.2.68). Rescued by the Prince, King Henry is delighted that his son has "redeem'd [his] lost opinion" (5.4.48) and now treats him as a colleague in war. Thus the prudential and calcu-lating streak in Hal's makeup in no way impugns his heroism, diminishes his patriotism, or lessens our hopes for his future kingship. But a super-lative irony of the play is that the son whom the King so misjudges has inherited his father's chilly expediency, including the view that "nothing can seem foul to those that win" (5.1.8). For Henry IV, as for his heir, right and wrong, loyalty and disloyalty, friendship and enmity, must always be considered in the context of success.

God is invoked four times during the reconciliation scene, and in two cases a casual prayer for forgiveness is involved (3.2.29, 130). Nevertheless, it is clear that Shakespeare portrays emotional reunion between King Henry and his heir as a family and political rapprochement largely free of religious content. No conscious insincerity manifests itself. Feelings on the part of both characters are genuine and deeply felt. But neither the King nor his son can confront moral issues without allowing dynastic self-interest and utility, even perhaps a degree of self-delusion, to complicate their relationship. Henry IV does not forgive Prince Hal because he has himself been forgiven or because he loves him as the Prodigal Son's father loves his lost child. Rather it is because he can now welcome the Prince as a successor and political ally, as a potential foe turned friend, and as an emerging national celebrity, who like himself at Ravenspurgh, has mastered the style of "pluck[ing] allegiance from men's hearts" (3.2.52).

The need for the second reconciliation scene (*2 Henry IV*, 4.5) has usually been explained in terms of Shakespeare's attempt to repeat his earlier success or to stage the completion of the Prince's progress from disobedient wastrel to "the mirror of all Christian kings" (*Henry V*, 2 Prologue, 6).[29] If Part I dramatizes the Prince's education in chivalry, Part II, so the orthodoxy runs, portrays his formation in the virtue of justice. At all events, the second reconciliation is so imbricated in the circumstances of Henry IV's death and in Hal's premature removal of the crown that, dramaturgically speaking, it would have been difficult to avoid. There is some suggestion, nonetheless, that relations between father and son have continued to be psychologically strained and that Harry's earlier pacification of the King remains insecure, especially now that Rumor presides uncertainly over the action and Henry IV is gravely ill.

Hal's supposed closeness to Falstaff in Part II has now dwindled to a single episode in which the Prince and Poins spy on Sir John with his doxy and then embarrass him for making disparaging comments. The Chief

---

[29] As Sherman H. Hawkins points out, "the parallel scenes between Henry and his son are based on distinct episodes in Holinshed"; see "*Henry IV*: The Structural Problem Revisited," *Shakespeare Quarterly* 33 (1982), 289.

Justice speaks truthfully, at least in spirit, when he observes to Falstaff early in the play that "the King hath sever'd" plump Jack from his royal playmate (1.2.203). But separations and alienations are the very stuff of *2 Henry IV*. "Division of . . . amity" (3.1.79), a phrase that the King applies to his falling out with Northumberland, extends to the entire kingdom and points to the failure of reconciliation at every level of society, from quarrels between Falstaff and Mistress Quickly or between him and Pistol to tensions within the Percy family and disunity among the highborn rebels. Falstaff bilks Shallow, his "old acquaintance" (3.2.294), of £1000, and the rebellious Archbishop, who is finally persuaded to "make . . . atonement" with his enemy (4.1.219), rejoices in communal drinking with Lancaster and Westmerland—peacemakers as he thinks—only to be dispatched to summary execution with the nauseating hypocrisy of the statement that "God, and not we, hath safely fought to-day" (4.2.121). Is it too far-fetched to regard the wine drinking, the ironic prelude to Prince John's treachery,[30] as a symbolic inversion of the Eucharist, the rite at which communicants were assumed to "be in love and charity with [their] neighbors"? At a lower stratum Coleville of the Dale, the only character more pusillanimous than Falstaff, yields peacefully to Sir John and is also sent unfeelingly to his doom. Falstaff's wry opinion of Lancaster—a "sober-blooded boy" who never laughs nor "drinks" for pleasure (4.3.87–89)—seems almost to understate his failure to connect with anyone apart from sharers in official policy. Given the prevailing ethos of suspicion and betrayal (Scroop asks, "What trust is in these times?" [1.3.100]), we can hardly be surprised by the King's distorted image of his son as even now a young man given over to "headstrong riot" (4.4.62).

Warwick's defense of Prince Harry is revealing. Hal's disreputable friends, he suggests, are like the vulgarities of a foreign language,[31] learned by the industrious student so that they may be avoided and discarded: "The Prince will in the perfectness of time / Cast off his followers," using "their memory" as a measurement of others, and thereby turn "past evils to advantages" (4.4.74–78). This forecast chimes resonantly with Hal's soliloquy in Part I. There the young man had promised to "falsify men's hopes," that is, their expectations (*1 Henry IV*, 1.2.211), by adopting misconduct as a means of acquiring useful experience, planning

---

[30] The drinking detail comes from Holinshed, III, p. 530.
[31] Warwick's euphemistic term is "immodest word[s]" (*2 Henry IV*, 4.4.70).

to dazzle detractors by unanticipated reform like the sun emerging from a cloud. The pragmatism of this attitude is much in harmony with the King's advice to Thomas of Clarence, namely that he must be careful not to "lose the good advantage of" the future Henry V by behaving coldly or neglectfully. If he is to thrive in the new reign, Thomas must learn to gauge the moods and "temper" of his brother so that he may reap the benefits of his "love," avoid his anger, and "prove a shelter" to friends and relatives who might otherwise feel the sting of regal displeasure. Nor does the dying King omit to remind Thomas that Hal has a softer side—"a tear for pity" and "a hand / Open as day for . . . charity" (4.4.27–42).

Hal, however, has clearly been avoiding his father. Although he feels "much to blame" for "idly . . . profan[ing] the precious time" (2.4.361–62) when he is needed to fight rebels, no chance for family intimacy offers. The Prince rises to the national emergency, but Shakespeare carefully isolates him from the shameful entrapment of the Archbishop. Though his "heart bleeds inwardly" for his father's sickness, Hal masks his grief lest he be thought a "princely hypocrite" (2.2.48–55). And while two of his brothers attend the ailing King, Hal goes hunting at Windsor (4.4.13) or "dines in London" (4.4.51), presumably with Poins and his déclassé companions.

Only after Shakespeare has established an ambience of confusion and mistrust and has shown Hal and the King as complex characters wrestling with love, guilt, obligation, self-interest, grief, incentives to power, the need to control others, and the burdens of state, does he bring us to the emotional climax of Part II—the powerful deathbed confrontation of father and son. The episode begins with a call for quiet and the playing of soft music. As Hal watches at the bedside of his sleeping father, he apostrophizes the crown on its pillow as a "polish'd perturbation" and "golden care" (4.5.23), only gradually coming to believe on the evidence of a feather that the King has just expired. Hal considers his abrupt accession in terms of a two-sided debt. What he owes his father is "tears and heavy sorrows" to be "plenteously" paid by "love . . . and filial tenderness"; what his father owes him as a lineal descendant is the "imperial crown" (4.5.38–41), which he now sets reverently on his own head. Hal's first concern as a monarch mindful of his father's perils is to prevent the crown from being "force[d]" from his possession so that he in turn may pass it on successively (4.5.45). Dynastic stability trumps private grief and national security envelops personal sorrow. The Prince then deserts his father's bedside in the conviction that he must urgently take up the burdens and authority of his new office.

Now the ironies proliferate. Only moments after Hal has achieved a new maturity, the King wakes in alarm to discover that the emblem of his power has disappeared and to assume that dangerous ambition has united with irresponsibility in his adolescent boy. Hal would appear to have "snatch'd" the crown, as the King himself will presently confess to having done when he supplanted Richard II (4.5.191). Henry thinks Hal desires his death, comparing himself to bees that spend their lives collecting honey and then are "murd'red for [their] pains" (4.5.78). Meanwhile the Prince in an adjoining room weeps for the father he believes he has lost forever. Summoned to face the living King, Hal must submit silently to a long rebuke for insensitive and unseemly aspiration together with a prediction of how England under his undisciplined control will revert to savagery and become "a wilderness again" (4.5.136). Almost speechless with sorrow, Hal returns the crown, begs for pardon on his knees, and prays that God, "He that wears the crown immortally" (4.5.143), will long guard his father's hold upon it. And the Prince, who had pretended to be a lover of low company so that he might impress "th' incredulous world" with his purposed "noble change," protests that in this case his sincerity is authentic: "If I do feign, / O, let me in my present wildness die" (4.5.151–54).

At this point Hal waxes eloquent on the paradox of the crown as something both to value and to shun, a precious symbol of honor and rule, yet an "enemy" (4.5.166) that victimizes and destroys its wearer. To be sure, he had removed the royal "garland" (4.5.201), but only to wrestle with it as his father's adversary, taking upon himself the "quarrel of a true inheritor" (4.5.168). He passionately disclaims a relish for "the might" of kingship, begging that God may "for ever keep [the crown] from [his] head" if the penitent who now kneels in "awe and terror" (4.5.173–76) had been motivated by pride or the joy of possession. By shifting responsibility from his own action to the crushing weight of what he had inadvertently stolen, the Prince casts himself in the role of his father's consoler and, at some subterranean level of consciousness, even perhaps of his confessor and absolver. But if Bolingbroke has "Put rancors in the vessel of [his] peace" (*Macbeth*, 3.1.66), it is his heir, not his divine Savior, who assimilates the guilt, for, as we learn from *Henry V,* the hero of Agincourt must continue to pray lest he be held accountable for "the fault /

suggesting that, ideally, a monarch's reconciliation with his realm calls for more encompassing, more charitable, and more communitarian values than can be expressed by a heartless rebuke to misconduct. Our final image of reconciliation in Part II comes to us by means of a negative example.

IV

Moving from the first to the second tetralogy, Shakespeare would appear to have come to terms with a politics divorced from a theological concept of history. Whereas the earlier chronicle plays tend to polarize piety and politics, the later ones depict a world in which the clear demarcation has nearly evaporated. Regime change in *Richard II* with its shift from a king who regards himself as divinely appointed to one who takes and holds power by virtue of human requirements and capacities seems to mark the transition. Although religious sentiment continues to play a role in the Henriad, reconciliation between human beings or between opposing interest groups is no longer seen to depend importantly upon the universal reconciliation wrought by God on behalf of His creation.

Erastianism predominates. The Bishop of Carlisle is instantly arrested for his religious objection to crowning Bolingbroke. Archbishop Scroop can be accused of "counterfeit[ing the] zeal of God" (*2 Henry IV*, 4.2.27) as a pretext for rebellion[36] and, having been tricked into surrender, can then hear his accuser pass off the result as divine protection of the realm. The worldly prelates of *Henry V* authorize an invasion of France to shelter Church property and privilege. And, as we have seen, Prince Hal's reconciliations with his guilty father involve elements of obfuscation and denial. It is surely no accident that Shakespeare omits an incident of Holinshed in which the Prince urges Henry IV to slay him with a proffered dagger rather than continue to suspect his loyalty: "I haue this daie made my selfe readie by confession and receiuing of the sacrament . . . and before God at the daie of the generall judgement, I faithfullie protest clearlie to forgiue you."[37] In Shakespeare, references to sacramental

---

[36] Cf. also Morton's statement: "now the Bishop / Turns insurrection to religion," is "Suppos'd sincere and holy in his thoughts," and "Derives from heaven his quarrel and his cause" (*2 Henry IV*, 1.1.201–6).

[37] Holinshed, III, p. 539.

forgiveness and the ultimacy of divine judgment are notably absent from the two encounters.

If a providential hand in the affairs of state can be credited at all in *Henry IV*, it is undercut by an appeal to necessitarian forces and a sense that kings and princes are the victims of destiny and false perception. Henry's revisionist take on usurpation is that "necessity so bow'd the state / That [he] and greatness were compell'd to kiss" (*2 Henry IV*, 3.1.73–74), while his heir asks pardon for presuming to wear the crown too soon, not as an eruption of culpable pride but as proof that he was shifting an intolerable burden from a king no longer capable of bearing it. Although perfunctory invocations of divine supremacy color the dialogue of *Henry IV*, values of humanism tailored to the competitive realities of dynastic power prevail. Debra Shuger, noting "the passage of sacred forms and practices . . . into the social and literary structures of secular culture," points out that biblical narratives such as that of the Prodigal Son "retained a certain . . . flexibility, . . . [an] extradogmatic surplus of undetermined meaning—or rather meaning capable of being determined in various ways."[38] Thus Prince's Hal's reformation, unlike that of the biblical Prodigal, becomes the story of a *gradus ad regnum*,[39] an ascent from premeditated libertinism to the wisdom of responsible government. And the reconciliation that the two plays ultimately celebrate is not merely the Prince's recovery of personal honor in his father's eyes but the popular rehabilitation of England under a warrior king who will expunge his predecessor's doubtful legitimacy in a freshly won unity of patriotic nationalism. In living up to his autochthonous identity as a future monarch, the Prince also rekindles the pride and shapes the destiny of the nation whose icon he becomes.

The famous theater critic Kenneth Tynan admired the Henry IV plays even above the tragedies as "the twin summits of Shakespeare's achievement . . . great public plays in which a whole nation is under scrutiny."[40] Undoubtedly implied in Tynan's encomium is the way in which public

---

[38] Shuger, *The Renaissance Bible: Scholarship, Sacrifice, and Subjectivity* (Berkeley, 1994), pp. 3–5.

[39] The phrase is Sigurd Burckhardt's; see *Shakespearean Meanings* (Princeton, 1968), p. 152.

[40] Kenneth Tynan, *Curtains: Selections from the Drama Criticism and Related Writings* (New York, 1961), p. 93.

needs and private sympathies create strains not only in the characters themselves but in our shifting responses to them. Although kings and princes, like anyone else, have souls accountable to God, the states that they represent or embody refuse to be judged exclusively according to the laws of heaven. As Cardinal Richelieu is reported to have said, "The salvation of States is in *this* world" rather than the next.[41] The two reconciliations of *Henry IV* inhabit a world of rich ambiguity in which success and failure, comedy and tragedy, are both present, depending on whether one's perspective is religious, social, domestic, political, national, or what is most likely, some admixture of these. In the theater, at least, Shakespeare makes it very difficult to choose. And the honest complexity thereby staged is a notable feature that marks the two parts of *Henry IV* as the supreme masterpieces of the chronicle genre.

---

[41] Quoted in W. H. Auden, "The Prince's Dog," in *The Dyer's Hand and Other Essays* (New York, 1948), p. 208. Auden is paraphrasing loosely. Richelieu actually wrote: "Man is immortal; his salvation is hereafter. The state has no immortality; its salvation is now or never." See Joseph R. Strayer and Hans W. Gatzke, *The Mainstream of Civilization Since 1500*, 4th ed. (New York, 1984), p. 420.

INDEX

Submission Guidelines

For current submission guidelines and calls for papers, please visit the *Studies in Medieval and Renaissance History* website at http://www.asu.edu/clas/clasjournals/smrh/submissionguidelines.htm.